KU-605-094

Britain's Birds in 1990–91:
the conservation and monitoring review

Edited by
John Andrews and Steve P Carter

Published in 1993
by the British Trust of Ornithology (Thetford)
and the Joint Nature Conservation Committee.

Copyright BTO/JNCC. ISBN 0-903-793-33-4

British Trust for Ornithology
National Centre for Ornithology
The Nunnery
Thetford
Norfolk IP24 2PU

Joint Nature Conservation Committee
Monkstone House
City Road
Peterborough
Cambridgeshire PE1 1JY

Typesetting by Prestige Typographics (BurySt Edmunds)
Printed by Reflex Litho (Thetford)

CONTENTS

Foreword

Jeremy Greenwood [1] & Mike Pienkowski[2]

[1]*Director, BTO*
[2]*Director, Life Sciences, JNCC*

The considerable public interest in Britain's birds might suggest that the conservation of their populations and habitats was assured. Regretfully this is far from the case. Although progress has been made in various areas, numerous threats remain. To overcome the threats we need to maintain a refined system for monitoring our bird populations and their habitats, so that we can detect untoward changes, understand their likely causes, and take effective action to reverse them. Recently, JNCC and BTO came together, with a number of other contributing bodies, to publish *Britain's Birds in 1989-90: the conservation and monitoring review*. This summarised not only the results from many bird monitoring schemes but also how the data are used for practical conservation purposes. Many of the schemes are funded by conservation bodies, both statutory and non-governmental, and provide the essential information basis to drive conservation forward within the UK. They also contribute to, and in many cases set a standard for, international co-operation in this field.

The 1989-90 'yearbook' received favourable comments, both in Britain and internationally. We welcome this successor volume. A wide range of material is reported and, as with last year's volume, much of this looks forward as well as back. It is unfortunate that the publication date has slipped from that intended. The slippage has been largely as a result of JNCC and its contractors being involved in a number of reviews, a necessary part of the re-organisation of the statutory conservation agencies. The purpose of the reviews has been to assess the scientific quality of the research and how it contributes to the conservation priorities of the statutory bodies. The quality of the research and conservation advice given by the British conservation movement can only benefit from such reviews, which focus the areas of work undertaken in terms of statutory needs and nature conservation priorities. It is intended that future issues of this publication will regain lost ground, such that *Britain's Birds* appears as soon as is practicable after the year to which it refers.

This volume draws together a wealth of information from a range of survey and monitoring schemes and is an important source of information for those people who wish to obtain an overview of the changes to our birdlife. Schemes such as the Common Birds Census, the Waterways Bird Survey, the Constant Effort Sites ringing scheme, and the Nest Records Scheme (organised by BTO with part funding by JNCC) and the JNCC's Seabird Monitoring Programme (also run in partnership with voluntary bodies) should enable us to identify whether changes in bird populations are due to natural fluctuations or whether they have been caused by man, particularly as the Integrated Population Monitoring programme is developed. The National Wildfowl Counts and the Birds of Estuaries Enquiry (involving partnership between BTO, WWT, RSPB and JNCC) provide essential information for the wetland habitats that are so widely threatened. In addition, special surveys to identify specific ecological requirements of selected bird species, such as the RSPB's research on Cirl Buntings, cast more light on the reasons for change. The next step is to implement conservation measures to protect the bird populations which are threatened and to assist the recovery of declining populations. We are very happy that reports from our partners in WWT and RSPB are well represented in this volume.

Successful partnership between JNCC and organisations in the voluntary conservation sector and research institutes is central to the scientific basis for site protection. In Britain and internationally the protection and management of sites is the cornerstone of bird conservation. During 1990/1991 considerable progress has been made in classifying Special Protection Areas and Ramsar sites in Great Britain and the notification or re-notification of SSSIs. These and other site protection measures go some way to sustaining the biodiversity of the wider countryside in general. It is, however, a common misconception that ecological evaluations are primarily for identifying and grading sites of biological interest.

Protected sites interact with their surroundings. Therefore there is a need to consider site protection in parallel with wider countryside management measures. The success of particular management options can in turn be assessed only if their effects on the bird populations are carefully monitored. This brings us back to the starting point of the need for an integrated monitoring programme.

Apart from the changes in the organisation of nature conservation bodies in recent years, there have been rapid changes in international laws and conventions. The Convention on Biological Diversity was signed on 5th June 1992 in Rio. This Convention states that each country should construct a plan for the conservation of biological diversity and for its sustainable use. Clearly the work of JNCC, BTO and the other bodies contributing to this volume will be very important to this strategy.

Within a strategy for biological diversity the collation and use of data collected on bird populations by volunteers will be crucial. Within the handling of data the development of a national biota database could be developed. A national database should be developed to handle conservation-related information on fauna and flora. Current work to improve accessibility and ways of interrelating existing databases should be continued. Modern technology means that the various components of such a national database need not be in one place but could be managed by those organisations responsible for its initial compilation. The work of BTO, JNCC and other organisations could be linked progressively to such a system and with other new initiatives as they arise.

The new arrangements for statutory nature conservation in Britain have encouraged much forward planning in the last year. A variety of exciting new initiatives are in hand which, when they come to fruition, will result in innovative new monitoring schemes and the interlinking of the existing ones to provide an even firmer base for practical conservation. We hope to report more fully on this in next year's *Britain's Birds*.

As in the past, future developments in the monitoring and survey work that provides the basis for the scientific framework of bird conservation in Britain will depend on the dedicated fieldwork of thousands of volunteers. We hope that the many publications which arise from their efforts, including this series of annual volumes, show clearly how their data is being used for the good of Britain's wildlife in general and birdlife in particular.

C.H. Gomersall, RSPB/Hambridge Drove, West Sedgemoor.

Acknowledgements

Our thanks must first extend to the veritable army of fieldworkers around the country who give so freely of their time and effort. Without such widespread grass-roots support this volume and much invaluable conservation and monitoring work in the UK would be impossible.

We are grateful to many people for their assistance in the preparation and production of *Britain's Birds in 1990-91*. Chief amongst these are the co-ordinators in each of the major bodies contributing material : Drs. David Stroud (acting on behalf not only of the JNCC but also the country agencies), Jeremy Greenwood (BTO), Mark Avery (RSPB) and Myrfyn Owen (WWT). It was their task to oversee the preparation of submissions from their own organisations, to act as the channels of communication with the editors and to referee draft texts from all contributors. Other staff from all organisations also provided helpful comments.

Editorial responsibilities were split. John Andrews was responsible for the editing original manuscripts and for overseeing all production work as far as the second proof stage. Steve Carter took on board the task of checking final proofs, organising page layouts, artwork and photographs, and final production. Assistance from Paul Green and Susan Waghorn was greatly appreciated.

We are grateful to Stephen Lings for providing the cover illustration. Joe Blossom, Steve Carter, Steve Cull, Andrew Mackay, BE Slade, Peter Scott, Thelma Sykes and D A Thelwell provided other artwork. Photographs are credited where they appear.

John Andrews
Steve P Carter

Acronyms used in this volume

BoEE	Birds of Estuaries Enquiry
BTO	British Trust for Ornithology
CBC	Common Birds Census
CCW	Countryside Council for Wales
CES	Constant Effort Site
DoE	Department of the Environment
DoE(NI)	Department of the Environment (Northern Ireland)
EA	Environmental Assessment
EN	English Nature
ESA	Environmentally Sensitive Area
EURING	European Union for Bird Ringing
FC	Forestry Commission
JNCC	Joint Nature Conservation Committee
IBBS	International Beach Bird Survey
ICBP	International Council for Bird Preservation (now BirdLife International)
IDB	Internal Drainage Board
IDP	Integrated Development Plan
IPM	Integrated Population Monitoring
IWRB	International Waterfowl & Wetlands Research Bureau
ITE	Institute of Terrestrial Ecology
IWC	Irish Wildbird Conservancy
MAFF	Ministry of Agriculture, Fisheries & Food
NCC	Nature Conservancy Council (now split into JNCC, EN, SNH, CCW)
NCCS	Nature Conservancy Council for Scotland (now SNH)
NERC	Natural Environment Research Council
NNR	National Nature Reserve
NRA	National Rivers Authority
NRS	Nest Record Scheme
NWC	National Waterfowl Counts
RSG	Raptor Study Group
RSNC	Royal Society for Nature Conservation
RSPB	Royal Society for the Protection of Birds
SNH	Scottish Natural Heritage (formerly NCCS)
SOC	Scottish Ornithologists' Club
SOTEAG	Shetland Oil Terminal Environmental Advisory Group
SPA	Special Protected Area
SSSI	Site of Special Scientific Interest
WBS	Waterways Bird Survey
WPWA	Western Palearctic Waterfowl Agreement
WWF	Worldwide Fund for Nature
WWRG	Wash Wader Ringing Group
WWT	Wildfowl & Wetlands Trust

Bird conservation challenges and successes in 1990 and 1991

This section briefly summarises some of the major bird conservation issues between April 1990 and March 1991. Although such a review cannot be comprehensive in such a limited space, it hopefully touches on most of the major bird conservation headlines that occurred in the period.

April 1990

Foresters protested against extending SSSIs in the Flow Country. The Scottish Office declared eight sites as new Special Protection Areas and/or Ramsar sites. The RSPB purchased another area of Abernethy Forest, making it the largest non-statutory nature reserve in Europe. The BTO and NCC jointly published *Population Trends in British Breeding Birds* which showed a decline in 39 breeding species over the last 30 years, but also increases in others.

May 1990

The Environmental Protection Bill was debated in the House of Lords. A spill of 1,100 tonnes of crude oil affected 12 miles of the south Devon coast causing serious pollution to marine life on the rocky shore. More Red Kites were imported to England and Scotland from Spain (11), Sweden (19) and Wales (2) for release as part of the continuing RSPB/JNCC re-introduction programme. Contrary to the NCC's advice, the Secretary of State for Energy granted a new oil exploration licence close to the internationally important seabird colony at Flamborough Head and Bempton Cliffs.

June 1990

A total of 299 ha of the Somerset Levels were declared a National Nature Reserve. Secretary of State Malcolm Rifkind turned down the proposal to extend skiing into Lurchers Gully in the Cairngorms. WWT, SOC and BTO organised a national survey of breeding Mute Swans.

July 1990

British Herpetological Society and Worldwide Fund for Nature took Poole Borough Council to court over plans to build 200 houses on Canford Heath. Pollution was suspected as the cause of death for hundreds of Kittiwakes found on the North Yorkshire coast. An Angus gamekeeper was fined £1,000 for killing two Peregrines. A Golden Eagle was found dead in Sutherland, having been killed using a poisoned bait.

August 1990

RSPB drew attention to the deliberate killing of Hen Harriers by some grouse moor managers, with at least 16 reports of nests and birds destroyed in Scotland in the first eight months of 1990. A Coventry man was fined £2,500 for stealing Osprey eggs from a nest in Perthshire. He was caught by Royal Marines guarding the nest. Two West Germans were sent to prison for attempting to smuggle 12 Peregrine eggs from Kent. Against extremely widespread opposition, the Forestry Commission approved an application to plant 873 ha of moorland at Glen Dye in Kincardine and Deeside District. The decision led to further calls for forestry to come under planning control.

September 1990

A major public enquiry into the development proposals on the Swale commenced. NCC and RSPB jointly opposed development on the Swale SSSI. RSPB launched their estuary campaign strategy document *Turning the tide - a future for estuaries*. Following earlier consultation, the Scottish Office declined to introduce a statutory ban on shooting the declining Capercaillie, but instead called for a voluntary ban and a package of research into habitat requirements and managment needs. The Forestry Commission published *The Forest Nature Conservation Guidelines* and the Government published their environmental white paper - *This Common Inheritance*.

October 1990

Second European Forum on Birds and Pastoralism held in Isle of Man: reported growing awareness of the role for traditional agricultural for bird conservation throughout Europe and urged reform of national agricultural policies. Environmental Protection Act received Royal Assent. Public inquiry started to investigate routing of another major road across Rainham Marshes SSSI. A consortium of nature conservation bodies purchased 530 ha of Blean Woods, now the largest ancient woodland reserve in England. NCC purchased the 684 ha Fens, Whixhall and Bettisfield Mosses from commercial peat diggers. RSPB plans to fell an oak tree on West Sedgemoor in the Somerset Levels were thwarted by a Tree Preservation Order imposed by South Somerset District Council. An RSPB report claimed that there are over 300 active egg-collectors in Britain.

November 1990

The out-going Chairman, Sir William Wilkinson, launched the 16th Annual Report of the NCC which detailed continuing damage to SSSIs. The Peat Producers' Association announced that, in future, members would not apply for new planning permissions to cut peat on SSSIs without the approval of the NCC.

December 1990

Red Data Birds in Britain was published on behalf of the NCC and RSPB by Poyser, and reviewed knowledge and conservation requirements of rare and specially protected birds in Britain. The Shetland sandeel fishery was closed - too late said many conservationists. The Government agreed to press the case of the Cairngorms as a World Heritage site.

January 1991

Swale Public Enquiry closed.

February 1991

House of Commons passed the Cardiff Bay Barrage Bill as amended by the Commons Select Committee. Bill was 'talked out' but Secretary of State for Wales announced that Government would publish a hybrid Bill in its place. Redgrave & South Lopham Fens designated as a Ramsar site. The High Court dismissed an attempt to save 17 ha of Canford Heath SSSI from builders - "a disaster for conservation" said WWF.

March 1991

Nature conservation and estuaries in Great Britain, published by NCC, revealed that 85% of estuaries have been damaged by human activity. MAFF launched a governmental campaign to combat the illegal poisoning of wildlife through education programmes, publicity and increased efforts at enforcement. Secretary of State Michael Heseltine revoked planning permission for Canford Heath housing in a move applauded by conservation bodies. RSPB employed a second team to manage heathland in Dorset. NCC and ICBP jointly convened an international seminar to consider conservation of dry grassland birds at University of Reading.

April 1991

Nature Conservancy Council RIP. Welcome to the Joint Nature Conservation Committee, the Countryside Council for Wales, Scottish Natural Heritage and English Nature. The BTO moved to Thetford, Norfolk.

M.B. Withers/Hen Harrier at nest

Progress in designating Special Protection Areas and Ramsar sites in Great Britain in 1990/91

Greg P Mudge

Vertebrate Ecology and Conservation Branch, JNCC

The public popularity of birds, as well as their spectacular migrations, have led to international commitments being made by governments including our own to conserve populations throughout their ranges. The increasing rate of habitat loss in recent years, coupled with declines in numbers of some bird species has stimulated the current world-wide concern, first to stop and, wherever possible, to reverse these declines.

For most bird species, international co-operation is essential for their conservation. For many species this is due to their migratory habits, depending on different countries at different times of the year. For some species even when habitat is good, populations are so low that urgent international measures are essential if the risk of major losses of range and numbers is to be avoided. Birds show little respect for country or administrative boundaries and we need to plan accordingly. The network of Special Protection Areas (SPAs) required under the EC Birds Directive and of wetlands under the Ramsar Convention give us one mechanism of achieving this international conservation co-ordination.

In Britain, a total of 44 Ramsar sites and 40 SPAs had been designated in part or wholly by 31 March 1991. A total of 141 candidate Ramsar sites and 222 candidate SPAs are eligible for designation. Table 1 gives the numbers and areas of SPAs designated by EC member states.

Designation procedures

The reorganisation of NCC into three Country Agencies and the JNCC has resulted in some changes in the operational procedures during the designation process. The main steps are now as follows:

- JNCC, in collaboration with the Country Agencies, maintains the formal list of designated and proposed SPAs and Ramsar sites. The current master list appears as *Ornithology Note*

4, Version 3. This was issued in March 1991 and copies are available from JNCC in Peterborough. This list was published in Hansard on 17 July 1991.

- An annual submission programme is agreed between JNCC, the Country Agencies and government departments.
- For each site, JNCC prepares the citations (summarising the international importance of the site) and Departmental Brief (giving a detailed account of the interest for governmental briefing purposes). These usually draw heavily on information supplied through JNCC contracts with BTO and WWT, and include additional information from RSPB and other sources.
- The Regional staff of the relevant Country Agency carry out consultations with the owners and occupiers of the site.
- Department of the Environment, Scottish Office or Welsh Office, as appropriate, consult with other Government Departments.
- Final designation is the responsibility of the relevant Secretary of State (Environment, Scottish or Welsh).

Sites awaiting designation

Table 2 lists those sites which have been formally submitted by NCC to Government and await designation. As at 29 February 1992, a total of 14 are in England; one overlaps England and Wales; one overlaps England and Scotland, and four are in Scotland.

New designations

Between April 1990 and March 1991 a total of nine sites were designated as SPAs and/or as Ramsar sites. One of these was in England - Redgrave and South Lopham Fens (Table 3). The other eight were in Scotland (Table 4). Details of these Scottish sites were given by Stroud & Mudge (1991). A further seven sites have been designated to the end of February 1992. Table 4 lists all sites designated from April 1990 to February 1992.

Optimistic signs for the future?

In contrast to the extremely slow progress of recent years, there now seems to be a much greater commitment being shown by Government towards rapid progress in the designation of remaining internationally important sites.

It is to be hoped that next year's *Britain's Birds* will be able to report a much healthier rate of designation.

Further information on internationally important bird sites in Britain

In order to ensure that decision-makers are more aware of the locations and special interests of all internationally important bird sites, the JNCC, Country Agencies and RSPB have collaborated in the production of a book which gives extensive details of each such site. *Important bird areas in the United Kingdom including the Channel Islands and Isle of Man* was published in October 1992 and is available from RSPB for £35.

References

Stroud, D.A. & Mudge, G.P. (1991). Slow progress in designating Special Protection Areas and Ramsar sites. Pp. 17-22. In: Stroud, D.A. & Glue, D. (Eds). *Britain's Birds in 1989/90; the conservation and monitoring review.* BTO/NCC, Thetford.

Table 1. Numbers and area of Special Protection Areas designated by Member States of EC pursuant to the Birds Directive as at 24 March 1991.

Member state	Number of SPAs	Total area of SPAs	Mean area of SPAs (ha)	Proportion of state area as SPA
Belgium	36	431,306	11,980	14.13%
Denmark	111	960,092	8,649	c5.80%
Spain[1]	135	2,324,926	17,222	4.61%
Portugal[2]	34	318,872	9,378	3.48%
Netherlands	9	52,865	5,873	1.56%
Greece	26	191,637	7,370	1.45%
Germany	390	324,640	832	1.30%
Italy	74	310,378	4,194	1.03%
France	61	519,741	8,520	0.96%
United Kingdom	40	128,848	3,221	0.53%
Luxembourg	4	356	'89	0.14%
Ireland	20	5,548	277	0.08%

[1]including sites in the Canary Islands
[2]including sites in the Azores

Table 2. Sites submitted by NCC to Government for proposed designation under the Ramsar Convention or the EEC Birds Directive in 1990/91 (also includes those sites formerly submitted but not yet designated).

Site name	Date of submission to Government	Proposed designation: EC SPA	Proposed designation: Ramsar site
Submissions up to 31 March 1990 and still with Government			
Mersey Estuary, Merseyside & Cheshire	25 November 1985	SPA	Ramsar
Stour & Orwell Estuary, Suffolk & Essex	16 January 1986	SPA	Ramsar
Medway Estuary and Marshes, Kent	1 April 1986	SPA	Ramsar
Burry Inlet, Dyfed & West Glamorgan	11 September 1986		Ramsar
Benfleet and Southend Marshes, Essex	27 May 1987	SPA	Ramsar
Burry Inlet, Dyfed & West Glamorgan	28 January 1988	SPA	
Upper Solway Flats and Marshes, Cumbria, Dumfries & Galloway	5 July 1988	SPA	Ramsar
Glannau Aberdaron and Ynys Enlli, Gwynedd	18 August 1989	SPA	
Exe Estuary, Devon	1 November 1989	SPA	Ramsar
Chippenham Fen, Cambridgeshire	21 December 1989		Ramsar
Caenlochan, Grampian & Tayside	21 December 1989	SPA	
Ynys Feurig, Cermlyn Bay and the Skerries, Gwynedd	4 January 1990	SPA	
Glannau Ynys Gybi, Gwynedd	4 January 1990	SPA	
Severn Estuary	2 March 1990	SPA	Ramsar
Humber Flats, Marshes and Coast, Humberside & Lincolnshire	20 March 1990	SPA	Ramsar
Lindisfarne, Northumberland	26 March 1990	SPA	Ramsar (extension)
Minsmere and Walberswick, Suffolk	27 March 1990	SPA	Ramsar (extension)
New Forest, Hampshire	28 March 1990	SPA	Ramsar
Traeth Lavan, Gwynedd	29 March 1990	SPA	
Submissions in 1990/91 (to end of March)			
Cairngorms, Highland & Grampian	15 August 1990	SPA	
Drumochter Hills, Highland & Tayside	15 August 1990	SPA	
River Spey-Insh Marshes, Highland	12 March 1991	SPA	Ramsar
Cors Caron, Dyfed	20 March 1991		Ramsar
Morecambe Bay, Cumbria & Lancashire	21 March 1991	SPA	Ramsar
Ribble and Alt Estuaries, Lancashire & Merseyside	1 March 1991	SPA	Ramsar
Lee Valley, Greater London	26 March 1991	SPA	
Crymlyn Bog, West Glamorgan	26 March 1991		Ramsar
The Swale, Kent (extension)	March 1991	SPA	Ramsar

Table 3. Site designated under the Ramsar Convention by Government on 15 February 1991.

Redgrave and South Lopham Fens, Norfolk and Suffolk

This 125 ha site qualifies for Ramsar status on account of its special wetland habitat features and associated species. It is an extensive example of a lowland base-rich valley mire and is the source of the River Waveney.

The site exhibits a zonation of vegetation types including dry birch woodland, species-rich fen grassland and areas dominated by reed and sedge. It is one of two British localities for the Fen Raft Spider.

Table 4. Sites designated under the Ramsar Convention or EEC Birds Directive from April 1990 to the end of February 1992.

Site name	Date of designation	Designation: EC SPA	Designation: Ramsar site	Area
Glac na Criche, Islay	25 April 1990	SPA	Ramsar	265 ha
Feur Lochain, Islay	25 April 1990	SPA	Ramsar	384 ha
Abernethy Forest, Badenoch & Strathspey	25 April 1990	SPA		5,796 ha
Firth of Forth Islands	25 April 1990	SPA		92 ha
Handa Island, Sutherland	25 April 1990	SPA		363 ha
Fala Flow, Lothian	25 April 1990	SPA	Ramsar	323 ha
Ailsa Craig, Strathclyde	25 April 1990	SPA		105 ha
Loch an Duin, Western Isles	25 April 1990		Ramsar	3,606 ha
Redgrave and South Lopham Fens, Cambridgeshire	15 February 1991		Ramsar	125 ha
Skomer and Skokholm, Dyfed	5 August 1991	SPA (extension)		422 ha
Rutland Water, Leicestershire	4 October 1991	SPA	Ramsar	1,540 ha
Llyn Tegid, Gwynedd	7 November 1991		Ramsar	484 ha
Llyn Idwal, Gwynedd	7 November 1991		Ramsar	14 ha
Esthwaite Water, Cumbria	7 November 1991		Ramsar	134 ha
Walmore Common, Gloucestershire	5 December 1991	SPA	Ramsar	51 ha
Abberton Reservoir, Essex	5 December 1991	SPA	[already Ramsar 1981]	716 ha

Sites of Special Scientific Interest in 1990 and 1991

David A Stroud

Vertebrate Ecology and Conservation Branch, JNCC

The principal legal mechanism for the protection of areas of nature conservation importance in Great Britain is notification as a Site of Special Scientific Interest. Whilst this does not confer absolute protection, it does ensure consultation with the statutory nature conservation agencies by those whose activities may be damaging.

Designations

By the end of March 1991, a total of 5,576 SSSIs had been notified or renotified by the NCC, covering 1,721,502 ha. By this date, NCC had virtually completed the renotification of SSSIs originally notified under the National Parks and Access to the Countryside Act 1949 (Table 1). The few remaining sites were largely of a complex nature.

During the year a total of 260 new sites covering 33,877 ha, not previously protected, were notified (Table 1).

A number of important sites for birds were amongst those SSSIs notified or renotified. A selection of these are listed in Table 2. They include several estuaries, including the Tamar-Tavy Estuary, Poole Harbour and the North Solent, as well as other coastal wetlands of importance for their resident or migratory bird populations (e.g. Newborough Warren - Ynys Llanddwyn and Penrhynoedd Llangawaladr in Anglesey, and Laugharne and Pendine Burrows in Dyfed).

A number of woodlands which were notified hold a diverse range of bird communities (according to their locality and management). Important seabird breeding colonies that were (re)notified included Boscastle to Widemouth in Cornwall, the Humberside Lagoons and Penrhynoedd Llangawaladr in Anglesey.

In recent years there has been much controversy over the conservation of the peatlands of Caithness and Sutherland or 'The Flow Country' (*Britain's Birds in 1989/90*, pp.13-14). It is pleasing to see many of the components of this area now coming through the SSSI designation procedure (Table 2). Other peatlands or moorlands noti-

fied during the year included the raised bog of Moine Mhor in Argyll and Bodmin Moor in Cornwall.

Sites designated as of international importance under the Ramsar Convention or Birds Directive have first to be notified as SSSI under domestic legislation. In this regard several of the sites notified during the year are, in whole or in part, of international ornithological importance and thus are candidate SPAs and/or Ramsar sites. With the faster rate of international designations it is to be hoped that recently designated SSSIs such as the Tamar - Tavy Estuary, Bodmin Moor, Poole Harbour, North Solent, Newborough Warren - Ynys Llanddwyn, Pevensey Levels and the component SSSIs of the peatlands of Caithness and Sutherland will soon obtain formal recognition of their international importance.

Loss and damage to SSSIs

SSSIs are the most important areas for nature conservation in Britain. Yet despite their fundamental role in the conservation of Britain's natural heritage, many are damaged each year. The most recent statistics on loss and damage are given in Table 3. This indicates that many cases of damage occur as the result of the activities of public bodies or are legally sanctioned through the planning process.

Summary figures for loss and damage are given in Table 4. Because of differences in the intensity of reporting however, inter-year comparisons are not valid. In all cases, because only part of the SSSI network was monitored in any year, these figures are minima.

Causes of loss and damage in 1990/91

The continued high rates of damage to the SSSI network are of considerable concern to all conservationists. Although no single site was so damaged in 1990/91 as to cause its complete loss, a number suffered partial loss or long-term damage.

There is ever greater recreational pressure on the countryside. With some parts of the country holding an increasing affluent society with greater leisure time, impacts from these activities on protected areas are increasing.

The list of activities that have resulted in damage to SSSIs in 1990/91 reflects the great range of today's 'countryside activities': walking, hound trailing, hang-gliding, mountain biking, off-road cycling, motorcycling, scrambling, horse-riding, construction of flight ponds, erosion of woodland rides by a fox hunt, car parking, erosion by all-terrain vehicles, construction of duck pens, watersports, power boating, construction of a tennis court, unauthorised falconry and the illegal encampment of travellers. This list is not exhaustive either! Although the damage resulting from such activities is usually of a short-term nature, solutions to recreational conflicts can be particularly problematic.

The cause of damage to the greatest area of SSSIs resulted from agricultural activities (Table 3). The principal causes of this damage were overgrazing (over 64% of all cases of agricultural damage) and nutrient pollution from farm slurry or other sources (11% of cases). A number of other activities were common to damage at several sites, including drainage of wetlands, uncontrolled burning, undergrazing allowing scrub encroachment on grasslands, dumping, and herbicide applications. Overgrazing, especially of upland SSSIs, has long been a problem. Other causes of agricultural damage included turf removal, chain harrowing and ploughing of grasslands, the dumping of brash and horse damage to a mire.

A number of damaging activities are authorised by planning consent, often given many years previously. In this category authorised peat extraction continues to damage important peatland sites such as Wedholme Flow, Hatfield Moor, Thorne, Crowle and Goole Moors and Bolton Fell, whilst continued drainage from abandoned peat cuttings on other sites damaged several SSSIs. Sand and

Table 1. The number and extent of SSSIs which NCC notified under Section 28 of the Wildlife and Countryside Act 1981, as areas of special interest by reason of their flora, fauna or physiographic features. Also given are the number and area of sites renotified or new sites notified in the year 1 April 1990 - 31 March 1991 and the total of all SSSIs, which includes sites notified under the National Parks & Access the Countryside Act 1949.

	ENGLAND		SCOTLAND		WALES		GREAT BRITAIN	
	No.	Area (ha)	No.	Area (ha)	No.	Area (ha)	No.	Area (ha)
SSSIs renotified under the 1981 Act by 31 March 1991	2,135	658,615	778	703,569	456	152,204	3,369	1,514,388
SSSIs renotified under the 1981 Act, 1 April 1990 – 31 March 1991	35	52,237	13	13,081	4	3,666	52	68,984
New SSSIs notified under the 1981 Act by 31 March 1991	1,340	82,674	523	92,753	344	31,687	2,207	207,114
New SSSIs notified under the 1981 Act, 1 April 1990 – 31 March 1991	148	9,438	61	19,490	51	4,949	260	33,877
Total SSSIs notified under the 1981 Act by 31 March 1991	3,475	741,289	1,301	796,322	800	183,891	5,576	1,721,502
Total SSSIs as 31 March 1991	3,536	781,526	1,319	803,906	816	193,042	5,671	1,778,474

Table 2. A selection of SSSIs of particular ornithological interest notified or renotified in 1990 and 1991.

Sites	County/District	Area (ha)	Ornithological interest
Finemere Wood	Buckinghamshire	45.7	Woodland birds
Bodmin Moor	North Cornwall	4,947.0	Breeding and wintering moorland birds
Boscastle to Widemouth	Cornwall	639.0	Breeding seabirds
Brendonmoor	Cornwall	11.7	Wintering Snipe
Tamar – Tavy Estuary	Cornwall	1,441.1	Wintering wildfowl and waders
Moss Valley	Derbyshire	25.9	Breeding woodland birds
Via Gellia Woodlands	Derbyshire	208.1	Breeding birds of woodland and limestone dales
Poole Harbour	Dorset	4,049.0	Breeding seabirds and waders, wintering waterfowl
Turners Puddle Heath	Dorset	390.1	Breeding heathland birds
Upton Heath	Dorset	215.8	Breeding heathland birds
Pevensey Levels	East Sussex	3,501.0	Wintering waders, breeding warblers of scrub
Tollesbury Wick Meadows	Essex	127.5	Waterfowl and wintering raptors
Dymock Woods	Gloucester	53.0	Woodland breeding birds
Twyning Great Hay Meadow	Gloucester	104.0	Breeding and wintering waders
Ruislip Woods	Greater London	305.4	Woodland breeding birds
Abram Flashes	Greater Manchester	39.6	Wintering waterfowl
North Solent	Hampshire	1,188.6	Wintering waterfowl, breeding seabirds and waders
Warren Heath Ponds	Hampshire	31.2	Breeding waders
Eastnor Park	Hereford/Worcester	147.5	Breeding woodland birds and waders
The Lagoons	Humberside	67.9	Breeding terns, migratory waders, winter sea ducks
Holborough to Burham Marshes	Kent	267.8	Breeding waders
Porlock Marsh	Somerset	165.1	Breeding waterfowl and migratory birds
The Perch	Somerset	72.1	Breeding woodland birds
Westhay Heath	Somerset	25.9	Breeding waterfowl and other wetland birds
Barnby Broad and Marshes	Suffolk	189.6	Breeding waterfowl
Chiddingford Forest	Surrey/West Sussex	543.9	Breeding woodland birds
Newborough Warren – Ynys Llanddwyn	Gwynedd (Anglesey)	1,552.0	Wintering waterfowl
Penrhynoedd Llagawaladr	Gwynedd (Anglesey)	180.0	Gull breeding colony
Nant Llech	Powys	42.1	Breeding woodland and riverine birds
Laugharne & Pendine Burrows	Dyfed	1,581.0	Breeding and wintering wildfowl, breeding wetland warblers and staging/wintering waders
Mynydd Ystyfflau-Carn	Dyfed	53.4	Wintering raptors
Shielton Peatlands	Caithness	5,593.0	Breeding waders, wildfowl and raptors
Stroupster Peatlands	Caithness	2,813.0	Breeding waders, wildfowl and raptors
Drium nam Bad	Sutherland	3,107.0	Breeding waders, wildfowl and raptors
Loch Meadie Peatlands	Sutherland	6,221.0	Breeding waders, wildfowl and raptors
Skinsdale Peatlands	Sutherland	7,069.0	Breeding waders, wildfowl and raptors
Slethill Peatlands	Sutherland	1,1440	Breeding waders, wildfowl and raptors
Loch Shiel	Lochaber	3,373.9	Greenland White-fronted Geese
Moine Mhor	Argyll & Bute	1,194.8	Greenland White-fronted Geese
Vallay	Western Isles	307.4	Breeding waders
Ben Lui	Argyll & Bute/ Stirling	2,982.2	Breeding upland birds

Table 3. Damage to SSSIs and proposed SSSIs: 1 April 1990 to 31 March 1991. Note that on 20 SSSIs, cases of damage fell into more than one category. The totals given at the foot of the table may thus be lower than the sum of the individual rows.

Cause of damage		SSSIs notified or renotified under the 1981 Act	Area (ha)	SSSIs awaiting renotification and proposed SSSIs (including extensions to existing SSSI)	Area (ha)
Agricultural activities	Sites lost	–	–	–	–
	Partial loss	–	–	2	5
	Long-term damage	1	45	–	–
	Short-term damage	47	28,011	1	430
Forestry activities	Sites lost	–	–	–	–
	Partial loss	–	–	–	–
	Long-term damage	1	6	–	–
	Short-term damage	3	5	–	–
Activities given planning permission	Sites lost	–	–	–	–
	Partial loss	2	2	–	–
	Long-term damage	6	997	1	316
	Short-term damage	–	–	–	–
Activities of statutory undertakers and other public bodies not included in above categories	Sites lost	–	–	–	–
	Partial loss	–	–	–	–
	Long-term damage	4	44	–	–
	Short-term damage	8	4,101	–	–
Recreational activities	Sites lost	–	–	–	–
	Partial loss	1	1	–	–
	Long-term damage	4	17	–	–
	Short-term damage	27	192	3	227
Insufficient management	Sites lost	–	–	–	–
	Partial loss	–	–	–	–
	Long-term damage	–	–	–	–
	Short-term damage	12	410	–	–
Miscellaneous activities (including pollution, unauthorised tipping and burning)	Sites lost	–	–	–	–
	Partial loss	1	1	2	4
	Long-term damage	3	2	1	2
	Short-term damage	46	2,485	1	0.3
Totals (sites)	Sites lost	–	–	–	–
	Partial loss	4	4	4	9
	Long-term damage	18	1,099	2	318
	Short-term damage	127	35,061	5	657.3

Grand total of 160 sites affected covering c37,148.3 ha

Totals (cases)	Sites lost	–	–	–	–
	Partial loss	4	4	4	9
	Long-term damage	19	1,111	2	318
	Short-term damage	143	35,204	5	657.3

Grand total of 177 sites affected covering c37,303 ha

Definitions:

Sites lost	Damage which will result in the denotification of the whole SSSI
Partial loss	Damage which will result in the denotification of part of the SSSI
Long-term damage	Damage causing a lasting reduction in the special interest
Short-term damage	Damage from which the special interest could recover

gravel extraction resulted in the partial loss or long-term damage to several sites.

In recent years there has been damage to a number of wetlands, especially in England, either from the excessive abstraction of groundwater or from other misuse of water resources. This has affected the hydrological regimes of many sites. It has proved a particular problem in the Somerset Levels where excessive pumping in spring has resulted in short-term damage to a number of SSSIs.

A significant number of SSSIs have been damaged as a result of insufficient management. At least in 1990/91, such damage was of a short-term nature although the potential for longer-term damage exists if such a situation persists. The majority of sites thus damaged were grasslands, with neglect, poor mowing management and scrub encroachment being recorded. Heathland sites were also damaged: pine invasion and scrub encroachment occurred at several sites.

A wide range of other 'miscellaneous' activities damaged SSSIs in 1990/91, although fire was a common theme. Fire damaged many sites - dunes, heaths, commons, grasslands and bogs. Causes included arson attacks and accidental fires resulting from a road crash and other causes.

Last years *Britain's Birds* highlighted the loss and damage to heathland SSSIs as being especially serious. This concern remains. In some areas, more or less all remaining heathland is within the SSSI network. When even these areas cannot be protected from damage, the situation is indeed serious.

Table 4. Summarised information in reported loss and damage to SSSIs 1983/83 – 1990/91. Information from NCC *Annual Reports* for the same period.

N.B. Because of differences in the intensity of reporting, inter-year comparisons of damage are not valid. Definitions as in Table 1.

	Total damaged	Short-term damage	Number of sites[1] Long-term damage	Partial loss[2]	Sites lost
1983/84	176	–	–	–	–
1984/85	255	161	86	–	8
1985/86	176	114	58	–	2
1986/87	228	166	46	22	2
1987/88	161	103	43	20	0
1988/89	241	181	39	20	1
1989/90	324	278	39	6	1
1990/91	160	132	20	8	0

[1] Including SSSIs awaiting renotification, proposed SSSIs and extensions, and notified sites.
[2] Prior to 1986/87, partial loss was included in 'long-term damage'.

Forestry proposals in Glen Dye

David Minns

Conservation Planning Department, RSPB

In 1988 the Fasque Estate, which is owned by the descendants of the Victorian Prime Minister Sir William Gladstone, applied for forestry grant for a scheme covering 1137 ha of heather moorland formerly managed for grouse.

Of this, 967 ha was to be conifers, mostly Sitka Spruce, and the remainder broadleaves, natural regeneration and unplanted land.

Monitoring during the 1980s, by Graham Rebecca and other members of the North-east Scotland Raptor Study Group, showed that there were three pairs of Merlins, three to four pairs of Short-eared Owls and around eight pairs of Golden Plovers on this ground. During the early part of this monitoring up to five pairs of Hen Harriers were also present. However, as in most other areas of Grampian, Harriers had declined by 1988 although the habitat was still suitable. All these species are listed on Annex I of the EEC Directive on the Conservation of Birds, and their habitats are therefore supposed to be given special protection by Member States' Governments, either as Special Protection Areas (SPA) or in other ways.

An Environmental Assessment was not requested by the Forestry Commission (FC) and the application was referred to Kincardine & Deeside District Council, who in turn consulted the NCC, the RSPB, the North-east Scotland Raptor Study Group and others. After consideration of the planting proposals and their likely effects on the birds, all three decided to object to them. Other objectors included the District Council, the Dee Valley Liaison Group and the Scottish Ornithologists' Club.

The case was referred to the FCs Regional Advisory Committee in August 1989 with a view to finding a compromise, and about a year later received approval, in a slightly modified form, having been referred to the relevant Government Minister for his opinion. The approved scheme consisted of 807 ha of planted conifers (reduced by 160 ha from the original proposals), 234 ha of unplanted land and 96 ha of regeneration and broadleaves, but it was still likely to affect at least two of the Merlin sites and most of the other raptors. Following advice from Graham Rebecca, the Estate agreed to further modifications, which should allow at least two of the three Merlin breeding areas to remain viable. Monitoring will continue with the agreement of the Estate.

The original grant application was submitted two days before the coming into force of the UK regulations which implemented the EC Directive on Environmental Assessment (EA). These gave the FC the responsibility for ensuring that an assessment of environmental effects was carried out for planting proposals which were likely to have significant effects. Despite the imminence of these regulations, and the strong objections from so many conservation organisations, the Commission decided against an EA despite having knowledge of the Annex I species. In December 1990 the Kincardine & Deeside District Council decided to apply to the Court of Session in Edinburgh for a judicial review of the FC approval of this scheme.

It is believed that this is the only time a FC decision has been subject to this procedure, which took place on three days in February 1991. The judge's decision was issued the following month, and he found in favour of the FC, ruling that the Directive gave sufficient discretion to Governments to allow them not to carry out any EAs at all for most types of development.

The RSPB then decided to refer the case to the European Commission as being in breach of both the Birds Directive and the EA Directive. Under the Birds Directive, it was argued that this was a high priority site for the species mentioned, particularly Merlin and Hen Harrier and that insufficient steps had been taken by the UK Government to protect the habitats of these species nationally as required by the Directive. Only about 15% of known Grampian Merlins breed within SSSIs and none of these is yet designated as an SPA.

Under the Environmental Assessment Directive the RSPB argued that although the application pre-dated the UK Regulations for EAs for forestry by two days, the Directive itself was already in force, the UK being late in implementing it, and the FC

13

knew this proposal was controversial and should have required the applicant to prepare an assessment of its effects, even if this was not a formal EA.

In June 1992 the European Commission indicated verbally that they would be taking up the case for an EA with the UK Government, and would consider the Birds Directive case thereafter. The outcome of this is awaited.

D. Minns: Afforestation in Glen Dye

Land management and conservation at West Sedgemoor

Graham Hirons

Conservation Management Department, RSPB

Summary

There has been a great decline in the ornithological importance of the Somerset Levels and Moors, despite SSSI designations and inclusion of the areas in an Environmentally Sensitive Area (ESA). West Sedgemoor is the most important ornithological site remaining in the area. Hydrological management of part of the RSPB reserve coupled with traditional pastoral agriculture has resulted in a tenfold increase in the numbers of wintering waterfowl to internationally important levels. The decline in breeding waders has also been halted and the one-sixth of West Sedgemoor that is hydrologically managed to provide high water tables now holds two-thirds of the Moor's breeding waders. New ESA Tier 3 conditions introduced in 1992 accord closely with those maintained within the hydrologically-managed area of the RSPB reserve.

The Somerset Levels and Moors

The 600 sq. km. of flat, low-lying grassland which comprise the Somerset Levels and Moors form the flood plains of several rivers draining into the Bristol Channel (Figure 1). They are one of Britain's largest remaining lowland wet meadow systems with 50% of the British resource of herb-rich grassland (Robins et al. 1991). Wet grassland has decreased by over 40% in the UK since 1930 (Williams & Bowers 1987).

RSPB surveys in 1976/77 (Round 1978) and 1982/83 (Murfitt & Chown 1983) revealed that collectively the Levels and Moors were internationally important in winter for Bewick's Swan, Wigeon, Teal and Lapwing and nationally important for Mute Swan, Golden Plover, Snipe and Black-tailed Godwit. Breeding wader surveys in 1977 and 1983 identified substantial populations of Lapwing, Snipe, Redshank and Curlew (Round 1978; Weaver & Chown 1983) making the area one of the five most important wet grassland sites in England and Wales in terms of wader numbers. The population of Snipe (4-8% of the grassland total for England and Wales) was of particular importance.

A repeat survey of breeding waders of the Somerset Moors by RSPB in 1987 (Robins 1987) revealed a 55% decline in total numbers, from 576 pairs to 258 pairs. The two species of national importance, Black-tailed Godwit and Snipe, suffered the greatest declines (83% and 69% respectively). The survey also demonstrated that wader distribution was closely correlated with the depth of the water table and vegetation communities characteristic of damp, unimproved grassland. However, the proportion of fields suitable for breeding waders (loosely defined as 'tussocky') had declined from 50% to 11% between 1977 and 1987. Since 1987 numbers of breeding waders have continued to decline and Snipe no longer breed on some moors (Robins et al. 1991).

Counts in the period 1976/77 to 1989/90 also demonstrated declines in the numbers of the key species of wintering waterfowl, while the botanical interest of the herb-rich grassland had also fallen (Robins et al. 1991).

To investigate the causes of the decline, long-term rainfall, sluice and pump station records have been examined. Within the Moors, water is carried by internal ditch systems to low spots whence it is pumped into high-level embanked channels and flows towards the sea. The NRA owns and operates the pumps, responding to the demands of the internal drainage boards (IDBs) in setting water levels. The investigation revealed that since the mid-1970s there had been a progressive lowering of the levels at which the pumps were started (Robins & Green 1988). This had lead to a reduction in the extent and frequency of shallow winter floods and to lower soil water tables in the spring. More rapid drying of the soil permits more intensive farming with heavier stocking rates and earlier hay or silage cuts all of which contributed to the creation of unsuitable conditions for breeding waders.

These changes had occurred despite the fact that the conservation importance of the Levels and Moors had been recognised by the designation of 10 grassland SSSI's covering 6,100 ha (Figure 1).

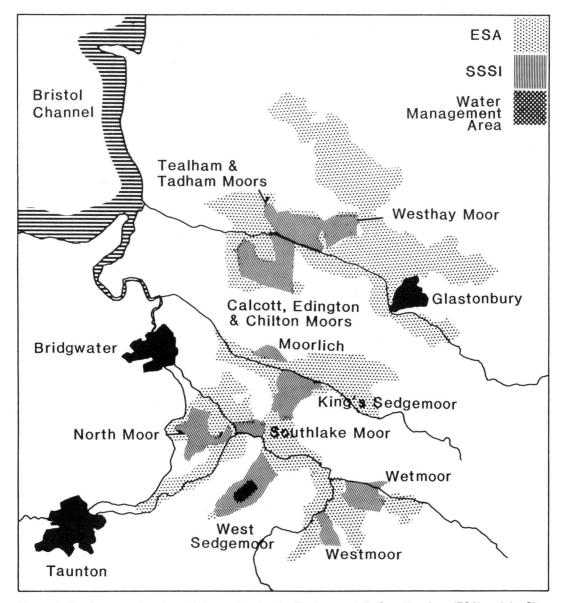

Figure 1. The Somerset Levels and Moors showing the Environmentally Sensitive Area (ESA) and the Sites of Special Scientific Interest (SSSI). After Robins, Davies & Buisson 1991.

In addition since March 1987, the majority of the farmed area of the Moors has been an ESA covering 27,000 ha. The area was selected for its wildlife and landscape value and because traditional farming methods would help to maintain these attributes. Farmers are invited to enter into agreements with MAFF involving the adoption or maintenance of practices which are judged to be compatible with the conservation of the area. In return they receive an annual payment on every eligible hectare included in the agreement. By February 1989, agreements had been concluded on 65% of the eligible land.

Restoring the conservation interest of the area clearly requires the adoption of water and land management practices more sympathetic to the needs of wildlife. The RSPB believes this can be achieved by promoting appropriate changes in agricultural policy (e.g. ESA prescriptions and changes in drainage standards) and providing appropriate advice to land management agencies (e.g. MAFF, NRA and IDB) and landowners. The adoption of appropriate reserve acquisition and management initiatives is also important, not least to provide a test-bed for practicable management methods. It is against this background that the RSPB has been acquiring and managing land on West Sedgemoor.

West Sedgemoor

West Sedgemoor comprises 1,016 ha of peaty, low-lying wet meadows with intervening droves and ditches. Shallow flooding occurs for brief spells in most winters. It has been designated a SSSI (Figure 1) and is the most important ornithological site remaining in the Somerset Levels and Moors in spite of suffering comparable decreases in wintering and breeding populations of wetland birds: there was a 64% decrease in breeding snipe and a 53% fall in all breeding waders combined between 1977 and 1987 (Robins 1987). The RSPB has been acquiring land on the Moor since 1979 and now owns over two hundred fields (425 ha) representing about 40% of the SSSI.

The basin of West Sedgemoor is lined by impermeable clay overlain by fen peat to a depth of at least 4m (average 5.25m). There is no river but water drains via an extensive ditch system (151 km.) into the NE corner of the moor whence it can be pumped into the River Parrett. Without pumping, the water table would produce a lake for much of the year. The IDB sets water levels: from April to November, water from the River Parrett is let onto the Moor to maintain a high summer level; from December to March water is pumped out at low tide. The aims of this regime are to reduce flooding in winter by providing 12-hour storage capacity in the ditches, to dry out the soil surface as quickly as possible in the spring and to provide optimum levels for wet fencing and drinking water for stock in the summer. Responsibility for the management of 47km of ditches rests with RSPB.

The reserve management plan (Street 1992) identifies the following principal habitat and species management objectives:

1. To rehabilitate West Sedgemoor so that it becomes a site dominated by damp lowland grassland with winter flooding, holding internationally important numbers of wintering wildfowl and nationally important breeding wader populations and plant communities.

2. To continue the traditional mowing and grazing regime to provide sward conditions which benefit the breeding and wintering bird assemblages, and to restore and retain the plant communities characteristic of unimproved lowland wet grassland.

3. To alter the hydrology of the RSPB holding to provide some surface flood water in winter and to maintain the soil water table over a high proportion of a core area (c180 ha) at about 20 cm below the surface from April to June.

Habitat requirements of key wetland birds on lowland wet grassland

An understanding of the habitat requirements of the important bird species is essential to the achievement of these goals and the RSPB has carried out research into the needs of breeding waders (Green 1986). Optimal levels of drainage and vegetation height in the breeding season differ between species. Snipe tend to be associated with wet and sedgy fields with soft, easily probed soil whereas Lapwings prefer drier, grassier, more closely grazed or mown fields. Surface water is an important feeding habitat for Redshank and Black-tailed Godwits.

In lowland wet meadows, waders settle to breed in April and May before most of the current year's growth of grass. The height and structure of the vegetation at this time is largely determined by management the previous year. Heavy summer grazing reduces the median height of grass in the following spring. Combinations of mowing and grazing can be used to produce effects on vegetation height similar to those from grazing alone.

Stocking rates of 2-3 cattle per ha or higher cause substantial nest losses through trampling, particularly of snipe and redshank. Postponing the start of summer grazing/mowing until mid-June increases wader breeding success, except for Lapwings for which tall vegetation in late May would reduce the amount of suitable foraging habitat.

The aim of management is to promote a range of vegetation structures and soil moisture conditions to cater for the requirements of the different species. Water levels should be managed to provide a scattering of shallow surface pools and an extensive area with a watertable about 20 cm below the soil surface in April, May and June. Management to maintain feeding conditions for waders longer into the summer permits them to extend their nesting season and allows replacement clutches to be laid after failure due to trampling or predation. However, extensive and prolonged surface flooding in spring should be avoided as it may kill vegetation, delay or prevent wader nesting and reduce the abundance of soil invertebrates on which the waders feed.

Wigeon and Bewick's Swans require a short, even,

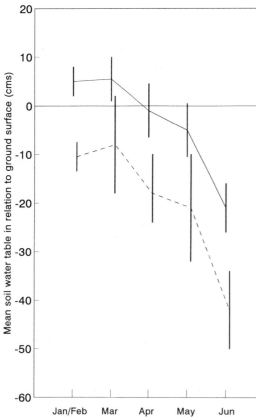

Figure 2. *Seasonal changes in the depth of the water table at the field centre within (solid line) and outside (broken line) the water management area at the West Sedgemoor RSPB reserve in 1991. Vertical bars represent 95% confidence intervals.*

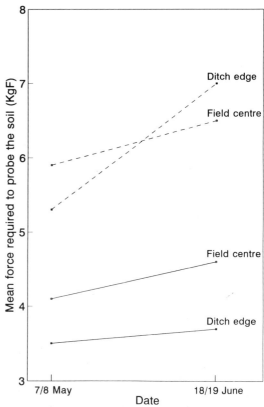

Figure 3. *The mean force required to probe the soil at five sites within (solid line) compared with four sites outside (broken line) the water management area at the West Sedgemoor RSPB reserve in 1991.*

grassy sward with some surface flooding (Thomas 1982). This is best achieved by mowing or heavy grazing of improved, drier grassland by cattle or sheep followed, if necessary, by mechanical topping.

How are these requirements to be met?

The first stage has been to begin to restore the required hydrological conditions. Since early 1989, 180 ha within the reserve has been isolated from the IDB (pumped-drained) ditch system by the use of dams with flexipipe sluices. Thus, in winter, water levels can be maintained 40-50 cm higher than in the IDB ditches and shallow flooding is possible, retained by low bunds and with areas inundated in rotation. In summer, ditch levels are held 30 cm higher than the IDB penning level. In April and May 1991 ditch water levels were almost all within 35cm of field height in the hydrologically managed area and almost exclusively more than 35 cm below field height over the rest

of the Moor (Chown 1991). The maintenance of higher ditch water levels meant that the soil water table was 10-30 cm higher within the water management area than outside (Figure 2).

A higher water table means that less force is required by waders to probe the soil. In the critical April to June period the water table remained within the target 20 cm of the surface. In contrast outside the water management areas the water table fell below 20 cm in early May, and by the middle of June the soil was harder at the ditch edges outside the water management area than it was at the field centre within it (Figure 3).

In late summer and autumn ditch water levels were allowed to fall thus lowering field watertables to facilitate farming activities. Most of the meadows on the reserve are farmed in the traditional way, usually starting with a hay cut in July, followed by aftermath grazing by cattle until the land becomes too wet in November. This is achieved by granting annual licences to local farmers. The conditions of the licences are set on a field-by-field basis to ensure specific habitat requirements are met. A secondary aim is to meet ESA prescription requirements. The terms of the licences specify dates between which grazing and/or mowing is permitted, the level, if any, of fertiliser application and any special conditions such as a requirement to top at the end of the season to provide suitable sward heights for wintering wildfowl and/or breeding waders the following spring. Fields on the higher ground are usually farmed from May/June, fields in the lowest areas from July.

All but 9.4 ha of the agricultural land was let to graziers in 1991 and farmed in compliance with ESA Tier 1 or Tier 2 prescriptions (L. Street pers comm.).

These management practices appear to have halted, and for several species already reversed, the decline in conservation interest.

Maintaining high ditch water levels in the autumn and early winter in the area isolated from the IDB ditch system has increased the frequency and extent of winter flooding. Even in comparatively dry winters a constant flood of 100-150 ha can be maintained through the winter. Rainfall in the winter which preceded hydrological management (1988/89) was similar to that in 1991/92 but there was extensive shallow flooding only in the latter period. This resulted in a ten-fold increase in the peak count of waterfowl which reached internationally important levels, with numbers of four species at nationally important levels (Table 1).

There is already evidence that the decline in the total numbers of waders breeding on West Sedgemoor has been halted for all species except snipe (Table 2). However, this reversal is not uniform and is dependent on the numbers of birds now concentrated into the hydrologically managed area within which there has been an 80% increase over 1977 figures (Chown 1991). Even though this area represents only one-sixth of the area of West Sedgemoor it now holds two-thirds of the Moor's breeding waders including 85% of the Snipe and 80% of the Redshank.

Research and monitoring

The hydrological and agricultural management outlined above is documented and its effects are closely monitored. This enables management prescriptions to be refined in the light of experience, the effectiveness of management to be demonstrated to others and specific recommendations to be made on how similar areas elsewhere should be managed.

Table 1. Peak counts of waterfowl on West Sedgemoor in two winters of similar rainfall before and after hydrological management. In 1991/92 the great majority of wintering birds were within the water management area of the RSPB reserve.

	Before management 1988/89	After management 1991/92
Rainfall (mm Oct.-Jan.)	235	219
Flooding	None	Extensive surface
Species		
Mute Swan	39	87
Bewick's Swan	62	165*
Wigeon	31	2000
Gadwall	2	15
Teal	250	2500*
Mallard	350	380
Pintail	2	12
Shoveler	2	58
Golden Plover	200	5000*
Lapwing	1200	12000*
Snipe	80	700
Total	**2250**	**22887****

** population internationally important
* population nationally important

Table 2. Changes in breeding wader populations of West Sedgemoor 1977-91. The figure in brackets is the percentage of the total breeding waders found within the hydrologically managed area in 1991. (Data from Round (1977), Robins (1987) and Chown (1991).

Species	1977	1987	1991
Lapwing (pairs)	50	20	34 (59%)
Snipe (drummers)	64	18	13 (85%)
Curlew (pairs)	10	5	9 (33%)
Redshank (pair)	16	4	10 (80%)
Black-tailed Godwit (pairs)	6	1	1 (100%)

The following research and monitoring programme has been established:

Hydrology

A topographic and field soil survey was undertaken and research started to determine:

(a) the proportion of the hydrologically managed area which needs to be in optimum condition for breeding waders in the period April - June and how this can be achieved e.g. by installing sub-surface irrigation pipes at particular spacings. Given the average ditch spacings on West Sedgemoor of 115m, the lateral flow of water through the soil is insufficient to replace water lost through evapotranspiration when the grass begins to grow in spring. This means that in dry summers the watertable at the field centre is likely to decline to well below 20 cm by the end of June, despite the maintenance of high ditch water levels.

(b) the extent of winter flooding and the soil watertable conditions which used to pertain on West Sedgemoor when wintering wildfowl and breeding wader numbers were much higher (by running existing theoretical watertable models with historical meteorological and penning level information).

There is regular monitoring of ditch water levels (by reading gauge boards) and watertable (by dipwell transects across fields) inside and outside the hydrologically managed area. Records are maintained of the operation of control structures such as sluices and pumps.

Birds

Research to determine the distribution of breeding waders on West Sedgemoor in relation to the soil watertable, soil penetrability, invertebrate densities and sward structure. Regular counts of wintering waterfowl and breeding waders over the whole Moor by standard methods every year.

Vegetation

Transects and quadrats to monitor changes in vegetation communities in relation to the changes in the water regime.

Soil invertebrates

Research into the effects of watertable management on invertebrate distribution and abundance.

Farming operations

For each field within the reserve records are kept of grazing intensity (cattle days/month, estimated by monitoring every two weeks), mowing (date and yield), topping and fertiliser application.

The future

The RSPB's ownership of a substantial block of land, some of which could be isolated from the IDB ditch system, provided an opportunity to demonstrate that traditional farming compliant with existing ESA prescriptions was not sufficient on its own to retain the conservation value of the

area (particularly for breeding waders, wintering wildfowl and the botanical communities characteristic of traditionally-farmed wet meadows). New ESA prescriptions introduced in 1992 now include a third tier attracting increased payments of £350 per ha and designed to further enhance the ecological interest of the grassland by the creation of wetter winter and spring conditions on the Moors. The conditions attached to Tier 3 include maintaining ditch water levels at not less than field level from 1 December to 30 April and not more than 30 cm below from 1 May to 30 November. These conditions accord closely with those maintained within the hydrologically managed area on West Sedgemoor RSPB reserve in 1991.

Where can further information be obtained?

Further information on the management of lowland wet grassland for breeding waders can be found in Green (1986). Robins *et al.* (1991) document the decline in the wildlife interest of the Somerset Levels and Moors. Both reports may be obtained from RSPB, Sandy.

References

Chown, D.J. (1991). *Report on breeding wader research, West Sedgemoor 1991.* Unpubl. rept. RSPB, Sandy.

Green, R.E. (1986). *The management of lowland wet grassland for breeding waders.* Unpubl. rept. RSPB, Sandy.

Murfitt, R.C. & Chown, D.J. (1983). *Somerset Levels and Moors winter bird surveys, 1981-82 and 1982-83.* Unpubl. rept. RSPB, Sandy.

Robins, M. (1987). *Somerset Moors breeding birds 1987.* Unpubl. rept. RSPB, Sandy.

Robins, M., Davies, S.G.F., & Buisson, R.S.K. (1991). *An internationally important wetland in crisis. The Somerset Levels and Moors: a case history of wetland destruction.* Unpubl. rept. RSPB, Sandy.

Robins, M. & Green, R.E. (1988). *Changes in the management of water levels on the Somerset Moors.* Unpubl. rept. RSPB, Sandy.

Round, P.D. (1978). *Bird Survey Somerset Levels 1976-77.* Unpubl. rept. RSPB, Sandy.

Street, L. (1992). *West Sedgemoor RSPB Reserve Management Plan.* Unpubl. rept. RSPB, Sandy.

Thomas, G, J. (1982). *Managing vegetation at wetlands.* Pp. 21-38. In: Scott, D.A. (Ed.). *Managing wetlands and their birds: a manual of wetland and waterfowl management.* IWRB, Slimbridge.

Weaver, D,.J. & Chown, D.J. (1983). *Somerset Moors breeding bird survey 1983.* Unpubl. rept. RSPB, Sandy.

Williams, G. & Bowers, J.K. (1987). Land drainage and birds in England and Wales. *RSPB Conserv. Rev. 1*, 25-30.

Woolston Eyes - past, present but no future?

J S Kirby & M Owen

Research and Conservation Department, WWT

Unless urgent remedial work is undertaken, and appropriate management plans are agreed, Woolston Eyes, one of the finest artificial wetlands in Britain and a Site of Special Scientific Interest (SSSI), will be permanently destroyed. The Wildfowl & Wetlands Trust, and others, cannot accept such losses and call upon the owners of the site, the Manchester Ship Canal Company (MSCC), to help retain and enhance its wildlife interest.

Where and what is it?

Woolston Eyes is situated some two miles to the east of Warrington, Cheshire. Lying alongside the Manchester Ship Canal it can easily be seen by commuters crossing the Thelwall Viaduct while travelling north or south on the M6 motorway. The area is some 200 hectares in extent and comprises four large deposit beds used in a 15-year rotation by the MSCC to hold dredgings from the ship canal. Such dredging is necessary to keep the canal open for shipping and for flood protection and takes place over three or four months of the year. Once in the beds, such materials are allowed to dry out, and have been extracted and sold commercially during the past 10-15 years.

The four deposit grounds vary in their attractiveness to wildlife. The Woolston Eyes Conservation Group (WECG), through active management and co-operation with the MSCC, have focussed attention on Bed No.3 which has been maintained in a shallow flooded state. As a result, it has attracted a diverse assemblage of wetland animals and plants. Indeed, it has certainly developed into one of the best wetland sites in northern England and, in some respects, one of the best in Britain as a whole.

Why is it important?

Woolston Eyes, and particularly Bed No.3, supports rich wetland plant and animal communities. Its wintering wildfowl populations, monitored for many years as part of the National Waterfowl Counts (NWC) scheme, number some 7,000 wild-fowl collectively. These include, on average, around 3,700 Teal and 300 Shoveler, numbers which easily exceed the levels required for the site to be considered nationally important for them (Kirby *et al.* 1991). Furthermore, such species have, at times, been present in concentrations deserving international recognition. Additionally, hundreds of Pochard, Pintail and Gadwall reside there, as well as up to 200 Ruddy Ducks, and a variety of other species.

In spring and summer, Woolston Eyes represents one of the most important breeding sites for waterfowl in Britain. The Eyes support a nationally important colony of Black-necked Grebes (4 pairs in 1991), the second largest in England and Wales and one of just four or five in Britain (information from the Rare Breeding Birds Panel). This species receives full protection under schedule 1 of the Wildlife and Countryside Act 1981, the EC Birds Directive and Appendix II of the Berne Convention (the Council of Europe Convention on the Conservation of European Wildlife and Natural Habitats). Other important breeding waterfowl include Pochard (13 pairs in 1991), certainly a concentration of national significance, and Ruddy Ducks (usually 10 pairs, but 21 broods in 1991). Of the non-wildfowl species, breeding birds include regionally important numbers of Sedge (50-100 pairs) and Reed Warblers (20+ pairs).

Woolston Eyes is not only important for birds. Of major interest are its Great Crested Newts, a schedule 5 species under the Wildlife and Countryside Act 1981, whilst commoner amphibia include the Smooth Newt, Common Frog and Common Toad. Amongst the reptiles, the Common Lizard and the Slow Worm can be seen, and numerous species of Odonata (dragonflies and damselflies) breed in good numbers. The rich plant community must not be forgotten. Indeed, Woolston Eyes would be unable to support its impressive fauna without it.

It was because of its nationally important wintering and breeding wildfowl that the four beds comprising Woolston Eyes were notified as an

SSSI in 1985. SSSI designation serves to label the importance of a site on a national basis. Unfortunately, however, SSSI status does not necessarily prevent the future development of a site as certain operations are permitted even if the site may effectively be destroyed.

What happened to Woolston Eyes?

Following survey work by consultant engineers in spring 1991, the MSCC decided that weaknesses in the north bank of Bed No.3 meant that there was no alternative but to drain it. During the regular meetings with the MSCC that ensued, the WECG tried desperately to dissuade the company from such drastic action and suggested that other less damaging alternatives could be pursued. This was to no avail and, in August 1991, despite formal protest from a variety of conservation groups including WWT, drainage began. Within three months, virtually all the water from Bed No.3 had been removed. Not surprisingly, this had catastrophic effects upon the wildfowl with some common species disappearing completely (Bowman *et al.* 1992).

Clearly, if there was a major safety problem then no one could have argued against this. Unfortunately, attempts to make an independent assessment of the engineers report have been rendered impossible by the MSCC's unwillingness to release anything other than selected sections of it. Attempts to allow other engineers to make an independent inspection of the banks were similarly refused. WECG suggested that, with time, an alternative area could be created to accommodate the birds from Bed No.3, but, as a result of the MSCC's wish to take immediate action, there was not the time to even discuss such possibilities.

The actions of MSCC have meant that Woolston Eyes has been severely damaged by drainage, and the landowners have so far refused to allow even shallow water, which is periodically pumped on to an adjoining deposit ground, to be retained. At the same time, other parts are being intensively drained for the extraction of soil and sand. As if this was not enough, Waste Management Limited (WML), who had a lease option on Bed No.1 from the MSCC, sought planning permission in 1991 to extend their present landfill site over the bed. Not surprisingly, this has been opposed by the WECG because the bed lies within the SSSI and is of considerable wildlife importance. Overall, one of Britain's most important wetlands, and an SSSI, is thus being systematically destroyed.

What now?

When indicating the need for drainage of Bed No.3, the MSCC proposed a new relationship with the WECG. They indicated that they were prepared to recognise, for the first time, the role of the WECG on the land, and gave an undertaking that they would take account of the needs of all wetland wildlife on the site, providing this did not conflict with their commercial interests. The WECG asked if there was any possibility of compensation for the loss of habitat but the MSCC felt that, since it was a safety requirement, they were not obliged to offer compensation. However, they have offered a small area, amounting to some 17ha, in the north-west corner of Bed No.4 on a 25 year lease. The condition was that the Group should pay for all excavation, bunding and other work necessary, provisionally estimated at £20,000. The Group is attempting to raise such funds.

Though not responsible for the destruction of Bed No.3, WML are also obviously feeling uneasy with the present situation. They, in recognition of the considerable loss of habitat from Bed No.1, the subject of their own planning application, and the drainage of Bed No.3, have agreed to fund investigations into the feasibility of creating a new wetland site within or close to Woolston Eyes as a means of mitigating the disastrous effects of recent developments. The WWT's consultancy wing, the Wetlands Advisory Service, are conducting such investigations and hope to gain some security for wetland wildlife in the area. The negotiations are still very much alive. However, it has to be said that these proposals represent piecemeal offerings on behalf of the MSCC and WML compared to what has been lost.

With careful thought, the compilers of a new book of Britain's most endangered and important birds offered suggestions for the wise management and protection of these populations. For the Black-necked Grebe, perhaps the most important bird at Woolston Eyes, they wrote that "there is a need to ensure that the main colony sites are adequately safeguarded" and that "these sites should have adequate safeguards either as nature reserves or SSSIs" (Batten *et al.* 1990). They must be disheartened to know that one of the few major colonies has now been destroyed. It would appear that the SSSI system provides relatively little protection to sites like Woolston Eyes. Admittedly, Woolston Eyes is an unusual SSSI since it was notified as a working industrial site where habitat change was perhaps inevitable and accepted. It is sad though that English Nature, who presumably recognise the importance of the area, appeared to have been somewhat powerless to prevent the landowners from destroying it. This begs the question: are other SSSIs equally vulnerable?

If the MSCC is genuine in wanting to work closely with the WECG, then perhaps there is still a future for Woolston Eyes. If however the importance of the site is not to be lost forever, then urgent remedial work on the weakened earth banks needs to be carried out. It is possible that some funds could be found from the conservation bodies, or raised by public donations, so the full cost did not fall on the company. So far, the WECG have not been given the encouragement to explore this possibility and the destruction of Woolston Eyes has continued at pace.

Hundreds of visitors to Woolston Eyes regard it as a magical place. The site has a very high educational value, an attribute to which the WWT, and others, attach great importance. If the will was there on the part of the MSCC then this magic could be retained for future generations. Sadly, time is running out and, to-date, there is no indication that the MSCC has any immediate plans to repair the weakened bank and allow water to return. Meanwhile, species such as Black-necked Grebes have returned only to stay for a day or so before moving on. It is unlikely that they will easily find another suitable water to meet their very particular requirements, and the British breeding population of this nationally scarce species will therefore suffer a severe setback, as will the important breeding numbers of other species and the thousands of wintering wildfowl.

References

Batten, L.A., Bibby, C.J., Clement, P., Elliot, G.D. & Porter, R.F. 1990. *Red Data Birds in Britain: action for rare, threatened and important species*. T. & A.D. Poyser, London.

Bowman, D., Linley, F. & Martin, B. 1992. *The Woolston Eyes Conservation Group Annual Report 1991*. Unpublished Report, 62pp.

Kirby, J.S., Ferns, J.R., Waters, R.J. & Prys-Jones, R.P. 1991. *Wildfowl and Wader Counts 1990-91*. The Wildfowl & Wetlands Trust, Slimbridge.

B. Martin: Woolston Eyes 1991, pre-damage

RSPB reserves management plans and monitoring

Ceri Evans, Gareth Thomas & Graham Hirons

Conservation Management Department, RSPB

A systematic approach to the planning of reserve management is essential. Broadly similar methods are followed by all conservation books in the UK. This article describes the process.

All RSPB reserves have a five-year management plan which identifies conservation priorities, and includes a work programme by which they can be attained. The progress of the management plan is monitored by the reserve annual report. The RSPB places high emphasis on recording and monitoring management experiments on reserves. Results are written up in the form of scientific papers and management case studies.

Objectives of acquisition and management

The RSPB's main mission is to conserve wild birds and the habitats upon which they depend. It strives to maintain bird numbers, diversity and geographical distribution and to increase these where general conservation values are enhanced by so doing (Prestt 1990). Habitat preservation is considered to be the most important means of conserving wild birds. The RSPB achieves this by influencing land-use practices and policy in the wider countryside for the benefit of wildlife and by the acquisition and management of land as nature reserves.

The RSPB acquired its first reserve at Dungeness in 1931. It now manages some 118 sites covering about 76,000 ha, half of which are owned with the remainder on lease or management agreement (Thomas 1991). Almost all are SSSIs and some 38,500 ha are of Nature Conservation Review quality (Ratcliffe 1977).

Over the last 10 years, the RSPB has spent an average of almost £2 million per annum on land purchase, and annual management costs for existing reserves amount to some £3 million (Thomas 1991). It is essential therefore to evaluate potential reserve acquisitions in terms of their contribution to bird conservation and to manage sites on sound ecological principles and in the most cost-effective manner.

Priorities for acquisition and management reflect the presence and requirements of bird species which qualify for Red Data status (Batten et al. 1990) and of scarce or threatened habitats (Thomas 1991). The RSPB manages significant amounts of some of Great Britain's scarcest habitats, e.g. more than 31% (730 ha) of all reedswamps larger than two ha, and 21.5% (2690 ha) of the native pinewood habitat (Thomas 1991). RSPB reserves hold significant breeding populations of the majority of British Red Data species especially colonial nesters and species dependent on scarce or diminishing habitats (Hirons & Lambton 1991). For example, our reserves hold peak winter count totals of 312,000 wintering wildfowl and 338,000 wintering waders. These totals represent more than 25% of the respective UK wintering populations which are themselves of world importance (Everett et al. 1988). The UK is also of world importance for its breeding seabirds and some 12% are located at RSPB reserves (Lloyd 1989; Hirons & Lambton 1991).

The role and content of management plans

Most reserves require management to maintain or increase their conservation value. This necessitates understanding the site, identifying the objectives to be attained, formulating programmes of work and monitoring their effectiveness to ensure that resources of cash, labour and skills are being efficiently used. A management plan is a convenient mechanism for bringing all these elements together and a good management planning system ensures the regional and national overview necessary to link work on reserves with other RSPB activities and aims. The RSPB has recently completed a three year programme to review and revise or initiate management plans for all of its reserves.

Management plans are prepared one or two years after acquisition when the warden has had time to assemble all the necessary background information (although outline plans are in position sooner) and the format is based on the system followed by the statutory nature conservation organisations in the UK (NCC 1988). The RSPB plan content (RSPB 1990) is shown in Figure 1 and the six-step system for plan production is summarized in Figure 2. The collection of background data and the processes of external and internal consultation are considered to be especially important in this sequence.

Adequate research and survey is essential for new acquisitions. As much information as possible is gathered on the site itself, its physical and biological character, habitat areas recorded to standard methods (NCC 1990), and past and present uses of the land as a basis for identification and evaluation of its conservation importance. These data are incorporated in Sections 1, 2 and 3 of the plan prior to consideration of management policy and methods.

This process pays full regard to the non-ornithological interest of sites. Many RSPB reserves have been designated as SSSIs on botanical, entomological and geomorphological grounds. These include such sites as North Hoy, Orkney which supports upland heath and mire vegetation communities of international importance, and Dungeness, Kent which is the largest natural shingle structure in western Europe, important not only for its physiographic features but also for its flora, particularly lichens, and insect fauna.

The RSPB places high emphasis on managing sites for their intrinsic nature conservation value and integrating management for birds with other important nature conservation goals. To support this and help ensure their continued well-being, resources are put into research, survey and monitoring of non-ornithological groups (Cadbury 1990; Evans 1991; Pickess 1989).

A quarter of RSPB reserves have been surveyed according to the National Vegetation Classification scheme (Rodwell 1991 et seq.). This scheme provides a means of mapping, describing, classifying and evaluating the vegetation resource of the reserve within a national context, in order to assist with management planning decisions and to demonstrate major changes.

General and environmental information pertaining to the reserve is reviewed and evaluated at special pathfinder meetings with representatives from the statutory nature conservation organisations. Their participation is particularly useful, since we receive advice on how to integrate management for birds with other important nature conservation

goals.

The main goals and strategies of management (Section 4 of the plan) are decided at these pathfinder meetings as is the general nature of the prescriptions to achieve these (Section 5). This gives the warden or site manager the framework within which to complete a draft plan, usually within about six months. An important element of this stage is to produce a work programme for the next five years which is an essential aid for the allocation of resources over this period. At the end of this time an audit is carried out automatically and a revised plan is produced.

There is a comprehensive system of consultation within the RSPB before the draft management plans are agreed. This provides an opportunity to incorporate elements that contribute to overall RSPB objectives including not only those for bird conservation now being set out in species and habitat action plans (Porter et al. 1990; Housden et al. 1991) but also those for education and marketing. It also ensures that the policies for individual reserves do not conflict with corporate goals.

How do we monitor the management plan?

An annual monitoring system is essential to assess progress towards the objectives of the management plans and the costs of achieving them. Currently, this is achieved through the mechanism of the Annual Report produced by the warden for each reserve. It contains progress reports on standard proformas for all the management operations set out in Section 5 of the plan (Lambton 1989). Standard codes and headings are used for all projects, following the recording system developed by NCC (1988). These help to ensure that information is presented in a consistent way from site to site and provide a basis for computerizing site records at all levels. At present records are held on paper systems. However, some of the key biological data are currently being computerized and trials are being held to evaluate a computerized management planning and project recording system.

Changes in the extent of different habitats are recorded according to a standardised system (NCC 1990). The breeding and overwintering populations of important bird species, and any others identified in the management plan, are monitored and the results are contributed, where appropriate, to the national schemes.

Special attention is paid to monitoring selected non-bird species, including all Red Data species and key indicator species, for which the reserve is important. This enables us to evaluate the effects of management for these groups. In addition, the status of the non-bird groups at the site is updated every five years by means of Biological Records Centre cards, to determine whether important species are present which might be sensitive to management intended to benefit key bird species, or merit management in their own right. Where appropriate, non-bird data are contributed to national monitoring schemes, for instance annual butterfly transect counts are sent to ITE.

A major effort goes into recording management methods and monitoring results. Projects are designed as experiments, so that changes in physical parameters and the responses of birds and other wildlife groups can be measured accurately. This enables management techniques to be refined, and exported to other reserves or conservation managers by means including scientific papers, Management Case Studies and training courses. Field work is usually done by wardens under guidance from Reserves Ecologists. However if the projects are large, contract ecologists are employed for periods of one to six months to carry out the field work and analysis. The following are examples of monitoring projects from the current work programme:

1. Monitoring of Red Deer numbers and tree regeneration to help determine correct grazing pressure to allow natural regeneration of native pinewood at Abernethy, Inverness-shire.

2. Monitoring the response to hydrological management by breeding waders, invertebrates and vegetation on six lowland wet grassland reserves.

3. The impact on birds, invertebrates and vegetation of creating rides in broadleaved woodland at Tudeley Wood, Kent and Highnam Wood, Gloucs.

For all monitoring projects, standard methodologies which conform to national schemes are used where they exist.

Where can more information be obtained?

Guidance notes for the preparation of Management Plans can be found in NCC (1988) and RSPB (1990). The standard project recording system, as used by the RSPB, is detailed in Lambton (1989) and NCC (1988). Information relating to current research, survey and monitoring projects carried out on reserves can be found in the RSPB's project register (RSPB 1992). A list of current RSPB Management Case Studies can be obtained from the Reserves Ecology Dept. at The Lodge, Sandy.

Advice on the management of land for important bird species is available from RSPB Regional Offices.

References

Batten, L.A., Bibby, C.J., Clement, P., Elliott, G.D. & Porter, R.F. (1990). *Red Data Birds in Britain, action for rare, threatened and important species.* T. & A. D. Poyser, London.

Cadbury, C.J. (1990). The status and management of butterflies on RSPB reserves. *RSPB Conserv. Rev.* 4, 40-46.

Evans, C.E. (1991). The Conservation Importance and management of the ditch flora on RSPB reserves. *RSPB Conserv. Rev.* 5, 65-71.

Everett, M.J., Cadbury, C.J., & Dawson, L. (1988). The importance of RSPB reserves for wintering and migrant wildfowl and waders. *RSPB Conserv. Rev.* 2, 57-63.

Hirons, G. & Lambton, S. (1991). The importance of RSPB reserves for breeding birds. *RSPB Conserv. Rev.* 5, 23-27.

Housden, S., Thomas, G., Bibby, C. & Porter, R. (1991). Towards a habitat conservation strategy for bird habitats in Britain. *RSPB Conserv. Rev.* 5, 9-16.

Lambton, S. J. (1989). *Reserves monitoring Programme and annual reporting.* RSPB, Sandy.

Lloyd, C. (1989). The importance of RSPB reserves for breeding seabirds. *RSPB Conserv. Rev.* 3, 35-40.

Nature Conservancy Council (1988). *Site management plans for nature conservation; a working guide.* Peterborough.

Nature Conservancy Council (1990). *Handbook for Phase 1 habitat survey.* Peterborough.

Pickess, B. P. (1989). The importance of RSPB reserves for dragonflies. *RSPB Conserv. Rev.* 3, 30-34.

Porter, R., Bibby, C., Elliott, G., Housden, S., Thomas, G. & Williams, G. (1990). Species action plans for birds. *RSPB Conserv. Rev.* 4, 10-14.

Prestt, I. (1990). The RSPB's mission. *RSPB Conserv. Rev.* 4, 5.

Ratcliffe, D.A. (1977). *A Nature Conservation Review.* Vols. I & II. CUP, Cambridge.

Rodwell, J.S. (ed.) (1991). *British Plant Communities. Vol.I Woodlands and Scrub.* CUP, Cambridge.

RSPB (1990). *Management plan guidance notes.* RSPB.

RSPB (1992). *RSPB Conservation Projects 1992/3.* RSPB.

Thomas, G. (1991). The acquisition of RSPB reserves. *RSPB Conserv. Rev.* 5, 17-2.

Table 1. The RSPB Management Plan format, based on that of NCC (1988).

0.	**SUMMARY**	3.9	Potential value for future development
1.	**GENERAL INFORMATION**	3.10	Intrinsic appeal
1.1	Location	3.11	Other criteria
1.2	Site status	3.12	Identification/confirmation of important features
1.3	Tenure	3.13	Operations likely to damage the special interests (PDO)
1.4	Site definition and boundaries	3.14	Main factors influencing the management of the site
1.5	Legal and other official constraints and permission	3.15	Potential acquisitions and extensions
1.6	Main fixed assets	**4.**	**MANAGEMENT POLICY**
2	**ENVIRONMENTAL INFORMATION**	4.1	Main management goals and strategies etc. including supporting rationale
2.1	**Physical**		
2.1.1	Climate	**5.**	**MANAGEMENT PRESCRIPTIONS AND OPERATIONS**
2.1.2	Hydrology	**5.1**	**Habitat and species management**
2.1.3	Geology	5.1.1	List of projects etc
2.1.4	Soils	**5.2**	**Visitor services, interpretation & education**
2.2	**Biological**		
2.2.1	Habitats	5.2.1	List of projects etc
2.2.2	Flora	**5.3**	**Estate services and major machinery**
2.2.3	Fauna	5.3.1	List of projects etc
2.3	**Cultural**	**5.4**	**Public relations and administration**
2.3.1	Commercial use	5.4.1	List of projects etc
2.3.2	Recreational use	**5.5**	**Research, survey, monitoring**
2.3.3	Research, survey, monitoring	5.5.1	List of projects etc
2.3.4	Conservation management		
3.	**EVALUATION**	**6.**	**5 YEAR WORK PROGRAMME**
3.1	Size	6.1	All projects and years of operation listed
3.2	Diversity		
3.3	Naturalness	**7.**	**APPRENDICES**
3.4	Rarity	7.1	References
3.5	Fragility	7.2	Maps/plans
3.6	Typicalness		
3.7	Recorded history		
3.8	Position in ecological/geographical units		

Table 2. Steps in production of RSPB Management Plan.

	Task	Responsibility	Main participants
1	Research and Survey 1/2 yrs	Warden. Ecologist	Contract and specialist staff
2	Plan meeting to decide policies	Manager	Warden. Manager Ecologist Land Agent. NCC Staff. Specialist Staff
3	Draft plan 3 months	Warden	Various
4	Consultation at H.Q. 3 months	Ecologist	Ecologist, Eductionalist. Marketing. Research. Scientist.
5	Revision of Draft plan 3 months	Warden. Manager, Ecologist	Various
6	Approved plan	Director	Heads of Ecology, Land Agency, Reserves management.

Plan operational for 5 years before automatic review. Monitoring by annual report.

Land management on RSPB reserves

Ian Bainbridge

Ecology Section, RSPB, Edinburgh

The RSPB was founded in 1889 to campaign against the plumage trade. The development of the idea that land purchase could protect birds and their habitats led to the acquisition of its first nature reserve at Dungeness in 1931. Since then, reserve acquisition has continued at a rate reflecting the rise in the Society's membership. By 1991, there were 118 reserves totalling 75,648 ha and covering almost the full range of important bird habitats to be found in the UK.

The current rationale for reserve acquisition and management

Both acquisition and management of reserves have been strongly influenced by changing attitudes to conservation over the years, and during the 1980s a series of reviews by RSPB conservation staff and discussions with other agencies led to the definition of a clear rationale for the Society's reserves activities.

The most important of these reviews was undoubtedly the production of *Red Data Birds in Britain* (Batten *et al.* 1990), and two closely related exercises to assess which of these birds are the most threatened (Bibby *et al.* 1989) and to review the threats to their habitats (Housden *et al.* 1991). These have enabled the RSPB to prioritise site acquisition and management relative to the status of birds and habitats and the degree of threat to them. In addition, the visitor and educational potential of possible reserves are also assessed. The overall process is summarised by Thomas (1991).

The application of this rationale has also involved an internal review of land management on all existing reserves, associated with the development of full management plans for them. The emphasis of management is now placed upon conservation and enhancement of the threatened habitats on reserves and of the Red Data Book birds associated with them. The contribution made by RSPB reserves to the conservation of these threatened habitats is shown in Table 1.

Management of semi-natural habitats

Some threatened habitats and some associated with

large numbers of Red Data Book birds require little physical management to maintain their wildlife value. Their conservation is normally achieved by acquisition, to reduce or remove threats associated with unsympathetic land-use. They include open waters and montane areas, as well as sea-cliffs which hold internationally important breeding seabird colonies. However, a number of habitats require substantial and careful management to maintain and enhance their conservation value, and the birds dependent upon them.

Lowland heaths

The management of lowland heath for conservation requires the maintenance of the plagioclimax vegetation, usually predominantly heathers and gorse, in a condition suitable for important bird species and other fauna, and prevention of invasion by non-native plants, scrub and trees. On Arne, rotational management of heather and gorse maintains the closed canopy conditions required by Dartford Warblers (Bibby 1978, Pickess *et al.* 1989) and several sites are managed for Nightjars, usually at the ecotone between woodland and heath (Burgess *et al.* 1990).

A more radical project currently underway is the restoration of Suffolk heathland from land that has latterly been used for arable farming, by depletion of nutrient levels and the re-introduction of seed of heathland plant species (Evans 1992).

Upland mires and heaths

Britain's heather moorlands are important breeding areas for many Red Data Book birds, including Merlin and Golden Plover, and the RSPB has undertaken a number of studies to determine the most appropriate grazing and burning management on its upland reserves. These vary depending on the bird species to be encouraged and on growth rates of vegetation, themselves influenced by local climate and soils. In Orkney, where grazing levels have been very low in the 20th century, and where an important requirement is deep heather for nesting raptors, a non-intervention approach is adopted, with no burning and low grazing levels.

Associated with the moorland habitats are

upland mires, many of which have suffered drainage in recent decades. On Fetlar, the restoration of high water tables to some of the few remaining mires, through a combination of bunds and sluices and the digging of small pools, has led to their re-occupation by breeding Red-necked Phalaropes, and it is hoped is that further hydrological manipulation will ensure the future of one of Britain's rarest birds. In Abernethy, the restoration of mires and pools within the pine forest and on moorland has provided nesting habitat for Goldeneye and other bird species, as well as valuable pools for northern dragonflies.

Native pinewoods

A series of acquisitions, beginning with the area around the famous Loch Garten Osprey site, has led to RSPB becoming one of the major owners of remaining native pinewoods in Britain; some 21% is within the RSPB Abernethy reserve. From the 1950s to the mid 1980s, native pinewoods suffered a 25% decline due to clear-felling, underplanting with non-native species and conversion to pine plantation (Bain & Bainbridge 1988) and RSPB's Abernethy reserve was previously subject to all of these pressures to some degree. The native pinewoods also suffer from the continuing increase in the Red Deer population, which in many areas is at such a high level that deer completely prevent natural regeneration.

At Abernethy, the RSPB has therefore begun a comprehensive management programme. This includes forestry work to remove exotic tree species and plantation trees from within the native pinewood to allow a natural woodland structure to develop by natural regeneration. Also, natural regeneration is being protected by the culling of deer on the reserve, in a programme designed to bring deer numbers down to levels at which pinewood regeneration and deer can co-exist.

Lowland wet grassland

Management of parts of the Somerset Levels to re-create conditions suitable for breeding waders is described by Hirons elsewhere in this volume. Often, a second aim is to provide shallow winter flooding as feeding and roosting areas for wildfowl. A number of hydrological studies are being undertaken to determine the most effective water control management for a range of RSPB reserves, from Pulborough Brooks in Sussex to the Loch of Strathbeg in Grampian. A key factor in this is the soil type as peats, clays and silts have different hydraulic characteristics which affect their suit-

ability as feeding habitat for different wader species (Burgess & Hirons 1990). Grazing intensity and timing are also critical in creating correct vegetation structures for nesting or feeding waders (Tickner & Evans 1992) and in avoiding trampling damage to nest sites (Green 1986).

Associated with lowland wet grassland are many important plant species found particularly in ditches and dykes and management programmes for their conservation, involving rotational cleaning, re-profiling and grazing, take place on a num-. ber of reserves (Evans 1991).

Sand and machair

In the last two years grassland management for Corncrakes has been implemented on part of the Loch Gruinart reserve on Islay, by excluding cattle from unimproved grassland from February onwards, and providing early spring cover by excluding cattle from iris beds for longer periods of time. The regeneration of deep, herb-rich hay swards has occurred surprisingly rapidly, and there are high hopes that Corncrakes will re-establish themselves. The recent acquisition of a substantial area of machair grassland on the island of Coll has also provided opportunities for Corncrake management. It is hoped that the population on the reserve will increase as a result of sensitive grassland management, retention of iris beds and late cutting of hay. The reserve will also provide an experimental and demonstration area for the development of best practice for implementation in other areas where corncrakes are declining or have been lost.

Swamp, fen and carr

Swamps are another group of habitats subject to rapid successional change. For example, as vegetation and debris accumulates in reedbeds, the ground becomes progressively drier, allowing scrub and carr encroachment. In recent years a number of reedbeds throughout the country have suffered from this process, and substantial rehabilitation work is currently underway, either by raising water tables or by the removal of the upper layers of the accumulated plant debris. These activities have been reviewed by Burgess & Evans (1989).

At Titchwell on the Norfolk coast the embankment of an area of estuarine reedbed to create a freshwater reedbed has led to the colonisation of the area by both Bitterns and Marsh Harriers (Sills 1988). At Strumpshaw Fen in Norfolk, the broad was rehabilitated by isolating it from polluted river waters, and this has also led to the regeneration of the important reedbed, which holds both Bearded Tits and Marsh Harrier (Tickner *et al.* 1991). At Leighton Moss, water control within reed bed areas has been facilitated by the creation of a series of shallow bunds to allow manipulation of water levels in different compartments, to benefit Bitterns.

Saltmarsh and intertidal habitats

One of the major problems of intertidal and salt-marsh management has been the spread of Spartina species and hybrids, either naturally or through their introduction into a number of estuaries as saltmarsh stabilisers in the course of this century. The RSPB reserves on the Dee and at Udale Bay on the Cromarty Firth are both experiencing problems of Spartina spread and experiments are underway for its control and removal (Garnett *et al.* 1992), to retain the high-level mudflats so important to Redshank and Dunlin.

Saltmarsh management depends on its existing vegetation types and the ornithological aims. Several sites, for example Morecambe Bay (Wilson 1991) and Frampton Marsh on the Wash, have been subject to the re-introduction of grazing to provide more suitable habitats for Wigeon and other wildfowl and waders.

At Titchwell, the creation of a brackish lagoon from saltmarsh has led to colonisation by breeding Avocets (Sills 1988). Management of the coastal lagoons at Minsmere and Havergate (Cadbury *et al.* 1989) also maintains Avocet populations at these reserves.

Management of agricultural habitats

Not all of the birds on RSPB reserves are reliant upon semi-natural habitats. On a number of sites, relatively intensive management of agricultural grassland is an important element in the provision of refuges for wildfowl. In Essex, the reseeding of coastal pasture and use of grazing sheep to produce short sward has provided conditions suitable for Dark-bellied Brent Geese. In contrast, experience in Norfolk has shown that the production of a relatively tall sward is the optimum management for Bean Geese (Allport 1989).

On Islay, the low ground on the Loch Gruinart reserve is subject to a programme of reseeding on a five-yearly basis to provide the nutrient-rich sward to feed large numbers of Greenland Barnacle Geese (up to 39% of the world population) which winter there. The high density of these flocks leads to the deterioration of the swards in a relatively short period, requiring the reseeding programme to maintain the necessary grass quality.

In eastern Scotland at Vane Farm and the Loch of Strathbeg management for Pink-footed and Greylag Geese is of a slightly lower intensity, providing permanent swards of moderately rich grassland and undertaking early spring fertiliser applications to provide the early growth of grass to enable geese to build up the necessary reserves for migration to Iceland and beyond.

Where can more information be obtained?

The RSPB places great importance on the exchange of management information between reserves, and on its dissemination to other conservation bodies. Many of the studies referred to in this paper have been detailed in case studies available from RSPB Ecology Section. Others have been outlined in the RSPB Conservation Review. The compilation of a Reserves Gazetteer, currently in draft (Parry 1991), will provide a comprehensive inventory of all RSPB reserve management activity.

Table 1. Extent of threatened habitats* on RSPB reserves.

Habitat	Area ha	% of GB resource
Lowland heaths	1,090	1.8
Upland mires and heaths	44,040	0.8
Native pinewoods	2,690	21.5
Lowland wet grassland	2,370	4.7
Sand and machair	2,520	?
Swamp, fen and carr	730	31.7
Saltmarsh	3,100	8.0
Intertidal	11,400	4.9

* As defined by Housden *et al.* 1991, from Thomas 1991.

References

Allport, G. (1989). Norfolk's Bean Geese and their management. *RSPB Conserv. Rev.* 3, 59-60.
Bain, C. & Bainbridge, I.P. (1988). A better future for our native pinewoods? *RSPB Conserv. Rev.* 2, 50-53.
Batten, L.A., Bibby, C.J., Clement, P., Elliott, G.D. & Porter, R.F. (1990). *Red Data Birds in Britain, action for rare, threatened and important species.* T. & A.D. Poyser, London.
Bibby, C.J. (1978). Conservation of the Dartford Warbler on English lowland heaths: a review. *Biol. Cons.* 13, 299-307.
Bibby, C.J., Housden, S.D., Porter, R.F. & Thomas, G.J. (1989). Towards a bird conservation strategy. *RSPB Conserv. Rev.* 3, 4-8.
Burgess, N.D. & Evans, C. (1989). Management of

reedbeds. *RSPB Conserv. Rev.* 3, 20-24.

Burgess, N.D. & Hirons, G.J.M. (1990). *Techniques of hydrological management at coastal lagoons and lowland wet grasslands on RSPB reserves.* RSPB Management Case Study.

Burgess, N.D., Evans, C. & Sorensen, J. (1990). Heathland management for Nightjars. RSPB *Conserv. Rev.* 4, 32-35.

Cadbury, C.J., Hill, D., Partridge, J. & Sorensen, J. (1989). The history of the Avocet population and its management in England since recolonisation. *RSPB Conserv. Rev.* 3, 9-13.

Evans, C.E. (1991). The conservation importance and management of the ditch flora on RSPB reserves. *RSPB Conserv. Rev.* 5, 65-71.

Evans, C.E. (1992 in press). *Heathland recreation on arable land at Minsmere. Proc. Heathland Habitat Creation Seminar.* Suffolk Wildlife Trust.

Garnett, R.P., Hirons, G.J.M., Evans, C.E. & O'Conner, D. (1992). The control of Spartina (Cord Grass) using Glyphosate. *Aspects of Applied Biology 29, Vegetation management in forestry, amenity and conservation areas.*

Green, R.E. (1986) Studies on ground nesting birds of the Somerset Levels. *Breeding waders of the Somerset Moors: factors affecting their distribution and breeding success.* RSPB Report to NCC.

Housden, S.D., Thomas, G.J., Bibby, C.J. & Porter, R.F. (1991) Towards a habitat conservation strategy for bird habitats in Britain. *RSPB Conserv. Rev.* 5, 9-16.

Parry, S. (1991) *Reserves management Gazetteer (draft).* Unpubl. rept. RSPB, Sandy.

Pickess, B.P., Burgess, N.D. & Evans, C. (1989). *Heathland management at Arne, Dorset.* RSPB Management Case Study.

Sills, N. (1988). Transformation at Titchwell: a wetland reserve management case history. RSPB *Conserv. Rev.* 2, 64-68.

Thomas, G.J. (1991). The acquisition of RSPB reserves. *RSPB Conserv. Rev.* 5, 17-22.

Tickner, M., Evans, C.E. & Blackburn, M. (1991). Restoration of a Norfolk Broad: A case study of Strumpshaw Fen. *RSPB Conserv. Rev.* 5, 72-77.

Tickner, M. & Evans, C.E. (1992). *Management of lowland wet grassland on RSPB reserves.* RSPB, Management Case Study.

Wilson, J. (1991) *The management of saltmarsh and lagoon creation at Morecambe Bay, Lancashire.* RSPB Management Case Study.

C.H. Gomersall, RSPB Reed Cutting at Radipole

Bird distributions and land use

Simon Gates

Habitats Research Department, BTO

Summary

For most if not all British bird species, the precise factors that influence their distributions are poorly understood. This is an obvious major gap in our understanding of the ecology of our birds, and one which must be rectified if we are to have any chance of understanding the reasons for changes in distribution or predicting the effects of future environmental changes. A major research project currently under way at the BTO aims to provide this information. Its objectives are threefold. First, to explore which factors may underlie the distributions of British birds. Second, to gain insights into reasons for changes in distributions over the last 20 years, and third, to produce predictive models of the effects of future changes in the environment on the distribution of birds. In all of these aims we will be focusing particularly on bird distributions in relation to land use. This has obvious conservation importance, as land use is under the direct control of man, and we hope to be able to provide scientific input to future decisions on agricultural and other land use policy.

The study of distributions

Ecologists' understanding of the causal factors that underlie the distributions of animals is generally poor. This subject has received little attention in the past, for a variety of reasons including the near-impossibility of performing meaningful experiments. Which factors are most important in determining distributions depends on the scale that is studied: the factors limiting a species' range across a continent will not be the same as those which determine which woods or fields it lives in. At the widest geographical scale, factors almost certain to play the most important roles include the area of evolutionary origin of the species and physiological factors, which will limit the types of climate in which the species can survive. In contrast, at the local scale, habitat preferences will control where a species is found. At an intermediate scale, many factors may have important and interacting influences. Distributions may be patchy, or a species may vary in abundance across

its range, and to understand these patterns we need to look at factors which vary across the range, such as the types of habitat available, the altitude and topography and interactions with other species, as well as factors which set outer limits on the range.

The influence of land use

In Britain, there is virtually no habitat which is not man made or strongly influenced by man's activities. Land use therefore provides an overriding influence on habitats available to birds, and is certain to have a profound impact on bird distributions. Furthermore, with the advance of technology, man has the potential to change land use more rapidly and more profoundly than at any time in the past. It is therefore important for us to understand the effects of land use on bird distributions in order to predict the effects of future changes.

Changes in agricultural practices or other forms of land use may have a dramatic impact on a species' range. There have been very large changes in range of several British breeding species over the last 20 years, and these are thought to be connected to changes in land use and agricultural practices. For example, a number of birds of agricultural land, including the Grey Partridge, Corn Bunting and Corncrake, are undergoing a decline in numbers and a contraction of range size. Figure 1 shows the distribution of the Grey Partridge in 1968-72 and 1988-91; in 20 years it has disappeared from a large part of its former breeding range, especially in Ireland and the west of Britain. Almost certainly this has been caused by changes in agriculture, particularly those, such as hedgerow removal and the use of pesticides, which have led to the eradication from crops of many weeds and invertebrates, and hence sources of food. Analysis of the changes in the birds' distributions in relation to changes in agriculture will provide evidence as to whether these factors have contributed to the decline. This will supplement the intensive research on the species already carried out by The Game Conservancy which has demonstrated the complexity of interactions between farming practices and the population dynamics of Grey Partridges (e.g. Potts 1986).

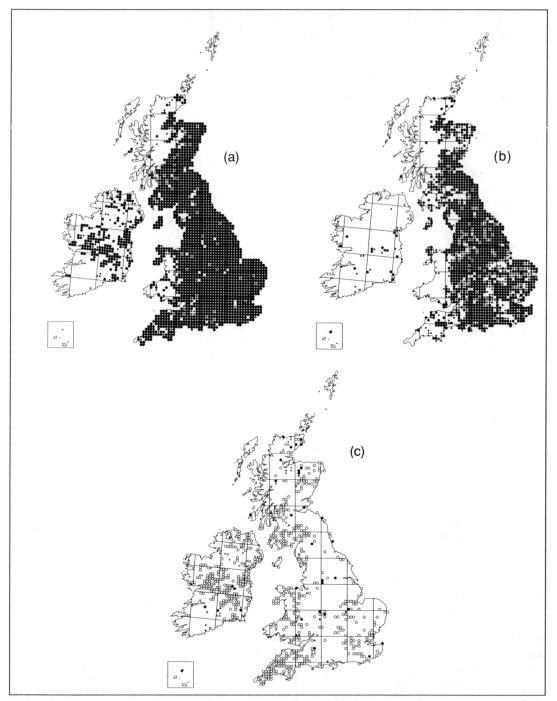

Figure 1. *The contraction of the breeding range of the Grey Partridge over the 20 years between the two atlases of breeding birds.*
(a) The distribution in 1968–72 (large dots = confirmed breeding, small dots = possible breeding).
(b) The distribution in 1988-91.
(c) The change in distribution between 1968-72 and 1988-91 (large open dots=confirmed or probable breeding in 1968-72 but absent in 1988-91; small open dots=possible breeding in 1968-72 but absent in 1988-91; large filled dots=absent in 1968-72 but breeding in 1988-91; small filled dots=absent in 1968-72 but present, although no evidence of breeding in 1988-91).

33

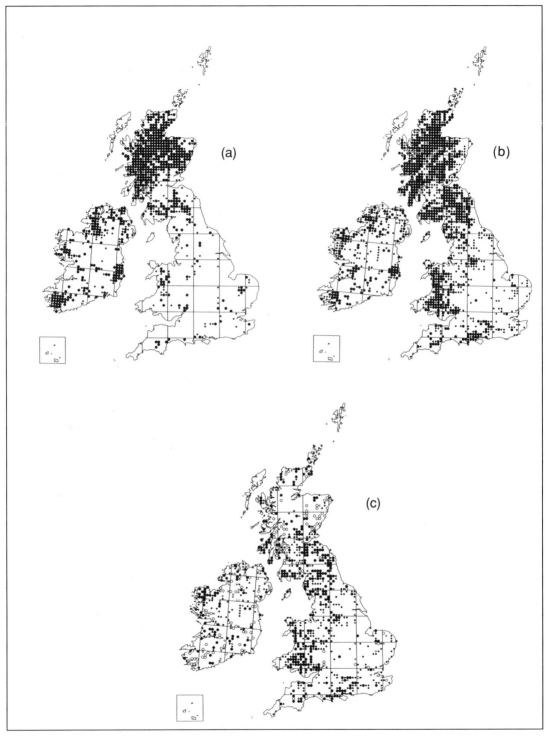

Figure 2. The expansion of the breeding range of the Siskin between 1968-72 and 1988-91. Dots as in Figure 1.
    (a) The distribution in 1968-72.
    (b) The distribution in 1988-91.
    (c) The change in distribution between 1968-72 and 1988-91.

In contrast, other recent changes in land use may have been beneficial to some birds. Afforestation has changed large areas of upland Britain from moorland and bog to coniferous woodland and, while this has been detrimental to some upland birds, it has undoubtedly benefitted others (Avery & Leslie 1990). The ranges of both the Siskin and Common Crossbill have expanded dramatically over the last 20 years. The change in the Siskin's distribution is shown in Figure 2. Its spread into new areas of northern England and Wales is thought to be linked to the growth to maturity of conifer plantations in these areas.

The BTO Bird Distribution Project

There has been very little rigorous scientific investigation of the factors influencing the distributions of birds, and most of our current ideas are based on extrapolation from small scale studies. The validity of this approach is questionable. Most previous work has concentrated on the factors determining range boundaries (e.g. Root 1988), and not on those determining variations in abundance across ranges. The main reason for the lack of work in this area is the dearth of detailed data on the distributions of species and environmental data at the same level of resolution. Such data simply do not exist for most species over most of the world, but the Atlases of Breeding and Wintering Birds in Britain and Ireland (Sharrock 1976; Lack 1986; Gibbons *et al.* in press) produced by the BTO, the Scottish Ornithologists' Club and the Irish Wildbird Conservancy have ensured that data on breeding and wintering birds in the British Isles are available. Moreover, environmental and land use data are also available for this region, and so we have the material to take a major step forward in understanding the causes of bird distributions. This research is being made possible by funding from the Natural Environment Research Council, the RSPB and Shell.

In addition to the bird distribution information from the two atlases, we are using climate and geographical data from the Institute of Terrestrial Ecology's Land Characteristics Data Bank (Ball *et al.* 1983) and data on land use and agriculture from the Ministry of Agriculture, Fisheries and Food's annual agricultural census. Because two atlases of breeding birds have been produced, separated by 20 years, we have obtained two sets of land use data, one from the period of each atlas. This enables us to assess changes in distribution over the period separating the two atlases and to correlate changes in bird distributions with changes in

land use. Analysis of these data sets will provide insights into the factors underlying bird distributions, but it is important to note that we cannot prove that a bird's distribution is determined by an environmental factor simply by uncovering a correlation between them. Our analyses will also enable us to quantify the effects of different habitats and environmental factors on bird distributions, and hence to produce predictive models of the distributional changes that would result from future environmental changes. Such models would have a valuable role to play in planning future agricultural strategies.

Acknowledgement

This work was funded by JNCC, RSPB, NERC, DoE, PowerGen, National Power, Nuclear Electric, National Grid Company and Shell.

References

Avery, M. & Leslie, R. (1990). *Birds and Forestry.* T. & A.D. Poyser.

Ball, D.F., Radford, G.L. & Williams, W.M. (1983). *A land characteristic data bank for Great Britain.* ITE Bangor Occasional Paper 13.

Gibbons D.W., Reid, J. & Chapman, R. (in press). *The New Atlas of Breeding Birds in Britain and Ireland.* T.& A.D. Poyser, London.

Lack, P.C. (1986). *The Atlas of Wintering Birds in Britain and Ireland.* T.& A.D. Poyser, London.

Potts, G.R. (1986). *The Partridge: pesticides, predation and conservation.* Collins, London.

Root, T. (1988). Environmental factors associated with avian distributional boundaries. *Journal of Biogeography* 15, 489-505.

Sharrock, J.T.R. (1976). *The Atlas of Breeding Birds in Britain and Ireland.* T. & A.D. Poyser, Calton.

Upland bird-habitat associations

Richard A Stillman & Andrew F Brown

Moorland Bird Study, JNCC

Summary

Results of upland bird surveys have been used to study the distribution and abundance of upland birds. Associations between bird numbers and habitat features have been used to predict bird distribution across large areas of the uplands. Survey results may be used to show how changes in the habitat may affect bird distributions.

Potential uses of survey data

JNCC's Moorland Bird Study has conducted surveys across most areas of upland Britain. These are primarily used to estimate the abundance of different bird species, thus allowing comparison of the ornithological interest of different areas. This information is vital if we are to identify areas of particular conservation value for designation as SSSIs or SPAs. However, more information can be obtained from these results. Survey results can show associations between different bird species and demonstrate how habitat features affect bird distribution. This makes it possible to predict effects of habitat change on bird distribution and to provide basic information concerning appropriate management of upland birds.

A knowledge of the associations between distribution and habitat may also allow us to predict numbers of birds based solely on habitat features. This is useful in that more intensive ground survey may not be viable.

During 1991, bird-habitat relationships were studied using results of surveys in the Grampian, Tayside and Central Regions of Scotland (Aspinall & Veitch 1991; Brown & Stillman 1991). These results were used to study distribution patterns of birds, bird-habitat associations and to predict the presence of birds in unsurveyed areas.

Upland bird distributions

The distributions of bird species were compared using survey data collected from 71 separate kilometre squares located in Grampian, Tayside and Central Regions (Figure 1). In the Figure the distance between two species gives an indication of how similar (for closely positioned species) or distance between two species gives an indication of how similar (for more separate species) are the distribution of two species. Those such as Golden Plover, Dunlin and Ptarmigan (being closely positioned) are therefore shown to have greater affinities with each other than they do to Curlew, Lapwing or Red Grouse (being more distant).

If species formed a number of assemblages then discrete groups of species (each with similar distributions) would be expected on the Figure. Since the species do not form any obvious groups but are scattered more or less evenly across the Figure, this suggests that, within the study area, upland birds do not form distinct assemblages. Thus it is unlikely that any single management practice would be favourable to a large number of species.

Bird-habitat associations

Information on both bird numbers and habitat features (topography, vegetation composition and structure) were recorded in each study site, so it was possible to express patterns in the distribution of bird species in relation to the habitat (Figure 2). As in Figure 1, the distance between two species is

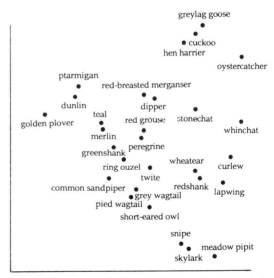

Figure 1. Patterns in the distribution of upland bird species, (produced using principal components analysis; redrawn from Brown & Stillman in press).

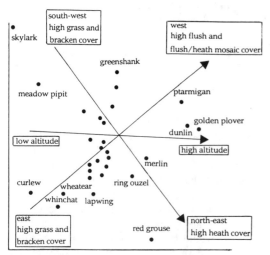

Figure 2. Upland bird-habitat associations, (produced using redundancy analysis; redrawn from Brown & Stillman in press).

related to similarity in their distributions, but in addition, the three arrows on the Figure refer to the directions of three sets of habitat features which were most strongly related to the distribution of the bird species. The location of a species relative to each of the arrows expresses its association with each set of habitat features. The Figure allows patterns in the distribution of birds to be directly related to the habitat.

The arrow directed from the top-left to the bottom-right of the Figure indicates a transition from south-western sites dominated by grass and bracken to north-eastern, heather dominated heaths. Skylark and Meadow Pipit are associated with south-western, grass and bracken dominated sites. Red Grouse is located towards the bottom-right of the Figure, indicating that this species is associated with north-eastern, heather dominated heaths.

A second arrow directed from the bottom-left of the Figure to the top-right represents a transition from eastern sites with high grass and bracken cover to western sites with high cover of flush and flush/heath mosaics.

Curlew, Whinchat and Wheatear are located to the eastern extremity of this gradient, in association with grass and bracken, and Ptarmigan, Dunlin and Golden Plover towards the western extremity, in association with flush and flush/heath mosaics.

The remaining arrow is directed from left to right across the Figure and indicates a gradient of increasing altitude. Species positioned towards the left of the Figure, such as Curlew, Skylark and Meadow Pipit, are associated with lower altitude areas, whilst those towards the right of the figure, such as Dunlin, Ptarmigan and Golden Plover, are associated with high altitudes.

Statistical approaches such as those summarised in Figure 2 are useful because they can represent the bird-habitat relationships of many species in combination. The results confirm our ecological knowledge that different birds show different preferences to habitat features. Changes in the habitat which favour one species may not therefore be of equal benefit to any other species. For example, Red Grouse is associated with heather-dominated heaths, in the north-east of the study area. This accords well with what is known of Red Grouse requirements and the distribution of the more intensively managed grouse moors in the study area. However, no other species are found in a similar area of the Figure, suggesting that none of the other species are as closely linked to the distribution of heather and thus that it would be dangerous to assume that management for Red Grouse would necessarily be of equal benefit to any other species. The other species are more closely linked to other habitat features.

Predicting upland bird distribution

Knowledge of bird-habitat relationships may be used to predict the distribution of birds in unsurveyed areas. These predictions may refer to individual sites (covering a few tens of square kilometres) or may cover large expanses of upland (reaching several thousand square kilometres). The bird-habitat associations apparent from Figure 2 were similar to those seen at a single site, Glen Clunie, in Grampian in 1991. In Glen Clunie, Golden Plover and Ptarmigan were found at high altitude, whereas Lapwing and Curlew were most abundant in the upland grasslands of the river floodplains at low altitude. These results would be expected from the locations of the species on Figure 2.

In order to predict bird distribution over large areas, knowledge of the habitats is required. The information required usually refers to the topography (i.e. altitude and slope) and vegetation composition.

Details of the topography of large areas can be obtained from digital contour data, and that for vegetation and other habitat features may be obtained from satellite imagery or ground surveys. The relationships between habitat features (derived from the contour data and satellite imagery) and the bird numbers recorded in 152 sites were extrapolated to predict the number of three wader species, Golden Plover, Dunlin and Curlew, throughout a 50 x 37 km area of Grampian Region (Figure 3). In the Figure, the bird species are predicted to be present in the dark-shaded squares and absent in the light-shaded squares. Each species is predicted to be distributed within different areas. These areas correspond approximately to low altitude for Curlew, medium altitude for Golden Plover and higher altitude for Dunlin.

These results make sense in terms of habitat preferences of these species in the study area, but further ground survey is required to determine the precise accuracy of the predictions.

Future work

The results show that survey data may be used for more than simply estimating the abundance of birds on a number of sites. However, the results are only based on survey data collected during a single field season in one geographical region and so show nothing of how bird distribution and populations may change through time and between different areas. Similar bird-habitat relationships are currently being studied from survey data collected in the south Pennines of England to determine whether or not the results found for the Grampian, Tayside and Central regions are consistent with those found in other areas. In addition, more detailed work involving monitoring populations over a number of years is required. A parallel study of how upland birds use different habitat patches is required in order to discover any trends in bird populations through time and to show how dependant different bird species are on different habitat types. Such work is planned for future years.

References

Aspinall, R.J. & Veitch, N.V. (1991). *Modelling the distribution and abundance of breeding moorland birds.* CSD Res. Rept. No. 998 (part 2). NCC, Peterborough.

Brown, A.F. & Stillman, R.A. (1991). *Bird-habitat associations in the eastern Highlands of Scotland.* JNCC Report No. 14. JNCC, Peterborough.

(a)   (b)   (c)

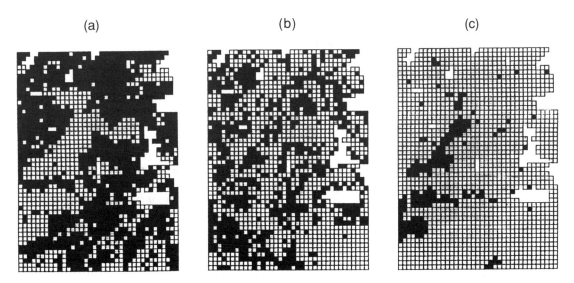

Figure 3. Predicted distribution of (a) Curlew, (b) Golden Plover and (c) Dunlin, (produced using pattern recognition; redrawn from Aspinall & Veitch 1991).

IPM - a new approach to identifying conservation problems

Stephen Baillie, Humphrey Crick & Will Peach

Populations Research Department, BTO

Summary

An Integrated Population Monitoring Programme for breeding birds in the wider countryside is being developed by the BTO under contract to JNCC. The IPM programme will bring together data on population levels, productivity and survival from different BTO schemes, principally the Common Birds Census, Nest Record Scheme, Constant Effort Sites Scheme and Ringing Scheme. The programme will develop threshold systems to assist in the identification of those changes which require conservation action. Measures of productivity and survival rates and correlations with environmental variables will help to identify the causes of population changes and thus indicate needs and priorities for further research.

The current emphasis is on the development of reliable estimates of population variables from individual schemes. A medium-term aim is to build population models that allow interactions between population and environmental variables to be investigated. Modelling will allow predicted population changes to be compared with observed ones so that deleterious population changes can be detected more effectively.

The importance of monitoring

Birds are greatly appreciated by a wide range of people from dedicated birdwatchers to those whose environment is enriched by the presence of common species. They are also valuable indicators of environmental changes, as was well illustrated by their role in highlighting the dangers in the use of organochlorine pesticides. It is valuable, therefore, to have reliable information on changes in our bird populations.

Considerable progress has been made in monitoring some rare breeding species and internationally-important seabird populations and relating changes to natural and anthropogenic factors. Vital as this work is, widespread species are likely to be most useful for detecting major environmental changes. Furthermore, a marked decline in one or more of our common species will have a much greater impact on those who derive enjoyment from birds than an equivalent decline in a very rare species. That is not to say that the monitoring of rare species in unimportant. There need be no conflict of priorities here, because in Britain and Ireland it should be possible to monitor most breeding bird species, thanks to the enormous efforts of many thousands of volunteer birdwatchers.

Conservation-oriented monitoring programmes aim to identify deleterious population changes that require conservation action, to suggest possible causes and to provide a means of checking on the effectiveness of remedial actions. In this article we introduce the BTO's Integrated Population Monitoring (IPM) Programme which is being developed to provide such monitoring for common species within the wider countryside.

The aims of the IPM programme

The IPM programme has four main aims, which are outlined in turn below.

1. To establish thresholds that will be used to notify conservation bodies of requirements for further research or conservation action.

If the monitoring system is to be effective in sounding 'alarm bells' to advise conservation bodies of particular problems there must be a system in place for identifying population changes which may require conservation action. There are two main aspects to the development of such threshold systems. The first is to implement statistical methods for identifying population declines and assessing their magnitude. The second is to devise systems for assessing changes in relation to the normal pattern of population fluctuations in the species concerned, including relationships with weather or other environmental variables.

We can generally allow greater population fluctuations in species with high reproductive rates and population turnover before we need to react. Heron populations decline sharply as a result of severe winters but recover rapidly afterwards. Thus a marked Heron decline following a series of severe winters would not require attention, but we should certainly be ringing the alarm bells if a similar decline were to occur during a series of mild winters. Analyses of long-term data from BTO monitoring schemes will provide the information that will be needed to establish these threshold systems. Such thresholds will not be 'cast in stone' but will be modified as our knowledge of the species involved increases.

2. To identify the stage of the life cycle at which changes are taking place.

This will often provide a first step towards identifying the causes of a particular problem. For many species we now monitor productivity (from nest records and ringing) and survival rates (from ringing). If we can pin down whether a particular problem is associated with a change in productivity or in survival then some possible causes will be highlighted and others eliminated.

Most bird populations have some ability to compensate for changes in reproduction or survival. In species which do not breed until they are several years old it may be a number of years before reductions in breeding success lead to changes in breeding population size. For both of these reasons monitoring breeding success and survival will sometimes allow us to detect changes at an earlier stage than would be possible if only breeding numbers were monitored. A particularly dramatic example of this was the recent seabird population declines in Shetland, where breeding failure provided the earliest indications that something was wrong (Monaghan *et al.* 1989, Lloyd *et*

al. 1991).

3. To provide data that will assist in identifying the causes of population changes.

Once the demographic variables that are responsible for a particular change have been identified, the next stage of analysis is to attempt to identify environmental variables that are related to the observed changes. Simple measures of winter weather in Britain are known to be strongly correlated with the population changes of some resident species (Greenwood & Baillie 1991), while population changes of some migrants, such as the Sedge Warbler, are explained by the rainfall in the Sahel region of Africa where they winter (Peach *et al.* 1991).

Land-use change is also an important consideration. For example, farmland covers over 70% of Britain and many of our birds live there. The effects of changes in cropping patterns and some other aspects of land-use can be investigated using the published agricultural statistics. We shall be giving increased emphasis to the recording habitat data as part of our own surveys or programmes. It is also likely that much more land-use data will be available in the next few years, particularly from satellites.

A lack of suitable environmental data often limits the analyses that we can perform. Statistics of pesticide use, for example, often do not exist or are difficult to obtain. We would like much better information on food availability, such as the abundance of fruit, seeds and insects, but such data are rarely gathered on a national scale. There is much scope for collaboration with other organisations

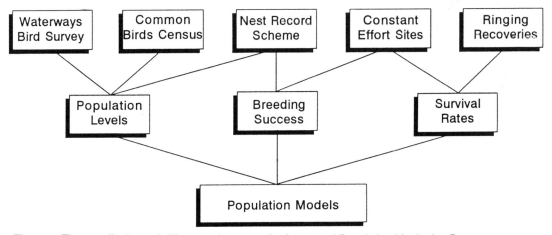

Figure 1. *The contributions of different schemes to the Integrated Population Monitoring Programme.*

here. For example, Percival (1990) was able to relate BTO data on the breeding performance of Tawny Owls to figures on small mammal abundance gathered by the Mammal Society.

The relationships between population variables and environmental variables which together bring about population changes are often complex. Modelling approaches will be developed in order to investigate these interactions (see below). It is also important to stress that correlations only provide weak evidence of causation. Monitoring results can often point towards probable explanations but where possible these should be tested by further observations or experiments. Monitoring programmes should aim to focus the limited resources available for intensive research on to the factors that are most likely to explain major population changes.

4. To distinguish changes in populations caused by human activity from 'natural' population fluctuations.

This is essentially part of objective three but is listed separately to stress the importance of identifying changes brought about by man, particularly those which it is possible to reverse.

Data needed for the programme

The IPM programme needs data on population levels, on breeding success and on survival rates (Figure 1). Data on population levels are provided by the Common Birds Census (CBC), the Waterways Bird Survey (WBS) and the Constant Effort mist-netting Sites (CES) scheme (Marchant *et al.* elsewhere in this volume). The CBC and WBS provide mapping censuses of farmland, woodland and waterways, while the CES provides standardised capture totals from scrub and wetland sites. The coverage provided by the CBC and WBS is currently restricted to certain habitat types and is poor in more remote areas. Work on the development of new census methods that will allow us to rectify some of these limitations is currently in progress (Marchant *et al.* 1991, Baillie & Marchant 1992).

The Nest Record Scheme provides data on timing of laying, clutch sizes, hatching success and fledging success. A major limitation is that usually only individual nesting attempts can be followed, so nest records do not provide information on the average number of nesting attempts per season. This problem is partly overcome by use of data from the CES scheme, which provides productivity indices based on the ratio of adults to juveniles captured. Recent results from productivity monitoring are given by Crick *et al.* elsewhere in this volume.

Two types of ringing data provide information on survival rates. First, recoveries of birds found dead by members of the public can be used to estimate first year and adult survival rates. Ideally

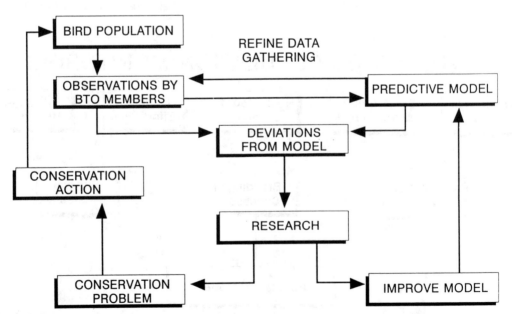

Figure 2. The role of population modelling within the Integrated Population Monitoring Programme.

information on the numbers of ringed birds, categorised at least by age and date, is needed because the chances of a dead bird being found and reported to the Ringing Office often vary with age and year. The fact that these ringing data are not yet computerised is a major limitation to such analyses, although data on the summer ringing of 22 passerines have been gathered since 1985.

A second source of information on adult survival rates is recaptures at Constant Effort Sites. Strictly speaking these should be described as return rates because any adult birds which do not return to the area where they were ringed are treated as if they were dead. This method cannot be used to measure first year survival rates because many birds do not return to breed in the area where they were ringed as juveniles. The CES methodology has great advantages for this type of analysis because the chances of individual birds being recaptured do not usually vary between years, as is often the case with recapture rates from less well standardised trapping programmes.

Habitat is an important variable which affects the breeding success and survival rates of birds. It is important, therefore, that habitat should be recorded in a comparable way by all schemes. A standard habitat coding system has been devised for this purpose (Crick 1992). It has been designed to allow birdwatchers with limited botanical knowledge to record the main features of a habitat that are important for birds. The system is largely compatible with the standard NCC/RSNC classification but omits some categories that could not readily be distinguished by birdwatchers while giving more detail on farmland and human sites. This habitat coding system has already been introduced to the Nest Record Scheme and Ringing Scheme, and will be introduced to other schemes in the near future.

How will the monitoring data be integrated and interpreted?

Patterns of variation in the size of bird populations can rarely be explained by single factors. It is important, therefore, to examine the combined effects of the different factors that influence each stage of the life-cycle.

It addition to identifying relationships with environmental variables it is important to determine how each population variable changes in relation to population density. This allows us to identify so called density-dependent processes that regulate populations (such as competition for territories). Analyses of long-term data on the popula-

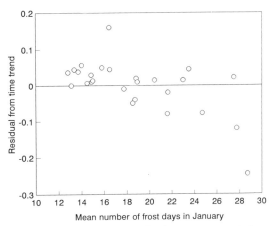

Figure 3. *Deviations from the long-term population trend for Song Thrushes plotted against the number of freezing days in the preceding January, showing that populations are higher than expected when there is little frost but lower when frost is extensive. r = –0.64, P < 0.001 (from Baillie 1990).*

tion dynamics of individual species are an essential cornerstone of this approach (Snow 1966, O'Connor 1980, Baillie & Peach 1992).

The next stage of analysis is to build population models which will allow the consequences of the relationships which have been established to be explored. Such models can be regarded as a mathematical summary of our knowledge of the qualitative relationships whose combined effects determine population changes. We can use such models to predict how we would expect the population to vary in future years on the basis of our current

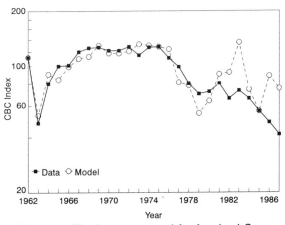

Figure 4. *The long-term trend for farmland Song Thrush populations compared with predictions from a model incorporating winter weather and density-dependence. The model is based on data from 1962 to 1976 (from Baillie 1990).*

knowledge. To make such predictions we generally need to supply the model with values for any environmental variables that are included.

Long-term BTO monitoring data will be used to construct initial population models (Figure 2). As further monitoring data are gathered they will be compared with the model predictions. Investigations of differences between model predictions and new observations will lead to an on-going process of model refinement. Such models will also allow us to identify those population variables that are the most important for predicting population changes.

This will help us to modify data gathering methods in ways that will make the most effective use of the voluntary fieldwork effort.

The main aim of investigating differences between model predictions and monitoring observations is to identify conservation problems. Hopefully it will be possible to take conservation action that will lead to the recovery of the population. Under these circumstances the monitoring system will be used to check that the conservation actions are having the anticipated effect.

An analysis of data on the decline of Song Thrush populations on farmland provides a simple example of the use of population modelling (Baillie 1990). An analysis of CBC data from 1962-1987 showed that fluctuations in Song Thrush populations were related to the number of days of frost in January (Figure 3). It was important to determine whether the decline in Song Thrush populations which had occurred since about 1976 was simply a consequence of a change in the pattern of winter weather. The CBC data from 1962-1976 were therefore used to construct a model incorporating winter weather and density-dependence. This model was then used to predict the population trend from 1962 to 1987 given the observed weather conditions in each winter (Figure 4). The model showed that while the decline between the mid-1970s and early 1980s appears to have been largely a consequence of colder winters, the continued decline through the 1980s, which the model did not predict, must also have involved some new factors. The causes of the continuing decline of this species urgently require further investigation.

Development of the IPM programme

The IPM programme is an ambitious project which will take much of the 1990s to develop fully. The current emphasis is on the analysis and reporting of data from individual schemes. New census methods are being developed so as to obtain improved geographical, habitat and species coverage combined with a more rigorous sampling framework. A new nest record card was introduced in 1989 to provide more objective recording and more efficient computerisation. Plans are in hand to ensure that all ringing data are computerised routinely from the mid-1990s. A computer-compatible ringing schedule has been introduced from the beginning of 1992 and ringers are being encouraged to enter their own data on micro-computers. A range of analytical methods are being developed and implemented to ensure that the best use is made of the data from each scheme (Baillie 1990, 1991).

Systems for defining action thresholds will be developed over the next two to three years. We shall also be developing computer programmes which will allow us to carry out annual screening of the data in an integrated manner.

All our main monitoring schemes already publish annual reports. We will develop integrated reporting procedures to complement the reporting of results from individual schemes. Analyses of our results for individual species, particularly those which are in long-term decline, will continue to form an important part of our work programme. The development of population models is dependent on many of these other building blocks being in place, and will occur mainly from the mid-1990s onwards.

Acknowledgements

Most of the work within the IPM programme is carried out under a contract from the Joint Nature Conservation Committee on behalf of English Nature, the Countryside Council for Wales and Scottish Natural Heritage, and under a similar contract from the Department of the Environment for Northern Ireland. We are very grateful to the thousands of volunteer fieldworkers who have made the IPM Programme possible through their contributions to its component schemes.

Where can more information be obtained?

More detailed accounts of the IPM programme are given by Baillie (1990, 1991). New contributors to the monitoring schemes which make up the IPM programme are always welcome. Please contact the Census Unit, Nest Records Unit or Ringing Unit at BTO headquarters as appropriate.

Figures 3 and 4 are reproduced from *Ibis* 132 (1990) by permission of the BOU.

References

Baillie, S.R. (1990). Integrated population monitoring of breeding birds in Britain and Ireland. *Ibis* 132, 151-166.

Baillie, S.R. (1991). Mônitoring terrestrial breeding bird populations. In: Goldsmith, F.B. (Ed.) *Monitoring for conservation and ecology.* Pp. 112-132. Chapman & Hall, London.

Baillie, S.R. & Marchant, J.H. (1992). The use of breeding bird censuses to monitor common birds in Britain and Ireland - current practice and future prospects. *Die Vogelwelt* 113, 172-182.

Baillie, S.R. & Peach, W.J. (1992). Population limitation in Palearctic-African migrant passerines. *Ibis* 134 (suppl. 1), 120-132.

Crick, H.Q.P. (1992). A bird-habitat coding system for use in Britain and Ireland incorporating aspects of land-management and human activity. *Bird Study* 39, 1-12.

Greenwood, J.J.D. & Baillie, S.R. (1991). Effects of density-dependence and weather on population changes of English passerines using a non-experimental paradigm. *Ibis* 133 (suppl. 1), 121-133.

Lloyd, C., Tasker, M.L. & Partridge, K. (1991). *The status of seabirds in Britain and Ireland.* T. & A.D. Poyser, London.

Marchant, J.H., Carter, S.P. & Baillie, S.R. (1991). CBC 2000. *BTO News* 174, 10-11.

Monaghan, P., Uttley, J.D., Burns, M.D., Thaine, C. & Blackwood, J. (1989). The relationship between food supply, reproductive effort and breeding success in Arctic Terns *Sterna paradisaea. J. Anim. Ecol.* 58, 261-274.

O'Connor, R.J. (1980). Pattern and process in Great Tit Parus major populations in Britain. *Ardea* 68, 165-183.

Peach, W.J., Baillie, S.R. & Underhill, L.G. (1991). Survival of British Sedge Warblers *Acrocephalus schoenobaenus* in relation to west African rainfall. *Ibis* 133, 300-305.

Percival, S.M. (1990). *Population trends in British Barn Owls, Tyto alba, and Tawny Owls, Strix aluco, in relation to environmental change.* BTO Research Report No. 57.

Snow, D.W. (1966). Population dynamics of the Blackbird. *Nature* 211, 1231-1233.

Action Plans for birds in the UK

Nicola J Crockford[1], Gwyn Williams[2] & Tony Fox[3]

[1] *Ornithology and Landscape Ecology Branch, JNCC[4]*

[2] *Conservation Planning Department, RSPB*

[3] *Research and Conservation Department, WWT[5],*

Role and coverage

In 1990, the RSPB and the NCC in association with the WWT began to develop strategies for the conservation of the most vulnerable and internationally important bird species in the UK, Channel Islands and Isle of Man.

The basic idea is to move away from the position of defensive protection to constructive or positive conservation. For threatened species this should lead ultimately to a situation where special protection measures are no longer so important because the populations have actually recovered. In the long-term, the implicit conservation objective is to maintain or adjust the population of each species to a secure level which corresponds to ecological, scientific and cultural requirements.

Action for each species is being planned, implemented and monitored through a Species Action Plan, which evaluates current knowledge of a species - its conservation status, ecology and the factors limiting its population size and distribution; identifies the major problems facing it, both in the UK and, as appropriate, elsewhere in its range; sets conservation objectives; identifies necessary actions; structures them into a programme for implementation within a reasonable time-span; and assigns managerial responsibilities.

The emphasis of the Plans is on the co-ordinated conservation application of scientific information. They are are dynamic internal working documents for the organisations which adopt them and are designed to be regularly reviewed and updated.

By the end of the decade plans will be produced for nearly 180 species. These are the 117 species

4. Current address: Conservation Planning Department, RSPB
5. Current address: Department of Wildlife Ecology, Natural Environment Research Institute, Kalø, DK-8410, Rønde, Denmark

of most conservation concern in Britain, plus the 30 `candidate' species, as identified by NCC and RSPB in *Red Data Birds in Britain* (Batten *et al.* 1990) and 30 additional 'problem' species which are mainly notable for alleged conflict with various human interests including agriculture and fisheries. Table 1 lists the selected species. Table 2 gives the criteria used for selection of species in *Red Data Birds in Britain.*

Benefits

There are several significant advantages in programming bird conservation through Species Action Plans. Most importantly, they provide a greater objectivity and focus to forward planning, enabling integration of a wide range of approaches and a more proactive approach which should, in the long run, reduce the need for reactive work. They also provide a mechanism to improve liaison and establish common standards throughout the statutory and non-governmental conservation organisations, nationally and internationally, for the management of these species and their habitats. Last but not least, they provide a definitive statement on the status and ecology of the species which will have many applications across the range of conservation work.

The format of Species Action Plans

The format of the Plans will be similar for all the bodies involved. However, the details of the actions may differ, reflecting differences between management structures and the statutory and voluntary remits. The Plan format for RSPB plans is outlined in Table 3 as an example.

Preparation, implementation and monitoring

Step 1: Pathfinder meeting - an initial 'brainstorm' meeting of ornithological experts and those responsible for plan implementation to identify the threats and limiting factors facing a species, decide the overall conservation priority of action for the species, define targets and identify main actions.

Step 2: Preparation of initial draft plan for comment and amendment.

Step 3: Formal adoption of plan and integration into work programmes/budgets.

Step 4: Implementation of plans; monitoring of actions; review in light of results and modification as necessary.

The staff attending pathfinder meetings consult widely in their organisations to ensure that the full range of expertise, concerns and current actions for the species are taken into account. In addition, other experts may be consulted over the plans as appropriate.

A considerable amount of work on implementation is already in progress within work programmes of the participating organisations. Examples include large scale projects, such as work on White-tailed Eagles, Red Kites, Corncrakes and Choughs, responses to planning applications so as to safeguard important bird sites and many smaller exercises, such as elements of management programmes on nature reserves or SSSIs to favour habitat for, say, Crested Tit or Brent Geese.

The actions from the Plans are cross-referenced so that similar actions for a range of species can be co-ordinated in a concerted effort. Though these are plans for species, they complement habitat-based approaches to conservation, often providing justifications for habitat protection and prescriptions for habitat management. The RSPB uses the relevant Species Action Plans as an input to its Habitat Action Plans (Housden *et al.* 1991).

Monitoring of species distribution, numbers and/or productivity is essential to assess whether the overall objectives of a plan are being achieved. In addition, monitoring of project implementation is necessary. Planned actions may be implemented effectively, but the biological objectives of the Plan not attained, in which case a major review of the Plan will be required. The process also enables the plan to function as a management tool if actions are not implemented effectively, due to external or internal factors. Ideally, the planned actions will be implemented effectively and will lead to the successful achievement of the Plan's objectives, which will then free resources for other priorities.

Priorities

Each species is afforded an overall priority for conservation action. Several factors are taken into account in determining this including: international legal status (particularly under the EC Directive on the Conservation of Wild Birds 79/409), domestic legal status (under the Wildlife and Countryside Act 1981 and the Wildlife (Northern Ireland) Order 1985 (Schedules 1 and 2)), degree of threat to the species (highest priority being given by RSPB to the 41 most threatened species in Britain identified by Porter *et al.* (1990)), and the likelihood of the identified actions resulting in the successful achievement of the objectives of the Plan.

Priority for Plan preparation has been given to those species for which the UK has a special conservation responsibility in international law (including the UK's three globally threatened species, Red Kite, White-tailed Eagle, Corncrake, and one endemic species, Scottish Crossbill) or which are under a high degree of threat.

Other species planning initiatives

Species Action Plans are equivalent in many ways to the species recovery plans which NCC prepared for certain vulnerable non-bird species listed on protected Schedules 5 and 8 of the 1981 Wildlife and Countryside Act (Whitten 1990). Some of these are now being taken forward in the statutory agencies' species recovery programmes.

Although the species recovery programme and action plan concepts are new to Britain, recovery programmes for threatened species have begun elsewhere, for example in the US under the 1973 Endangered Species Act. The Netherlands has published action plans for Black Grouse and Grey Partridge and is producing plans for several other indicator species. New Zealand launched a programme with the publication of the Kakapo Recovery Plan 1989-1994 (Powlesland 1989).

In addition, international species action plans are now being produced at the population level. The International Waterfowl and Wetlands Research Bureau (IWRB) has produced, in 1990, a conservation action plan for the White-headed Duck and the JNCC, contracted by IWRB and the Irish Government, is to produce an international conservation plan for the Greenland White-fronted Goose. RSPB is assisting the International Council for Bird Protection to produce international species action plans for the 28 globally threatened species in Europe.

Further information

Published summaries of several Species Action Plans are available, including Red Kite (Lovegrove *et al.* 1990), White-tailed Eagle (Elliott *et al.* 1991), Corncrake (Williams *et al.* 1991) and Cirl Bunting (Smith & Evans elsewhere in this volume, Smith *et al.* in press).

The statutory agencies are currently considering ways in which the Species Action Plan approach could benefit their conservation programmes for threatened species. The main contact is John Holmes of the Vertebrate Ecology and Conservation Branch, JNCC.

At the RSPB the Conservation Planning Department co-ordinates the production of the plans. Robin Wynde, Nicola Crockford and Peter Newbery are each responsible for a set of plans. Gwyn Williams has overall responsibility.

At the WWT Jeff Black is the main contact.

References

Batten, L.A., Bibby, C.J., Clement, P., Elliott, G.D. & Porter, R.F. (1990). *Red Data Birds in Britain: action for rare, threatened and important species.* T. & A.D. Poyser, London.

Housden, S., Thomas, G., Bibby, C., & Broad, R. (1991). Towards a habitat conservation strategy for bird habitats in Britain. *RSPB Conserv. Rev.* 5, 9-16.

Elliott, G., Dennis, R., Love, J., Pienkowski, M., & Broad, R. (1991). A future for the White-tailed Eagle in Britain. *RSPB Conserv. Rev.* 5, 41-46.

Lovegrove, R., Elliott, G., & Smith, K. The Red Kite in Britain. *RSPB Conserv. Rev.* 4, 15-21.

Porter, R., Bibby, C., Elliott, G., Housden, S., Thomas, G., & Williams, G. (1990). Species Action Plans for Birds. *RSPB Conserv. Rev.* 4, 10-14.

Powlesland R. 1989. *Kakapo Recovery Plan 1989-1994.* Department of Conservation, Wellington, New Zealand.

Smith, K., Walden, J., & Williams, G. (In press). Action for Cirl Buntings. *RSPB Conserv. Rev.* 6.

Whitten, A.J. (1990). *Recovery: A proposed programme for Britain's protected species.* NCC CSD Rept No. 1089.

Williams, G., Stowe, T., & Newton, A. (1991). Action for Corncrakes. *RSPB Conserv. Rev.* 5, 47-53.

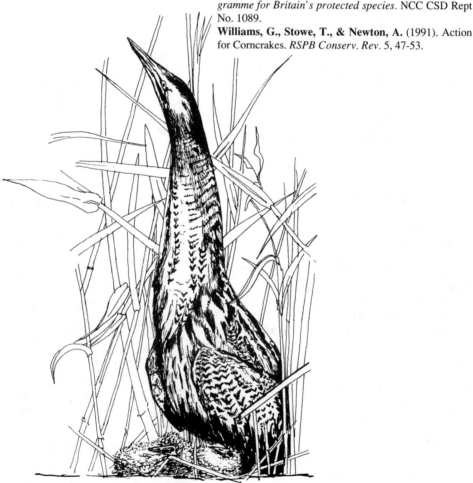

Table 1. List of Species Action Plans.

	Annex	Schedule G. Britain	Schedule N. Ireland
RED DATA BIRDS			
Red-throated Diver	1	1	1
Black-throated Diver	**1**	**1**	
Great Northern Diver	1	1	
Slavonian Grebe	**1**	**1**	
Black-necked Grebe		1	1
Manx Shearwater			
Storm Petrel	1	1	
Leach's Petrel	1	1	
Gannet			
Bittern	**1**	**1**	**1**
Bewick's Swan	1	1	1
Whooper Swan	1	1	1
Bean goose	**2.1**		
Pink-footed Goose	2.2	2.1	2.1
Greenland White-fronted Goose	1		
Greylag Goose	2.1	1.2[1], 2.1	2.1
Barnacle Goose	1		
Brent Goose (races)			
Shelduck			
Wigeon	2.1	2.1	1.2, 2.1
Gadwall	2.1	2.1	1.2, 2.1
Teal	2.1	2.1	2.1
Pintail	2.1	1.2, 2.1	1.2, 2.1
Garganey	**2.1**	**1**	**1**
Shoveler	2.1	2.1	1.2, 2.1
Pochard	2.1	2.1	1.2, 2.1
Scaup	**2.1**	**1**	**1.2, 2.1**
Long-tailed Duck	**2.2**	**1**	
Common Scoter	2.1	1	1
Velvet Scoter	**2.2**	**1**	
Goldeneye	2.2	1.2, 2.1	1.2, 2.1
Honey Buzzard	1	1	
Red Kite	**1**	**1**	
White-tailed Eagle	**1**	**1**	**1**
Marsh Harrier	1	1	1
Hen Harrier	**1**	**1**	**1**
Montagu's Harrier	**1**	**1**	
Goshawk		1	1
Golden Eagle	**1**	**1**	**1**
Merlin	**1**	**1**	**1**
Peregrine	1	1	1
Red Grouse	**2.1**		
Black Grouse	**2.2**		
Capercaillie	**1, 2.2**	**2.1**	
Grey Partridge	**2.1**		
Quail		1	1
Spotted Crake	1	1	
Corncrake	**1**	**1**	**1**
Crane	1		

Table 1. Continued ... /2

	Annex	Schedule G. Britain	Schedule N. Ireland
Oystercatcher			
Avocet	1	1	
Stone Curlew	**1**	**1**	
Ringed Plover			
Dotterel	1	1	1
Golden Plover	**1, 2.2**	**2.1**	**1.2, 2.1**
Grey Plover	2.2		
Knot			
Sanderling			
Temminck's Stint		1	
Purple Sandpiper		1	
Dunlin			**1**
Ruff	1	1	1
Black-tailed Godwit		**1**	**1**
Bar-tailed Godwit	**2.2**		
Whimbrel	2.2	1	1
Curlew	2.2		2.1
Redshank	**2.2**		
Greenshank		**1**	**1**
Wood Sandpiper	1	1	
Turnstone			
Red-necked Phalarope	**1**	**1**	**1**
Great Skua			
Mediterranean Gull	1	1	
Sandwich Tern	1	1	
Roseate Tern	**1**	**1**	**1**
Arctic Tern	1	1	
Little Tern	1	1	1
Guillemot			
Razorbill			
Barn Owl		**1**	**1**
Nightjar	**1**	**1**	
Wryneck		1	
Woodlark	1	1	
Black Redstart		1	
Fieldfare		1	1
Redwing		1	
Cetti's Warbler		1	
Savi's Warbler		1	
Marsh Warbler		**1**	
Dartford Warbler	**1**	**1**	
Firecrest		1	1
Bearded Tit		**1**	**1**
Crested Tit		1	
Golden Oriole		**1**	
Red-backed Shrike	**1**	**1**	
Chough	1	1	1
Brambling		1	
Serin		1	
Twite			1

Table 1. Continued ... /3

	Annex	Schedule G. Britain	Schedule N. Ireland
Scottish Crossbill	1	1	
Snow Bunting		1	
Cirl Bunting		1	
OCCASIONAL BREEDERS			
Red-necked Grebe			
Little Bittern	1	1	
Black-winged Stilt	1	1	
Kentish Plover		1	
Little Gull		1	
Black Tern	1	1	
Snowy Owl	1	1	
Hoopoe		1	
Bee-eater		1	
Shore Lark		1	
Bluethroat	1	1	
Parrot Crossbill		1	
Scarlet Rosefinch		1	
Lapland Bunting		1	
CANDIDATE RED DATA BIRDS			
Buzzard			1
Red-legged Partridge	2.1		
Lapwing			
Snipe	2.1	2.1	
Herring Gull		2.2	2.2
Arctic Skua			
Kittiwake			
Puffin			
Rock Dove	2.1		
Turtle Dove			1
Short-eared Owl	1		1
Kingfisher	1	1	1
Sand Martin			
Swallow			
Yellow Wagtail			1
Dipper			
Nightingale			
Redstart			1
Whinchat			
Stonechat			
Wheatear			
Ring Ouzel			1
Sedge Warbler			
Whitethroat			
Spotted Flycatcher			
Raven			
Tree Sparrow			
Linnet			
Corn Bunting			1

Table 1. Continued ... /4

	Annex	Schedule G. Britain	Schedule N. Ireland
"PROBLEM" SPECIES			
Woodcock	2.1	2.1	
Moorhen	2.2	2.1	
Tufted Duck	2.1	2.1	2.1
Coot	2.1	2.1	
Canada Goose	2.1	2.1	
Woodpigeon	2.1	2.2	2.2
Starling		2.2	2.2
House Sparrow		2.2	2.2
Great Black-backed Gull		2.2	2.2
Lesser Black-backed Gull		2.2	2.2
Collared Dove		2.2	
Jay		2.2	
Magpie		2.2	2.2
Rook		2.2	2.2
Jackdaw		2.2	2.2
Crow		2.2	
Feral/racing Pigeon		2.2	2.2
Cormorant			
Black-headed Gull			
Mute Swan			
Heron			
Red-breasted Merganser			
Goosander			
Sparrowhawk			
Stock Dove			
Tawny Owl			
Bullfinch			
Chukar			
Ring-necked Parakeet			

KEY

Annex. Species listed on Annex 1, 2/1 or 2/2 of the EC Directive 79/409 on the Conservation of Wild Birds.

Schedule G. Britain. Species listed on Schedules 1, 2 part 1, 2 part 2 of the 1981 Wildlife and Countryside Act.

Schedule N. Ireland. Species listed on Schedules 1, 2 part 1, 2 part 2 of the 1985 Wildlife (Northern Ireland) Order.

Species in bold type are amongst the 41 most threatened species in Britain.

[1]In Outer Herbrides, Caithness and Sutherland and Wester Ross only.

Table 2. Criteria for selection of species in *Red Data Birds in Britain* (Batten *et al.* 1990).

International significance of British Populations: more than 20% of the western European population breeds or winters in Britain.

Scarcity as British breeders: fewer than 300 pairs breed regularly in Britain.

Declining breeding numbers: species whose breeding numbers have declined by more than 50% since 1960.

Restricted distribution in vulnerable sites or habitats: species often confined to rare and vulnerable habitats with more than half the population occurring at 10 or fewer sites.

Species of special concern: for current data is inadequate to be confident of their exclusion from the above four categories and the species are believed to be potentially at risk.

Candidate Red Data birds: those which do not quite meet the criteria for inclusion in *Red Data Birds in Britain*, often because information on their status is not good enough. (*Red Data Birds in Britain* is unlike other Red Data Books in including species of international importance because of the significant numbers - in European or global terms - which regularly occur in the British Isles, in addition to including those species that are rare, very local or rapidly declining. The inclusion of these internationally important species is irrespective of whether or not they are threatened).

Table 3. The Format of Species Action Plans.

Part 1: Summary

1.1 Conservation status of the species: reasons for concern and inclusion in the Action Plan process, population size, range, trends, level of population and conservation knowledge, limiting factors and threats, conservation importance.

1.2 Legal status.

1.3 Priority statement: importance attached to overall action for the species in terms of high, medium or low priority categories.

1.4 Objectives: goals at which to aim in taking conservation action.

1.5 Broad policies: as to how to achieve the objectives.

1.6 Summary of actions: titles of actions proposed in Part 3 with priority and responsibilities for implementation.

1.7 Review: timetable and procedures for monitoring effectiveness and for reviewing and updating the Plan.

Part 2: Biological Assessment

2.1-3 "Introduction", "Ecology" and "Distribution and Population" sections from *Red Data Birds in Britain* updated and amended to take account of new information and of populations within the British Isles but outside Great Britain.

2.4 Discussion of limiting factors and threats thought to affect population numbers and distribution with classification (high, medium, low, unknown) as to their relative importance. Each is cross-referenced, by Action number, to the actions proposed to affect the impact of the factor on the species.

2.5 Summary of conservation action undertaken and in progress.

Part 3: Actions and Work Programme

Proposed actions are listed in the categories: 1. Policy and Legislative; 2. Site Safeguard; 3. Land Acquisition and Reserve Management; 4. Species Management and Protection; 5. Advisory; 6. International; 7. Future Research and Monitoring; 8. Communication and Publicity

For quick reference by those implementing the plan, each action is given a priority rating according to its cost-effectiveness and achievability, and is assigned to a particular work programme (or work programmes) specifying who does what and when. Each action is individually identified by a Species Action code to assist referencing and cross-referencing.

Red Kite re-introduction progresses well

I M Evans[1] & T S Stowe[2]

[1]Vertebrate Ecology and Conservation Branch, JNCC
[2]North Scotland Office, RSPB

Background

The Red Kite is a favourite bird with birdwatchers, but unfortunately this magnificent raptor is now rare over much of its limited world range (Evans & Pienkowski 1991). It is one of only three British breeding species which are threatened on a global scale (Collar & Andrew 1988).

In Britain, the small relict population in central Wales has increased from half a dozen pairs at the beginning of this century to 77 pairs in 1991. However, its isolation, small size and comparatively low productivity make this population particularly vulnerable to pressures such as food shortages or persecution (Lovegrove 1990). Factors such as these are preventing the Red Kite from colonising parts of its former range in Britain.

In the last *Britain's Birds* Pienkowski & Evans (1991) outlined the background to the joint JNCC/RSPB re-introduction programme. By conserving the species in its existing range in Wales and encouraging it to re-colonise parts of its former British range, we are making an important contribution to its future. This article reports on progress so far and emphasises again the importance of this programme for the long-term survival of the Red Kite in world terms.

Release scheme

An experimental programme to evaluate whether viable breeding populations could be established in England and Scotland was set up in 1989. The JNCC, working with English Nature, manages the releases in England, whilst Scottish releases are carried out under RSPB direction.

Since the Red Kite is rare in global terms, it is important to ensure that the re-introduction programme has no adverse effects on the donor populations. Young birds are taken from healthy populations in Sweden and Spain and young are also reared artificially by Dr Nick Fox from Welsh eggs taken from nests that have failed or where failure is anticipated.

The following birds have so far been released:

| | RELEASE AREA | SOURCE | | |
		Sweden	Spain	Wales
1989	England	4	-	1
	Scotland	6	-	-
1990	England	13	-	-
	Scotland	19	-	-
1991	England	-	11	4
	Scotland	20	-	-

Young birds, aged from 4-7 weeks are brought to Britain where they spend a 35 day quarantine period in specially designed aviaries at their intended release site. The birds are reared in brood-sized groups of no more than four and fed on a diet of rabbit, squirrel, corvid and fish obtained mostly from local gamekeepers. Direct contact with birds is kept to a minimum during this period to avoid conditioning to humans.

Before release, each bird is fitted with a BTO ring, a tail-mounted radio transmitter and a coloured plastic tag visible on the upper surface of each wing so that its fate can be closely monitored. Once released, birds are dependent upon food stations near the release aviaries but soon learn to forage for themselves, becoming totally independent within about two weeks.

Dispersal and survival

Table 1 gives release and survival statistics for Red Kites during the first three years of the programme. The radio transmitters have only a limited lifespan and monitoring of older birds therefore relies on visual records. As a result, some birds are currently unaccounted for but may well still be alive.

In 1989, the five birds from the English site dispersed west and were encountered in Cornwall, Somerset and Shropshire. At least three returned to southern England but at this early stage showed no signs of settling. Birds from the Scottish site showed similar behaviour, dispersing widely across south-west, south-east, central and eastern Scotland. At least three returned to the Highlands the following summer. Two birds were known to have been killed by illegal poisoning, one in

Table 1. Red Kite release and survival statistics, 1989-1991.

		1989	1990	1991
Total released	Scotland	6	19	20
	England	5	13	15
Recently Accounted	Scotland	3	14	20
	England	-	7	15
Unaccounted	Scotland	2	2	-
	England	4	3	-
Captivity	Scotland	-	-	-
	England	-	1	-
Poisoned	Scotland	1	2	-
	England	1	1	-
Dead (other than poisoned)	Scotland	-	1	-
	England	-	1	-

England and one in Scotland. Successful prosecutions resulted.

In 1990, the Spanish Red Kites released in England tended to disperse over much shorter distances than their Swedish counterparts, with nine over-wintering in southern England. Some late-summer dispersal was evident with one bird leaving the release site after only two days of freedom to be re-discovered in north Norfolk. Three birds left in September, with one reported caught in a fence in Shropshire and another found dead in northern France in January 1991. Of the birds which over-wintered, one was found illegally poisoned, another was taken into captivity after developing a flight impairment and another dispersed the following spring, paying a brief visit to the RSPB headquarters at Sandy before turning up in Essex.

Just one of the birds released in Scotland remained in the Highlands throughout the winter, with birds recorded in southeast Scotland, Sutherland, Yorkshire and Ireland (where two were poisoned). At least 14 returned to the Highlands during spring 1991 but quickly dispersed to favoured wintering areas.

Five 1991 releases left southern England on 12 August 1991 with one settling briefly in the Midlands and four in Clwyd, North Wales. During autumn 1991 three returned to join the other ten which were dispersed across several southern English counties. By the autumn of 1991, 12 Scottish releases were outside the Highlands, with one in Ireland, two in central and south-west Scotland, six in southeast Scotland and three in eastern Scotland (Duncan Orr-Ewing, pers. comm.).

Success

We are greatly encouraged by the survival rate of the released birds so far. The scheme has successfully demonstrated that:
1. translocation of Red Kites can be carried out without jeopardising donor populations;
2. the release methods are a practical way of establishing Red Kites in the wild;
3. southern England and the Highlands of Scotland are still capable of supporting Red Kites and,
4. birds which disperse widely can and will return to suitable areas in southern England and the Highlands of Scotland where, hopefully, nucleus populations will be established.

Further releases will continue for at least two more years to ensure that there are enough individuals of suitable age and condition to initiate breeding. The goal of the programme is to establish self-sustaining populations in England and Scotland. Clearly this will require a long-term commitment to monitor the fate of released birds. The information gathered will be crucial to the future management of the project.

How can you help?

Any sightings of Red Kites (noting location, date and colour of wing tags if present) are useful in assessing the current status of the population, particularly now that a proportion of the older birds can no longer be located by radio tracking. Please send any records of birds in England to Ian Evans, JNCC, Monkstone House, City Road, Peterborough. PE1 1JY, and in Scotland to Duncan Orr-Ewing, RSPB, North Scotland Regional Office, Munlochy, Ross-shire, IV8 8ND.

When watching Red Kites, please remember not to stray from public rights of way, since this may disturb the birds and alienate landowners.

Acknowledgements

We are grateful to the following organisations who assist with the provision of Red Kites: the Swedish National Environmental Protection Board, WWF-Sweden, Skanes Ornitologiska Forening, Servicio de Medio Ambiente (Navarra), Instituto Nacional para la Conservacion de la Naturaleza, the Royal Air Force and British Airways Assisting Nature Conservation, all of whom recognise the importance of widening the distribution of the Red Kite throughout its former range.

References

Collar, N.J. & Andrew, P. (1988). *Birds to watch: the ICBP world checklist of threatened birds.* ICBP, Cambridge.

Evans, I.M. & Pienkowski, M.W. (1991). World status of the Red Kite: a background to the experimental reintroduction to England and Scotland. *British Birds* 84, 171-187.

Lovegrove, R. (1990). *The Kite's Tale: the story of the Red Kite in Wales.* RSPB, Sandy.

Pienkowski, M.P. & Evans, I.M. (1991). Red Kite reintroduction to Scotland and England. In: Stroud, D.A. & Glue, D. (Eds). *Britain's Birds in 1989/90: the conservation and monitoring review.* Pp. 124–127 BTO/NCC Thetford.

C.H. Gomersall, RSPB/Red Kite

Cirl Buntings in Britain

K W Smith & A D Evans

Research Department, RSPB

Summary

In Britain the Cirl Bunting is now largely limited to south Devon where, in 1990, around 132 pairs bred. The recovery of the population is now the subject of an action plan involving habitat manipulation, advice, research and monitoring.

Colonisation and decline

The Cirl Bunting is essentially a Mediterranean species and is at the northern edge of its breeding range in Britain. It was first reported as breeding in Britain near Kingsbridge in south Devon in 1800. It then colonized southern England until, in the 1930s, it was locally common in many areas south of a line between the Thames and Severn estuaries with an additional group in North Wales. After the 1940s numbers declined with the distribution becoming progressively more patchy and eventually contracting to south-west England (Sitters 1982). In 1982, when the BTO conducted a national survey, there were thought to be only 167 pairs of Cirl Buntings in the whole of Britain with 78% in Devon (Sitters 1985). The numbers of 10 km squares occupied by Cirl Buntings fell from 174 in 1968-72 (Sharrock 1976) to only 32 in 1982 (Figure 1 and Table 1).

A number of explanations have been put forward for this change including climatic factors such as severe winter weather, interspecific competition with Yellowhammers and adverse habitat changes. However no detailed studies had been undertaken to investigate these possibilities until 1988 when the RSPB began work on the detailed ecology of Cirl Buntings. A number of projects were set up to look at diet and habitat requirements throughout the year and it is the results of this work (Evans 1991) which have formed the basis of the action being taken to help Cirl Buntings.

Current status

The first task was to assess the remaining numbers and distribution and so, with the help of members of the Devon Birdwatching and Preservation Society (DBWPS), a full survey was carried out in 1989. A total of around 114 pairs was found in Devon (Table 1) (Evans 1992). This was significantly lower than the numbers found in the 1982 survey but, more importantly, the distribution had become more restricted, with the loss of birds from many inland sites and only 15 10 km squares occupied in the county. There had also been severe losses from counties other than Devon. Annual monitoring of breeding Cirl Buntings is now carried out jointly by the RSPB and DBWPS and, as the figures in Table 1 show, the numbers of pairs increased to 132 in 1990. Much of this apparent increase has been the result of improved coverage and knowledge of traditional sites but in some areas there is thought to have been a small real increase between 1989 and 1990.

Habitat requirements

One of the key findings of the research work is that in winter the birds form flocks and show very strong selection for weedy cereal stubbles and other weed-rich areas. Their diet is dominated by weed seeds and cereal grains. Birds rarely venture far from dense cover so fields bordered by large mature hedges are preferred.

Table 1. The estimated numbers of pairs of Cirl Buntings in Devon and elsewhere in Britain (excluding the Channel Islands) from 1968-74 until 1990. Because of the methods employed, the figures for 1968-72 and 1982 are likely to be under-estimates. In 1989 and 1990 very thorough coverage of a relatively restricted area was obtained so the figures are more likely to reflect the true numbers. The total number of occupied 10 km squares have been included to indicate the severe contaction of range that has occurred over the twenty year period.

Year	Numbers in Devon	Numbers elsewhere	Number occupied 10 km squares
1968-72	140-150	112-169	174
1982	130	37	32
1989	114	4	17
1990	132	2	17

In periods of severe weather, when stubble fields are snow covered, Cirl Buntings are forced to feed elsewhere and are likely to move to stock feeding areas or garden feeders. It is probable that the loss of mixed farming systems and the stock yard have had a major impact on them. With modern farming systems they often have no alternative feeding areas in periods of cold weather. The current distribution in south Devon, an area of the country experiencing some of the mildest winters, may well be linked to this.

Colour-ringing of birds in winter flocks and young fledglings has shown that, in general, birds nest within a few kilometres of their wintering sites. Hence, to be effective, winter feeding habitat must to be provided in close proximity to the breeding areas.

Work continues to understand better the ecology of the Cirl Bunting, but this now forms just one element of an RSPB 'Action Plan' designed to secure the existing population and ultimately bring about a recovery of numbers. The plan encompasses many elements including monitoring of numbers, safeguard of existing sites against adverse developments, the experimental creation of wintering and breeding habitat and the promotion of schemes in the wider countryside such as Environmentally Sensitive Areas and Set Aside which will benefit Cirl Buntings.

Advice and information

Advice and information on Cirl Buntings and their requirements can be obtained from the RSPB Southwest Regional Office, 10 Richmond Road, Exeter, Devon, EX4 4JA.

Acknowledgements

H. Sitters provided much help and access to his original survey data. A. Cole has organised a large part of the annual survey and has contributed many original observations to our studies. Members of the DBWPS have contributed enthusiastically to the cause and carried out the bulk of the surveys. Our work would not have been possible without the willing support of many farmers and landowners.

References

Evans, A.D. (1991). *Cirl Buntings - report on research project 1988-91*. Unpubl rept. RSPB, Sandy.

Evans, A.D. (1992) The numbers and distribution of Cirl Buntings breeding in Britain in 1989. *Bird Study* 39, 17-22.

Sharrock, J.T.R. (1976). *Atlas of Breeding Birds in Britain and Ireland*. T & A D Poyser, Calton.

Sitters, H.P. (1982). The decline of the Cirl Bunting in Britain 1968-80. *British Birds* 75, 105-108.

Sitters, H.P. (1985). Cirl Buntings in Britain in 1982. *Bird Study* 32, 1-10.

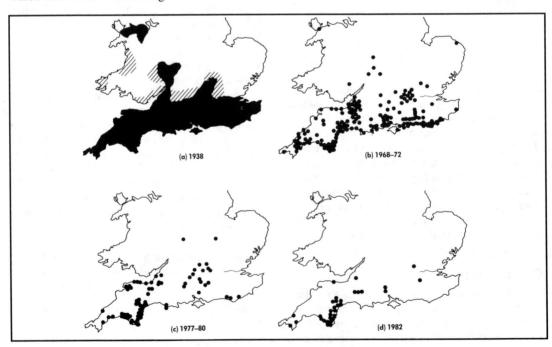

Figure 1. *Distribution of the Cirl Bunting in Britain 1938–82.*
Sources (a) Sharrock 1976 (b) and (d) adapted from Sitters 1985 (c) Sitters 1982.

Greenland White-fronted Goose international conservation plan

David A Stroud

Vertebrate Ecology and Conservation Branch, JNCC

Summary

International management plans for migratory populations of waterfowl complement site-related co-operation formerly undertaken at an international level. Work on the development of such a plan for the Greenland White-fronted Goose is described. This population and the draft international management plan for it may provide a useful model for the development of further such plans. The Western Palearctic Waterfowl Agreement being developed under the Bonn Convention provides a suitable mechanism for the implementation of the Greenland White-fronted Goose plan and will hopefully encourage the development of further plans for other biogeographic populations.

Population management plans

Migratory birds require international co-operation for their effective conservation, a fact that underlies many international wildlife conventions. However until recently, the focus of international co-operation has tended be the designation of protected areas in each of the countries signatory to an international convention. Such site-based protection is clearly important, and if sufficient sites are protected in a sufficiently large number of countries, then this approach gives major opportunities to enhance the conservation of migratory populations.

For most bird populations however, such a site-related approach, in itself, is insufficient. There is a need for a population-based approach which identifies the major problems and develops a specific set of actions to enhance population status and provide for a more secure future in an uncertain and ever-changing world. This is especially important for waterfowl such as geese which may depend on agricultural or other artificial habitats not normally amenable to conventional site-protection measures.

One mechanism for achieving such an objective is the development of population-specific international management plans, which draw together the actions of all the states along the migratory range of the birds.

These plans would not only identify the problem but, importantly, analyse these in terms of the opportunities and potential for action in each Range State. They should also give a set of clear guidelines which would enable each country to operate complimentary conservation policies: this co-operation is to everyone's advantage - not least in terms of making the most cost-effective use of ever- limited conservation resources.

The plan for Greenland White-fronts

For some years, those involved in Greenland White-fronted Goose conservation have been keen to promote a management plan for the population as a whole. This would address the various problems and opportunities facing the population at an international scale and would facilitate co-operation between the four nations (Greenland/Denmark, Iceland, Ireland and the United Kingdom) responsible for the well-being of this small population.

The first steps in this direction were taken at the 1990 Montreux meeting of the parties to the Ramsar Convention. A meeting of representatives of the four Range States was held to discuss co-operation under Article 5 of the Convention which encourages international co-ordination in the conservation of wetlands and their fauna.

An outcome of this meeting was that the Republic of Ireland agreed to be host to a further meeting of Range States at Wexford, Ireland in March 1992. Ireland further agreed to sponsor an international management plan and contracted IWRB to co-ordinate the meeting and develop the plan, which has been prepared by the JNCC.

The plan provides a significant opportunity to make real progress. Aside from its value for this small population, the exercise provides a valuable model for the development of future plans for the following reasons:

● the population is small, well-monitored in winter, and has a simple flyway through four nations;

- much survey work on the wintering grounds has resulted in a good knowledge of wintering sites and site-specific conservation problems;
- there is a range of different conservation policies in the four countries, and in particular, a wide range in the level of statutory and non-governmental conservation provision;
- there is a wide range of conservation problems to be faced, but all are potentially soluble given co-operation and appropriate structures;
- there is already a high degree of co-operation between Greenland White-fronted Goose workers through the flyway, both from governmental and non-governmental organisations. This provides an excellent basis for further international co-operation and collaborative studies;
- all the Range States are party to the Ramsar Convention, and all but Iceland are party to the Bonn Convention.

Development of a plan for Greenland White-fronted Geese thus brings one up against many of the problems of international waterfowl conservation; but in microcosm.

Plan development

The plan is being developed in consultation with interested parties in all the Range States. The structure of the plan follows that of the Project Planning and Recording System developed by the former NCC. This was originally developed for use in site-related management plans (e.g. for nature reserves), but has proved robust in its adaptation for a species approach.

The plan is structured in three parts:

Part 1 gives the descriptive background necessary to justify the plan's actions. It covers areas such as population size and distribution, population dynamics, relevant environmental information such as background on past and present land-uses within the range, diet and habitat selection, and information on the past and present history of human perception, utilisation and nature conservation. Where appropriate, many sections present information broken down for each Range State separately.

Part 2 then evaluates this background against a range of criteria. The requirement to address the evaluation criteria (e.g. naturalness, rarity, fragility, potential value etc.), results in a clear understanding of the justification for cooperation. Deriving from this evaluation are a set of ideal

management objectives. These may not necessarily be achievable, but are a clear statement of the ideal that the parties to the plan wish to achieve.

Following this statement of the ideal is an outline of the various constraints or opportunities that will either hinder or help in their achievement. These cover, for each of the Range States, the various management constraints such as resources for statutory conservation, existing policies for conservation and wildlife management, anthropogenic impacts such as shooting and habitat loss, as well as a range of other factors. On the positive side is a description of the various relevant obligations under national and international law.

With a clear idea of these constraints, 'operational objectives' are identified, which may be a step back from the ideal, but will hopefully be on the same road. The careful separation of the ideal from the constraints, and from the realisable operational objectives is important. It allows re-assessment of the plan targets in the light of any future change in constraints.

At the time of writing, and subject to ratification by the Range States, there are five ideal objectives for this population: the need to conserve the range of the population, the need to maintain numbers at least at the present level, the need to avoid conflict with agricultural interests, the need for 'wise use' of the population, and the need for international co-operation and liaison.

The third part of the plan develops the necessary prescriptions to implement the operational objectives, and the identification of work programmes and project recording systems. To a major extent these need to be developed individually in each Range State according to their own conservation management systems. The objective of the plan is to provide an common international outline, which will then be implemented in more detail by a series of national plans.

In effect, the international plan is a road map to a destination: it will be for each country to use it to navigate themselves towards the goal, and clearly some countries may take longer to make this journey than others.

However, at least they all will now be travelling in the same direction!

Where to from here?

The writing and agreement of such plans is merely the start of the process. Indeed, the hard work comes later in using the plan to influence events. To be effective, it is clear that a key long-term need is to monitor, maintain and enhance liaison between the Range States. Likewise, there is no such thing as a finalised management plan since such plans should always be seen as a draft in revision.

The stages of feedback and revision are crucial to its effectiveness, although clearly they have resource implications that cannot be neglected.

The draft plan will be discussed at the intergovernmental meeting in Wexford between 4-6 March 1992. It is to be hoped that agreement can be reached at this meeting on the principles of the plan. The relationship of the plan to the range of relevant international conventions will be a matter for that meeting and the concerned governments. Whilst Article 5 of the Ramsar Convention is clearly relevant in this context, the plan relates more closely to the Western Palearctic Waterfowl Agreement (WPWA) being developed under the Bonn Convention. It would obviously be appropriate for the Greenland White-front Plan to become the first plan developed under the WPWA, not least since that agreement will provide a Secretariat to service such plans.

Should the Greenland White-front plan be linked to the WPWA, the role of the Secretariat will clearly be of particular importance in ensuring such plans move forward. Equally it will hold in pivotal position in providing support for further such plans, and in the provision of advice on 'best practice', as well as in the sharing of international experience in plan development and implementation.

Conservation of geese in relation to agricultural damage

Myrfyn Owen

WWT

In the first volume of *Britain's Birds*, we reported on a workshop on the conservation management of our internationally important populations of geese, in relation to agricultural damage. This was organised by the Wildfowl & Wetlands Trust and held in April 1990. The proceedings of this workshop were published early in 1991 (Owen & Pienkowski 1991).

As a result of its participation, the Ministry of Agriculture, Nature Management and Fisheries of the Netherlands decided to host a further, international, workshop to examine the problems in an international light and to produce recommendations as to how they might be solved. This was held in Lelystad, the Netherlands in October 1991, and organised jointly by the Ministry and IWRB. About 70 participants came from 16 European countries and from Canada.

A number of review papers were presented, and 16 national reports outlined the conditions and problems in the different countries. One of the most striking aspects of these accounts was the variety of problems and ways of dealing with them within the ranges of individual goose species and sub-species, the differences in the legislative framework in different countries and the general lack of international co-ordination.

In the context of increasing goose populations in Europe and increasing conflicts with farmers, it was recognised that some action had to be taken. Discussions were very constructive and the proceedings are to be published by IWRB. There was a general consensus that we should be looking for a strategic solution at an international level.

The recommendations of the workshop can be summarised as follows:

1. Conservation and species management depends on detailed monitoring throughout the range.
2. Species and populations differ in ecology and behaviour and this must be recognised when management proposals are being formulated.
3. The damage issue is not directly related to bird numbers. Distribution across the flyway and agricultural practices are also important.
4. The agricultural problems are largely man-made, with intensive agriculture and rich feeding causing concentrations of birds. One aim of management should be to disperse these concentrations.
5. International co-operation should aim to re-establish the traditional ranges of population by ensuring that feeding and resting areas are available.
6. An international framework should be developed, which must be sufficiently flexible to encompass different national and local requirements. The IWRB was identified as the international body which should take responsibility for setting up such a framework. The Bonn Convention and the Western Palearctic Waterfowl Management Agreement would be suitable instruments to incorporate it.

One of the most interesting ideas is that we should try to break up large concentrations of geese such as those which have become established in the Nord-Rhein Westfalia area of Germany and parts of the Netherlands. These have become large because of the measures taken to conserve geese, including making compensation payments to farmers for goose damage. However, experience of dispersal attempts in North America are not encouraging; once geese establish a tradition to visit an area where the food supply is rich, they are difficult to dislodge (Owen 1980). We may end up with a international network of conservation areas, but dispersing the birds so that they re-establish their former ranges is a more difficult challenge.

References

Owen, M. 1980. The role of refuges in wildfowl management. In: Wright, E.N., Inglis, I.R. and Feare, C.J. (eds) *Bird Problems in Agriculture*. Pp 46–61. British Crop Protection Council, Croydon.

Owen, M. & Pienkowski, M.W. 1991. *Proceedings of the Goose Damage and Management Workshop, Martin Mere, April 1990*. JNCC, Peterborough.

Pink-footed Goose research

A D Fox

Research and Conservation Department, WWT[1]

The reasons for research

The world stock of Pink-footed Geese comprises two discrete populations. The smaller of these nests in Svalbard and winters in Denmark, the Netherlands and Belgium, while the larger population (some 80% of the world total) breeds in Iceland and Greenland and winters in Britain. The Pink-foot is a British Red Data Book species because of its highly restricted distribution in this country and is protected under Annex 1 of the EC Birds Directive (Batten *et al.* 1990). The British Government therefore has a special obligation to protect the population on the wintering grounds.

On arrival in autumn from their northerly breeding areas, Pink-feet glean spilled grain from cereal stubbles. As the stubbles become exhausted of food or are ploughed in preparation for drilling of winter cereal, the geese progressively move to grassland to feed. Waste potatoes, carrots and other root crops may also be taken, as is the new growth of spring cereals in some areas. However, generally, the species exploits grassland for virtually all the latter part of the winter (Newton and Campbell 1973, Forshaw 1983, Bell 1988). Because this affects the availability of early spring grazing for livestock, such feeding activity brings Pink-feet into conflict with agricultural interests. Partly for this reason, considerable effort has gone into studies of the birds' population trends and distribution and their causes.

Abundance and population trends

An annual census of the Iceland/Greenland population has been undertaken on the wintering areas by the Wildfowl & Wetlands Trust since the early 1950s. This work is now carried out under contract to the JNCC, which also co-funds a range of studies on the reasons for changes in the numbers of birds wintering here. The counts have shown an increase from around 30,000 in 1950 to 76,000 in 1966, climbing to over 200,000 by autumn 1991.

1. Current address: Department of Wildlife Ecology, Natural Environment Research Institute, Kalø, DK-8410, Rønde, Denmark.

It is important to understand the reasons for this increase. From ringing information, we know there is relatively little movement of geese between the two populations, so it would appear that the expansion is due to increased survival or an increase in breeding productivity (or both) by the birds which winter here. We have attempted to answer this question by a number of studies.

Has breeding success increased?

To see if the increase has been brought about by improved breeding success, analysis of the proportion of young birds arriving here each autumn (the young birds can be identified in the field by plumage characteristics) has been carried out. There is no trend in the pattern of productivity since the mid-1960s. Many of the year-to-year fluctuations in breeding success can be explained by meteorological conditions on the wintering grounds prior to departure and on the breeding areas in spring as geese reach their nesting grounds (Fox *et al.* 1989).

Studies of Pink-feet on their arrival in Iceland show that the timing of snow melt has considerable consequences for the geese. In a late spring, the grass hayfields, which are the predominant habitat used by geese, are covered in snow. Birds may lose condition whilst waiting for their snow-bound nest sites to become available. The geese make finegrained choices about where to forage, even to the extent of grazing around the edges of snow-fields to exploit the first flush of green growth which has started under the greenhouse-like protective mantle of snow (Fox *et al.* 1991). In a mild spring, the Pink-feet arrive to good forage and nest sites which are free from snow and ready for immediate occupancy. In this way, clutch initiation commences earlier and breeding success tends to be higher. It would therefore seem that breeding success is determined to a large extent by weather and hence pre-nesting feeding forage quality which affects both the condition of the female and the timing of her breeding. Whilst we may speculate that climatic amelioration in Iceland in the future might increase breeding success, there is no evidence from the past of any sustained increase in productivity to account for the increase in the population.

Has annual mortality declined?

The alternative explanation is that annual adult mortality has declined. We have examined estimates of survival rates based on census information and find that annual adult mortality rate has apparently declined from 22% in the early 1960s and is presently nearer to 12% (Fox *et al*. 1989). Little is known about the relative importance of different causes of mortality of geese, with one exception. We know from this species, and other geese, that hunting is responsible for more than three quarters of deaths in quarry populations. Under a sub-contract to the British Association for Shooting and Conservation, we obtained information on the numbers of geese shot by a random sample of their membership. Retrospective analysis of these data suggest that there has been little change in the numbers of Pink-feet shot in Britain throughout the 1980s (Murray-Evans & Harradine 1991). Information from earlier decades is lacking, but it is possible that the hunting bag of Pink-feet may have been more or less constant for rather longer. Therefore, in proportional terms, this source of mortality has actually fallen over at least the last decade (Fox *et al*. 1989). Although the population has increased, many more are now wintering on refuges and are less accessible to hunters; this is partly responsible for the fact the kills are not keeping pace with the population growth.

Effects on distribution

Pink-feet in winter are highly dispersive; they tend to arrive initially at traditional sites and then disperse more widely during mid-winter before aggregating again at regular spring gathering areas during the pre-migration phase. They therefore appear to be opportunist in their exploitation of food resources within their overall wintering range. Although restricted to Britain, their distribution has changed greatly during the last 40 years. In particular, the more southerly parts of the range (Lancashire and Norfolk) hold considerably greater numbers now than in the 1960s. An individual marking scheme was started in Lancashire in 1987 to try to assess patterns of movement of these birds, apparently the most mobile of the wintering population.

The changes in distribution could be due to movements of birds between areas from year to year, or to different survival rates of different sub-units of the population causing some segments to increase while others declined or remained stable.

We require considerably more information relating to inter-site movements of individually marked geese, profitability of different feeding opportunities and differential breeding success and mortality patterns in different parts of the range before we can understand the impact of these factors on the numbers and distribution of the population on as a whole and how this might change in the future.

And what of the future?

In recent years, Pink-footed Geese have been found nesting in parts of lowland Iceland, utilising habitat more usually associated with Greylag Geese (Fox & Madsen 1991). Competitive interactions during the pre-nesting period and competition for nest sites could possibly limit breeding success in future (Fox *et al*. 1992), but there are areas of potentially suitable habitat, such that availability of breeding sites seems unlikely to limit the population in the foreseeable future.

The prospect of ever-increasing numbers of Pink-feet exacerbates the issue of agricultural conflict and this problem was addressed at a workshop organised by the Wildfowl & Wetlands Trust at Martin Mere in April 1990 (Owen & Pienkowski 1991). At this meeting Owen reviewed a number of possible solutions and suggested that the designation of Environmentally Sensitive Areas to support a proportion of the wintering population of Pink-feet would offer a farmer the opportunity to opt into the scheme, accept payments and tolerate geese on his land, or opt out and bear the losses or the costs of preventing their use of his crops.

The success of the research programme on Pink-feet depends very heavily upon the efforts of a great many voluntary observers, ranging from the South-west Lancashire Ringing Group, plus staff from our Martin Mere Centre and Carl Mitchell who help catch the Pink-feet, through the mighty team of counters who contribute to the census every year, to people like Andy Stewart and Paul Shimmings who devote so much time to reading ring combinations in the field. Their contributions and the accumulated information from the past 40 years combine to give us the data essential for decisions on the future conservation of this important population.

References

Batten, L.A., Bibby, C.J., Clement, P. , Elliot, G.D. & Porter, R.F. (1990) *Red data birds in Britain: action for rare, threatened and important species.* T. & A.D. Poyser, London.

Bell, M.V. (1988) Feeding behaviour of wintering Pink-footed and Greylag Geese in north-east Scotland. *Wildfowl* 39, 43-53.

Forshaw, W.D. (1983) Numbers, distribution and behaviour of Pink-footed Geese in Lancashire. *Wildfowl* 34, 64-76.

Fox, A.D. & Madsen, J. (1991) *Pre-nesting studies of Pink-footed Geese in Europe.* IWRB Goose Research Group Bulletin 2, 7-13.

Fox, A.D., Gitay, H., Boyd, H. & Tomlinson, C. (1991) Snow-patch foraging by Pink-footed Geese *Anser brachyrhynchus* in south Iceland. *Holarct. Ecol.* 14, 81-84.

Fox, A.D., Boyd, H. & Warren, S.M. (1992) Spatial and temporal feeding segregation of two Icelandic goose species during the spring pre-nesting period. *Ecography* 15, 289–295.

Murray-Evans, J. & Harradine, J. (1991) *The Wildfowl and Wetlands Trust/BASC Contract. 1st Annual Report 1990/91: Grey Goose Shooting Kill.* BASC/Rossett.

Newton, I. & Campbell, C.R.C. (1973) Feeding of gesse on farmland in east-central Scotland. *J. Applied. Ecol.* 10, 781-801.

Owen, M. & Pienkowski, M.W. (1991) Goose Damage and Management Workshop. *Research and Survey in Nature Conservation* 33, 1-86.

S.P. Carter: Pink-footed Geese

Progress on lead-free shot in the UK

Myrfyn Owen

WWT

Britain is at last moving positively on the replacement of lead shot, a matter which, for some years, has been a rather contentious issue between conservationists and shooting interests.

Over the last few years, there has been a great deal of discussion, especially in the shooting press, about the problem of lead poisoning in wildfowl and the need to replace lead in shotgun cartridges and for coarse fishing weights. As long ago as 1979, the Wildfowl & Wetlands Trust, together with RSPB and the NCC and in collaboration with the British Association for Shooting and Conservation, carried out studies on the incidence of lead shot ingested by wildfowl, the lead levels in their tissues and the density and settlement of lead in wetland soils (Mudge 1983). Although the figures were rather imprecise, it was estimated that some 8,000 Mallard may be dying from lead poisoning in Britain each year. At the same time, concern was growing about the widespread deaths of Mute Swans poisoned by lead fishing weights. As many as 4,000 swans may have been affected annually (Goode 1981).

Taking note of these studies, in 1983 the Royal Commission on Environmental Pollution report 'Lead in the Environment' stated: "Lead shot from spent cartridges and lead fishing weights poison wildlife. We recommend that as soon as substitutes are available the Government should legislate to ensure their adoption and use." (RCEP 1983).

The lead poisoning in Mute Swans from lead fishing weights has been substantially reduced since their sale was banned in 1987 and their use has since been banned in most areas of England and Wales, but not in Scotland. The problem of lead poisoning from shotgun lead remains. An international workshop, organised by the International Waterfowl and Wetlands Research Bureau in Brussels on 12-16 June 1991, with support from JNCC and others, (Pain 1992) attracted more than 100 people from 20 countries to discuss the problem and possible solutions. Delegates were from shooting organisations, government agencies, conservation bodies and also included ballistics experts concerned with the manufacture and testing of ammunition. Surprisingly, although the problem has been recognised in the USA and Europe for at least half a century, this was the first time that such a gathering had come together.

The first session focused on the problem. There was not much dispute that lead poisoning was a problem, though its effects were patchy. I was surprised, though, how important it was for non-wetland birds. Most of the pressure for substitutes in the USA came because of poisoning of Bald Eagles which had ingested lead while scavenging on unretrieved kills. The last three California Condors to die in the wild died from lead poisoning (Locke & Friend 1992).

There were also potential problems for humans; in acid soils, dissolved lead from heavily shot areas was liable to leach into watercourses or be taken up by crops and pose a health risk. There was a consensus that as lead is a persistent poison it should be eliminated from all unnecessary uses.

Replacement of lead shot

The next session, which examined possible solutions, concluded: "The wise use of non-toxic shot is the only measure, other than the cessation of hunting, proven to be effective in restricting the availability of lead shot to waterfowl.....".

Many years of trials in the USA had led to the conclusion that steel was the only acceptable alternative currently available. A recent innovation in Britain - tungsten shot - has now been tested and rejected because of problems of ballistics and safety when fired.

The replacement of steel with lead is not without its problems. Among those focused on at the meeting were the relative lightness of steel, which means that a larger charge is needed to gain the equivalent downrange velocity, thus inducing pressures which are dangerous in some guns, and its hardness which, combined with increased charge, leads to problems of barrel wear and bulging of the barrel.

There were also potential problems with increased wounding. The killing power of steel is less than lead at the same load charge, which means that clean kills would be possible at reduced range. Unless there is an adjustment by the shooter, a larger proportion of birds would be hit but not brought down, or brought down and not retrieved by the shooter. The experience in the USA was that there was no conclusive evidence one way or the other about relative wounding rates of lead and steel. However, the steel cartridges used in the USA were unsuitable for most guns used in the UK because their barrels are thinner and more vulnerable to damage. The situation at the time of the meeting was that there were no lead-free cartridges available which were suitable and safe for use here.

There was general agreement that using lead in cartridges was not 'wise use' of the wildfowling resource and all possible steps should be taken to introduce lead-free shot and to phase out lead. Many countries, including Denmark and the Netherlands in Europe, led by the USA, had definite plans already agreed. The main feeling from the workshop was very optimistic; the problem was capable of solution given determination and goodwill. It was felt that there was no reason why many countries should not ban lead for waterfowl shooting in a very few years, and for all shooting soon afterwards.

Good progress in Britain

After the workshop, the Department of Environment and JNCC formed a group to work on a planned programme of implementation. The Lead Poisoning in Waterfowl Working Group has representatives from shooting organisations, weapon and ammunition manufacturers and a proof and safety expert, as well as representatives of statutory and voluntary conservation interests. It was given a year to draw up recommendations for government and first met in November 1991.

The diverse interests worked constructively together and by the third meeting in May 1992 good progress had been made. The press releases following the second (January) and third (May) meeting of the group made statements to the following effect:

-viable non-toxic shot cartridges for most guns used in wildfowling can be commercially available within three years;

-gun safety and proofing requirements will be re-assessed once viable non-toxic cartridges have been developed;

-from September 1995, there will be an agreement between shooting and conservation organisations to phase out the use of lead over wetlands;

-subject to the achievement of these objectives, the aim is to eliminate the use of lead gunshot for 12-bore shotguns in wetlands by September 1997

Problems remain; for example, no lead-free ammunition is being developed for use in guns other than 12-bore. However, the use of these in wildfowling is thought to be very minor. A constructive attitude by shooters and a realisation by manufacturers that there will be a market for non-toxic shot in the near future, mean that we are well on the way to seeing lead phased out of use over wetlands and eventually for all shooting.

References

Goode, D.A. (1981). *Lead poisoning in swans. Report of the NCC Working Group.* NCC, London.

Locke, L.N. & Friend, M. 1992. Lead poisoning of avian species other than waterfowl. In: Pain, D.J. (Ed.) *Lead poisoning in Waterfowl. Proc. IWRB Workshop, Brussels, Belgium, 13-15/6/91.* Pp. 19-22 IWRB Spec. Publ. 16.

Mudge, G.P. (1983). The incidence and significance of ingested lead pellet poisoning in British wildfowl. *Biol. Cons.* 27, 333-372.

Pain, D.J. (Ed.) (1992). *Lead poisoning in Waterfowl. Proc. IWRB Workshop Brussels, Belgium, 13-15/6/91.* IWRB Spec. Publ. 16.

Royal Commission on Environmental Pollution *(1983). Ninth Report - Lead in the Environment.* HMSO, London.

Auk mortality causes and trends

Chris Mead

Populations Research Department, BTO

In *Britain's Birds in 1989-90* attention was drawn to the reduction in the proportion of ringing recoveries of Razorbill and Guillemot reported as shot and the increase in casualties in fishing nets. Oiling had also decreased for Guillemots but only slightly for Razorbills. The results from 1990 (Table 1) show the proportions hunted remaining low for both species and oiling affecting a slightly higher percentage of birds. Recoveries in fishing nets were much reduced for Razorbills to a level very similar to that reported in the historic recoveries of 1909-70. The percentage of Guillemots recovered in fishing nets was also reduced but the rate was still almost five times that for birds recovered from 1909-70.

Table 1. Recovery methods for Guillemots and Razorbills.

Guillemot	* 1909-70	** 1987-89	1990
Found dead	44.8%	42.7%	53.5%
Oiled	28.2%	15.1%	17.0%
Hunted ***	22.2%	5.3%	4.0%
Fishing nets	4.8%	36.9%	25.4%
Total recovered	504	662	495
Razorbill	*** 1909-70**	**** 1987-89**	**1990**
Found dead	50.2%	57.6%	75.0%
Oiled	7.8%	15.3%	16.9%
Hunted ***	25.4%	1.4%	1.2%
Fishing nets	6.5%	25.7%	7.0%
Total recovered	611	144	172

* Data from Mead 1974.
** Recoveries reported from July 1987 to June 1989.
*** Mostly shot but all recoveries deliberately taken by Man are included.

It is important to investigate where these birds are being killed over the fairly extensive range that they occupy through the year. Table 2 shows the areas where the 495 Guillemots reported during 1990 were found and the percentage, within each area, of those recoveries found dead, hunted, oiled, and netted. For hunted birds, the Faeroes are the most important area; 14 of the 16 birds so reported were from there rather than waters off Norway,

where shooting is now illegal. On Channel and North Sea coasts (not east coast of Britain) Guillemots seem to be at particular risk of oiling. In the Channel, 17 of the oiled birds were on the English and 22 on the French shores. Overall 87 of the 126 recoveries in fishing gear (69%) came from Scandinavian waters and only two other areas contributed more than ten. All but one of the North Sea recoveries in fishing nets were from Denmark and 10 of the 14 reported from the Irish Sea and Ireland were from Co. Cork.

Where increased proportions of recoveries are now being reported from fishing nets there is most likely to be increased mortality from this cause. However, an alternative explanation is that other mortality methods, as reported by finders, may have diminished in importance as is the case with the hunting ban in Norway. However, it seems very likely that netting has increased greatly in importance for Scandinavia. This applies both to the traditional areas, off Norway, and Swedish waters where many British Guillemots are now found. Up to 1976 only one of 144 recoveries reported was in Swedish rather than Norwegian waters. During the next ten years 109 of 515 recoveries were from Sweden. On a world scale there are grave conservation problems for seabirds, cetaceans and turtles following the introduction of monofilament nets. These seem to be invisible to the animals in the water and cause their death by drowning. Such nets are banned from some areas, for instance Scottish waters but may be responsible for increased mortality in other areas which BTO ringed Guillemots visit.

The interpretation of these results must be treated with caution since the recovery method is taken from the report of the finder. Fishermen who realise that the capture of birds in their nets might cause public disquiet are unlikely to report recoveries and may simply throw the bodies overboard. Subsequent strandings, if the rings had not been removed, would then not be reported as netted birds. Provided that post-mortem oiling had not taken place such reports would inflate the number of recoveries reported as Found Dead. This category is highest in the British and Irish regions. Despite such problems information from the recoveries remains the only means by which seabird casualties can be related to birds of particular ages and to their colonies of origin. As in so many other instances, ringing is able to provide uniquely useful information to address a conservation problem.

References

Mead, C.J. (1974). The results of ringing auks in Britain and Ireland. *Bird Study* 21, 45-86.

Table 2. Recovery area and cause of mortality (%)* for Guillemots reported during 1990.

	Found dead	Hunted	Oiled	Netted	Total Recoveries
Recovery area **					
Scandinavia	21	12	5	64	136
North Sea	45	3	37	15	71
East Coast of Britain	87	1	5	7	75
Irish Sea & Ireland	80	–	2	17	81
Channel Coasts	45	–	52	5	75
Southern Coast	79	2	8	10	48
Totals	53.5	4.0	17.0	25.4	495

* Healthy live birds reported by ringers are omitted. Hunted includes birds shot, snared or trapped deliberately.

** Scandinavia includes Iceland, Faeroes, Norway and Sweden. North Sea is Denmark, Germany, the Netherlands and Belgium. The East Coast of Britain includes the whole of Orkney and Shetland, and from Cape Wrath south to Essex. Channel includes northern France west to Finisterre and southern England from Kent to Cornwall.

The effects of Magpie predation on songbird populations

Stephen Baillie[1], Stephen Gooch[2] & Tim Birkhead[3]

1. Populations Research Department, BTO
2. Populations Research Department, BTO & Department of Animal and Plant Sciences, University of Sheffield
3. Department of Animal and Plant Sciences, University of Sheffield

Summary

Magpie populations increased at an average rate of 4-5% per annum between 1966 and 1986. Rates of increase were highest in south-west England and in suburban and scrub habitats. Data on numbers of Magpies and of eleven species of open-nesting songbirds were obtained from the Common Birds Census. Data on songbird breeding success were obtained from the BTO's Nest Record Scheme. Songbird nesting success increased between 1966 and 1986 in Song Thrush, Greenfinch and Yellowhammer, and showed no trend in the other eight species. Songbird nesting success was not related to Magpie density on either farmland or woodland. Songbird population changes were not related to Magpie population density or rates of increase on farmland. In woodland songbird numbers increased most where Magpie numbers were high and where Magpie numbers were increasing most rapidly. Thus this study does not support the hypothesis that Magpie predation is adversely affecting songbird populations. The limitations of the study are discussed. In particular, it was not designed to detect local effects or effects that are restricted to suburban and urban habitats.

Introduction

Magpies are very conspicuous nest predators of small songbirds. They often raid nests in gardens and this habit in particular has invoked the wrath of many birdwatchers and others who derive enjoyment from their garden birds. Magpie populations have been increasing over at least the last three decades, giving rise to public concern about the increase in predation of songbird nests which may have resulted.

Individual predation events, even though they might be distressing to watch, cannot be regarded as a conservation problem. The key question that needs to be answered is whether the increase in Magpie numbers has caused reductions in songbird populations by reducing nesting success. It may seem inevitable that an increase in nest losses will bring about a population decline. However, most bird populations are maintained at relatively constant levels through the operation of density-dependent processes. For example, competition for food might result in proportionately lower winter mortality when the population at the beginning of the winter was low. Such a process could compensate for a reduced abundance of juveniles at the end of the summer, brought about through increased nest predation. Thus increased nest predation might alter the abundance of songbirds in late summer but have a proportionately much smaller effect on the size of the breeding population.

However, there are certainly some bird populations for which nest predation does have a marked influence of the number of breeding pairs. One of the best examples is the Grey Partridge (Potts 1986).

The long-term monitoring schemes operated within the BTO's Integrated Population Monitoring Programme (Baillie 1990) provide data on the numbers and breeding success of Magpies and songbirds. We used these data to test whether changes in the numbers or breeding success of songbirds are related to Magpie densities or population trends.

Magpie population changes

We measured rates of increase in Magpie populations between 1966 and 1987 using data from the Common Birds Census (CBC). Over this period Magpie populations increased at very similar rates in both farmland (4.2% per annum) and woodland (4.9% per annum). However, in suburbia they increased almost twice as rapidly (8.6% per annum) as in these rural habitats. The Garden Bird Feeding Survey and studies in the Sheffield area have also shown rapid increases in suburban

Magpie populations.

The census data from farmland and woodland were further subdivided into four regions of England and six habitat categories (Table 1). Magpie populations increased little in the north while rates of increase in the three southern regions did not show statistically significant differences between regions and between farmland and woodland (farmland 4.9% per annum, woodland 4.7% per annum). Rates of increase in the three farmland habitats did not differ significantly. However, Magpie populations increased about twice as rapidly in scrub as in broadleaved and mixed woodland.

Comparisons of relative densities were only made within the farmland and woodland categories because woodland densities are likely to be exaggerated relative to those for farmland (Gooch *et al.* 1991). On both farmland and woodland densities were highest in the south-west, intermediate in the north and lowest in the Midlands and south-east. Densities were higher on grazing land than on arable or mixed farmland, a result that would be expected from the Magpies foraging requirements (below). Densities were higher in scrub than in the other two woodland types, again reflecting a higher availability of open grass for foraging.

The rapid increase in Magpie populations over the last three decades is probably due to a reduction in persecution (Birkhead 1991), although insufficient data are available to prove it. If numbers were limited previously by persecution then

we would expect the population to increase until it reached a new equilibrium determined by the revised level of persecution and by environmental factors such as food supplies or the availability of suitable nesting territories.

At the time of our detailed analysis, for which we used data up to 1986, there was little evidence that the rate of increase was levelling off nationally, although the data did suggest that it had declined in the Midlands and in woodland in south-west England. CBC trends updated to 1990 now show that Magpies numbers on both farmland and woodland have been stable since about 1986 (Figure 1). Thus it appears that Magpie populations have now reached a new equilibrium level although further years of data are needed to confirm this.

How important are songbirds in the Magpie's diet?

All studies of the food taken by Magpies have found that birds are a small component of the diet (Birkhead 1991). For example, Holyoak (1968) reported that only nine out of 60 adult gizzards examined between March and August contained remains of birds eggs, eight of which were gamebirds. Similarly Tatner (1983) found that of 34 adult gizzards and pellets examined between March and May only 5 contained bird remains and only two included remains of eggshells. Most birds that are taken are eggs or nestlings, full-grown birds being taken rarely.

Adult Magpies feed mainly on grain and fruit

Table 1. Average rates of increase of Magpie populations in different regions and habitats between 1966 and 1986. Increases are expressed as percent per annum. Sample sizes are given as the number of plot/years of data used in the analysis. Tests that the increase is statistically significant: * P<0.05, ** P<0.01, N.S. Not significant. For further details see Gooch *et al.* 1991.

a. Regional variation

	Farmland			Woodland		
	Increase	Plot/years	sig.	Increase	Plot/years	sig.
North	1.6%	357	N.S.	0.5%	193	N.S.
Midlands	2.9%	355	**	5.4%	122	*
South-east	5.7%	812	**	5.3%	858	**
South-west	5.0%	349	**	4.8%	226	**

b. Habitat variation

	Increase	Plot/years	sig.
Arable farmland	1.8%	157	*
Grazing farmland	2.8%	339	**
Mixed farmland	5.4%	735	**
Broadleaved woodland	4.0%	922	**
Mixed woodland	4.6%	324	**
Scrub	9.7%	173	**

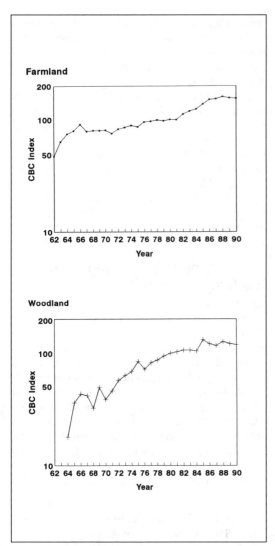

Figure 1. The Common Birds Census index for Magpies on farmland (1962-1990) and in woodland (1964-1990). Numbers within each habitat are shown relative to an arbitrary value of 100 in 1980. The index is plotted on a logarithmic scale.

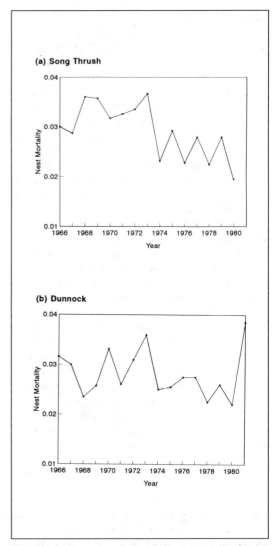

Figure 2. Annual variation in nest mortality for (a) Song Thrush, 1966-1980 and (b) Dunnock, 1966-1981. Nest losses are calculated as the average daily nest mortality rate over the whole nesting period. There is a statistically significant trend for Song Thrush (r=-0.658, P<0.01) but not for Dunnock (r=-0.100). After Gooch et al. 1991.

during the winter and on ground living invertebrates during the summer. Thus they show a marked preference for foraging on pasture, particularly that occupied by domestic stock. This appears to be related to the higher densities of soil invertebrates that long-term leys and permanent pasture support.

Magpie nestlings are also fed mainly on invertebrates, particularly beetles and caterpillars. Owen (1956) did not record birds or eggs in the

diet of nestlings in Wytham Wood, Oxfordshire. Tatner (1983) identified 4092 prey items from 92 nestling gizzard and faecal samples collected in Manchester, of which 0.3% were birds and 0.5% eggs.

Thus eggs and nestlings form only a small part of the diet of most Magpies, and are generally taken opportunistically. However, this does not preclude the possibility of Magpies taking a high proportion of the nests in some areas.

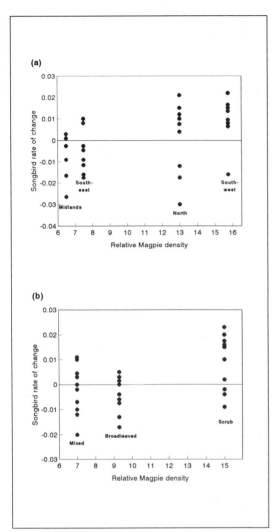

Figure 3. Population changes of woodland song-birds from 1966 to 1986 against Magpie density. Each point on the graphs represents the average rate of change for one species in one region or habitat relative to the average rate of change of that species over the country as a whole. (a) regional subdivision, $r_S=0.581$, P<0.001 (b) habitat subdivision, $r_S=0.445$, P<0.05.

Are the numbers and breeding success of songbirds related to Magpie numbers?

There is widespread concern that the increase in Magpie populations has had a detrimental effect on songbird numbers over large areas of the country. We made use of the fact that Magpie rates of increase and densities have varied between different regions and habitats to test four predictions that we would expect to be true if Magpies were having

a major impact on songbird populations.

We know that Magpies only predate songbird eggs and nestlings (as opposed to adults) and would therefore expect any effect of Magpies on songbird populations to come about through a reduction in songbird nesting success. We therefore predicted that:

1. Songbird nest losses would increase as Magpie density increased.
2. Songbird nest losses would be greater in regions and habitats where Magpies were more abundant.

If songbird populations were unable to compensate for any increase in nest losses caused by Magpie predation we predicted the following effects on songbird breeding populations:

3. Songbird populations would decline more (or increase less) in areas where Magpies were more abundant.
4. Songbird populations would decline more (or increase less) in areas where Magpies increased most rapidly.

All these predictions are subject to the qualification of all other things being equal. While this is unlikely to be strictly true, we would expect the predictions to be upheld if Magpie predation were a dominant factor effecting songbird populations. We used data on the numbers and breeding success of 11 species of open-nesting songbirds, provided by the CBC and by the BTO Nest Record Scheme, to test these predictions. Our study species were Blackbird, Song Thrush, Mistle Thrush, Dunnock, Robin, Chaffinch, Greenfinch, Goldfinch, Skylark, Wren and Yellowhammer.

1. Have songbird nest losses increased as Magpie density increased ?

Eight of the 11 songbird species showed no trend in nest losses with time while Song Thrush, Greenfinch and Yellowhammer actually showed a long-term decrease in nest losses over the period when Magpie numbers had increased (Figure 2). These improvements in nesting success are obviously due to factors that are not connected with the increase in Magpie numbers. The prediction is not supported.

2. Are songbird nest losses greater in regions and habitats where Magpies are more abundant than where they are less abundant ?

Analyses were carried out within the two major habitat types (farmland and woodland), with separate analyses for regional and habitat subdivisions. Data for all 11 songbird species were included in each analysis, after the removal of average differences between species. Thus four tests were possible, none of which showed a statistically significant relationship between songbird nesting success and Magpie density. Therefore, our second prediction is also not supported.

3. Have songbird numbers increased more (or decreased less) in areas with lower Magpie densities ?

This analysis was carried out in a similar way to that described under prediction two, but using songbird population changes rather than nesting success. Analyses for the regional and habitat subdivisions of farmland showed no relationship between songbird population changes and Magpie densities. However, contrary to our prediction, the woodland data showed that songbird population changes were positively related to Magpie density, using both regional and habitat subdivisions (Figure 3). This is presumably because those areas which provide good habitat for songbirds also provide good habitat for Magpies. It is unlikely that Magpie densities are determined directly by the density of songbirds because songbirds are not the Magpies main food (above). The main point here is that neither the analyses for farmland or woodland support prediction three.

4. Have songbird numbers increased more (or decreased less) in areas where Magpie numbers have increased more slowly?

This is the weakest of our four predictions because a rapid increase in Magpie numbers from a low starting density might have only a small effect, while a low rate of increase from a high starting density might have a large effect. Nevertheless we considered this prediction to be worth testing, particularly in view of frequent suggestions that recent increases in Magpie populations have adversely affected songbird populations. The method of analysis was similar to that used for predictions two and three. For both the regional and habitat subdivisions of farmland, and for the regional subdivision of woodland, there was no significant association between the rates of change of Magpies and songbirds. However, for the habitat subdivision of woodland there was weak statistical evidence that songbirds had increased more rapidly in areas where Magpies had increased more rapidly. This result is consistent with the woodland results noted under prediction 3. Overall the data provide no support for prediction 4.

Thus we made four predictions arising from the hypothesis that songbird populations are being reduced through Magpie predation of eggs and nestlings. None of these predictions are upheld by extensive national data on songbird numbers and breeding success. Similar conclusions have been reached by workers in Germany (Bastian 1989, Witt 1989, Kooiker 1991). Does this mean that Magpies never have any effect on songbirds ?

What effects of Magpies on songbirds might not have been detected by this study?

Our four predictions all depend on the assumption that other factors are equal. Thus our ability to detect the effects of Magpie predation will depend on its strength relative to other regional and habitat related factors affecting songbird populations. If Magpie predation is one of the main factors affecting the size of songbird populations then we would certainly expect to detect it in our analyses. However, if it is a relatively minor factor its effects might be masked. We do not regard this as a major limitation because our main aim was to test whether Magpie predation is reducing songbird populations on a wide scale.

The analyses we have performed only provide information on a regional and national scale. It is quite possible that Magpies could have marked effects on a minority of local populations (Møller 1988). This study was not designed to detect such local effects. Most of our analyses are restricted to data from farmland and woodland habitats in predominantly rural areas. Therefore they cannot be used to draw conclusions about the effects of Magpie predation on songbirds in suburban and urban areas. Many of the complaints about Magpies relate to suburban and urban gardens, where predation events are particularly likely to be observed.

Very many ecological studies must rely on correlative analyses of the type presented here. However, where experiments can be carried out effectively they will generally provide stronger evidence of causation. The obvious experiment that is needed in relation to this problem is to manipulate Magpie density (by removing Magpies from a limited area) and to record the effects on songbird nesting success and numbers. While we think that such an approach would be very useful, it would only address the problem on a local scale.

Where can more information be obtained?

The full results of the analyses presented above were published in the Journal of Applied Ecology in 1991 (Gooch, Baillie & Birkhead 1991). Studies of the ecology and behaviour of Magpies are reviewed in the recent Poyser book "The Magpies" (Birkhead 1991). The Common Birds Census and Nest Record Scheme always welcome new participants. For further details write to the Census Unit or Nest Records Unit at BTO head-quarters.

Acknowledgements

This work was supported by the RSPB and by a NERC CASE studentship. The BTO Integrated Population Monitoring Programme is supported by the contract from the JNCC. Special thanks are due to all the BTO fieldworkers who gathered the data on which these analyses are based.

References

Baillie, S.R. (1990). Integrated population monitoring of breeding birds in Britain and Ireland. *Ibis* 132, 151-166.

Bastian, H.-V. (1989). Are corvids able to exterminate populations of Whinchats (*Saxicola rubetra*)? - a computer-simulation. *Die Vogelwelt* 110, 150-156.

Birkhead, T.R. (1991). *The Magpies*. T. & A.D. Poyser, London.

Gooch, S., Baillie, S.R. & Birkhead, T.R. (1991). Magpie *Pica pica* and songbird populations. Retrospective investigation of trends in population density and breeding success. *J.Appl.Ecol.* 28, 1068-1086.

Holyoak, D. (1968). A comparative study of the food of some British *Corvidae*. *Bird Study* 15, 147-153.

Kooiker, G. (1991). Study on the influence of Magpie *Pica pica* on urban bird species in the city of Osnabräck. *Die Vogelwelt* 112, 225-236.

Møller, A.P. (1988). Nest predation and nest site choice in passerine birds in habitat patches of different sizes: a study of magpies and blackbirds. *Oikos* 53, 215-221.

Owen, D.F. (1956). The food of nestling Jays and Magpies. *Bird Study* 3, 257-265.

Potts, G.R. (1986). *The Partridge: Pesticides, Predation and conservation.* Collins, London.

Tatner, P. (1983). The diet of urban Magpies *Pica pica*. *Ibis* 125, 90-107.

Witt, K. (1989). Do Magpies (*Pica pica*) control the population of passerines in a city? *Die Vogelwelt* 110, 142-150.

Mike Weston: Magpie

Trends in the hunting of migratory birds in Europe

Neil McCulloch[1], Graham Tucker[1] & Stephen Baillie

Populations Research Department, BTO

Summary

Broad patterns of hunting of migratory birds in Europe and North Africa were documented using recovery data from European bird ringing schemes. More detailed data were available from western Europe than for eastern Europe due to the larger number of birds ringed and the greater availability of computerised recoveries. There can be no doubt that large numbers of birds continue to be killed in many areas, especially in Iberia, Italy and north-west Africa. In Europe this hunting is carried out predominantly in autumn and winter, while in North Africa spring hunting is equally prevalent. Many of the birds killed in southern Europe come from northern and central Europe, including Britain and Ireland. The recovery data suggest that there has been a decline in the intensity of hunting of protected species during the last ten years, though levels of hunting of legitimate quarry species show little change. There is some uncertainty about the magnitude of the decline in hunting because of the potential problem of changes in attitude by hunters towards the reporting of ringed birds. Many protected species continue to be hunted in some areas. The international legislation and conventions that should provide protection for these birds are outlined. This study demonstrates the value to bird conservation of the work of the thousands of volunteer ringers who operate throughout Europe.

Background to the study

It is well known that large numbers of birds are killed annually by hunters while on migration through Europe and the Mediterranean basin. In recent years this has been the subject of much controversy, with hunters fiercely defending their "traditional" practices while conservationists have been concerned that hunting may have contributed to the declines of many migratory species throughout the continent (Berthold *et al.* 1986, Marchant

1. Current address: ICBP (Birdlife International)

et al. 1990, Marchant 1991).

The hunting of migrant birds has a long history. In southern Europe particularly, spring and autumn migrations once provided an important seasonal food source. Today, hunting is almost entirely a recreational pursuit. Modern transport has opened up previously less accessible areas to the hunters while sophisticated firearms have increased their efficiency. Also, people are more numerous and have more leisure time. In some areas trapping, using older methods such as bird-lime, clap-nets and spring traps, continues and may be augmented by mist-nets.

It has proved extremely difficult to obtain hard information on the numbers of birds killed by hunters and, consequently, to assess the effect of hunting on bird populations as there is frequently no legal requirement for bag records to be kept. Previous investigations have concentrated on single countries or smaller political units (e.g. Magnin 1986, 1989; Massa & Bottoni 1989). Only Woldhek (1979) has attempted a major comparative study of hunting covering the entire Mediterranean basin. Most of these analyses have attempted to estimate the intensity of hunting and numbers killed by obtaining the opinions of local ornithologists or by extrapolation from sales of shotgun cartridges and hunting permits. They have resulted in widely varying figures of unknown accuracy though all suggest that the annual mortality of migratory birds due to hunting in Europe is numbered in hundreds of millions.

A new approach - ringing recovery analysis

One source of information on bird deaths due to hunting has not previously been utilised on a European scale. This is the records of recoveries of ringed birds held by European ringing schemes. Recoveries are reports of ringed birds found dead by members of the public. These reports are recorded throughout Europe in a standardised format which includes the date and place of finding

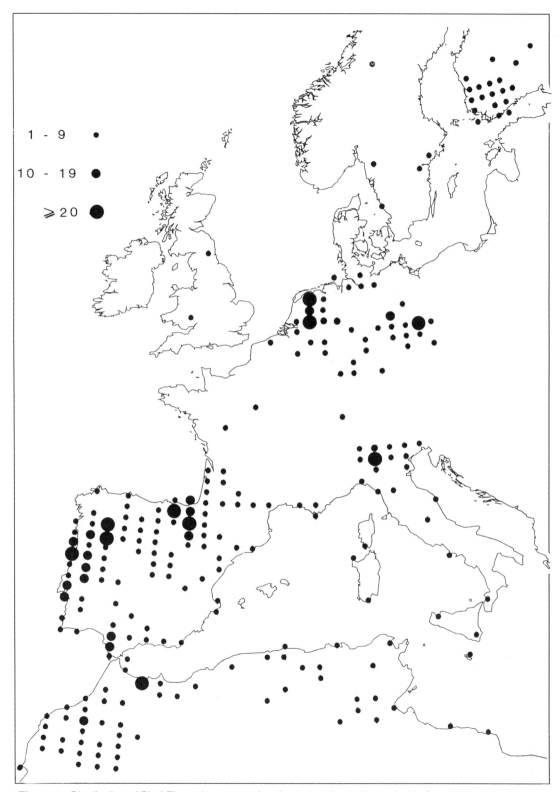

Figure 1. Distribution of Pied Flycatcher recoveries due to hunting in the period before 1980.

and the immediate cause of death, where known. Although it is not possible to use this information to determine the absolute number of birds killed, it can be used to investigate variation in the intensity of hunting between countries and over time.

What did the project involve?

We carried out a study at the BTO of geographical and temporal variation in hunting intensity for five species of raptor (Black Kite, Red Kite, Marsh Harrier, Sparrowhawk, Buzzard) and 15 passerines (Skylark, Meadow Pipit, Robin, Redstart, Wheatear, Fieldfare, Song Thrush, Redwing, Reed Warbler, Garden Warbler, Blackcap, Willow Warbler, Pied Flycatcher, Goldfinch, Linnet). We classified all records of birds taken by man as being hunted, regardless of whether they were shot, trapped or caught with bird-lime. Most of the passerines were taken in the course of recreational hunting activities but some of the raptors will have been taken for reasons of game preservation, particularly in northern Europe. The ringing recovery records do not generally indicate the reasons for which birds were taken.

The European Union for Bird Ringing and 18 individual European ringing schemes generously contributed data to the project enabling a database of some 140,000 recoveries for the 20 species to be established. The work was funded by the EC and was carried out in collaboration with ICBP and RSPB.

The aims of the project

The principal objectives of the project were:
1. to investigate geographical variation in the intensity of hunting in order to identify areas where hunting is particularly severe.
2. to examine seasonal patterns of hunting for each species in individual countries.
3. to determine long-term trends in the intensity of hunting and to compare the situation over the last ten years with that prevailing earlier in the century.
4. to investigate whether hunting affects the population dynamics of selected species by examining the relationship between annual adult survival rates and the intensity of hunting to which populations are exposed during migration. We are still working on this aspect of the project which is therefore not discussed in this article.

Identifying the main hunting areas

After a preliminary screening of the data for records with insufficiently accurate date or place

of ringing or finding, the initial step of the analysis was to map the finding localities of all hunted recoveries for each species. This enabled the major areas of hunting activity to be located (e.g. Figure 1). Large numbers of hunted recoveries from a particular area do not necessarily reflect particularly intense hunting. It is important to determine whether such concentrations of hunted recoveries represent a small fraction of a very large number of birds passing through the area or a relatively high proportion of birds available to the hunters. A better comparison of hunting intensity between countries can be obtained by expressing hunting recoveries from each country as a proportion of all ringed birds found dead there.

The Hunting Index

If the proportion of recoveries due to hunting is to be compared between countries it is desirable for the underlying non-hunted recovery rate to be as similar as possible throughout, since local factors causing unusually high non-hunted recovery rates might cause the proportion attributable to hunting to be misleadingly low. To counter such effects common causes of recovery were examined for regional bias. Where strong regional biases were detected recoveries due to these factors were excluded from the analysis. Details of excluded categories are given in McCulloch et al. (1992).

After these exclusions the proportion of recoveries due to hunting was re-calculated and used as an index of hunting intensity. This can range from 0 (no recoveries due to hunting) to 100 (all recoveries due to hunting). It is however still necessary to interpret patterns of variation in these indices with caution. Such indices provide the best available comparisons of hunting intensity between samples, but it is never possible to be certain that all bias has been removed. For this reason we have concentrated on identifying broad patterns with the available recovery data rather than on the details of what happens to particular species in particular regions.

Where is hunting most severe?

Index values showed hunting to be an infrequent cause of mortality in northern Europe but in Mediterranean countries, particularly Italy, Spain and Portugal, indices were high (over 50) for many species (Figure 2). Within the Mediterranean region most hunted recoveries came from "bottle-neck" areas where large numbers of migrating birds are concentrated by geographical features such as gaps in mountain ranges and narrow sea-

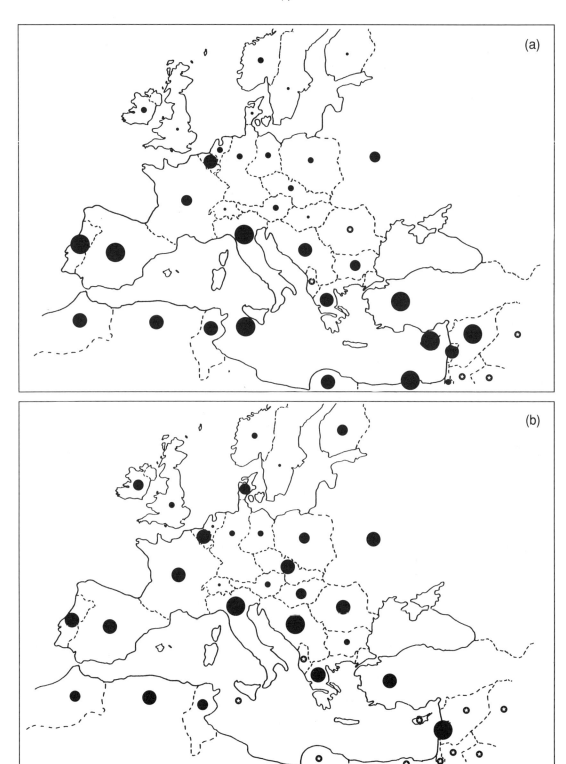

Figure 2. Geographical variation in hunting indices for (a) raptors and (b) passerines in the pre-1980 period. Stars indicate insufficient recoveries for index calculation. (Figures 2, 3 and 4 are reproduced from Ibis 134 (1992) by permission of the BOU).

78

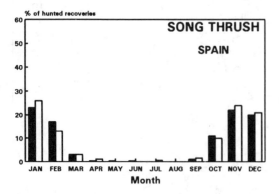

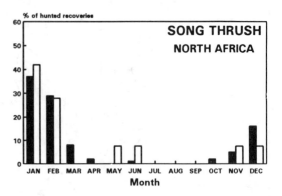

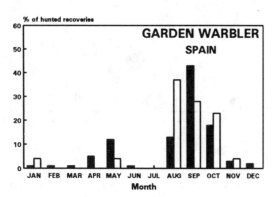

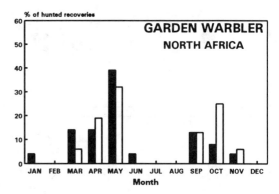

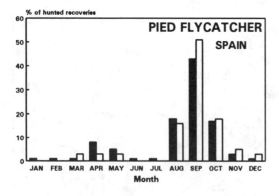

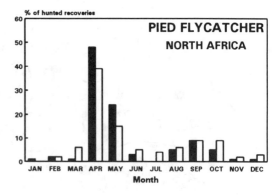

Figure 3. *Differences between western Europe and North Africa in the seasonal pattern of hunting of Song Thrush, Garden Warbler and Pied Flycatcher. The number of hunted birds recovered in each month in Spain and North Africa (Tunisia, Algeria, Morocco) is expressed as a percentage of the total. Filled bars represent the period before 1980, open bars after 1980.*

crossings. The areas around the Straits of Gibraltar, both ends of the Pyrenees and the southern ends of the Alpine passes in Italy were particularly prominent in this respect. More surprising perhaps was the large number of hunted recoveries from North Africa, especially Morocco, Algeria and Tunisia. It appears that the hunting of migrants in this area may be more significant than was previously thought.

Unfortunately few data were available for the eastern European bird populations that mainly use migratory flyways through the Balkans and Middle East, because relatively little ringing is carried out in the region. Furthermore much of the information that does exist was not computerised or otherwise available. The small amount of information that was analysed did, however, suggest that hunting around the eastern end of the Mediterranean, from Greece to Egypt, is at least as intense as that farther west.

The three thrush species (Fieldfare, Song Thrush, Redwing) are legitimate quarry for hunters in many southern European countries and this is reflected in their having the highest average index values.

Seasonal patterns in hunting

In most European countries the legal hunting season occurs during autumn and winter. This is reflected strongly in the seasonal distribution of recoveries of hunted birds, of both quarry and protected species (Figure 3). The majority of migrants are hunted from August to November, the peak month for recoveries for each species becoming progressively later with decreasing latitude of the country analyzed. The thrushes, most of which spend the winter within Europe, are also hunted throughout the winter months. Spring hunting, which is potentially more damaging to populations because the returning birds are all potential breeders, is allowed in Malta and was legal in Cyprus until 1991.

The seasonal distribution of recoveries resulting from shooting and trapping in North Africa is quite different from that occurring in Europe, with almost as many birds taken by hunters in North Africa in spring as in autumn. This may be because birds that winter to the south of the Sahara stop off in the area for long periods in spring in order to replace depleted fat reserves after the long Saharan crossing.

Have levels of hunting changed?

The results of this study suggest that the overall level of hunting in Europe may be declining for the majority of species analysed, though the magnitude of the decline varies between countries (Figure 4). Index values for each species in the last ten years were compared with the figures based on earlier recoveries for each country in turn: a total of 391 comparisons in all. Of these, 289 showed a decline. This was most marked among raptors: 80% of comparisons involving raptors showed a decline compared with 70% for passerines.

The hunting indices for legitimate quarry species mostly showed little change, however, and the proportion of recoveries attributable to hunting for Song Thrush in France, Spain and Italy, and for Skylark in France, actually increased significantly. It may be that recent legal protection of a wider range of species has resulted in a compensatory increase in the hunting of remaining quarry species.

Trends in index values for five-year periods since 1950 for all countries combined revealed

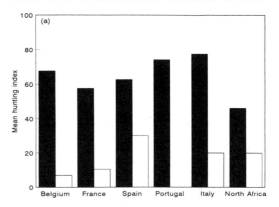

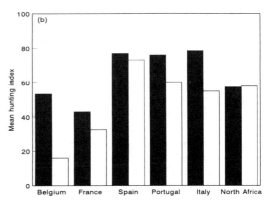

Figure 4. Changes in mean hunting index for (a) raptors and (b) passerines before and after 1980 for countries from which large numbers of hunted recoveries have been reported. North Africa = Morocco, Algeria, Tunisia. Filled bars represent the period before 1980, open bars after 1980.

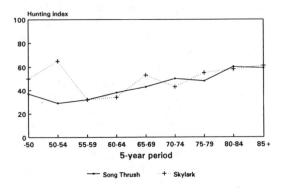

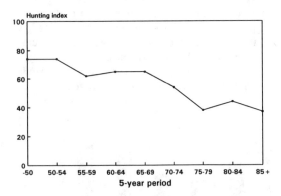

Figure 5. Trends in hunting indices for 5-year periods since 1950. (a) Skylark and Song Thrush, (b) Linnet.

statistically significant declines in hunting indices for 13 of the 20 species. Song Thrush alone was subject to increasing hunting pressure (Figure 5). The species for which no significant trend could be demonstrated were Skylark, Meadow Pipit, Redstart, Wheatear, Fieldfare and Redwing.

The reduction of index values over the last 40 years in countries where large numbers of birds were known to have been shot or trapped certainly suggests that fewer birds are now being hunted. However, it is possible that such an effect could be generated if hunters in those countries either suppressed recoveries of ringed birds or reported them without indicating that the birds had been hunted. This would be understandable in the case of illegally hunted non-quarry species, especially considering the growth of opposition to hunting in many parts of Europe. Such practices are, however, more likely to apply to locally ringed birds, when the finder is less inquisitive about their origins or may wish to avoid drawing the attention of the local

authorities to the hunting of protected species. At present we cannot be absolutely certain that the reductions in indices are due to fewer birds being hunted rather than to deliberate under-reporting, but the former is supported by the fact that the majority of low indices found for recent years follow a long-term decline rather than an abrupt change and by the magnitude of the reduction in a number of countries. Reductions in index values for Italy are coincident with a decline of over 10% in the number of licensed hunters since 1980 (Massa & Bottoni 1989, Lambertini & Talloni 1990).

Current protective legislation

The seasonal mobility of migratory birds creates difficulties for the effective conservation of breeding populations of such species as protective legislation, unlike the birds themselves, is frequently confined by political boundaries. Thus protection of bird populations on their breeding grounds alone may be insufficient to safeguard species if they are subjected to threats from human activities in other parts of their annual range.

These problems have been addressed in recent years by three major items of international legislation.

The Directive and Resolution of the Council of the European Community on the Conservation of Wild Birds (1979) requires member states to maintain populations of naturally-occurring wild birds and to preserve sufficient diversity and area of habitats for their conservation. Enforcement is supervised by the EC. The Directive restricts the number of species that may be hunted or used in trade. Amongst passerines only Skylark and thrushes may be hunted for sport in some member countries, though there is provision for pest species to be controlled under licence. A small amount of trapping of finch and bunting species is still permitted in Belgium and some northern provinces of Italy.

The Bern Convention came into force in 1982. States party to the Convention are required to maintain populations of native flora and fauna, particularly those considered endangered or vulnerable, including migratory species. Article 4,3 of the Convention requires contracting states to "give special attention to the protection of areas that are of importance for the migratory species specified in Appendices II and III which are appropriately situated in relation to migratory routes, as wintering, staging, feeding, breeding and moulting areas".

The Bonn Convention seeks to protect migratory species throughout their range by international co-operation and legislative action. States party to the Convention are required to "conserve and, where feasible and appropriate, restore those habitats of the species which are important in removing the species from danger of extinction" and to provide for "the maintenance of a suitable network of such habitats appropriately disposed in relation to the migration routes".

Despite this legislation it is generally recognised that the hunting of protected species remains widespread in Mediterranean countries, particularly during the autumn migration.

Where can more information be obtained?

The results of this study are summarised in a paper in Ibis (McCulloch, Tucker & Baillie 1992). Full details of the analysis are presented in BTO Research Report No. 58 *The conservation of migratory birds in the western Palaearctic-African flyway: Review of losses incurred to migratory birds during migration*" (Tucker *et al.* 1990). This contains data on the geographical distribution of hunted recoveries for each country of origin, hunting indices for each country of recovery and for national breeding populations, seasonal patterns of recovery in major hunting countries and trends in index values over the last 40 years.

References

Berthold, P., Fliege, G., Querner, U. & Winkler, H. (1986) Die Bestandsentwicklung von Kleinvögeln in Mitteleuropa: Analyse von Fangzahlen. *J. Orn.* 127, 397-437.

Lambertini, M. & Talloni, G. (1990). *Bird killing in Italy.* LIPU, Parma.

Magnin, G. (1986). *An assessment of illegal shooting and catching of birds in Malta.* Study Rept. No.13. ICBP, Cambridge.

Magnin, G. (1989). *Falconry and hunting in Turkey during 1987.* Study Rep. No.34. ICBP, Cambridge.

Marchant, J.H., Hudson, R., Carter, S.P. & Whittington, P.A. (1990). *Population Trends in British Breeding Birds.* BTO, Tring.

Marchant, J.H. (1991). Recent trends in the breeding populations of some common trans-Saharan migrant birds in northern Europe. *Ibis* 134 suppl. 1, 113-119.

Massa, R. & Bottoni, L. (1989). The killing of passerine migrant birds in Italy. *Sitta* 3: 27-36.

McCulloch, M.N., Tucker, G.M. & Baillie, S.R. (1992). Hunting of migratory birds in Europe: a ringing recovery analysis. *Ibis* 134 suppl 1, 55-65.

Tucker, G.M., McCulloch, M.N. & Baillie, S.R. (1990). *The conservation of migratory birds in the Western Palaearctic-African flyway: Review of losses incurred to migratory birds during migration.* BTO Research Report No.58. BTO, Tring.

Woldhek, S. (1979). *Bird killing in the Mediterranean.* European Committee for the Prevention of Mass Destruction of Migratory Birds, Zeist, Netherlands.

Changes in reproductive performance of some seed-eating birds, 1962–89

Jeremy J D Greenwood, Humphrey Q P Crick & Paul F Donald

BTO

Introduction

A number of British seed-eating bird species have declined in numbers and the pattern of decline has been linked to changes in agricultural practices (O'Connor & Shrubb 1986a; Marchant *et al.* 1990). The reasons postulated for the declines (e.g. pesticide poisoning, eradication of weeds by herbicides) are plausible but need testing through deeper analyses and further study.

One approach is to analyse existing data to get a more detailed knowledge of the birds' ecology. We have recently conducted such an analysis to discover whether there have been long-term changes in the timing of breeding, in the number of eggs laid and in breeding success in various seed-eating finches and buntings (Crick *et al.* 1991). This account presents a summary of the methods and results, with some examples of the results shown in graphical form.

The species

Six species of finches and buntings, differing in ecology and in their recent population trends, were investigated. They were the following.

Chaffinch. Farmland populations have remained fairly stable (Marchant *et al.* 1990). It is possible that this species has been less affected than some others by the reduction in seeds available on farmland because it feeds its young mainly on insects (O'Connor & Shrubb 1983). Alternatively, it may be that the population of Chaffinches on farmland has never been more than an overspill from the species' main habitat, woodland, in which case one would expect farmland populations not to be influenced markedly by conditions on farmland itself.

Greenfinch. Populations have also remained fairly stable (Marchant *et al.* 1990), even though they feed largely on farms in the winter and might have been expected to have suffered from the reduced availability of grain in winter stubbles (as a result of cleaner harvesting and autumn ploughing). It is possible that increased cereal acreages

and the use of bird-table food in winter have compensated for this (O'Connor & Shrubb 1986a,b; Marchant *et al.* 1990).

Linnet. The population has fluctuated over the years but with a considerable general decline over the last thirty years (Marchant *et al.* 1990). This species uses farmland during winter and its population decline has been linked with the availability of weed seeds on farmland, perhaps because such small seeds are particularly important as food for Linnets (O'Connor & Shrubb 1986a,b).

Yellowhammer. Populations have remained fairly stable, perhaps because increased cereal acreages have compensated for cleaner stubbles and earlier ploughing (likes Greenfinches) (Marchant *et al.* 1990).

Reed Bunting. Farmland populations have declined, perhaps because of the decline in weed seeds (like Linnets) (Marchant *et al.* 1990; O'Connor & Shrubb 1986a).

Corn Bunting. There has been a marked decline (Marchant *et al.* 1990), apparently associated with the decline in barley acreage (O'Connor & Shrubb 1986a).

Methods

The basic data were gathered through the BTO Nest Record Scheme (Baillie 1991, Crick *et al.*, this volume). We used all the computerised data for 1962–89, the years for which we had population data from the BTO's Common Birds Census (Marchant *et al.* 1990). Since the regional distribution of nest recording activity has varied over the years and since it seemed likely that there would be differences between regions in breeding time and productivity, the data were analysed by region. They were also broken down by altitude, since this was thought likely to affect laying date. The regional division, although reflecting main divisions of farm types, was somewhat arbitrary (Figure 1), as was the division into altitude classes (0–49m a.s.l., 50–99m, above 99m), these regional and altitude classes mainly being chosen such that they divided the datasets roughly equally.

Figure 1. *The regional divisions used in this study. S = Scotland, N = Northern England, SW = Southwest England and Wales, SE = South-east England. Offshore islands were included in the nearest mainland region.*

In this analysis, we were interested in long-term trends rather than annual fluctuations. We have assessed these by fitting both linear and quadratic regression lines to the annual data. Linear regressions describe more-or-less steady trends during 1962–89. Quadratic regressions describe rather more complex trends such as an increase in early years and a decline later, but even they ignore patterns more complex than that.

Timing of breeding was measured as the date on which the first egg of each clutch was laid. Differences between years, regions, or altitude classes in average time of breeding could result from differences in the time at which breeding started or from differences in the proportion of replacement or second clutches, since such clutches cannot be distinguished from first clutches in

nest record card data.

Breeding success was measured as the daily rate of loss of whole clutches of eggs or whole broods of chicks using the standard Mayfield (1961, 1975) technique. Using a standard statistical method (analysis of covariance), we have tested for differences between regions and between altitudes – and also whether the effects of altitude are the same in all regions.

Samples sizes available for the analyses were different for different aspects of the breeding biology, since most cards do not record complete nest histories. They lay between 1500 and 3500 per species for most analyses, though were only one-tenth this size for Corn Buntings.

In this account, for simplicity, we present no details of the statistical tests applied. Suffice it to say that all the results we present are significant at the 5% level. Also for simplicity, we have omitted individual data points from many of the graphs.

Timing of breeding

Chaffinches tended to nest later in more northerly parts of Britain and at higher altitudes. They tended to lay slightly later in the 1970s than in the 60s or 80s.

Greenfinches also tended to nest later at higher altitudes but they did not show regional differences in date of breeding. Breeding has advanced on average by about six days over the last three decades.

The timing of breeding of Linnets was similar in all regions and at all altitudes. It did not change systematically during 1962–89.

Yellowhammers had an earlier distribution of laying dates in the north than in the south, possibly because they lay fewer second clutches there than in the south. Altitude had no significant effect on the timing of Yellowhammer breeding. There is some evidence that breeding has become later as the years have gone by.

Reed Buntings tended to breed latest in the north. The impact of altitude differed between regions: Reed Buntings breed in the north of England at the same time as in Scotland when at high altitude but at the same time as in southern England at low or medium altitudes. There were no long-term trends in the timing of breeding in this species.

The data for Corn Buntings indicated not only marked differences in the timing of breeding between different altitudes and different regions but also a marked tendency for breeding to be later in the 1970s than in the '60s and '80s (Figure 2).

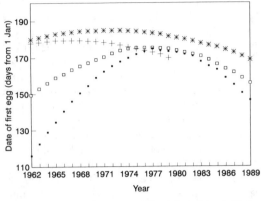
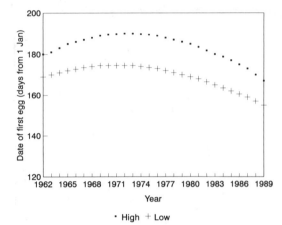

• Northern England + Scotland ＊ South East □ South West   • High + Low

Figure 2. *Temporal trends in date of first egg for Corn Bunting and year during 1962–89 for various regions (a) and altitudes (b). Curves fitted by quadratic regression. Note that day 140 is 20 May.*

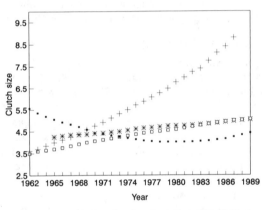
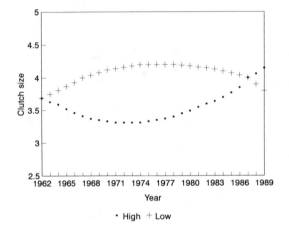

• Northern England + Scotland □ South East ＊ South West   • High + Low

Figure 3. *Temporal trends in clutch size of Corn Bunting during 1962–89 for various regions (a) and altitudes (b). Curves fitted by quadratic regression.*

Clutch size

The clutch size of Chaffinches slightly declined at low altitudes during 1962–89 and slightly increased at high altitudes, but there was no general trend in the country as a whole. There were no overall differences in clutch size between regions or between altitudes, but this masked the fact that high altitudes were associated with large clutches in some regions but with small clutches in others.

Greenfinches and Linnets showed almost identical patterns to those shown by Chaffinches.

Similarly complex interactions between region and altitude also affected clutch size in Yellowhammers but in this species there were no long-term trends.

Reed Bunting clutch sizes in Scotland and northern England were somewhat lower in the middle part of the period under review but there were no long-term trends in south-east or south-west England.

Of all six species, the Corn Bunting revealed the most dramatic variation in clutch size (Figure 3). There was a huge increase in Scotland, a substantial decline in northern England and a slight increase in southern England.

Nest losses

The daily rates of loss of Chaffinch clutches declined considerably over the three decades. There was no such overall change in losses at the chick stage (though there were some differences between altitudes in this respect).

Greenfinches also showed a decline in rates of loss at the egg stage, particularly during the '60s.

In contrast, the rates of loss for Linnets increased markedly during 1961–89.

For Yellowhammers, losses declined over the years at both egg and chick stages (Figure 4) but in Reed Buntings this was true only at the chick stage: losses at the egg stage (and over the whole nesting period) showed no long-term trend. The figures suggest that there were no major trends in the rates of loss of Corn Bunting nests but the sample sizes were so small that this result must be interpreted with caution.

Discussion

Our results will be presented and discussed in more detail elsewhere. However, it is clear that, at a national level, there have been no major trends in clutch size in most of the species considered. Thus the decline in population of Linnets and Reed Buntings cannot be ascribed to any reduction in clutch size. The decline in Corn Buntings could be associated with declining clutch sizes in northern England – but clutch sizes have increased in Scotland and southern England.

Turning to losses of eggs and chicks, Chaffinches, Greenfinches and Yellowhammers seem to have fared increasingly better in recent years. Since their populations have not increased, nor clutch sizes decreased, this suggests that mortality at other stages of the life cycle may have increased. Conversely, Corn Bunting populations have declined but, averaged over all regions, nest survival has been constant. Only in the Reed Bunting and Linnet have there been long-term changes in nest survival that could have led directly to the observed changes in population levels.

The analyses presented here have shown that breeding performance may be as variable as population levels. If we are to understand population processes in our commoner birds and to attain more insight into the possible causes of population changes, two extensions of our work on breeding are required: more detailed analyses of individual species and more comprehensive analyses of a wider range of species. To extend our understanding of the dynamics of each species' population, we need to study survival as well as reproduction – as is being done in the BTO Integrated Population Monitoring Programme.

References

Baillie, S.R. (1991). Monitoring terrestrial breeding bird populations. In: Goldsmith, F.B. (Ed.), *Monitoring for Conservation and Ecology*. Pp. 112–132. Chapman & Hall, London.

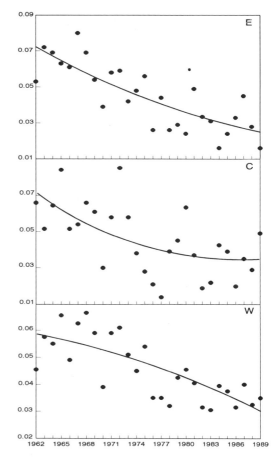

Figure 4. Temporal trends in daily rates of nest losses for Yellowhammer during 1962–89 for all regions and altitudes combined. E = egg stage, C = chick stage, W = whole nest period. Points show annual values; curves fitted by quadratic regression.

Crick, H.Q.P., Donald, P.F. & Greenwood, J.J.D. (1991). *Population processes in some British seed-eating birds*. BTO Research Report No. 80. BTO, Thetford.
Marchant, J.H., Hudson, R., Carter, S.P. & Whittington, P.A. (1990). *Population Trends in British Breeding Birds*. BTO/NCC, Tring.
Mayfield, H.F. (1961). Nesting success calculated from exposure. *Wilson Bull.* 73, 255–261.
Mayfield, H.F. (1975). Suggestions for calculating nest success. *Wilson Bull.* 87, 456–466.
O'Connor, R.J. & Shrubb, M. (1983). Some effects of agricultural development on British bird populations. *Proc. Symp. Birds & Man, Johannesburg 1983*: 131–152.
O'Connor, R.J. & Shrubb, M. (1986a). *Farming and Birds*. Cambridge University Press, Cambridge.
O'Connor, R.J. & Shrubb, M. (1986b). Recent changes in bird populations in relation to farming practices in England and Wales. *Journal of the Royal Agricultural Society of England* 147, 132–141.

The weather in Britain during 1990-91

David E Glue

Populations Research Department, BTO

1990 was an exciting year for students of weather and ornithologists alike with several major meteorological events occurring and records broken: another Great Storm, peak summer temperatures, low rainfall in the south and late snowfalls. All events will have affected Britain's bird-life, though different species in different ways. Weather has a profound influence overall on the timing of nesting and migration, breeding success, patterns of dispersal, survival and ultimately population sizes. An appreciation of the timing and extent of the major features of the weather will help one to interpret the ornithological happenings during 1990 and the subsequent 1990-91 winter.

JANUARY:
the second Great Storm

The New Year opened with settled anticyclonic conditions until the 6th when vigorous cyclones dominated for a spell along the interface of cold polar air and warmer southern air that straddled the country. It was surprisingly mild in all regions with very few air frosts, conditions that will have enhanced the over-wintering prospects of lingering Little Egret, Chiffchaff and Firecrests. All regions except parts of the east were very wet. Highlight was the memorable Burn's Day storm on 25th January which produced gusts of 145-160 kph, most severely along coastal parts of southern England. Loss of life, destruction of property and over 10 million trees was similar in scale but more widespread than the Great Storm of October 1987. Cornwall, Devon, Hampshire and Dyfed were the worst affected counties this time. The storm caused the destruction of many old trees with nesting cavities, reducing the availability of nesting sites in some areas. With few frozen fields, large flocks of soil invertebrate-feeding Fieldfare, plovers and gulls patronised parts of central and western England.

FEBRUARY:
very mild, wet and windy

Remarkably the very disturbed wild, wet and windy westerly airflow persisted across Britain throughout the month, interspersed with just a few days of quieter weather. Temperatures since the New Year remained above average in all regions, being as much as 2.5°C above normal for much of south and east England. The mild conditions prompted some early nesting by thrushes, wildfowl and doves, but most attempts will have failed through damage and desertion. Westerly gales continued to track farther south over the winter sweeping seabirds inland, including auks and Nearctic ducks, notably American Wigeon and Ring-necked Duck. Higher sea temperatures in offshore British waters will have affected food for seabirds: more northern gulls - notably Glaucous, Iceland and Sabine's - were noted. Midmonth saw an early return movement of Bewick's Swans. Storms were frequent, the worst on the 26th with winds exceeding 145 kph and hitting mainly northern England, south-west Scotland and the Western Isles.

MARCH:
unseasonably hot spells

The damp south-westerly airflow with gale force winds at times continued to dominate the weather in northern England and Scotland, but from the 11th, warm anticyclones situated to the south pushed northwards, bringing unseasonably hot spells of weather to southern England and Wales. Northern Britain continued to be influenced by winds and rain with above-average rainfall but, in sharp contrast, most of southern England received only 10% of its usual rainfall. Temperatures everywhere were well above average, but most strikingly in central southern England which recorded its third mildest March in 350 years. The unseasonably warm temperatures brought unprecedented early influxes of spring migrants from Africa, especially after the 18th, mainly involving Sandwich Tern, Willow Warbler, Sand Martin, House Martin and Redstart. Many county records for first arrival dates of spring migrants were broken. The southerly airflow also drew a scattering of south European over-shooting vagrants, notably Black-winged Stilt and Red-backed Shrike. The month ended with an anticyclone centred over Britain giving dry, warm, settled conditions.

APRIL:
destructive frosts, unusual warmth

Calm, mild anticyclonic weather persisted through the first week before low pressure deepened over Scandinavia causing a dramatic change. A cold northwesterly airflow, brought on by a succession of depressions, crossed all regions from the 9th, with snow in many places and widespread very low temperatures. England and Wales saw some of the severest night frosts of the winter (lowest -7.3°C St Harmon, Powys on 9th), causing the loss of some early nests, migrants and tender plants. Rainfall was below average in all regions. Winds in the second half of the month turned easterly, then northeasterly and by the 20th sunny, warm weather returned as the Azores high pressure area developed to the southwest of Britain. Conditions helped a continuation of the spring passage of many common migrants together with unusual numbers of European vagrants, notably southern herons, Black Tern and Serin.

MAY:
a sweltering start to summer

With high pressure established south of Scandinavia producing an easterly airstream during much of the month, calm conditions started off the month with temperatures reported in the upper 20°s C on each of the first five days, making it the hottest May since comprehensive records began in 1875. The temperature reached 28.6°C at Barbourne (Hereford and Worcester) on the 3rd. Easterly winds aided a continuing arrival of overshooting birds from the Continent, notably Red-footed Falcon, Red-backed Shrike and Golden Oriole. Nesting activities proceeded largely unhindered, except that hard ground affected thrushes, martins and corvids. The three spring months of March, April and May combined gave the warmest spring period since 1945, and the driest since 1893.

JUNE:
cool and dismal

Euphoric birdwatchers were brought back to reality with a duller, cooler, and wetter month than usual. It was cool, often cold, notably in Scotland, and with little rainfall until mid-month. Westerly and northerly winds were prevalent and temperatures in southern parts averaged only 16°C. Wind backed southwesterly on the 17th as a succession of depressions swept in from the Atlantic causing widespread heavy rains, especially in Wales and western Scotland. Hundreds of Crossbills that had arrived on Orkney and Shetland in late May now spread south and west over the mainland. Most resident and early-nesting spring migrants will have reared first broods before the adverse conditions arrived. High pressure situated to the south of Britain shifted eastwards on the 26th feeding in much warmer air from the Continent.

JULY:
Mediterranean summer begins

A warmer, sunnier and drier month than normal. An unsettled northwesterly airflow produced ground frosts and cool conditions, mainly in parts of central and eastern England over the first ten days. The second half turned considerably warmer with high sunshine totals and small rainfall amounts in all regions. High pressure established north of Scotland from the 22nd drew hot Continental air from the eastern sector and on each day from the 11th some locality in the country topped 26°C. Marshes and meadows baked hard as rainfall dwindled, producing Mediterranean conditions. Settled conditions with gentle easterly winds aided an early return movement of some northern waders while the exodus of summer visitors proceeded unhindered. The month ended with a short spell of wet weather brought to Western parts by a depression over the Atlantic from the 26th.

AUGUST:
Britain bakes

Settled, very dry, anticyclonic conditions persisted during the first half of the month as a very hot southerly airflow was drawn up across the country: during each of the first ten days 32°C was exceeded somewhere in Britain, breaking many long-term records. It was the warmest August in central England since 1975 and the third warmest this century. In sweltering heatwave conditions endured by man and birds alike, the 37.1°C (98.8°F) temperature reached at Cheltenham on the 3rd was the highest ever recorded at an official UK weather station. From the 15th a temporary respite came in the form of a deepening depression that crossed Scotland bringing strong winds and some much-needed rain to much of Britain. The long hot summer, however, left low water levels and large muddy expanses for migrant waders at inland water bodies. Passerine migration and seabird movements proceeded largely unaffected by the weather.

SEPTEMBER:
a mixed bag

A varied month with some marked regional variations. Much of south and eastern England continued to receive lower than average rainfall but northwest Scotland became very wet, while unusually early sharp night-frosts were experienced in many districts over the last week. A deepening depression crossed north Scotland on the 5th bringing strong winds to all northern parts, followed by severe gales during 18th and 20th with 180 kph winds recorded on Orkney. This intense cyclonic activity was confined largely to the north, southern Britain experiencing lacklustre, calmer autumn conditions. Leach's Petrels and Long-tailed Skuas were notable coastal birds encountered, while Curlew Sandpipers and Little Stints exploited many muddy margins of inland and coastal waters.

OCTOBER:
mild and changeable

A warmer and wetter month than average in most regions. The remarkable fine hot summer and autumn of 1990 came to a close on the 12th and 13th when temperatures exceeded 24°C in England and Wales for the last time. For much of the month a string of depressions brought on a westerly airflow off the Atlantic, giving welcome periodic heavy rain to most regions. From the 12th the wind veered to the south and by the 17th from the east, drawing a cooler airstream from the Continent. This persisted until the last few days of the month when milder cyclonic westerlies returned. There were no great storms, though a gust of 155 kph was reported in Sussex on the 28th. The strong westerlies will have aided the passage of a scattering of Nearctic vagrants that appeared, while the strong easterly winds that swept across the North Sea on the 18th produced a large-scale arrival of Scandinavian thrushes and prompted an influx of Waxwings, while more Long-eared Owls were observed than usual.

NOVEMBER:
mists and mellow fruitfulness

Worries about low water tables continued as parts of central and western Britain experienced a month with considerably less rainfall than usual, the exceptions being parts of Kent, East Anglia, Borders and the Moray Firth. Early cool north-easterly winds from Scandinavia gave way to a milder southerly airflow from the 8th but by the 15th a much colder northwesterly airstream returned. This brought the first snow of the winter to northern hills, even some lower parts. In the absence of severe storms, large scale bird movements were not a feature, the exception being a large passage of Little Auks along the east coast, while Waxwings and Crossbills dispersed widely inland. During mild interludes, fog and mists became a regular feature in parts of central and southern England.

DECEMBER:
surprise snowfalls

The extraordinarily snow-free run over the previous three years came to an abrupt halt on the 8th when many parts of Britain were hit by major snowstorms. The relatively mild, moisture-laden southwesterly airflow that had dominated during the early days of the month was suddenly confronted by a blocking anticyclone over Scandinavia which generated opposing gale-force northern Arctic air. Substantial accumulations of drifting snow fell over much of Scotland, north England, the Midlands and parts of south-west England causing severe damage to power supplies, transport and loss of human life during three days of subzero conditions. Birds were reported killed by high winds and low temperatures but the cold spell was too short to have caused major mortality. The bumper fruiting crop ripened by the hot summer will have helped many birds to survive. After a thaw and settled spell, heavy rains, storms and damaging gales returned over England and Scotland from Christmas into the New Year giving above average rainfall amounts.

Weather during January-March 1991

The weather experienced over the second half of the 1990/91 winter will have affected the survival, movements and numbers of Britain's wintering bird populations - chiefly the waders and wildfowl. The major meteorological features of each month are given below to help interpret changes in these populations. Overall, the 1990/91 winter see-sawed from notably mild to unexpectedly cold spells. The severe spells with associated snowfalls in December 1990 and February 1991 were the most significant events for our bird-life. The first was intense but short-lived. The second covered two weeks, produced severe ground frosts and glazed-ice conditions and is likely to have influenced birds adversely to a far greater extent.

JANUARY: storms before the calm

The stormy weather of late 1990 was maintained over the first 10 days so that most regions received their allotted ration of rainfall before mid-month. Thereafter, quieter anticyclonic conditions prevailed with a return to near average temperatures and rainfall in most regions but colder than normal in parts of Scotland.

FEBRUARY: a bitterly cold spell

A very severe cold spell with bitter, strong easterly winds of Siberian origin gave penetrating ground frosts and affected all parts during the first half of the month. Conditions were at their worst in the eastern half of Britain and in south coast counties. The overnight temperature of -16.0°C at Caward, North Yorkshire on the 14th was the lowest UK temperature of 1991. Snowfall was patchy but locally heavy, the 200mm that fell in central London on the 8th was believed to be the heaviest since the winter of 1962/63. It was the coldest February since 1986.

MARCH: spring beckons

As in 1990, a warmer month than average, most notably in the Midlands and East Anglia. The south-east was very dry but regular cyclonic conditions in N England and Scotland gave higher rainfall than normal.

J. Cadbury: The Wash, December 1981

Changes in numbers of common breeding birds, 1989-90

John Marchant, Steve Carter & Will Peach

Populations Research Department, BTO

Summary

Since 1962 the British Trust for Ornithology, under contract to JNCC and its predecessors, has been monitoring changes in the numbers of common breeding birds in Britain and Ireland. Here we review changes in breeding populations between 1989 and 1990 using results for the Common Birds Census, the Waterways Bird Survey and the Constant Effort Sites ringing scheme. Despite another mild winter during 1989-90, populations of many resident songbirds declined from their very high levels of 1989. Changes in the numbers of long-distance migrants were variable; fewer Tree Pipits and Spotted Flycatchers were recorded in 1990 than in any year since monitoring began. Long-term declines in the populations of several seed-eating species continued, although Tree Sparrows, Goldfinches and Linnets increased. The dramatic decline in the Starling population continued. Plans for an improved and more extensive monitoring scheme are described.

The purposes of monitoring common birds

While population declines and conservation successes for rare breeding birds more often attract the headlines, knowledge of changes in numbers of the commoner species is also of special conservation importance. Because they are typically widespread, these are the species which make the best indicators of the general health of the environment. They are also the species which give most pleasure to most people who enjoy the countryside and who are concerned about bird conservation. Aside from its applied value in drawing attention to situations where conservation action may be required, information on changes in population size for a wide range of bird species is in itself of considerable biological interest and gives insights into how our familiar birds cope with an ever-changing environment.

Rarer birds, and highly clumped species like the colonial seabirds, can be monitored by specially directed studies. Some programmes of this kind are reported in this volume. For the rarest species we can even attempt to count the entire breeding population every year, through county bird recorders and the Rare Breeding Birds Panel. But common species must be monitored by widespread sample surveys of the kind that the British Trust for Ornithology, with its thousands of volunteer fieldworkers, is uniquely equipped to carry out.

In this report, the results comparing the breeding seasons of 1989 and 1990 are drawn together from three separate BTO monitoring schemes. These results have already appeared as separate annual reports in BTO News (Carter & Musty 1991, Marchant *et al.* 1991b, Peach & Baillie 1991).

Why have three schemes?

The primary scheme for monitoring breeding numbers of the commoner farmland and woodland birds in the United Kingdom is the Common Birds Census (CBC), which began in 1962. Between 200 and 300 plots of land, mostly either farmland or woodland, are censused each breeding season (late March to early July) using the territory-mapping method. The observer records the positions and activities of all birds encountered on each of ten visits, then transfers results for each species onto a separate map. The resulting species maps show both the numbers and the distribution of breeding territories of each species in each year. Between-year changes in the numbers of each species are used to calculate indices of population change, while the maps themselves provide raw data for studies of bird distribution in relation to habitat.

Currently, population levels of 76 species are indexed by the CBC. These include all of the commonest and most widespread British breeding species except Feral Pigeon and Swift, which have very large urban populations which are not monitored, and Rook and Sand Martin, which are too strongly colonial for mapping to be a suitable census method. All species encountered are included in the counts, although samples tend to be small for species having more specialised habitat requirements.

The Waterways Bird Survey (WBS) was launched in 1974 to help fill some of the gaps in CBC coverage relating to waterside bird species. It was also recognised that rivers and canals were important but vulnerable habitats and that a scheme was needed which would provide information on the habitat features of most value to waterside birds and the effects of waterway management. Like the CBC, the WBS uses the mapping census method, so that comparisons can be made between detailed maps of territory distribution and elements of the habitat. The WBS method differs from the CBC mainly in that plots are linear, along the river or canal, rather than covering an area of country, and in that only certain waterside groups and species of birds are recorded. Up to 120 stretches are censused each breeding season.

Recent collaborative research, initially with the Water Research Centre and subsequently with the University of Newcastle, has examined relationships between the abundance of waterways birds and habitat characteristics using data collected by the WBS. Water quality data, collected by the National Rivers Authority, were also utilized and this proved to be the most important factor in influencing the distribution of many species. A detailed appraisal of results is currently in hand.

The third scheme reported here is the Constant Effort Ringing Sites scheme, which began as a national programme in 1981. It aims to monitor changes in the populations and breeding performance of a range of common songbirds. Each summer volunteer BTO ringers are asked to visit their study site once in each of 12 ten-day periods between early May and the end of August. On each visit mist-nets are set in standard positions and for a standardised period of time. Provided there are no major changes to the habitat, changes in the numbers of birds trapped should reflect changes in the numbers of birds present. By combining data from a large number of such sites, change in the size of the adult catch is used as a measure of population change. Only this aspect of the CES results is reported here. In addition, the proportion of young birds in the total summer catch is used as an index of breeding performance (see elsewhere in this volume). Since every bird is uniquely identifiable by its ring number, the CES also provides information on return rates and individual survival. Survival of individual Sedge Warblers has been shown to be closely linked with the amount of rain in the south-western Sahel region of West Africa (Peach *et al.* 1991) - the greater the rainfall during May to October, the greater the proportion of Sedge Warblers that survive the ensuing winter and return to their British breeding sites the following spring.

All of the 23 species indexed by the CES are also monitored by the CBC, and three species (Sedge Warbler, Whitethroat and Reed Bunting) are covered by all three schemes. The relationships between population changes detected by CES and those from breeding bird censuses have not yet been investigated in detail, but in most cases the results are broadly similar. To some extent, differences between the CBC and CES results are to be expected because of differences in habitat coverage: CBC aims to cover ordinary patches of farmland and woodland, while CES sites tend to be in scrubland or reedbed sites which are unusually rich in birds and therefore likely to provide good catches. Such sites may attract many passage birds, particularly during late July and August when CBC and WBS fieldwork has already finished - although most of the adult captures on which the information in this article is based occur in May and June. CES ringers are likely to catch non-breeding as well as breeding adults, while the efforts of CBC and WBS observers are directly mainly towards the territory-holding (breeding) sections of the populations.

How did our birds fare in 1990?

Common Birds Census

A grand total of 182 plots (85 farms, 78 woods and 19 of other habitats - "special" plots) were available for the comparison of the 1989 and 1990 breeding seasons. As always, the plots that could be used were those where observer effort was consistent between the two seasons and where comparisons between the results would therefore be valid. They were thus a subsample of the grand total of 218 plots (97 farms, 96 woods and 25 "specials") censused in 1990, excluding chiefly those that were covered for the first time in that year. The samples of plots had changed very little in character from those of previous years (Marchant *et al.* 1991b), but as usual there was turnover in the sample amounting to about 12% of the total. As in all previous years, the geographical distribution of the plots was biased strongly towards "Southern England" (south of Bristol and the Thames) and "Eastern England" (between the Thames and the Humber).

The CBC estimates of population change are based on paired counts, tabulated and summed for all plots where coverage was consistent in the two years under review. Table 1 presents the sums of these paired counts as "year totals" for each species, together with the percentage change between the two year totals, and its 95% confidence limits, the number of plots contributing data and a condensed summary of previous trends. The confidence limits give an indication of the certainty of each estimated percentage change. Where the confidence limits are both either above or below zero, we can be 95% confident that there was a real change in population level and the change is statistically significant. Such cases are marked with an asterisk in the left margin. Small changes, and those which are not statistically significant, may nonetheless be biologically important as part of longer-term trends.

The number of plots available for each species varies greatly. Where it is high, it is possible to give separate estimates for the farmland and woodland samples. For the scarcer species it is possible to gather a sufficient sample only by combining plots of all habitat types. For some, a combination of chance sampling effects and population decline has brought the number of plots to a much lower level than is desirable: data based on fewer than an arbitrary 30 plots are marked with a cross.

Waterways Bird Survey

A total of 101 waterways plots were surveyed in 1990 of which 73 were suitable for inclusion in the calculations of population changes. Comparing this sample with the equivalents from previous years shows only minor changes (Carter & Musty 1991). No plots combining both river and canal sections were included in 1990, while the proportion of all index sites which were canals increased from 17% to 24%. Despite the total number of plots being unaltered from 1989, the number available for the index calculations continued downwards. Plots not suitable include those being covered for the first time - for 1990 there were ten such plots, more than in recent seasons. The geographical distribution of WBS plts in 1989 is presented in *Britains Birds in 1989–90*, and has altered little since.

Population changes for the 19 species monitored by the WBS are shown in Table 2. Of these, 12 showed population increases between 1989 and 1990, six decreased and one remained stable, but for only the three commonest species did the change reach statistical significance.

Constant Effort Sites scheme

The results presented here are based on the 85 CES sites worked in a consistent way during 1989 and 1990. This sample comprised 44 ringing sites in reedbed or wetland habitats, 31 in dry scrub and ten in deciduous woodland. The distribution of these sites in 1989 was given in *Britain's Birds in 1989–90*.

The percentage changes in catches of adult songbirds at CES sites in 1989 are summarised in Table 3. The large increases in the populations of many species recorded on CES sites during the 1988 and 1989 seasons were not continued in 1990. Significant declines were recorded for Wren, Dunnock, Blackbird, Sedge Warbler and Lesser Whitethroat, all of which had increased between 1987 and 1989. Despite the small (though statistically significant) decline in the catch of Wrens, numbers were still relatively high in 1990. Only Garden Warbler and Chiffchaff were significantly more abundant in 1990 than in 1989. Along with Robin, Blackcap and Long-tailed Tit, for which smaller increases were recorded, adults of these five species were more abundant during 1990 than in any other year since the start of CES ringing in 1981.

Table 1. Population changes between 1989 and 1990, as measured by the BTO's Common Birds Census.

Species	Habitat	Year totals 1989	1990	% change	95% confidence limits		Number of plots	Five-year trends					
+ Mute Swan	A	21	24	+14	−15	+54	17	.	.	.	=	=	+
* + Shelduck	A	33	48	+45	+4	+107	18	.	.	.	+	+	=
Mallard	F	236	247	+5	−10	+21	62	+	+	+	=	=	=
+ Tufted Duck	A	28	31	+11	−38	+101	13	.	.	.	.	=	=
Sparrowhawk	A	38	39	+3	−26	+43	57	.	.	.	+	=	=
+ Buzzard	A	20	21	+5	−25	+48	20	.	.	.	=	−	+
Kestrel	A	71	65	−8	−23	+9	79	.	+	=	−	−	+
* R-1 Partridge	F	67	83	+24	+4	+48	32	.	=	=	+	=	=
Grey Partridge	F	86	88	+2	−18	+28	39	−	−	=	=	−	−
* Pheasant	F	281	335	+19	+7	+33	72	+	+	+	−	=	+
* "	W	132	154	+17	+1	+35	46	.	=	+	+	+	+
Moorhen	F	158	170	+8	−5	+23	52	−	+	=	=	−	+
+ Coot	A	97	99	+2	−13	+20	26	.	.	=	=	=	=
Lapwing	F	121	118	−2	−25	+27	34	−	+	=	=	=	−
+ Woodcock	A	13	12	−8	−51	+69	16	.	=	=	−	−	=
+ Curlew	A	38	41	+8	−12	+32	21	.	.	.	=	=	=
+ Redshank	A	18	19	+6	−34	+69	15	.	.	.	=	=	−
Stock Dove	F	101	103	+2	−14	+21	43	.	+	+	+	+	=
" "	W	97	102	+5	−11	+24	33	.	.	.	+	=	=
Woodpigeon	F	472	509	+8	−2	+19	57	.	.	.	+	+	+
"	W	366	377	+3	−9	+17	42	.	.	.	+	+	+
Collared Dove	F	126	133	+6	−106	+24	48	.	.	+	+`	=	−
* + " "	W	48	37	−23	−41	0	24	.	.	.	+	=	=
+ Turtle Dove	F	39	42	+8	−30	+66	29	+	+	=	−	−	−
+ " "	W	51	47	−8	−38	+36	20	.	+	=	=	−	−
Cuckoo	F	76	65	−14	−31	+6	58	=	=	+	+	=	=
* "	W	47	31	−34	−51	−12	38	.	=	+	+	=	=
Little Owl	A	41	29	−51	−51	0	36	=	=	=	+	=	−
Tawny Owl	A	55	56	+2	−19	+29	67	+	+	=	−	=	=
+ Green Woodpecker	F	29	24	−17	−48	+28	27	.	=	+	=	−	+
" "	W	71	63	−11	−24	+3	51	.	+	=	=	=	=
Gt S Woodpecker	F	32	35	+9	−18	+46	31	.	.	+	+	=	=
" " "	W	104	101	−3	−16	+13	60	.	=	+	+	=	=
+ Lr S Woodpecker	A	18	19	+6	−33	+67	21	.	.	+	+	=	−
Skylark	F	748	787	+5	−2	+13	75	=	=	=	=	−	−
Swallow	F	239	256	+7	−5	+21	68	=	=	−	+	−	+
+ House Martin	A	85	71	−16	−39	+13	22	.	=	=	=	=	=
+ Tree Pipit	A	63	53	−16	−33	+5	22	.	=	=	=	=	−
Meadow Pipit	A	178	185	+4	−6	+14	37	+	=	=	=	−	+
+ Yellow Wagtail	A	51	53	+4	−17	+30	24	=	=	=	+	−	=
+ Grey Wagtail	A	24	23	−4	−36	+43	25	.	.	=	−	=	=
Pied Wagtail	F	107	113	+6	−13	+28	62	−	=	+	−	−	=
Wren	F	2000	2021	+1	−4	+6	82	−	+	+	−	=	+
"	W	2157	2061	−4	−9	+1	77	.	+	+	−	=	+
Dunnock	F	1032	1005	−3	−8	+3	83	+	=	+	−	−	=
"	W	467	448	−4	−12	+4	66	.	+	+	−	−	=
* Robin	F	1328	1480	+11	+4	+19	83	+	=	+	−	=	=
"	W	1715	1718	0	−4	+5	77	.	=	=	=	=	=
+ Redstart	A	116	103	−11	−28	+9	27	.	−	−	+	=	+

Table 1. Continued .../2

Species	Habitat	Year totals 1989	1990	% change	95% confidence limits		Number of plots	Five-year trends					
Blackbird	F	1662	1597	−4	−8	+1	85	+	=	=	−	−	=
* "	W	1089	1028	−6	−10	−1	75	.	+	=	=	−	=
* Song Thrush	F	321	283	−12	−22	−1	77	−	+	=	−	−	−
" "	W	392	371	−5	−15	+5	76	.	=	−	−	−	=
Mistle Thrush	F	84	96	+14	−5	+38	61	−	+	=	=	−	−
" "	W	89	79	−11	−25	+5	64	.	+	+	+	−	=
+ Sedge Warbler	F	93	93	0	−41	+68	25	.	=	−	=	−	+
+ Reed Warbler	A	234	235	0	−10	+11	22	.	.	.	+	=	+
Lr Whitethroat	F	68	64	−6	−29	+24	42	.	=	+	=	=	+
Whitethroat	F	362	415	+15	+4	+26	67	=	−	−	=	−	+
"	W	99	98	−1	−15	+15	30	.	−	=	=	−	+
Garden Warbler	F	69	53	−23	−48	+12	36	=	−	−	−	+	+
" "	W	152	155	+2	−15	+22	49	.	−	−	+	+	=
Blackcap	F	223	242	+9	−5	+24	61	.	+	+	+	+	+
"	W	468	471	+1	−7	+9	71	.	=	=	+	=	=
+ Wood Warbler	A	55	64	+16	−6	+44	19	.	.	=	=	−	+
Chiffchaff	F	243	262	+8	−7	+25	49	+	+	−	+	−	+
"	W	414	414	0	−9	+9	70	.	+	−	+	−	+
* Willow Warbler	F	683	613	−10	−18	−1	77	+	+	=	=	=	=
* " "	W	841	718	−15	−20	−9	73	.	=	=	=	=	=
Goldcrest	F	76	60	−21	−44	+9	34	.	+	+	−	=	−
"	W	280	292	+4	−6	+16	64	.	+	+	−	−	−
Spotted Flyc.	F	37	34	−8	−35	+29	32	=	−	−	−	−	=
+ " "	W	46	32	−30	−56	+6	29	.	−	−	+	−	=
Long-tailed Tit	F	114	129	+13	−4	+33	58	+	+	+	−	=	=
" " "	W	125	148	+18	+2	+37	66	.	+	+	−	=	=
Marsh Tit	W	82	85	+4	−14	+25	36	.	=	−	=	−	=
Willow Tit	A	51	40	−22	−41	+3	32	.	+	+	−	=	=
+ Coal Tit	F	50	61	+22	−6	+60	26	.	=	+	−	+	+
" "	W	350	348	−1	−11	+11	68	.	+	+	=	=	−
Blue Tit	F	1096	1048	−4	−10	+1	83	+	=	+	=	=	=
* " "	W	1337	1252	−6	−12	−1	76	.	=	+	=	=	=
* Great Tit	F	602	542	−10	−17	−2	83	+	=	+	=	+	=
* " "	W	766	707	−8	−14	−1	77	.	=	=	+	=	=
* Nuthatch	W	127	146	+15	+4	+27	49	.	=	=	+	+	+
* Treecreeper	F	48	33	−31	−51	−25	34	+	+	+	−	+	−
"	W	146	148	+1	−11	+16	61	.	+	+	=	+	−
Jay	F	49	41	−16	−33	+4	32	.	+	=	=	=	=
"	W	120	106	−12	−22	0	66	.	=	=	=	=	=
Magpie	F	284	281	−1	−12	+11	73	+	=	+	=	+	+
"	W	141	138	−2	−11	+7	61	.	=	+	+	+	=
Jackdaw	F	150	168	+12	−3	+30	50	=	=	+	+	+	=
"	W	82	75	−9	−23	+9	30	.	.	.	+	=	=
Carrion Crow	F	258	276	+7	−2	+17	72	+	+	+	+	=	+
" "	W	112	117	+4	−11	+23	63	.	+	+	+	+	=
* Starling	F	376	320	−15	−27	−1	66	+	−	+	=	−	−
* + "	W	209	135	−35	−49	−19	29	.	−	+	=	−	−
House Sparrow	A	306	281	−8	−21	+7	61	.	.	.	+	−	+
+ Tree Sparrow	F	59	76	+29	−5	+76	29	+	−	=	−	−	−

Table 1. Continued .../3

Species	Habitat	Year totals 1989	Year totals 1990	% change	95% confidence limits		Number of plots	Five-year trends					
Chaffinch	F	2048	1969	−4	−8	0	84	=	=	+	=	=	+
"	W	1194	1177	−1	−8	+5	77	.	=	=	+	=	=
Greenfinch	F	321	319	−1	−9	+9	72	+	=	=	=	=	=
"	W	120	117	−3	−24	+24	40	.	=	+	+	=	=
Goldfinch	F	143	169	+18	−2	+43	60	=	=	+	=	−	+
Linnet	F	269	261	−3	−16	+12	69	+	−	+	−	−	−
+ "	W	59	71	+20	−5	+54	24	.	=	=	−	−	−
+ Redpoll	A	33	28	−15	−47	+34	22	.	+	+	=	−	−
Bullfinch	F	81	67	−17	−36	+6	47	+	−	+	−	−	=
"	W	138	143	+4	−11	+21	58	.	+	=	=	−	=
* Yellowhammer	F	747	672	−10	−16	−4	69	=	=	=	=	=	=
"	W	162	145	−10	−22	+3	33	.	+	=	=	−	=
Reed Bunting	F	119	111	−7	−22	+11	44	=	+	+	−	−	=
+ Corn Bunting	A	85	76	−11	−32	+17	19	=	=	=	=	−	−

Key

Significance: * significant at the 5% level, + treat results with caution (data are drawn from fewer than 30 plots). Because percentage figures in the Table are rounded to the nearest whole number, a confidence limit recorded here as zero does not necessarily indicate a statistically change.

Habitats: F farmland only, W woodland only, A all habitats combined.

Trends: no information, + increase, = no real change, − decrease. Each symbol represents a subjective assessment of the trend during each four- or five-year period of CBC data during 1962–90 (two each for the 1960s, 70s and 80s). The symbols give no information on the magnitude of changes, and may conceal short-term fluctuations (see *Population Trends* for CBC and WBS data up to 1988).

Some trends to watch

Each year's percentage change figures reveal how our bird populations have responded to the latest environmental influences, but do not indicate how the levels stand in relation to previous years' results. For that, we need to examine the long-term trends. The BTO/NCC book *Population Trends in British Breeding Birds* (Marchant *et al.* 1990) gives details of CBC and WBS trends for all relevant species up to 1988. Only a small fraction of the data available can be updated in a short report, so we have concentrated on those species and groups where we feel the long-term trends are of special interest.

Small residents

CBC results since 1962 have shown that winter weather is a strong determinant of population changes in several species of resident birds. In these terms, "residents" include species which may move appreciable distances on occasion but of which many or most individuals breeding here

also winter in the UK or neighbouring countries. Those most at risk from severe weather are those very small species with a high surface area to volume ratio, so that their rate of heat loss is high, and their capacity to store fat is relatively low. Several of these, including Wren, Robin and Goldcrest, reached peak populations in the 1975 CBC season, following a series of mild winters which enabled the population levels to build up.

The 1989/90 winter was generally mild, and in some parts of the UK even warmer than the record-breaking winter of 1988/89. Following such benign conditions, our smaller resident birds could reasonably be expected to have shown continued increases. But after several such seasons of mild weather, with numbers of many residents unusually high, breeding habitats may well have been occupied almost to capacity and further increases in the territory-holding section of the population severely limited. CBC results for 1990 were therefore anticipated with unusual interest to see whether the populations had been able to expand beyond the previously recorded maxima.

Table 2. Population changes for waterside birds between 1989 and 1990, as measured by the BTO's Waterways Bird Survey.

Species	Year totals 1989	Year totals 1990	% change	95% confidence limits		Number of plots	Five-year trends		
+ Little Grebe	36	43	+19	−7	+55	14	=	=	=
Mute Swan	52	59	+13	−12	+47	32	+	−	+
* Mallard	988	1211	+23	+6	+42	71	+	+	+
+ Tufted Duck	48	43	−10	−42	+37	21	+	=	−
* Moorhen	585	648	+11	+3	+19	61	=	=	=
Coot	250	277	+11	−1	+24	39	+	=	+
+ Oystercatcher	144	135	−6	−21	+11	17	+	+	=
Lapwing	126	131	+4	−16	+29	34	.	+	−
+ Curlew	66	58	−12	−29	+8	18	.	+	=
+ Redshank	78	82	+5	−10	+23	17	=	=	=
+ Common Sandpiper	139	147	+6	−6	+19	27	=	+	−
+ Kingfisher	42	42	0	−24	+32	28	−	−	+
+ Yellow Wagtail	43	50	+16	−12	+54	19	=	−	−
Grey Wagtail	157	177	+13	0	+28	50	−	−	+
Pied Wagtail	232	219	−6	−15	+5	54	−	−	=
Dipper	113	104	−8	−17	+3	33	=	+	=
* Sedge Warbler	418	376	−10	−19	0	34	=	−	+
Whitethroat	88	98	+11	−9	+37	34	=	−	+
Reed Bunting	200	202	+1	−10	+13	39	−	−	=

Conventions are in Table 1. Five year trends cover the period 1974–90.

In the event, Wren numbers fell slightly in woodland and also on CES plots, where the decrease was statistically significant; on farmland CBC plots the index increased a little but may be levelling off at marginally below the 1975 value. Recent CBC increases for woodland Robins and farmland Dunnocks also appeared to be levelling off. On farmland, Robin numbers were at a new peak but only a little higher than their 1975 level. On CES sites, the Robin index was the highest for the ten years of the scheme, while Dunnocks were significantly fewer than in 1989.

Following their astonishing increase of 79% on farmland in 1989, Goldcrest numbers fell sharply by 21%, although there were still five times as many farmland territories as in 1986. In that year there had been heavy mortality of Goldcrests during an exceptionally cold February, but the crash in population was followed by a rapid increase and overspill onto farmland which is a secondary breeding habitat. In woodland, where Goldcrests increased by over a third in 1989, the relatively high populations were maintained in 1990.

With strong increases in both CBC indices in 1990, Long-tailed Tit numbers were, as for Wren, just short of the peak levels of the mid-1970s. A smaller increase was recorded on CES sites. Coal Tits, stable in woodland, expanded further onto farmland than ever before. Another strong increase in Nuthatches brought their numbers to a level double that of the early 1970s. Treecreepers decreased on farmland to reach marginally the lowest level since 1968, but were stable in woodland which is their primary habitat; CES ringers recorded a small increase. Willow Tits were also scarcer, perhaps as a continuation of a shallow longterm decline. The CBC recorded decreases in both habitats for Blue and Great Tits, with three of the four changes being statistically significant. However, 1990 indices were close to recent average values. By contrast, small increases in both species at CES sites brought a halt to the downward trends recorded since 1981.

Mistle Thrush, Song Thrush and Blackbird all fared rather badly, although the CBC showed that more Mistles held territory on farmland than in 1989. On CES sites, an 18% decrease for Blackbirds was statistically significant. Kingfisher, a species affected adversely by prolonged freezing weather, was stable on WBS plots in 1990.

Table 3. Changes in captures of adult birds by BTO ringers on Constant Effort Sites between 1989 and 1990.

Species	Year totals 1989	Year totals 1990	% change	95% confidence limits		Number of plots	Five-year trends	
* Wren	560	513	−8	−16	−1	68	=	+
* Dunnock	535	467	−13	−22	−2	67	−	=
Robin	308	344	+12	−2	+30	66	=	+
* Blackbird	782	642	−18	−29	−3	68	−	−
Song Thrush	260	249	−4	−19	+15	65	−	=
* Sedge Warbler	811	687	−15	−26	−4	51	−	+
Reed Warbler	1195	1176	−2	−14	+11	41	=	−
* Lesser Whitethroat	181	146	−19	−35	−2	44	=	=
Whitethroat	296	280	−5	−20	+18	50#	−	+
* Garden Warbler	220	274	+25	+3	+51	55	=	=
Blackcap	502	542	+8	−4	+22	60	=	=
* Chiffchaff	213	270	+27	+4	+67	51	−	+
Willow Warbler	1320	1202	−9	−16	+1	66	−	=
Long-tailed Tit	289	303	+5	−11	+27	58	=	=
Blue Tit	425	444	+4	−10	+22	67	−	−
Great Tit	252	280	+11	−9	+36	64	−	−
Treecreeper	57	61	+7	−30	+82	36	−	+
Chaffinch	314	299	−5	−21	+15	59	=	=
Greenfinch	167	166	−1	−33	+56	38	=	=
+ Linnet	145	97	−33	−63	+8	21	−	=
+ Redpoll	111	148	+33	−2	+87	29	−	=
Bullfinch	408	429	+5	−9	+21	63	=	=
Reed Bunting	313	280	−11	−29	+9	49	−	−

Key to Table 3

two sites excluded after major habitat changes distorted catches for this species.

Five-year trends cover the period 1981–90. Other conventions are as in Table 1.

Long-distance migrants

It was the crash of Whitethroats on CBC plots in 1969 that first alerted ornithologists to the effects of African rainfall on bird population levels in western Europe. The West African Sahel zone, immediately south of the Sahara, is particularly important for European migrants, and in years of plentiful rains during the May-October wet season migrants return to an abundance of habitat and food. Since then, as droughts have persisted and even worsened, we have become increasingly aware of the scale of their effects here. The species we believe to be most susceptible to drought (e.g. Sedge Warbler, Whitethroat, Sand Martin) are those of which many or most individuals spend the whole winter in the Sahel. All trans-Saharan migrants wintering south of the Sahel must traverse the drought-prone areas on spring and

autumn passage and may therefore be adversely affected to some degree. Population changes for long-distance migrants are therefore of special interest.

Sahel rainfall conditions were a little less severe for migrants during the 1989/90 winter, though this did not result in general increases in migrant population levels.

On CBC plots, Cuckoo index values for both farmland and woodland were the lowest since the early 1970s. Tree Pipits fell sharply to a new low, while Swallows continued their slow recovery from the low points of 1984 and 1987. Spotted Flycatchers in woodland were at an all-time low in 1990, at about one-third the level recorded as recently as 1983; the decrease of 30% followed one of 24% in 1989. On farmland the 1990 index fell back almost to the low point of 1984. Yellow Wagtail increased for the third successive year on WBS plots; CBC numbers were also marginally higher.

Warbler fortunes were mixed according to CBC results: of the seven species monitored on farmland, three showed declines, three increased and one remained stable, while in woodland two species were down, two up and one stable. Both Reed and Sedge Warblers maintained their relatively high 1989 levels on CBC plots. With declines for Sedge Warbler on both CES sites and WBS plots, stability on farmland, regarded as a suboptimal habitat for this species, was surprising.

Catches of adult warblers on CES sites decreased for five species and increased for three. As on CBC plots, Blackcaps and Chiffchaffs increased and Willow Warblers, a species whose numbers since 1962 have been generally remarkably stable, decreased. The increase in Chiffchaffs on CES sites was large and statistically significant; on CBC plots high numbers were maintained in woodland and numbers increased on farmland (for the sixth successive year) to a level second only to the peak year of 1970.

Whitethroats increased on both CBC and WBS plots, though CES catches were slightly down. Garden Warblers also show habitat-specific population changes: an increase on CES was significant, but a decline was apparent on CBC farmland plots. The decline in Lesser Whitethroats might be related to severe drought conditions in the wintering grounds of Sudan and Ethiopia during 1989.

Vulnerable birds on farmland

The need for quantification of bird population changes on farmland, in the light of pesticide kills of birds in the 1950s and the continuing habitat loss and changes in farm husbandry, was the initial impetus for the setting up of the CBC in 1961. Since then there has been no repetition of the wide-scale mortality incidents of the 1950s and indeed the CBC has charted the strong recovery of several species. Throughout the CBC period, however, there has been an almost continuous decline in the numbers of Grey Partridges which has been attributed largely to poor chick food supplies brought about by the use of pesticides and other changes in farming practice (Potts 1986). Grey Partridges enjoyed a second successive annual rise in 1990, but the recent increase is negligible in the face of this species' long-term decline.

Since the late 1970s, serious declines have become apparent in a number of other farmland birds including a suite of small seed-eating species. The reasons for these declines are as yet unknown.

There were more Skylarks on farmland than in 1989, but numbers remained at about half the level of the late 1970s. The large percentage increase in Tree Sparrows was both unexpected and welcome although it was not statistically significant and was based on data from only a small number of plots. In any case, it was not enough to reverse the losses in 1988-89. Goldfinch and Linnet also increased substantially on CBC plots, although for the latter the increase was largely in woodland where it was the third successive annual rise of more than 20%. In contrast, the CES showed a non-significant decrease of 33%. Goldfinch numbers on CBC plots were the highest since 1977 and more than double those of the 1986-87 trough. The continued collapse in the number of Redpolls brought them back almost to the levels of the mid-1960s and to less than a third of the 1977 peak; again in contrast, CES ringers caught one-third more Redpolls in 1990 than in 1989.

Farmland Bullfinches, and Yellowhammers in both woodland and farmland habitats, were scarcer than previously recorded by the CBC, although for the latter species the indices have varied little over the years and the present low levels may just represent short-term fluctuations. The decrease for Corn Bunting, on the other hand, continued the alarming downward trend evident particularly since 1981. This species is to be the subject of special new fieldwork in 1992-93, aimed at gaining a better understanding of the present decline and its causes.

Waders

1990 was a year of mixed fortunes for the five wader species covered by the WBS. Oystercatcher numbers fell slightly, while Curlew numbers were down for the second year in succession. Despite spring and summer drought conditions, Lapwing, Redshank and Common Sandpiper all maintained their numbers or increased a little. On CBC plots, both Woodcock and Lapwing continued to decline, and for each species the index value has fallen to about half the level of a decade ago. The picture was a little brighter, however, for Redshank and Curlew both of which improved a little on their relatively low population levels in 1989.

With the discontinuation of the Breeding Wader Monitoring Scheme, the population changes reported here represent the best broad-scale documentation of the changing abundance of this important group of species. Unfortunately, however, with the current restriction of fieldwork to farmland, woodland and river and canal habitats, census coverage for waders is very limited in its scope. Important concentrations of waders on coasts and moorlands are not included, while sample sizes of plots from CBC and WBS habitats are often barely sufficient for annual monitoring.

Pigeons and doves

The four British breeding species of pigeons and doves have shown remarkably dynamic population levels on CBC plots since 1962. Stock Dove and Collared Dove have shown very high rates of increase, the former as recovery from pesticide kills in the 1950s and the latter following colonisation of Britain from mainland Europe. Indices for both species appear to have reached relatively stable levels by the mid-1980s. Unexplained decreases in Turtle Doves are currently a cause for concern. The species is killed in large numbers on migration through southern Europe and North

Africa, and may also be susceptible to the effects of drought in the Sahel, but the reasons for the decline are unknown and might also lie on the breeding grounds.

Woodpigeon and Stock Dove showed population increases on both farmland and woodland CBC plots in 1990. There is now some sign that the continuous rise in the numbers of Woodpigeons recorded since 1976 may be levelling off, at least in woodland, while Stock Doves in woodland appear to be enjoying a further phase of increase. The smaller doves also increased on farmland. In woods, however, Collared Dove showed a significant decline of 23%, following high numbers in 1989, and the 8% drop for Turtle Dove took the woodland index to a new all-time low at less than half its value in 1980.

Corvids

Long-term increases in the numbers of Magpies and Carrion Crows have given rise to speculation about the impact of these nest predators on the population levels of some smaller open-nesting species, particularly the possible effects of Magpies on Song Thrushes (see elsewhere in this volume). There is evidence now that the Magpie population may have peaked around 1988, following a period of almost continual increase since the start of the CBC indices in 1962. The Carrion Crow population is showing no sign yet of levelling off, however. Jays were fewer on farmland than in any year since 1964, but in woodland only a little below the average level of the 1980s.

Starling

One of the most dramatic population changes recorded by the CBC in 1990 was the drop in Starling numbers on both farmland and woodland. This annual change was not an isolated event but part of a downward trend which began in about 1980.

Feare (1987) expressed an uneasy feeling about the future of the species as a nesting bird here, and described how changes in the UK fitted into the wider European context. The basic story, now updated in *Population Trends in British Breeding Birds* (Marchant *et al.* 1990), is of widespread decline and range contraction throughout northern Europe. Climatic shifts, changes in the pattern of mortality, and lower productivity as a result of intensive farming practices and more effective agrochemical use are each likely to be playing a part in driving the decline.

The results of a Finnish study (Tiainen *et al.* 1989) have recently thrown some light on the effect of changes in farmland management practices on Starling breeding success. In essence it was shown that there was a more than three-fold reduction in breeding success in areas of specialised monoculture compared to mixed farming. The decline in mixed farming, and consequent loss of permanent pasture which is the prime feeding habitat for breeding Starlings, could be affecting Starlings in the UK in the same way that it appears to be doing in Finland.

The future of monitoring censuses

Since the early 1960s, BTO census workers have contributed enormously to our knowledge of changes in abundance of our familiar birds. A recent milestone has been the publication of the BTO/NCC book *Population Trends in British Breeding Birds* (Marchant *et al.* 1990). The continuation of monitoring work is important both to the BTO and to the funding bodies co-ordinated by the Joint Nature Conservation Committee. As Integrated Population Monitoring develops, the CBC will become an essential part of a wider network involving also the Nest Record Scheme and bird ringing. In "CBC2000", Marchant *et al.* (1991a) described a continuing programme of pilot fieldwork which will lead to considerable improvements in the way in which breeding populations of common birds are monitored in the United Kingdom. We are aiming for a system which will cover more habitats and species than the current CBC and be more representative of the United Kingdom as a whole.

A new pilot scheme, the Pilot Census Project (PCP) is being launched in the 1992 breeding season and will continue for several more years. Sampling is based on random selection of one-kilometre squares of the National Grid. In 1992, point counts, transects and a combination of these two methods are on trial.

Thank you

The contribution of every census worker and CES ringer in 1989-90 is gratefully acknowledged. We are especially grateful to Phil Whittington, a CBC

analyst of ten years' standing, who left the staff on the occasion of our move to Thetford.

These schemes form part of the BTO's Integrated Monitoring Programme carried out under a contract from the JNCC, on behalf of EN, the CCW, and the SNH, and under a contract from the DoE(NI).

Where can more information be found?

The book, *Population Trends in British Breeding Birds*, which includes all CBC and WBS trend data for 1962-88, is available from BTO headquarters for £15 members, £17 non-members including postage and packing.

All the schemes would welcome new participants. If you feel you might be able to contribute to any of them or would like more information on CBC, WBS or CES, or on the new Pilot Census Project, please telephone or write to us at BTO headquarters.

References

Carter, S.P. & Musty, L. (1991). Waterways Bird Survey: 1989-90 population changes. *BTO News* 175, 10-11.
Feare, C.J. (1987). Where have all the Starlings gone? *BTO News* 149, 6.
Marchant, J.H., Carter, S.P. & Baillie, S.R. (1991a). CBC 2000. *BTO News* 174, 10-11.
Marchant, J.H., Musty, L. & Carter, S.P. (1991b). The Common Birds Census: 1989-90 index report. *BTO News* 177, 11-14.
Marchant, J.H., Hudson, R., Carter, S.P. & Whittington, P.A. (1990). *Population Trends in British Breeding Birds*. BTO/NCC, Tring.
Peach, W.J. & Baillie, S.R. (1991). Population changes on Constant Effort Sites 1989-90. *BTO News* 173, 12-14.
Peach, W.J., Baillie, S.R. & Underhill, L. (1991). Survival of British Sedge Warblers *Acrocephalus schoenobaenus* in relation to West African rainfall. *Ibis* 133, 300-305.
Potts, G.R. (1986). *The Partridge: Pesticides, Predation and Conservation*. Collins, London.
Tiainen, J., Hanski, I.K., Pakkala, T., Piiroinen, J. & Yrjölä, R. (1989). Clutch size, nestling growth and nestling mortality of the Starling in south Finnish agro-environments. *Ornis Fennica* 66, 41–48.

Breeding performance in 1990

Humphrey Q P Crick, Will Peach, Caroline Dudley, David E Glue & John Turner

Nest Records and Ringing Units, BTO

Summary

Overall 1990 was an early but short breeding season. For some passerine species reduced numbers of breeding adults resulted in lower numbers of young birds being reared. The late summer drought may also have affected the survival of young fledglings. It is likely that the relatively small output of young in 1990, coupled with the effects of a brief but severe period of cold winter weather in Britain and the continuing drought in the Sahel region of Africa, led to widespread population declines in 1991 (Peach & Baillie 1992).

How the BTO monitors breeding performance

There are two volunteer schemes that contribute information on breeding performance. One is the Nest Record Scheme (NRS) which is suitable for all birdwatchers from beginner to professional, and the other is the Constant Effort Ringing Sites scheme (CES) which can only be undertaken by trained and licensed ringers.

All that is required to participate in the NRS is to find a nest (or occupied nest box), describe the site and habitat, and then record its progress on a Nest Record Card by counting eggs and young and detailing the outcome. CES ringing involves the use of a standard set of mist nets to catch birds for a standard period on twelve mornings between May and August. Changes in capture rates of juveniles from year-to-year can then be monitored. The two schemes are complimentary, the NRS measuring success to fledging and the CES providing an index of overall success which also depends on the frequency of repeat-nesting and on post-fledging survival of young birds.

In 1990, a new style Nest Record Card was introduced to replace one that had seen little change over the past 50 years. BTO nest recorders took to the new card with a gusto that surprised even the staff at the Nest Records Unit. Over 32,000 cards were sent in, making 1990 one of the best years ever. The new card is a great leap forward. For the first time, it provides nest recorders with a set of defined choices to tick off for habitat and nest site. No longer do they have to ponder over how much and what detail to put down: the choices are clearly laid out in their handy pocket-sized coding card (Crick 1992). The new card is also very timely for the development of the BTO's Integrated Population Monitoring Programme (Baillie 1990) because it allows for quick computerisation. The tick-boxes can be automatically read into the computer without the need for typing. Analysis can be undertaken sooner than before, allowing speedier reporting to the scheme's major contractor, the JNCC.

The NRS provides a reasonable geographical coverage, although locally patchy at the county level. The top ten counties/regions in 1990 were, in order: Highland, Cheshire, Nottinghamshire, Dumfries and Galloway, Lothian, Surrey, Norfolk, Merseyside, West Yorkshire and Hertfordshire. The NRS results reported below are for the 26 species listed in Table 1. Breeding records from 1990 were compared with a sample taken from the previous 12 years (1978-89), except for four species that were not fully computerised: Lapwing (1972-81, 1987-89), Moorhen (1972-81, 1986-89), Dipper (1978-80, 1982-88), and Grey Heron (1973-74, 1986-89).

Table 1. List of Nest Record Scheme species covered in this report.

Grey Heron	Swallow
Mute Swan	Meadow Pipit
Hen Harrier	Grey Wagtail
Sparrowhawk	Dipper
Kestrel	Dunnock
Peregrine	Redstart
Moorhen	Song Thrush
Oystercatcher	Sedge Warbler
Lapwing	Willow Warbler
Stock Dove	Spotted Flycatcher
Barn Owl	Magpie
Tawny Owl	Starling
Skylark	Linnet

Table 2. Changes in the percentage of juveniles caught at CES sites from 1989 to 1990 .

		Paired sites 1989–1990				
Species	n	Total 1989	% juv 1989	Total 1990	% juv 1990	Diff in % juv
Wren	68	1780	69	1690	70	+1
Dunnock	67	1311	59	1102	57	−2
Robin	65	1293	76	1411	75	−1
Blackbird	67	1205	35	970	34	−1
Song Thrush	57	433	40	366	32	−8
Sedge Warbler	46	1949	58	1564	56	−2
Reed Warbler	41	2437	51	2119	45	−6
Lesser Whitethroat	38	355	49	295	51	+2
Whitethroat	50	727	59	701	60	+1
Garden Warbler	51	441	50	446	38	−12*
Blackcap	58	1132	56	1224	56	0
Chiffchaff	52	960	78	921	71	−7
Willow Warbler	66	3509	62	3355	64	+2
Long-tailed Tit	53	817	65	917	67	+2
Blue Tit	60	1972	78	1858	76	−2
Great Tit	65	780	68	988	72	+4
Treecreeper	39	177	68	230	74	+6
Chaffinch	50	569	45	561	47	+2
Greenfinch	26	277	40	260	36	−4
Linnet	16	190	24	130	25	+1
Redpoll	16	173	36	220	33	−3
Bullfinch	56	617	34	616	30	−4
Reed Bunting	40	525	40	427	34	−6

n = number of paired sites
Total = total number of adults plus juveniles captured
% juv = percentage of captures which were juveniles
Diff in % juv = % juveniles in 1990 minus % juveniles in 1989
* = statistically significant change at 5% level

The CES Scheme covers Britain and Ireland but tends to have a geographical bias to eastern England (Peach 1991). The results come from 85 sites operated in 1989 and 1990 (44 in wetland habitats, 31 in dry scrub and 10 in woodland). Changes in the percentages of juveniles caught in 1990 are presented Table 2.

An early but a short year

Exceptionally mild mid-winter conditions allowed several species such as Great Crested Grebe, Tawny Owl, Blackbird and Woodpigeon to start nesting in January. Many of these nests were lost during the great storms in late January and early February but then dry and warm weather stimulated much nesting in March and early April. The Edward Grey Institute's famous nest box programme in Wytham Woods, Oxfordshire, saw the first Great Tit egg laid on the 1st of April, the earliest ever, by sever-

al days, since the project started over 40 years ago.

An early end to breeding was brought about by frosts in late May, the cool weather in June and then prolonged hot drought in many places thereafter. This combination of early start and early stop limited the number of second and third broods recorded in 1990 and for many species this was reflected in the overall distribution of laying dates being more concentrated in the early part of the season than in the last 13 years (see Table 3). (It should be noted that the figures in Table 3 are averages for all nests. Although these are rather crude measurements, there are certain statistical problems associated with the analysis of laying date distributions which are under review. However, the overall average is useful for broad comparative purposes and inspection of the frequency distributions indicated the occurrence of fewer late nests than in earlier years.)

Table 3. Significant changes in average laying dates of first eggs in a clutch between 1990 and the previous 12 years.

Species	1990	1978–89	Sig
[Grey Heron	2 May	20 April	*]
[Skylark	29 April	17 May	**]
Swallow	1 June	17 June	**
Grey Wagtail	15 April	30 April	**
Dipper	5 April	11 April	*
Redstart	12 May	19 May	***
Sedge Warbler	19 May	27 May	***
Willow Warbler	12 May	15 May	*
Spotted Flycatcher	1 June	7 June	**
Linnet	10 May	17 May	***

NB   The probabilities that such differences could have occurred by chance are:
* 1 in 20; ** 1 in 100; *** 1 in 10,000

(The average dates given for 1978–89 are medians and the differences were statistically significant using Wilcoxon tests. The data include repeat clutches and multiple broods. Species with very small samples are placed in square brackets.)

Table 4. Changes in average clutch size between 1990 and the previous 12 years.

Species	Month	1990	1978–89	Sig
Hen Harrier	All	4.00(29)	4.70(149)	**
Sparrowhawk	All	4.79(70)	4.58(613)	
Kestrel	All	4.94(50)	4.71(672)	*
Oystercatcher	All	2.39(61)	2.71(1621)	***
Skylark	April	3.73(11)	3.05(40)	***
Song Thrush	May	3.93(15)	4.34(719)	*
Redstart	All	6.62(50)	6.27(806)	*
Linnet	May	5.00(24)	4.74(551)	*

(The averages given above are means with sample sizes given in brackets. See Table 3 for details of significance probabilities. The result for Sparrowhawk was non-significant at the 5% level).

Three species associated with watery habitats were particularly affected: fewer Grey Wagtails nested in June than normal, more Dippers nested in March and fewer in May and there were no records for Sedge Warbler laying in July. Moorhens too laid eight days earlier than usual, starting fewer nests than normal from May to August. Amongst landbirds, the long-distance migrants seemed to be particularly affected by the

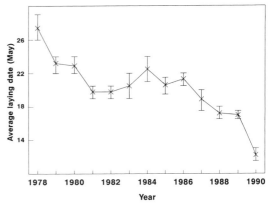

Figure 1. *Average laying date (±SE) for Redstart measured from Nest Record Cards.*

weather: Swallow and Spotted Flycatcher both nested significantly early, compared with the previous twelve years, though this was mainly because there were few second and third broods from June onwards. Redstart and Willow Warbler also had their laying periods concentrated towards the first part of the season and, for the former, 1990 seemed to be part of a long-term trend towards an earlier season (Figure 1). This seems to be a genuine trend rather than the result of any shift in the geographical distribution of nest records.

How clutch sizes changed

Bird populations usually lay the same average clutch size each year, refined by natural selection to be the optimum for the average conditions that the parents and young will find after hatching and fledging. Birds generally cannot predict how good an individual season will be, which is why only 8 of the 26 species investigated showed any change in clutch size (Table 4).

Two raptors showed very interesting trends in clutch size from 1978-90. Clutches of the Kestrel have increased in size over the past thirteen years and the high value in 1990 probably indicated that it was a good year for voles. However, the Hen Harrier has shown a progressive decline in clutch size (Figure 2). The increase in clutch size for the Sparrowhawk (nearly significant) was almost certainly due to the high numbers of some species of their songbird prey. Tawny and Barn Owls also did better than in 1989 when reports suggested that vole numbers were low. Amongst other birds, Oystercatchers showed a dramatic drop in clutch size which was unparalleled in the last twelve years (Figure 3). It is possible that this was due to the effect of the dry weather on the availability of

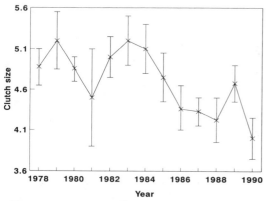

Figure 2. *Average clutch size (±SE) for Hen Harrier measured from Nest Record Cards.*

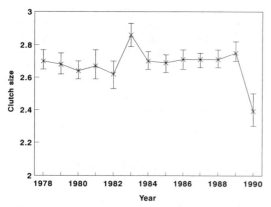

Figure 3. *Average clutch size (±SE) for Oystercatcher measured from Nest Record Cards.*

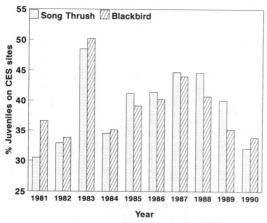

Figure 4. *The percentage of young Blackbirds and Song Thrushes caught at CES sites since 1981.*

their food - soil-dwelling invertebrates. This may have also affected the clutch size of Song Thrushes in May 1990.

It was good to see an upturn in clutch size for the Linnet after the alarming series of falls that was reported in Crick *et al.* (1991a), although there are indications that overall nesting success has been falling for this species (Crick *et al.* 1991b). The larger than average clutch size for Redstarts was because there were few late nests (which tend to contain smaller clutches).

Juveniles less abundant but productivity similar to 1989

Significant changes in the numbers of young birds caught were detected for Dunnock (-18%), Blackbird (-22%), Song Thrush (-32%), Sedge Warbler (-23%), Reed Warbler (-24%), Great Tit (+34%) and Treecreeper (+41%). In the cases of Dunnock, Blackbird, Sedge Warbler, Lesser Whitethroat, Linnet and Reed Bunting, declines in the abundance of young birds were partly a consequence of declines in the size of adult breeding populations (Peach & Baillie 1991). Great Tits made up for a poor year in 1989 whilst young Reed and Sedge Warblers were relatively abundant though well down on the spectacular numbers of 1989.

As the numbers of juveniles reared each year depends partly on the numbers of breeding adults, the percentage of young birds in the total catch is used as an index of breeding productivity. Changes in productivity were generally small in 1990, the only significant change being recorded for Garden Warbler which suffered a massive 12% reduction in the proportion of juveniles (Table 2). The proportion of young Garden Warblers caught in 1990 was the lowest since 1985.

Despite the abundance of adult Chiffchaffs on CES sites in recent years, the percentage of young birds fell for the third year in succession. Also down for a third consecutive year were the proportions of young Song Thrushes and Blackbirds, both of which were lower in 1990 than during the previous six years. Figure 4 shows that changes in the proportions of young Song Thrushes and Blackbirds coincide closely from year-to-year suggesting that some common factor may determine the survival of young birds during the post-fledging period. Sustained dry weather in recent springs and summers is likely to have reduced the availability of earthworms and other important foods for young thrushes.

Where can more information be obtained?

Free starter packs for the Nest Record Scheme are available from Caroline Dudley at BTO HQ. Questions about NRS analysis and monitoring can be sent to Humphrey Crick. For more information on the CES Scheme contact Will Peach, also at BTO HQ.

References

Baillie, S.R. (1990). Integrated population monitoring of breeding birds in Britain and Ireland. *Ibis* 132:151-166.

Crick, H.Q.P., Dudley, C., Glue, D.E. & Fisher, S. (1991a). The Nest Record Scheme in 1989. In: Stroud, D.A. & Glue, D.E. (Eds.), *Britain's Birds in 1989/1990: the conservation and monitoring review.* Pp.62-67. BTO/JNCC, Thetford.

Crick, H.Q.P., Donald, P.F. & Greenwood, J.J.D. (1991b). Population processes in some British seed-eating birds. *BTO Research Report No. 80.* BTO, Thetford.

Crick, H.Q.P. (1992). A bird-habitat coding system for use in Britain and Ireland incorporating aspects of land-management and human activity. *Bird Study* 39, 1-12.

Peach, W.J. (1991). The Constant Effort Sites scheme. In: Stroud, D.A. & Glue, D.E. (Eds.), *Britain's birds in 1989/90: the conservation and monitoring review.* Pp. 73-78. BTO/JNCC, Thetford.

Peach, W.J. & Baillie, S.R. (1991). Population changes on constant effort sites 1989-90. *BTO News* 173, 12-14.

Peach, W.J. & Baillie, S.R. (1992). Population changes on Constant Effort Sites 1990-1991. *BTO News* 179, 12-13.

M.S. Wood/Oystercatcher at nest

Bird ringing in 1990

Chris Mead & Jacquie Clark

Populations Research Department, BTO

Origins and objectives

The first properly formulated scientific programme of bird ringing, each bird being marked with a ring inscribed both with an unique registration number and a return address, was started in Denmark in 1899. The British and Irish scheme, operated by the British Trust for Ornithology for more than 50 years, in part evolved from two separate schemes founded by Harry Witherby and Landsborough Thomson in 1909. It has become a highly co-operative enterprise with the BTO, the ringers, JNCC and the public all having their part to play. The BTO organises and administers the scheme; the ringers, who are almost all volunteers, catch and mark the birds; the ringers, the BTO and JNCC provide the funds needed to run the scheme; and the public, worldwide, report the majority of the recoveries of ringed birds. In 1990, there were almost 1,800 ringers operating with permits which allowed them to ring unsupervised, while a further 463 held Trainee permits. The training process, which has evolved over many years, seeks to ensure that they apply the highest standards of care for the birds and of accuracy in the gathering of data.

The main aims of the Scheme are to provide information on the survival rates and movements of wild birds in Britain and Ireland. Much of the work is now directed towards the BTO's Integrated Population Monitoring Programme and towards other conservation-related studies of particular groups, especially raptors, seabirds and waders. Results from some elements of this programme, such as the Constant Effort Sites Scheme and analyses of mortality due to hunting, are detailed elsewhere in this volume.

In addition to its own objectives, the Scheme provides data to individuals researching many aspects of bird biology. It also provides services for those undertaking studies that necessitate bird marking, particularly through the review and licensing of marking techniques and the co-ordination of colour marking.

This article provides a brief review of work and results of the Scheme during 1990. A more detailed account, including comprehensive totals of birds ringed and recovered and an extensive list of the more interesting recoveries reported, is given in the Report on Bird Ringing for 1990 (Mead & Clark 1991).

Numbers ringed

Some 840,615 birds were ringed in 1990. This figure is 38,714 less than the record total for 1988, reflecting a small reduction in the numbers of both full grown birds and nestlings ringed. This change results from a complex interaction between ringing effort, catching success and the breeding productivity of the commonest species. Most of the variation in the numbers of small birds ringed is attributable to fluctuations in the numbers of juveniles caught in the late summer and autumn. Severe winters are the factor that has most influence on the ringing totals for resident species through direct mortality and less juveniles later being available from the reduced breeding population. All of the winters from 1987/88 to 189/90 were relatively mild, resulting in many resident birds being available for ringing.

The bulk of ringed birds are the most abundant species and these are usually of greater importance for research and conservation but variations in numbers of scarce migrants are also of interest. Table 1 shows the totals for scarce migrants ringed in Britain and Ireland from 1987 to 1990. The numbers of Waxwings and Crossbills ringed during 1990 were exceptional. Both species are prone to invade Britain, irregularly, from the east. Waxwings arrive in the autumn and winter following a good breeding season combined with subsequent failure of the berry and fruit crops on which they depend for winter food. Crossbill arrivals consist of families reared in areas where spruce and pines have fruited well. To settle to breed they have to find new areas where the next crop will be good, because it is very seldom that conifers in the same area have good crops in successive years. The 1990 total for Waxwings was 42.9% of the previous grand total; the equivalent figure for Crossbill was 41.1%.

Table 1. Scarce migrant totals ringed in Britain and Ireland from 1987 to 1990: only the annual totals for full-grown birds are shown.

Species	1987	1988	1989	1990
Little Stint	6	48	6	19
Curlew Sandpiper	6	280	4	74
Wryneck	30	39	15	19
Waxwing	35	130	42	429
Bluethroat	33	32	11	9
Aquatic Warbler	5	8	19	26
Icterine Warbler	26	24	20	11
Melodious Warbler	5	7	5	7
Subalpine Warbler	6	13	7	5
Barred Warbler	17	24	17	20
Pallas's Warbler	11	11	5	7
Yellow-browed Warbler	61	128	35	27
Red-breasted Flycatcher	20	20	13	9
Red-backed Shrike	18	58	24	11
Great Grey Shrike	3	4	5	4
Crossbill	7	29	3	592
Scarlet Rosefinch	13	32	20	13

1990 was a poor year for numbers of many of the scarce passerine migrants that are usually encountered on migration at coastal or island bird observatories. It was a moderate year for the two Siberian waders, Little Stint and Curlew Sandpiper, whose numbers show annual fluctuation due to varying presence on autumn migration, mainly at estuarine sites. Aquatic Warblers were at their highest level for 14 years with 26 individuals caught and ringed (and, in addition, two Polish birds controlled - see below). This species is usually caught in reed-beds in southern England by ringers trapping *Acrocephalus* warblers and does not generally occur in other habitats at Bird Observatories.

Ringing recoveries

A total of 13,523 recoveries was reported during the year. The most dramatic change in the number of reports for a single species came from Roseate Tern. The 1989 total was one; 90 were reported in 1990! This came about because it proved possible for the warden to read the ring numbers of adult birds through a telescope at the main Irish Sea colony. Many of the breeding birds had come from other colonies, mainly in the Irish Sea. Two other species showing major increases in recoveries were Razorbill (47 in 1989 and 174 in 1990) and Long-tailed Tit (32 in 1989 to 94 in 1990). These results reflect the high numbers of Razorbill ringed in 1989 and Long-tailed Tits in 1990.

Ringing recoveries provide the fundamental data about the movements and mortality of our birds but, in general, each is only useful when considered as part of the total information for the species. However there are, each year, a few individual recoveries of particular interest, either because they demonstrate unusual movements for a relatively well-known species or because they are among the first to provide the meaningful information for the species concerned.

For example, two recoveries in England of Polish-ringed Aquatic Warblers were of particular significance. None of the 453 ringed in Britain has been recovered nor had there been a previous record in Britain of one of the birds ringed abroad. These two birds wore consecutive rings and had been marked, as youngsters, in Lomza, Poland as part of a research project. They were found, within an hour of each other, on 25th August, by ringers in Avon and Cornwall. Three further Polish ringed birds were recovered in France, and Polish ringers also caught a Belgian bird. These records all result from the same project. It seems to suggest that members of this very rare species migrate westwards before turning south to Africa. Its stronghold may be in Poland where there are 1,300 - 1,500 pairs; otherwise it possibly only breeds in Austria, Germany, Hungary and the USSR (Collar & Andrew 1988).

Some records transmitted to us by the Moscow ringing office are of particular interest. These included two breeding-season reports of Grey Plover, only our third and fourth ever. They were ringed in winter on Teesmouth and the Wash respectively, found more than 4,000 kms away in Siberia. One was shot in Tyumen Oblast in SW Siberia and the other was recaptured on the nest by a Polish ornithologist on Sibriakov Island off the Taimyr Peninsular. The record of a male Mandarin, ringed in the Berkshire breeding area, and reported from Pskov, south of St Petersburg, Russia, was wholly unexpected but a search of the ringing records provides a precedent, because a Mandarin from St James's Park, London was reported in Hungary during 1931. Perhaps this species acts as a financial indicator and leaves Britain in times of severe recession. However, no precedent could be found for the most unusual recovery, reported in autumn from the Ukraine, of a Turtle Dove ringed as a nestling the previous summer in Hampshire. An extensive series of autumn recoveries of British-ringed Turtle Doves show that British populations of this species generally undertake a fairly concentrated movement down the very west of Europe including the west coast of Portugal.

Notable recoveries in Africa included three birds of high conservation interest in Britain that were shot on their wintering grounds. Two were Ospreys ringed in Scotland. One was shot in Guinea (our first from that country) within four months of being ringed in the nest. The other, our third from Senegal, was more than ten years old. One of the breeding female Black-tailed Godwits from the Ouse Washes, ringed in 1984, was shot in November 1990 in Guinea Bissau and provides the first evidence of the wintering area of our breeding birds in Africa. Two other recoveries, unfortunate for the conservation of the species, were closer to home. Red Kites brought from Sweden and introduced to Scotland were found poisoned in Co. Waterford in December and in Co. Longford in February. The use of strychnine baits has now been banned in the Republic of Ireland.

Each year we receive only a handful of records of our passerine summer migrants from sub-Saharan Africa - out of hundreds of thousands that winter there wearing rings. Apart from Swallows, which often provide a number of such recoveries, those reported in 1990 were Sedge Warblers in Ghana and Burkina Faso, a Reed Warbler in Mauritania and a Sand Martin in the Canary Islands. However the end of 1990 saw the start of an important development with a British-led expedition of ringers to an extensive wetland area in Senegal. Although only a few weeks of 1990 were included in their initial season, which extended to early April 1991, British and Irish ringed birds which they caught included 18 Sand Martins, four Sedge Warblers, three Reed Warblers and four Chiffchaffs. By the time that they returned home, over 300 ringed birds from Europe had been controlled - the majority being Sand Martins from Britain and Ireland. A further expedition to the same site is taking place from autumn 1991 to spring 1992.

Developments and products

One important role of ringing is to provide information on bird survival rates, which have a profound influence on population size. Detection of changes in survival rates may provide the first warning of a threat to the species due to natural events or human activity. Statistical methods for estimating survival rates using ringing and recovery data are well-established. They require totals

of birds ringed to be split at least by age and by year, season and region of ringing. In 1985 the Trust began to collect these data for 22 common passerines. The run of data collected will allow analyses of age-specific totals in 1992. The Ringing Unit is now moving towards full computerisation of the ringing data so that more detailed analyses may be carried out in the future.

Data on productivity are also derived from the work of ringers. These are important in predicting the ability of a species to cope with environmental change or recover from catastrophe. For example, wader catchers now report the adult and juvenile numbers in each catch they make and these data are analysed to give a measure of breeding success for each species or, where practicable, subspecies and populations.

Ringers also collect biometrics on many of the birds they catch. In order to make these data as valuable as possible, the Ringing Committee has set up a working group to recommend measurements that can best be used in the determination of age, sex or race and in the calculation of condition indices using a combination of weight and measurements. The working group is due to report in 1992. At the same time, work is now nearing completion on a guide to ageing and sexing non-passerines. This will be an invaluable tool for ringers throughout Europe, allowing them to assign more birds to the correct age and sex classes.

Data from the BTO Scheme and information from individuals' own studies are used by both BTO staff and other workers in the production of scientific papers and reports. Papers which were published in 1990 covered many topics including population monitoring, behaviour, ecology, migration, moult and survival. Examples include work on *Waterfowl Migration and Distribution in North-West Estuaries* (Clark *et al.* 1990) and *Population Trends in British Barn Owls and Tawny Owls* (Percival 1990). Ormerod (1990) used ringing to look at the time of passage, habitat use and mass change of *Acrocephalus* warblers in a south Wales reedswamp and Milwright (1990) investigated the sex differences in breeding colony fidelity of House Martins. Elsewhere in this ?issue? are brief reports on some of the work undertaken by staff in analysing some of the data gathered recently. In *The effects of the severe weather in February 1991* Jacquie Clark describes work undertaken on the exceptional number of waders, particularly on the Wash, found dead, which included a high proportion of ringed birds. In *Auk Mortality Causes and*

Trends Chris Mead, draws attention to the changes in reported mortality causes from ringing recoveries of Razorbills and Guillemots.

The success' of ringing studies is greatly increased by effective international co-operation. Close links are maintained with other schemes, particularly through EURING. These links provide the exchange of data about birds moving between countries and there are regular meetings to discuss common problems. At the EURING meeting, which took place in September 1990 in Hungary, 23 different schemes were represented. Recent political changes in Eastern Europe may have a profound effect on the organisation of its ringing schemes. Such changes are important since they could have a significant effect on the quantity and quality of the data from the breeding areas of many species which winter in Western Europe.

References

Clark, N.A., Kirby, J.S., Langston, R.H.W., Donald, P., Mawdesley, T. & Evans, J. (1990). *Waterfowl migration and distribution in north west estuaries.* BTO Research Report No. 54 to the Energy Technology Support Unit of the Department of Energy.

Collar, N.J. & Andrew, P. (1988). *Birds to watch.* ICBP Technical Publication No. 8. ICBP, Cambridge.

Mead, C.J. & Clark, J.A. (1991). Report on Bird Ringing for Britain and Ireland for 1990. *Ringing & Migration* 12, 139-176.

Milwright, R.D.P. (1990). Sex differences in breeding colony fidelity of House Martins *Delicon urbica.* *Ringing & Migration* 11, 2, 101-103.

Ormerod, S.J. (1990). Time of passage, habitat use and mass change of *Acrocephalus* warblers in a South Wales reedswamp. *Ringing & Migration* 11, 1-11.

Percival, S.M. (1990). *Population trends in British Barn Owls, Tyto alba, and Tawny Owls, Strix aluco.* BTO Research Report No. 57. BTO, Tring.

The effects of the severe weather in February 1991

Jacquie Clark

Populations Research Department, BTO

When unusual bird mortalities occur, the Ringing Unit is often the first to find out - as a result of reports of ringed birds from members of the public. During and after the severe weather of mid February 1991 the Ringing Unit was deluged by recoveries of waders from south-east England, notably the Wash, although there was little change to the usual pattern of passerine recoveries.

One of the Wash Wader Ringing Group's (WWRG) aims is to study the effects of cold weather on waders. A routine visit to the Wash, shortly before the onset of this spell of cold weather, had concentrated on catching those species normally affected by cold spells, such as Redshank and Grey Plover. A total of 400 birds had been caught, weighed and measured during the weekend and plans were made to return for further catching if cold weather occurred. Two weeks later, as the brief but very extreme spell of cold weather was ending, WWRG members returned to the Wash and discovered many waders dead on the tideline. Over 800 corpses were collected immediately and samples of those which survived were caught. Special care was taken to ring, weigh and measure these birds very quickly so that they were not deprived of feeding time. Group members then organised a massive tideline search of the whole of the Wash, enlisting the help of local Birds of Estuaries Enquiry counters and wildfowlers. In all nearly 3000 corpses were counted (see Table 1); 2,500 were of these were collected and stored in freezers for detailed analysis.

These have subsequently been sexed, by dissection, and measured. The sex and biometric data will be analysed to see if particular portions of the population died. For example, were the larger Icelandic breeding Redshank less susceptible to the cold than the smaller birds that breed in Britain? The measurements of the casualties will also be compared to those of birds caught in previous years and to the live birds caught during and after the cold spell. The origins of the hundreds of previously ringed birds which perished will also be studied. Most had been marked on the Wash in previous years - many more than 10 and some more than 20 years ago. All this information will give us a much better insight into the effects of such cold weather episodes on wintering waders.

Table 1. Dead waders counted on the Wash in February/March 1991.

	West Wash	South Wash	East Wash	Total
Redshank	130	336	1,060	1,526
Grey Plover	24	45	311	380
Dunlin	55	149	392	596
Knot	20	24	90	134
Oystercatcher	40	41	46	127
Curlew	5	35	25	65
Turnstone	5	3	16	24
Other Waders	7	1	15	23
Grand Total	286	634	1,955	2,875

This was clearly an exceptional event. Whilst other areas were affected, Figure 1 shows that it was the Wash populations which bore the brunt of the cold weather. About two-thirds of the Redshanks wintering on the Wash died. The impact can be gauged by comparing the monthly counts of Redshank on the Wash during winter 1990-91 with the average for 1984–89 (Figure 2).

This event presented an unique opportunity to study the subsequent reoccupation of the area and funding was obtained from the Departments of Energy and the Environment for the BTO and ITE to undertake this work. The study, which will be completed in late 1992, may provide insights into, for example, the timescale of recolonisation of parts of an estuary following the building of a barrage.

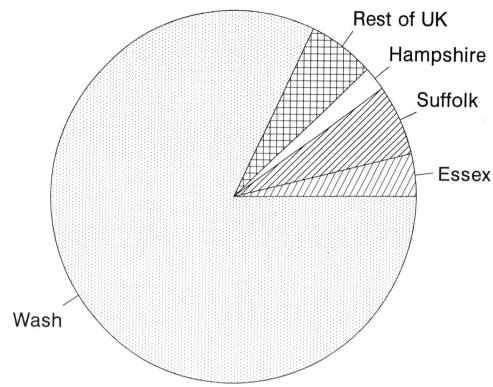

Figure 1. *Distribution of Redshank cold weather recoveries of dead ringed birds (n = 221).*

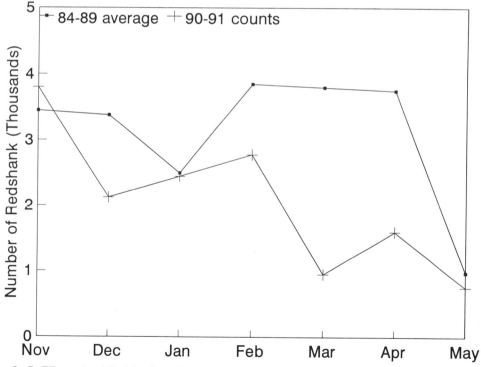

Figure 2. *BoEE counts of Redshank on the Wash. (The February 1991 count preceded the cold snap.)*

Monitoring of seabird numbers and breeding success

Paul M Walsh[1], Jane Sears[2] & Martin Heubeck[3]

[1]Seabirds Team, JNCC
[2]Research Department, RSPB
[3]SOTEAG, University of Aberdeen

Seabird numbers and breeding success are monitored annually at many colonies throughout Britain and Ireland. A brief history of seabird monitoring in Britain and an outline of the methods used were given in *Britain's Birds in 1989-90*. Most of the relevant monitoring is carried out by (or under contract to) JNCC, RSPB and the Shetland Oil Terminal Environmental Advisory Group (SOTEAG), with JNCC's Seabird Monitoring Programme in a coordinating role. Information from these and other sources is collated for an annual JNCC/RSPB/SOTEAG report and the following summary is taken from the 1990 report (Walsh *et al*. 1991). Patterns and trends for individual species are outlined more fully in relevant Species Accounts at the end of this volume.

Monitoring efforts are particularly directed at the numbers and breeding success of cliff-breeding species and of terns. Breeding success of widespread, wholly marine species such as Kittiwake, Fulmar and Shag may provide an effective means of monitoring changes in aspects of the wider marine environment (including food availability). The information collected is also of use in formulating conservation policies. Terns are of particular conservation importance in that breeding numbers are relatively small, and colonies are highly subject to disturbance, predation and other factors. The results of tern monitoring in relation to long-term population trends are described in more detail by Sears & del Nevo elsewhere in this volume.

Summary of results

In 1990, several seabird species in Shetland-experienced near-total breeding failure, for the third year in succession. This continues a decline in breeding success evident since 1984 (with Arctic Terns in particular rearing very few chicks from 1984 onwards). Detailed studies confirm that a reduction in the availability of small sandeels in Shetland waters has been responsible. Breeding numbers of a range of species in Shetland have also been in decline since the early 1980s, and rates of decline may have accelerated recently.

Breeding success of cliff-breeding species in Orkney and Caithness in 1990 was, in general, much higher than in Shetland. Terns and Arctic Skuas had a poor season, however, in part a result of predation and bad weather.

Populations of cliff-breeding species were not assessed in Orkney in 1990, but showed little change (and generally upward recent trends) in Caithness.

At other east Scottish colonies, breeding success of terns (especially Arctic Tern) was very poor in 1990. Kittiwakes also showed a substantial reduction in success (to the lowest levels recorded on these coasts during 1986-90), as did several other species in the Firth of Forth. Numbers of a range of (mainly cliff-breeding) species fell at SE Scottish colonies in 1990, although 1986-90 trends have been for numbers to increase in general.

Populations of terns and *Larus* gulls have fluctuated to a greater degree.

Cliff-breeding species (especially Kittiwake) on the east coast of England generally reared more chicks than on the east coast of Scotland, and showed a less marked reduction in success compared to 1989. Population trends of these species have generally been upward during 1986-90, with only slight increases or decreases seen in 1990. Tern populations on this coastline seem to have been declining slowly in recent years, and this continued for most species in 1990. Breeding success of terns was generally higher than in Scotland.

Off the west coast of Scotland, some reduction in breeding success of cliff-breeding species was seen compared to 1989, but this was not consistent between species or colonies. Population trends generally indicate stable, fluctuating or declining numbers. Tern success was generally low in 1990 (largely reflecting predation), though (for SW Scotland at least) better than in 1989 or on North Sea coasts of Scotland. Population trends for terns have been variable during 1986-90.

Cliff-breeding species in SW Britain/SE Ireland have generally shown stable or decreasing numbers during 1986-90. Some reversal of the general decrease for many species between 1988 and 1989 was seen in 1990. Breeding success of Kittiwakes and most terns remained low in 1990, but Roseate Terns at the large Rockabill colony continue to rear large numbers of chicks. Most tern populations in these southwestern regions are small, and have fluctuated markedly during 1986-90. Lesser Black-backed Gulls in south Wales reared very few chicks, as in 1989.

Where can more information be obtained?

Copies of the report on seabird numbers and breeding success in 1990, briefly summarised here, are available from P.M. Walsh, Seabirds Team, JNCC, 17 Rubislaw Terrace, Aberdeen, AB1 1XE at £4 (including postage). Contributing observers and organisations are fully acknowledged there. Details of methods used in seabird monitoring are also available on request, and we would welcome any offers of help or data.

References

Walsh, P.M., Sears, J. & Heubeck, M. (1991). *Seabird numbers and breeding success in 1990*. CSD. Rept. No. 1235. NCC.

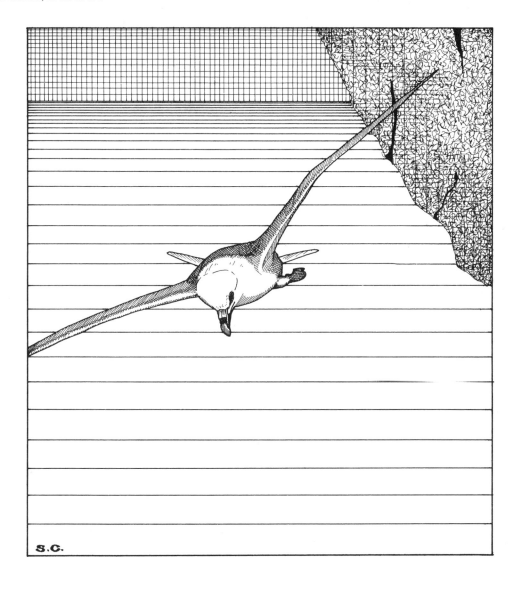

S.C.

Tern monitoring

Jane Sears & Adrian del Nevo

Research Department, RSPB

Summary

A large proportion of the British population of three tern species, Sandwich, Roseate and Little, is monitored each year, enabling the long-term trends in numbers of pairs and breeding success to be assessed. Sandwich Tern and Little Tern populations have remained relatively stable in recent years although there have been large changes within regions due to colony shifts. Roseate Terns have declined steeply since 1969 and are one of the most threatened bird species in Britain.

There is less comprehensive monitoring of Arctic Tern and Common Tern colonies but studies in Orkney, Shetland and other parts of Scotland have demonstrated problems of food shortage, predation and severe weather limiting their breeding success.

Background to monitoring

Britain has special responsibility for four of our regularly breeding tern species. Sandwich, Arctic and Little Terns all breed in internationally important numbers (i.e. more than 20% of the north-west European population) (Batten *et al.* 1990). Roseate Terns have declined dramatically since the 1960s and are now such scarce breeders that the British population may no longer qualify as internationally important.

We need to monitor populations and their breeding success over a number of years in order to detect significant changes. Terns have a habit of shifting colonies between years and it is therefore important to monitor a large number of sites each year rather than a few sample colonies. Regular monitoring of most Common Tern and Arctic Tern colonies poses quite a challenge due to their wide distribution in remote locations and their habit of shifting between sites. Roseate, Sandwich and Little Terns are easier to monitor since they occupy fewer colonies in more accessible locations. Unfortunately this accessibility is to the terns' disadvantage and most colonies require protection against human disturbance and mammalian predators.

Each year since Operation Seafarer's national

survey in 1969/70 (Cramp *et al.* 1974), tern colonies have been counted by many people, including reserve wardens and amateur recorders, and as part of scientific studies. The number of breeding pairs has usually been recorded by counting the maximum number of occupied nests during the mid-incubation to early nestling period. Productivity has been estimated by counting the number of young fledged for the whole colony and dividing by the number of breeding pairs (Walsh *et al.* 1990). The RSPB has collated these records into a comprehensive database for British terns. The following accounts examine the 1990 records in the context of long-term trends in numbers and breeding success.

Sandwich Tern

The British Sandwich Tern population has been comprehensively monitored since 1969 with over 90% of the total population counted each year, in 24 major colonies. After a 15% decline in numbers in 1989 there was little overall national change in 1990. The population has fluctuated between about 8000 and 13000 pairs during the last 20 years (Figure 1) but overall the population has been stable, at least in our sample colonies.

Regional totals varied, as some colonies gained

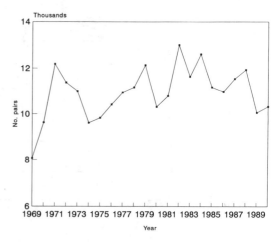

Figure 1. *Population trend of Sandwich Terns breeding in 24 major colonies in Britain, 1969-90.*

several hundred pairs and others lost them. Sandwich Terns have a history of shifting between colonies. This has been particularly apparent within the Norfolk population. Continuous records beginning in 1952 illustrate the exchanges between Scolt Head Island, Blakeney Point and, in a few years, Stiffkey. For the first time, in 1990, all 3000 Norfolk Sandwich Terns nested at Blakeney Point, making it the largest colony in Britain and Ireland.

The average productivity recorded at 16 colonies in 1990 was 0.79 chicks per pair; the same as the average annual productivity for 1969-90 (Sears & Walsh in prep). Two large colonies, at Blakeney Point (Norfolk) and Coquet Island (Northumberland), enjoyed good breeding success in 1990.

Roseate Tern

During 1990 the number of breeding pairs of Roseate Terns and their reproductive success were monitored at all European colonies (UK 8; Irish Republic 2; France 3; Portugal 28). It was a very poor year for Roseate Terns in Britain as only 109 pairs attempted to breed. Breeding success was around one chick per pair. All was not gloom and doom however, as there was clear evidence from sightings of ringed birds that Roseate Terns from some British colonies had shifted across the Irish Sea to breed on Rockabill Island in Dublin Bay. Breeding success at this isolated and well-protected spot was very good with an average of 1.5 chicks per pair.

Such shifts between breeding sites are a feature common to the species throughout its European range. Sometimes these movements take place over considerable distances and then in subsequent years birds may return to their 'original' colony.

The number of breeding Roseate Terns within Britain has undergone a steady decline since the late 1960s (Figure 2). Similar reductions have taken place throughout the European breeding range, particularly in Ireland. To investigate the reasons behind this decrease and to assess what can be done to reverse it, an international programme of research and conservation has been established and co-ordinated by the RSPB.

On the breeding grounds a number of problems have been identified, such as disturbance and predation. All British Roseate Tern colonies are now protected and wardened and detailed studies are underway to monitor factors which may influence breeding success.

Ringing studies have been invaluable in following Roseate Terns between colonies and in examining other aspects of their ecology. Ringing revealed the trapping for sport and food of Roseate and other terns in West Africa thus identifying a potential threat to their numbers and a possible explanation for their decline. Studies of the range and extent of tern trapping will show how seriously tern populations are affected by this activity.

Ringing and systematic observations have shown that all tern species spend around three months of the winter period in Ghana. However, the distribution of Roseate Terns (and other tern species) on leaving Ghana in November/December is completely unknown. Further research is required to identify the location of these birds and the factors liable to influence their survival from the time that they leave Ghana until they return to the breeding quarters in late April (the Azores) and late May (NW Europe).

Common Tern

The problems of tern monitoring are accentuated for Common Terns which breed at a large number of sites including inland ones, often in remote locations, move between colonies and get 'lumped' with Arctic Terns in some colony counts. As a result, coverage is incomplete and care has to be taken in interpreting population changes.

The indications are that there was little change in overall numbers in Britain between 1989 and 1990. The English and Welsh population has declined since 1986, particularly in East England. The colony at Scolt Head declined from 160 pairs in 1989 to 14 in 1990, largely as a result of increasing predation by foxes. Round the coast at

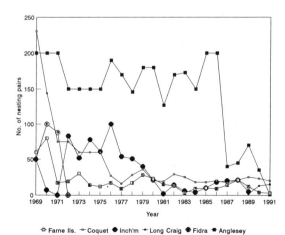

Figure 2. Roseate Tern numbers (pairs) at major colonies (those holding at least 20 pairs in at least one year in the period 1969-1990) in Britain during 1969-90.

Breydon Water in the Yare Estuary, the colony on artificial rafts grew by 30 pairs to a total of 129 pairs. English colonies raised an average of 0.5 chicks per pair. Three colonies were monitored in Wales and all failed completely; two due to gull predation and another for unknown reasons which caused a mass desertion during incubation.

There was relatively little change in the Scottish population. Breeding success in Scotland was higher than in 1989 but was still very low at 0.4 chicks per pair. Around half the Scottish colonies monitored in 1990 failed completely, many due to predation by mammals on the west coast and poor weather and gull predation elsewhere. There are concerns about the level of predation at some Scottish west coast colonies. The terns appear to be concentrating into fewer, larger colonies on the more remote off-shore islands, away from predators such as Mink. We need to ensure that these islands remain Mink-free.

Arctic Tern

In 1989 the RSPB organised a complete survey of Arctic Terns in Orkney and Shetland. This indicated that numbers had declined by 55% in Shetland and by 40% in Orkney since 1980 (Avery et al. in prep). A sample of colonies was resurveyed in 1990 and the indications were that the Shetland population had decreased by a further 35% since 1989 whilst numbers on Orkney remained stable. Elsewhere in Britain the available records suggested there had been no major changes between 1989 and 1990 at the larger colonies.

The major problem on Shetland has been a lack of food, causing widespread breeding failure, and 1990 was the seventh successive year of disastrous breeding; none of 300 monitored pairs fledged any young and only two are believed to have fledged from the whole of Shetland. Most colonies failed during incubation but a small number of chicks hatched. Most of these died within a few days during a period of bad weather.

Other factors caused breeding failure in Arctic Terns around the country. On Orkney the success was low due to severe weather at the time of hatching, combined with heavy predation by gulls and Hedgehogs. Bad weather and mammalian predators also caused problems in west Scottish colonies and all the Scottish east coast colonies fared badly. The more southerly colonies, in Northumberland and Wales, were generally more successful, although Herring Gull predation caused one large colony on Anglesey to fail completely.

More detailed monitoring of breeding success at Arctic Tern colonies is needed. High chick mortality in Arctic Terns can provide an early warning of food shortages that may also affect other seabird species.

Little Tern

In recent years over half the estimated British population of 2400 pairs of Little Terns (Lloyd et al. 1991) has been counted each year. At 53 colonies counted in both 1989 and 1990 the number of pairs decreased by 4% from 1611 pairs to 1552, continuing the slight decline recorded in 1989. To put this into perspective, we need to look at the long-term population trend. Most colony records are incomplete and terns move between colonies, so rates of change in numbers have been estimated by comparing colonies counted in consecutive years. Such chain indices have been calculated using records from 87 colonies counted more than once between 1969 and 1989 (Sears & Avery in prep.). They indicate that the Little Tern population in Britain increased during the mid 1970s but has remained relatively stable since 1977 although with some fluctuations in recent years.

It is difficult to know what caused the population increase in the 1970s. It coincided with the introduction of many Little Tern protection schemes which reduced recreational disturbance. The schemes involve a variety of measures ranging from signs and fences through to full-time wardening. One way to evaluate these schemes is to see if they cause an increase in breeding success.

The average productivity in 1990 of 53 colonies in Britain and Ireland was 0.40 young per pair, below the average annual productivity of 0.56 for 1969-89 (Sears & Avery in press). Low breeding success often causes concern, but we need to look at the long-term trends to assess how significant it is. Average productivity has fluctuated widely over the last 20 years (Figure 3), ranging between 0.18 and 0.88 young fledged per pair. There is no obvious relationship between the annual fluctuations and the population trend. Neither is there any indication that productivity increased at the time the protection schemes were introduced. Indeed the records from individual colonies continue to show large fluctuations in breeding success even after the introduction of full-time wardening. Wardening usually reduces human disturbance but it is difficult to prevent failure due to flooding or predation and in some years even wardened colonies fail to produce any young.

The terns' usual strategy appears to be to move to another colony if the present site becomes unsuitable. Disturbance has limited the number of

117

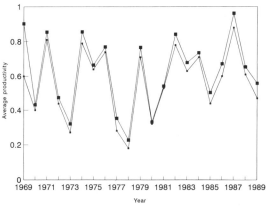

Figure 3. *Average annual productivity, recorded as number of young per pair, of Little Tern colonies in 1969-89. Large symbol = excluding colonies which failed to fledge any young, small symbol = including colonies which failed to fledge any young.*

available sites and in some areas Little Terns are concentrated into a few protected colonies. One such site is on the beach at Great Yarmouth, where the colony expanded from nine pairs in 1982 to 201 pairs in 1990 and was the largest colony in Britain in both 1989 and 1990. It was first wardened in 1986 and enjoyed high breeding success up to 1988 but then suffered predation by Kestrels in 1989. There were more predators in 1990 as the Kestrels were joined by a Hedgehog and Cats and the 201 pairs only fledged 15 chicks.

There is concern that the concentration of so many Little Terns at one site is making life very easy for the predators and causing a large part of the British Little Tern population to fail. Other large colonies were also predated in 1990. For example, Foxes prevented the colony of 145 pairs at Langstone Harbour from fledging any young. There have been many attempts to control predation but with little success. It is therefore important that we ensure that Little Terns have suitable alter-

native sites to move to when predators make the birds' present sites temporarily unsuitable.

Where can more information be obtained?

Reports summarising the annual population and productivity data for all five tern species are presented with other seabird records in joint JNCC/RSPB/SOTEAG (Shetland Oil Terminal Environmental Advisory Group) annual reports on seabird numbers and breeding success (Walsh *et al.* 1990, 1991). Copies are available from P.M. Walsh, Seabirds Team, JNCC, 17 Rubislaw Terrace, Aberdeen AB1 1XE at £4 (including postage). The RSPB would welcome any offers of help or data and can provide details of methods on request. Anyone wishing to use original data presented here should first contact Jane Sears.

References

Avery, M.I., Burges, D., Dymond, N.J., Mellor, M., & Ellis, P.M. (in prep). The status of Arctic Terns, *Sterna paradisaea*, in Orkney and Shetland in 1989.

Batten, L.A., Bibby, C.J., Clement, P., Elliot, G.D. & Porter, R.F. (1990). *Red data birds in Britain: action for rare, threatened and important species*. T. & A.D. Poyser, London.

Cramp, S., Bourne, W.R.P., & Saunders, D. (1974). *The seabirds of Britain and Ireland*. London, Collins.

Lloyd, C., Tasker, M.L. & Partridge, K. (1991). *The status of seabirds in Britain and Ireland*. London, Poyser.

Sears, J. & Avery, M.I. (in prep). Population and productivity trends of Little Terns (*Sterna albifrons*) in Britain, 1969-89.

Sears, J. & Walsh, P. (in prep). Population and productivity trends of Sandwich Terns (*Sterna sandvicensis*) in Britain and Ireland, 1969-90.

Walsh, P.M., Avery, M.I. & Heubeck, M. (1990). *Seabird numbers and breeding success in 1989*. Nature Conservancy Council CSD Report No. 1071.

Walsh, P.M., Sears, J. & Heubeck, M. (1991). *Seabird numbers and breeding success in 1990*. Nature Conservancy Council CSD Report No. 1235.

Moorland bird surveys in 1990

Andrew F Brown & Richard A Stillman

Moorland Bird Study, JNCC

As part of its 1990 programme of research and survey, NCC's Moorland Bird Study conducted two surveys covering very large moorland areas in England and in Scotland.

South-west Scotland

In conjunction with NCC's South-west Scotland Region, 435 km^2 of the remaining unafforested moorland in Dumfries & Galloway and south Strathclyde were surveyed. The major aim was to evaluate moorland breeding birds as part of NCC's contribution to the Regional Indicative Forest Strategies for the two Regions (Galbraith & Bates 1991). The survey generally confirmed knowledge of the area (assessed principally using raptor data) but new information allowed conservation recommendations to be made. A further survey is planned to assess the extent of an area found to be particularly important.

South Pennines

In England, we conducted a survey of 725 km^2 of moorland in the south Pennines: this was the entire extent of unenclosed moorland in the south Pennines (between Skipton (Yorkshire) in the north and Leek (Staffordshire) in the south).

Taking place between 12 April and the 28 June, the survey was largely NCC-funded, but received considerable additional funding from Yorkshire Water, North-West Water, Severn-Trent Water and Lancashire County Council. Ten surveyors visited each part of the moors twice during the season, once in the first half and once in the second, spending equal amounts of time in each area and using standard census methods. The report (Brown & Shepherd 1991) provides the first comprehensive review of the important breeding birds of these moors.

Data were collected and mapped for some 30 breeding or important non-breeding species. The maps, at various scales, have helped us evaluate the extent and distribution of the moorland birds here. As an example, Figure 1 shows the distribution of breeding Golden Plover.

There is no doubt as to the great regional, national and international importance of this area.

The moors support more than 1% of the British breeding populations of no less than eight species. In addition the area is the stronghold of the southernmost English populations of breeding Merlin, Red Grouse, Golden Plover, Dunlin, Twite, and Short-Eared Owl (only a few Red Grouse, Golden Plover and Dunlin nest on Dartmoor and Merlin are scarce or irregular breeders any further south). Furthermore, together with scattered populations of Golden Plover in Ireland, 12 pairs on Dartmoor and the rapidly declining Welsh population, the south Pennines is at the south-western edge of the world range of this species. Twite is similarly at the edge of its range here. It is isolated from Twite breeding further north in Britain, which is in itself separate from others breeding in coastal Scandinavia. This is quite disjunct from the next and only other breeding population stretching across Asia from Turkey to China.

With a number of species at the edge of their range and at high density or high overall numbers, protection of the breeding bird assemblage is critical if traditional ranges of these species are to be maintained. Populations at the fringe of their ranges may be particularly responsive to environmental change and close monitoring of the south Pennine populations may well offer a sensitive indicator.

Numbers and trends

The south Pennines have suffered greatly from the effects of industrial pollution, outdoor recreation on a huge scale, overgrazing and other poor moorland management. These impacts are obvious on the vegetation, where wide-scale footpath erosion, conversion of heather moor to acid grassland and the almost total loss of the bog-forming *Sphagnum* mosses can clearly be blamed on man. Remarkably, however, there is clear evidence of rapidly increasing Merlin and Curlew populations, a small increase in Peregrines, no evidence of any significant change in the distributions of Red Grouse, Golden Plover and Twite, and no significant change in numbers of breeding Golden Plover over approximately the last 20 years. Yalden (1974), using methods similar to our own, estimated 380-400 breeding pairs of Golden Plover in the

Peak District National Park in 1970-73, distributed across 214 one-kilometre squares of moorland. In 1990 we estimated the same population as 456 pairs in 242 one-kilometre squares. The eastern moors hold much of this increased population and we know also from other information that numbers have increased here during this period.

Such good news should not allow us to be complacent about the protection afforded our upland breeding birds. In the context of major Scottish losses of Golden Plover and many other moorland breeding species in the same period (notably for example in our 1990 south-west Scotland study area), the adequate protection and management of the south Pennine moorlands is a priority. The greater part of the area is not protected as SSSI.

Data gathered during 1990, coupled with the invaluable locational information provided in confidence by groups and individuals monitoring breeding raptors, have allowed us to make scientifically-based and justified recommendations to further protect the breeding birds of the south Pennine moors. Amongst these measures is the recommendation that a significant part of the area should be designated as the South Pennine Moors Special Protection Area under the terms of the EC Directive on the Conservation of Wild Birds.

References

Brown, A.F. & Shepherd, K.B. (1991). *Breeding birds of the south Pennine Moors*. JNCC Res. Rept 7.

Galbraith, C.A. & Bates, M. (1991). Regional Forestry Strategies and bird conservation. In: Stroud, D.A. & Glue, D (Eds): *Britain's Birds in 1989/90: the conservation and monitoring review*. Pp. 23–24. BTO/NCC, Thetford.

Yalden, D.W. (1974). The status of Golden Plover (*Pluvialis apricaria*) and Dunlin (*Charadrius alpina*) in the Peak District. *Naturalist* 922, 89-102.

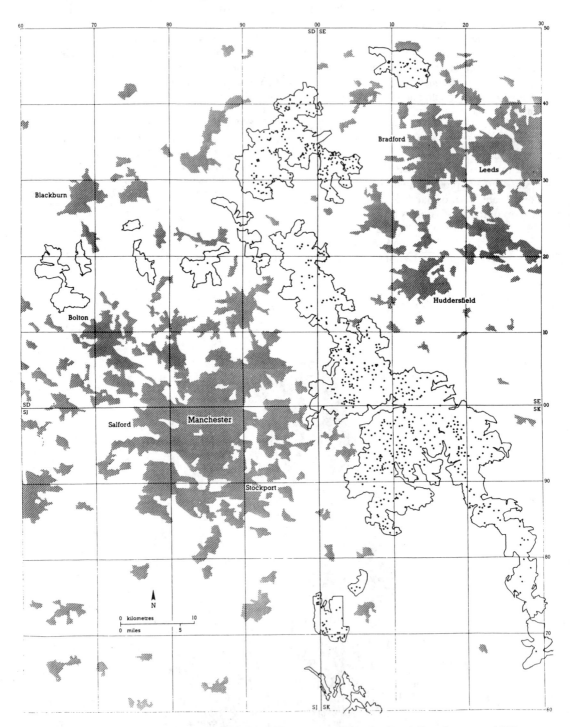

Figure 1: *Distribution of breeding pairs of Golden Plover recorded in the South Pennines area 1990.*

Studies of moorland birds: Merlin and Golden Plover

Humphrey Q P Crick

Nest Records Unit, BTO

Introduction

Moorland areas hold significant populations of birds of conservation interest and there is widespread concern over the future viability of these populations because of large-scale changes in land-use including losses of moorland to forestry, conversion of heather into grassland, decreases in grouse management interests and increasing levels of other forms of recreational use (Ratcliffe 1990).

This report describes the long-term trends in breeding success of two moorland bird species of conservation interest: the Merlin and the Golden Plover. It is based upon analysis of the historical records collected by the BTO's Nest Record Scheme over approximately fifty years. Contributors to the Scheme complete nest record cards to provide both details of a nest's location and habitat and a record of its contents at each visit made by the observer. The information is computerised and estimates of laying date, clutch size and nest survival rates are calculated.

Is the Merlin in decline?

The Merlin is the smallest falcon breeding in Europe. It is monogamous and nests on traditional home ranges, usually in old crow's nests in trees or on rocky crags. In Britain an unusually high proportion of Merlins nest on the ground, particularly in heather or bracken. During the breeding season their main prey comprises small passerines such as Meadow Pipit, Skylark and Wheatear (Cramp & Simmons 1980).

The Merlin population has been in apparent gradual decline throughout the twentieth century in Britain. This decline became more marked in the 1950s and 60s, coincident with widespread use of organochlorine pesticides (Newton & Haas 1988). Such pesticides affected most raptor populations in Britain, either by direct poisoning or through causing egg shell thinning and breakage. After the progressive withdrawal of organochlorine pesticides in the 1970s and 80s, populations of other birds of prey, such as Sparrowhawk or Peregrine, have sig-

nificantly recovered, but Merlins have not (Bibby & Nattrass 1986).

The only nationwide population census of Merlins was undertaken in 1983-84 and provided an estimate of 550 to 650 pairs (Bibby & Nattrass 1986). Since that survey, populations have further declined and there is a general concern for the conservation of this species in Britain (Batten *et al.* 1990), although some recovery is apparent from recent clutches showing the Merlins increasing use of old crow nests in the edge of conifer plantations (Parr 1991, Little & Davison 1992).

Although there have been a number of detailed long-term breeding studies in localised areas of Britain, the overall trends of breeding productivity are not readily apparent. The 1,400 nest histories collected by the BTO Nest Record Scheme from 1937-89 allow just such a national overview.

Is there a regional divide?

Clutch size could be calculated for 615 nests and 85% of birds laid four or five eggs (mean = 4.16). There were no discernable differences in clutch size between regions or habitats nor any trends through time.

The maximum brood size of successful nests is a measure of partial losses from nests during incubation and hatching, given that clutch size varies

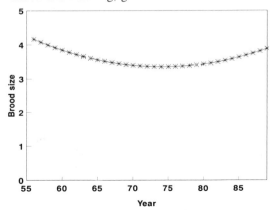

Figure 1. *Changes in successful Merlin brood size.*

so little. 61% of nests produce four or five nestlings (mean = 3.63, N = 280). Following the introduction of organochlorine pesticides in 1947 there was a decline in brood size until the early 1970s and then a recovery (Figure 1). However, when the data are broken down by regions, it is apparent that, while there have been increases in productivity since the early 1970s in Scotland and the Midlands, productivity in north England and Wales has declined gradually.

The causes of these changes need to be investigated by comparative studies of breeding Merlins in mainland Scotland and in northern England and Wales. It is possible that the changes could be associated with regional differences in the time-course of exposure to DDT; one would need to investigate birds on their wintering areas also, to examine this. Breeding studies should concentrate on the possible impacts of changes in habitat quality. There has been a loss of the Merlin's favoured habitat (heather moors) due to conversion into sheep pasture (Newton *et al.* 1986, Meek 1988) or conifer plantation (Bibby & Nattrass 1986), although the latter need not be detrimental (Parr 1991, Little & Davison 1992). Decreases in predator control (especially of foxes) with a decline in game-keeping interests (Haworth & Fielding 1988) and increasing levels of disturbance from recreational walking may be further factors that could affect nesting success.

Finally, it will be important to increase the integration of monitoring efforts by volunteers and professional ornithologists across the country (e.g. Crick *et al.* 1990). This would ensure that any general worsening of the current situation would be noticed as early as possible.

Golden Plover

The Golden Plover is the characteristic upland bird of flat, gently sloping heather and grass moorland and bog. The British and Irish breeding populations are considered distinct and relatively isolated from the populations of Scandinavian birds that visit in winter. Concern has been expressed that the Golden Plover population in Britain has declined, with numbers falling from 30,000 pairs in the early 1970s (Ratcliffe 1976) to 23,000 pairs in the late 1980s (Marchant *et al.* 1990). Indeed, there is anecdotal evidence for a general decline of its southern populations throughout Europe (Ratcliffe 1976, 1990).

There have been very few detailed studies of Golden Plovers in Britain and they provide evidence and reasons only for local population declines due, for example, to increasing populations of egg predators (Parr 1989) and to increasing disturbance from recreational walkers (Yalden & Yalden 1989). An analysis of the 669 nest record cards collected by the BTO over the period 1943-89 allows the examination of trends in breeding performance over the years and a comparison of incubation and hatching success among major regions and habitats. Success cannot be followed beyond hatching because the young disperse from the nest soon after hatching and are very cryptic.

Heather is best

Golden Plovers nesting on heather moorland and bog lay, on average, 11 days earlier than those on grass moorland. Furthermore, clutch size is slightly larger on heather than on grass. This could be due to fewer early partial egg-losses (before observers found the nests) or to a real difference in the numbers of eggs laid. Grassland may be a less productive habitat generally than heather moor and bog for Golden Plovers. Egg laying is energetically costly for them: they have one of the largest eggs of the Charadriidae at 16.2% of the female's weight and a clutch of four eggs can weigh up to 73% of the female's weight (compared to 46% for the Lapwing) (Nethersole-Thompson & Nethersole-Thompson 1986). Prior to egg-laying, females spend 60-90% of their time feeding, which compares with 20% at later stages of the nesting cycle (Byrkjedal 1985). The delay in laying shown by Golden Plovers on grassland may be due to poorer food supplies, perhaps also explaining why they occur at lower densities there than on heather and bog (Ratcliffe 1976).

Although nest failure rates have not changed over the years for Golden Plovers nesting on heather moorland and bog, they have increased significantly in north-west England and Wales on grass moorland in the 1980s (Crick 1992). This may be due to increased stocking rates of sheep on upland grass in response to economic factors. Stocking rates have been increasing faster in these areas than in Scotland, despite being already up to three times higher (Crick 1992). Nesting Lapwings have suffered increasingly from trampling and desertion due to sheep on upland areas (Shrubb 1990) and it is possible that Golden Plovers have been similarly affected. It is also possible that this result was the effect of either increased recreational pressure (although similar effects might have been expected on heather moors) or increased corvid predation, although populations of crows levelled off in the 1980s after big increases in the previous two decades, at least in farmland and woodland; moorland habitats have not been censused (Marchant *et al.* 1990). The effect of altitude could not be investigated because samples were too small, although no effect of altitude was found on laying date, probably because very few truly montane nests were recorded. Further detailed work is needed to discover the reasons for regional and habitat differences in nesting success.

One of the main threats to Golden Plover populations is that of afforestation of moorland and bog (Ratcliffe 1990). In the flow country of Sutherland and Caithness, forestry has already caused the loss of 19% of Golden Plovers (Stroud *et al.* 1987). It is not just the loss of breeding habitat but also the avoidance of moorland near plantations that might affect Golden Plover populations (Thompson *et al.* 1988, but see Avery 1989).

If forestry tends to occur preferentially on heather moors and bog, and if heather moor continues to be turned into grassland, then Golden Plovers may have to depend increasingly on the less-productive grass moors. If these areas are subject to increasing stocking rates and the remaining heather moors are subject to more recreational disturbance, the national population of Golden Plovers may be expected to decline yet further as the average breeding success declines.

References

Avery, M.I. (1989). Effects of upland afforestation on some birds of the adjacent moorlands. *J.Appl.Ecol.* 26, 957–966.

Batten, L.A., Bibby, C.J., Clement, P., Elliott, G.D. & Porter, R.F. (1990). *Red Data Birds in Britain: action for rare, threatened and important species.* T. & A.D. Poyser, Calton.

Bibby, C.J. & Nattrass, M. (1986). Breeding status of the Merlin in Britain. *British Birds* 79, 170-185.

Byrkjedal, I. (1985). Time-activity budget for breeding Greater Golden Plovers in Norwegian Mountains. *Wilson Bull.* 97, 486-501.

Cramp, S. & Simmons, K.E.L. (1980). *Handbook of the birds of Europe, the Middle East and North Africa.* Vol 2: Hawks to Bustards. Oxford University Press, Oxford.

Crick, H.Q.P. (1992). *Trends in the breeding performance of Golden Plover in Britain.* BTO Research Report No.76. BTO, Thetford.

Crick, H.Q.P, Baillie, S.R. & Percival, S.M. (1990). *A review of raptor population monitoring.* BTO Research Report No. 49. BTO, Tring.

Haworth, P.F. & Fielding, A. (1988). Conservation and management implications of habitat selection in the Merlin *Falco columbarius* L. in the South Pennines, UK. *Biol. Conserv.* 46, 247-260.

Little, B. & Davison, M. (1992). Merlins *Falco columbarius* using crow nests in Kielder Forest, Northumberland. *Bird Study* 39, 13-16.

Marchant, J.H., Hudson, R.H., Carter, S.P. & Whittington, P.A. (1990). *Population Trends in British Breeding Birds.* BTO, Tring.

Meek, E.R. (1988). The breeding ecology and decline of the Merlin *Falco columbarius* in Orkney. *Bird Study* 39, 209-218.

Nethersole-Thompson, D. & Nethersole-Thompson, M. (1986). *Waders: Their breeding haunts.* T. & A.D. Poyser, Calton.

Newton, I. & Haas, M.B. (1988). Pollutants in Merlin eggs and their effects on breeding. *British Birds* 81, 258-269.

Newton, I., Meek, E.R., & Little, B. (1986). Population and breeding of Northumbrian Merlins. *British Birds* 79, 155-170.

Parr, R. (1989). *Demographic effects of nest predation on Golden Plovers and other waders.* NCC, CSD Report No. 1026.

Parr, S.J. (1991). Occupation of new conifer plantations by Merlins in Wales. *Bird Study* 38, 103-111.

Ratcliffe, D.A. (1976). Observations on the breeding of the Golden Plover in Great Britain. *Bird Study* 23, 63-116.

Ratcliffe, D.A. (1990). *Bird Life of Mountain and Upland.* University Press, Cambridge.

Shrubb, M. (1990). Effects of agricultural change on nesting Lapwings *Vanellus vanellus* in England and Wales. *Bird Study* 37, 115-127.

Stroud, D.A., Reed, T.M., Pienkowski, M.W. & Lindsay, R.A. (1987). *Birds, bogs and forestry.* NCC, Peterborough.

Thompson, D.B.A., Stroud, D.A. & Pienkowski, M.W. (1988). Afforestation and upland birds: In: Usher M.B. & Thompson, D.B.A. (Eds.) *Ecological change in the Uplands.* Pp. 237–260. Blackwell Scientific Publications, Oxford.

Yalden, D.W. & Yalden, P.E. (1989). The sensitivity of breeding Golden Plovers *Pluvialis apricaria* to human intruders. *Bird Study* 36, 49-55.

Black Grouse census and monitoring

John T Cayford

Research Department, RSPB[1]

Summary

Recent surveys suggest that there are less than 1,000 male Black Grouse in England and Wales. Numbers in Scotland are higher but unknown. Thus the status of the species is a matter of concern. Monitoring its populations is of great importance since it provides a yardstick against which habitat changes (natural or induced) and their effects can be measured. In Wales, the RSPB has set up a monitoring programme which combines annual and bi-annual counts in a restricted part of the species' range with full census every 6 years. The RSPB is currently working with the Forestry Commission (FC) in Wales to undertake management in forests which should favour Black Grouse.

Introduction

The Black Grouse is a large bird, best known for the elaborate early morning displays of males at traditional leks. It typically favours habitats transitional between moorland or heath and forest. Widely distributed throughout continental Europe and Siberia, its numbers are declining over much of this range with the exception of northern Sweden and Finland.

In Britain, Black Grouse now occur in the uplands of north Wales, the moorlands and rough grazings of northern England and the Peak District, but only in Scotland are they numerous over large areas. At the turn of the century the species was more widespread (Gladstone 1924). Changes in agricultural practice and land use have been implicated in its decline. The ploughing of lowland heaths, drainage of mires, increased levels of grazing and the abandonment of traditional farming practices in the uplands have probably all had an effect. Concern over its status has led to its inclusion in the British 'Red Data Book' (Batten *et al.* 1991) and to comprehensive surveys in England and Wales.

Counting Black Grouse

Black Grouse are difficult birds to census: they occur at low densities often in remote, upland areas, the sexes vary in their conspicuousness and birds do not always flush easily. The two main census methods are to count displaying males in spring or to walk transects with dogs and count the number of birds seen. Both methods have been used to estimate the densities, range and numbers of black grouse in Wales, Scotland, northern England and the Peak District.

Male Black Grouse gather on traditional lek sites in spring to display and their distinctive calls can be heard over several kilometres. Counting displaying males may therefore be the easiest census method, but there is potentially a source of error in population estimates derived from such counts because not all birds display on traditional leks. The age and social status of males influences attendance at leks, with juveniles tending to display solitarily. The problem is that solitary displaying males tend not to be consistent in their choice of display site, but these birds can, in some years, form a large part of the male Black Grouse population. Therefore, in the absence of full coverage, lek counts may provide imperfect evidence of overall numbers or population change. Another potential source of bias is that the number of males attending individual leks varies depending on the time of day and season. Arrival of birds on leks gets progressively earlier with the onset of spring and attendance at the lek is shorter later in the season (Figure 1). The highest counts are obtained in April and early May, one hour either side of sunrise (Cayford & Walker 1991). Transects with dogs can provide accurate indices of abundance and are therefore potentially useful for comparing different sites or monitoring changes within sites over time but they cannot give a total population estimate.

Recent surveys of Black Grouse

It is only in the last five years that conservation groups have attempted comprehensive surveys of Black Grouse in Wales, northern England and

1. Current address: Estuaries Unit, BTO

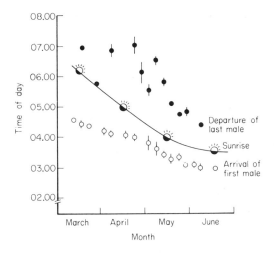

Figure 1. Seasonal changes in the timing of lek attendance by male Black Grouse. These data collected in Wales provided valuable information on the behaviour of birds which was used to establish standardised counting procedures. (Figure reproduced from Cayford & Walker 1991).

parts of Scotland. As a result, reliable data on the distribution and numbers of this important species now exist for most of England and Wales, but more information is needed for the main stronghold in Scotland.

Black Grouse were surveyed in Wales by the RSPB in 1986 following pilot questionnaire work in 1985 which collected information from foresters, shooting estates and county bird reports (Grove *et al.* 1988). The purpose of this work was to describe the distribution and numbers of Black Grouse throughout Wales, an objective never previously attempted. Leks were visited at dawn in April and May and displaying males counted. A total of 91 leks were located, including 41 solitary displaying males. The two northern counties of Gwynedd and Clwyd held most of the population which was estimated at between 264 and 300 males. The results of this extensive survey confirmed a marked retraction in range from that described by Sharrock (1976) in the 1968-1972 Breeding Atlas (Figure 2). The distribution of leks showed that the majority of Black Grouse in Wales were associated with young conifer plantations, particularly those bordering moorland. Research carried out by the RSPB and funded by the Forestry Commission established the critical habitat requirements of Black Grouse in these plantations (Cayford 1991). Both organisations are now collaborating to implement management which

should favour the species.

Members of the Tyneside Bird Club, Durham Bird Club and FC staff carried out a survey of Black Grouse leks in Durham, Northumberland and Cumbria in the springs of 1987 and 1988. As in Wales, the survey was the first of its kind in the region. In 1987, 43 leks were located and 207 males counted. The area covered was extended in 1988 and the total population of males estimated at 440 on 91 leks (Garson & Starling 1990). The survey showed considerable variations in density with the majority of the population between the Tees valley in the south and the south Tyne Valley in the north. Most of the leks occurred where sheepwalk and/or open coniferous forest were the major habitats.

The Game Conservancy obtained estimates of Black Grouse densities on 16 shooting estates throughout Scotland and northern England between early April and mid-May 1989. Transects were walked with pointing dogs and the number of birds flushed either side of the observer were counted and converted to birds seen per km^2 (Baines 1990). Highest densities were found in Tayside with eight birds flushed/km^2 and the lowest densities of one bird/km^2 were recorded for north and west Scotland.

The most recent counts of Black Grouse in the Peak District suggest that this isolated population is at risk of extinction. Counts in 1985 estimated there were as few as 26 males remaining and, more significantly, this figure represents a 64% reduction in the population over a period of 13 years.

Monitoring Black Grouse populations in Wales

Extensive surveys like that in Wales in 1986 cannot realistically be repeated on a frequent basis. In view of this, the RSPB has set up a 3-tiered monitoring programme for Black Grouse in Wales which includes national survey and local census. The original extensive survey which aims to locate every male is to be repeated every 6 years, with the next in spring 1992. In addition, the important "core" area (see Figure 2) which holds most of the population in the Berwyns, is surveyed every other year by RSPB staff and volunteers. All known lek sites are visited at least once between late April and early May, counts are made one hour either side of sunrise and every effort is made to locate all solitary displaying males in the area. These biannual counts are carefully standardised so that these data can provide a reliable index of population change in the highest density area of the birds'

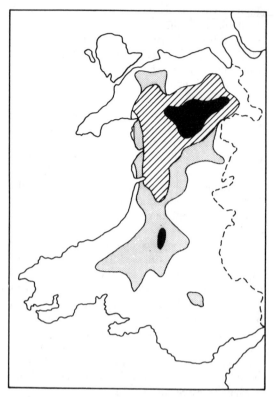

Figure 2. *Distribution of Black Grouse in Wales. Black (core area) = area sampled in 1988 corresponding to the distribution of leks with four or more males in 1986. Hatched area = distribution of leks with two to three males and solitary display sites in 1986. Stippled = distribution of Black grouse in Wales in 1968-1972. (Figure reproduced from Cayford & Walker 1991).*

current range. Finally, annual surveys are conducted by FC rangers in selected forestry blocks in an attempt to correlate changes in numbers with conservation initiatives.

In May 1988, 45 of the 91 leks recorded in 1986 were re-surveyed as part of the bi-annual monitoring programme. The results showed that 29% of leks had more males in 1988, 47% had fewer males and 24% were unchanged. Overall, 148 males were counted on the 45 sites and 15 males were located opportunistically, representing an overall increase of 4% on the 1986 total. The data suggest that the population of Black Grouse in this important area in north Wales has probably not declined since 1986. Interestingly, forest display sites had fared worse than those on moorland and it was suggested by Cayford & Walker (1991) that this could be related to the very dynamic nature of forest habitats, or more likely, high den-

sities of grouse predators in young plantations.

Where can more information be found?

Further information on census methods for Black Grouse and the results of recent counts in Wales can be found in Cayford & Walker (1991). Details of management for Black Grouse in forests is summarised in a FC Bulletin shortly to be published by HMSO titled: Black Grouse and Forestry: Habitat Requirements and Management by J.T. Cayford.

References

Baines, D. (1990). The ecology and conservation of black grouse in Scotland and Northern England. In: Lumeij, J. T. & Hoogevegen, Y.R. (Eds.) *The future of wild galliformes in the Netherlands.* pp 106-118.

Batten, L.A., Bibby, C.J., Clement, P., Elliot, G.D. & Porter, R.F. (1991). *Red Data Birds in Britain; action for rare, threatened and important species.* T. & A.D. Poyser, London.

Cayford, J.T. (1991). The distribution and habitat preferences of black grouse, *Tetrao tetrix* in commercial forests in Wales: Conservation and management implications. In: Myberget, S. (Ed.) *Transactions of the XIXth International Union of Game Biologists Congress.* Vol.2 pp 435-447.

Cayford, J.T. (in press). *Black Grouse and Forestry: Habitat Requirements and Management.* Forestry Commission Bulletin. HMSO Publications.

Cayford, J.T. & Walker, F. (1991). Counts of male Black Grouse *Tetrao tetrix* in North Wales. *Bird Study* 38, 80-86.

Garson, P.J. & Starling, A.E. (1990). Explaining the present distribution of Black Grouse in North-east England. In: Lumeij, J. T. & Hoogeveen, Y.R. (Eds.) *The future of wild galliformes in the Netherlands.* pp 97-105.

Gladstone, H.S. (1924). The distribution of Black Grouse in Great Britain. *British Birds*, 18, 66-68.

Grove, S.J., Hope Jones, P., Malkinson, A.R., Thomas, D.H. & Williams, I. (1988). Black Grouse in Wales, spring 1986. *British Birds* 81, 2-9.

Sharrock, J.T.R. (1976). *The Atlas of breeding birds in Britain and Ireland.* T. & A.D. Poyser, Berkhamsted.

The breeding performance of Black-throated Divers in Scotland, 1983-1991

Roger Broad[1], Colin Crooke[2], Greg P Mudge[3], Alison Rothwell[2] & Ron Summers[2]

[1] *South and West of Scotland Office, RSPB*

[2] *North Scotland Office, RSPB*

[3] *Vertebrate Ecology and Conservation Branch, JNCC*

The breeding success of Black-throated Divers was monitored annually from 1983-1991 in the Highland Region of Scotland and for fewer years in Tayside, Central, Strathclyde and the Western Isles. In the Western Isles, 43-55% of pairs raised young and average production per pair was 0.83 young. By contrast, an average of only 23% of pairs raised young on mainland Scotland and their average production was 0.25 young. In an attempt to increase breeding success on the mainland, floating artifical islands were provided for divers on lochs where there has been a history of egg loss through flooding. Productivity was 0.65-0.73 young per pair when divers bred on these rafts.

The need for monitoring

The Black-throated Diver has a British population of only 150-160 territorial pairs, occurring mainly on the larger lochs of the Scottish Highlands (Campbell & Talbot 1987). There is evidence from surveys (Mudge *et al.* 1991) that the population has declined in some areas. It has been suggested (Nilsson 1977) that productivity needs to be 0.4-0.5 young per pair per year to maintain numbers. This value is close to some productivity levels for Black-throated Divers in Scandinavia but higher than for Scottish birds (Campbell & Talbot 1987).

In order to monitor breeding success of this important bird, a variable number of lochs where breeding was regular was surveyed each year, coverage depending on manpower. In the Highland Region between 27 and 65 lochs were surveyed each year from 1983 to 1991. In Strathclyde, Central and Tayside eight to 15 lochs were surveyed annually between 1986 and 1991 and in the Western Isles 11 to 16 lochs were covered in 1989-1991.

Territories were visited in May and/or June to check for occupancy (Campbell & Talbot 1987).

Some territories encompassed more than one loch, thus requiring surveys of neighbouring lochs. Additional visits were made in late July/early August to count the number of young raised. Although some chicks were not yet fully grown by this time it was assumed that they would survive to fledge.

Regional differences in productivity

In the Highland Region an average of nearly 23% of pairs using natural nest sites (as distinct from rafts - see below) raised at least one young. There were significant differences between years but no trend in the success rate over the whole period (Figure 1). Productivity averaged 0.25 young per pair and only 12 (11.2%) pairs reared two chicks

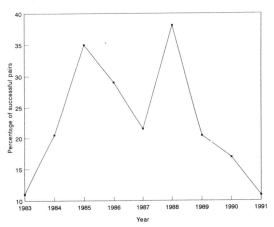

Figure 1. *The percentage of successfully breeding Black-throated Divers on natural sites on Highland lochs. There was a significant difference between years ($X^2_8 = 20.7$, P = 0.008) but no time trend in the data ($X^2_1 = 0.4$, n.s.; tested for a linear trend within the contigency table, Everitt 1977)*

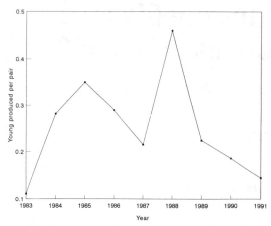

Figure 2. *The number of young produced per pair by Black-throated Divers on natural sites on Highland lochs.*

(Figure 2).

Tayside, Central and Strathclyde have fewer Black-throated Divers. No differences were found between years, partly because the sample sizes were small. On average, 25.4% of pairs bred successfully and 0.28 young were reared per pair. Two pairs (11.8%) produced broods of two.

The breeding success in the Western Isles was better than on mainland Scotland. Between 1989 and 1991, 43%, 50% and 55% of pairs were successful, with average productivity of 0.83 chicks per pair. There was a much greater frequency of broods of two than on the mainland (Table 1).

Table 1. Brood sizes of Black-throated Divers on the Scottish mainland and Western Isles.

	Broodsize		
	1	**2**	**Sample size**
Mainland	35 (89.7%)	4 (10.3%)	39
Western Isles	6 (30.0%)	14 (70.0%)	20

Are the divers maintaining their numbers?

Breeding success on the Scottish mainland was below the level (0.4-0.5 fledged young per pair) assumed necessary for the population to be self-sustaining (Nilsson 1977). This figure, based on work in Scandinavia, is probably an over-estimate as it was based on a minimum adult survival rate calculated from ringing recoveries and ring loss would cause an under-estimate of survival which was not taken into account. Some Scandinavian

studies have shown production levels around 0.4-0.5: in Finland and south-west Sweden average production was 0.41 and 0.4 young per pair respectively (Lehtonen 1970, Eriksson 1987). Other studies in Sweden show low productivity (0.04, Anderson and Anderson 1980; 0.24, Lindberg 1968). Heavy distubance by people in one area reduced production to 0.08 but this increased to 0.38 after the establishment of sanctuaries (Gotmark *et al.* 1989).

Divers on the Western Isles had over twice the productivity of those on the Scottish mainland. Conceivably this could help to offset, through immigration, any decline in the mainland populations. However, until we have an accurate assessmemnt of the adult survival rate we cannot tell if production on the mainland is inadequate.

Success with artificial sites

The main causes of breeding failure are flooding of nests after heavy rain and predation on eggs (Campbell 1988, Campbell & Mudge 1989). Building on the pioneering work of David Merrie, who worked mainly with Red-throated Divers in Argyll (Merrie 1979), in an attempt to reduce losses to flooding, floating islands were set in breeding lochs by the RSPB and the Forestry Commission, from 1987 onwards. Sites with a history of nest flooding were selected. These 2 x 3 m rafts were made from three blocks of polystyrene surrounded by a wooden frame and wire netting to bind the structure together. The edges were chamfered to give a slope of about 45°. Rafts were turfed to make them resemble natural islands and anchored in position with concrete blocks close to previous natural nest sites to increase the likelihood of use. Storms and ice can damage the rafts in winter so vulnerable rafts were towed to sheltered inlets after each breeding season. Although the rafts have been provided for only a few years their results have been encouraging (Table 2). So far, breeding has been attempted on 11 of 18 sites and once a raft had been used, breeding attempts usually continue there annually. There have been 26 breeding attempts and the productivity has been significantly greater than for natural sites on the Scottish mainland (Table 2).

At the moment there are insufficient rafts to make a substantial addition to the overall number of chicks produced, but the Forestry Commision and RSPB now intend to increase the total to over 50 in the hope that productivity can be markedly improved.

Table 2. The use of artificial islands by Black-throated divers in Scotland.

	1987	1988	1989	1990	1991	1987-91
Number of rafts provided	5	11	14	17	19	-
Number of rafts used for nesting	0	2	4	9	11	26
Number of pairs to raise young	0	1	2	5	5-6	13-14
Number of chicks reared	0	2	36	6	6-8	17-19
Number of chicks per pair using raft	0	1.0	0.75	0.67	0.55-0.73	0.65-0.73

In a test for independence between success rate, nest site and year for Black-throated Divers on artificial islands and natural sites over the period 1988 to 1991, it was found that the success rate was not independent of nest site; G= 8.4, 3 df, P<0.05.

Who helped

The monitoring was co-ordinated by staff of the Forestry Commission, JNCC, NCC and RSPB. We are grateful to B. Anderson, K. Brockie, E. Cameron, M. Canham, T. Clifford, R. Downing, J. Dunn, M. Hancock, W. Henderson, A. Hinde, R. McCurley, W. Mattingley, S. Payne, G. Rebecca, K. Shaw, T. Talbot, S. Witts and others who contributed to the field work. The draft was commented on by L. H. Campbell, R. E. Green, D. B. Jackson, K. Shaw and T. J. Stowe.

References

Anderson, G. & Anderson, Å. (1972). Häckfågelfauna i sjön Järnlunden, 1956-1970. *Vår Fagelvärld* 31, 96-110.

Campbell, J.H. (1988). *Loon conservation in the British Isles.* In: Strong, P.I.V. (Ed.). Papers from the 1987 conference on Loon research and Management. pp 78-85.

Campbell, J.H. & Mudge, G.P. (1989). Conservation of the Black-throated Diver in Scotland. *RSPB Conserv. Rev.* 3, 72-74.

Campbell, L.H. & Talbot, T.R. (1987). Breeding status of Black-throated Divers in Scotland. *British Birds* 80, 1-8.

Eriksson, M.O.G. (1987). The production of young in Black-throated Diver, *Gavia arctica*, in south-west Sweden. *Vår Fagelvärld* 46,172-186.

Everitt, B.S. (1977). *The Analysis of Contingency Tables.* Chapman & Hall, London.

Gotmark.F., Neergaard,R. & Åhlund,M. 1989. Nesting ecology and management of the Arctic Loon in Sweden. *Journal of Wildlife Management* 53, 1025-1031.

Lehtonen,L. (1970). Zur Biologie des Prachttauchers, *Gavia a. arctica* (L.). *Ann. Zool. Fennici* 7,25-60.

Lindberg, P. (1968). Något om storlommens (*Gavia arctica* L.) och smalommens (*Gavia stellata* L.) ekologi. *Zool. Revy* 30,83-88.

Merrie, D. (1979). Success of artificial island nest sites for Divers. *British Birds* 72, 22–32.

Mudge, G.P., Dennis, R.H., Talbot, T.R. & Broad, R.A. (1991). Changes in the breeding status of Black-throated Divers in Scotland. *Scottish Birds* 16, 77-84.

Nilsson, S.G. (1977). Adult survival rate of the Black-throated Diver *Gavia arctica.* *Ornis Scandinavica* 8,193-195.

The 1990 national Mute Swan survey: provisional results

Simon Delany[1] & Jeremy Greenwood[2]

[1]Research and Conservation Department, WWT
[2]BTO

Summary

The 1990 Mute Swan survey found a total British population of about 25,750 birds, an increase of 37% since 1983. In England and Wales the increase was probably attributable in part to the banning of the sale of lead fishing weights, but both there and in Scotland, a succession of mild winters is likely to have been significant.

Findings must be regarded as provisional since not all the counts have yet been submitted and formal statistical analysis is still incomplete.

Previous surveys

The 1955/56 survey was one of the first for any species to use 10km squares in the presentation of results (Campbell 1960, Rawcliffe 1958). The 1961 count (Eltringham 1963) was only partial and relied mainly on aerial survey. The 1978 survey (Ogilvie 1981) was the first "modern" census and the fieldwork technique proved so satisfactory that it was hardly changed in 1983 or 1990 (Ogilvie 1986, Delany et al. 1992). In all surveys to date, the major problem has been the impossibility of obtaining 100% coverage of many regions, making it necessary to adjust population estimates by extrapolating from areas with good coverage.

Reason for the survey

In the late 1970s and early 1980s it became apparent that Mute Swan numbers were declining, and that this was a result of lead poisoning caused by the ingestion of anglers' fishing weights (e.g. Goode 1981). In 1987 the sale of most sizes of lead weights for fishing was banned by law in England and Wales. The National Wildfowl Count totals for Mute Swans increased markedly in two successive winters following the ban, and NCC asked the WWT and BTO to undertake a national Mute Swan survey during the 1990 breeding season. The main objectives were to assess population changes since earlier surveys and to estimate the sizes of local and national populations and describe their geographical pattern, particularly in relation to the ban on lead weights for fishing.

Fieldwork techniques in 1990

Volunteer counters were asked to visit all wetland habitat suitable for Mute Swans in their squares between 1 April and 31 May 1990. For each square, two forms were completed, one for territorial birds and one for non-breeders, with details of localities, dates and numbers of birds present. For territorial birds, the total was broken down according to the breeding status of each pair, whether merely holding territory, at a nest, with cygnets or failed breeders. Completed paperwork was returned to the Regional Organiser, who filled in a Regional Summary Sheet, including estimates for squares that were not covered, before submitting the results.

Because non-breeders are mobile and because failed breeders may join non-breeding flocks and be counted twice, the analysis of non-breeders was restricted to counts made between 25 March and 15 May 1990 and, where multiple counts were made at a site during this period, to the count closest to 15 April.

Coverage

85% of 10km squares in Great Britain were covered or were considered to comprise habitat unsuitable for Mute Swans (Figure 1). Overall coverage was so good that the estimates made to allow for areas not covered only comprise a small proportion of the results.

Overall abundance

Table 1 shows the provisional population totals, broken down by country and breeding status. Just 12.5% of the overall total comprise subjective (but carefully considered) estimates made, usually by the Regional Organiser, for areas that were not covered. In all, 31% of the population comprised breeding birds, a further 9% held territory without

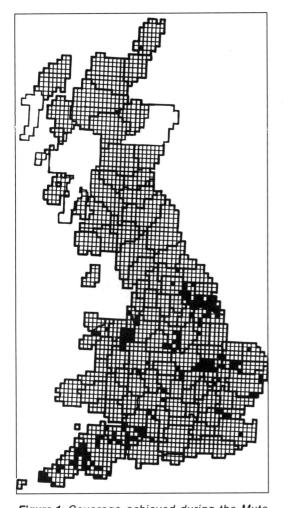

Figure 1. *Coverage achieved during the Mute Swan Survey 1990.*
Filled squares = 10km square not covered.
Blank areas = data not yet available.

being recorded breeding, and 60% were non-breeders.

10km squares with high densities of Mute Swans

Figure 2 shows the overall distribution of paired and non-breeding Mute Swans and Figure 3 shows the 10km squares that produced the highest densities of birds (nine or more pairs and 36 or more individuals). Of the 10km squares covered, 41 held more than 20 pairs of Mute Swans, or more than 100 non-breeders (or both). Thus 0.16% of 10km squares in Britain held 17% of paired and 29% of non-breeding birds. A few squares for which information is not available in the Outer Hebrides, Somerset Moors and Levels, Huntingdonshire and Lincolnshire probably held similarly high densities.

For probably the first time, the most densely populated 10km square recorded was not SY58, which contains the artificially maintained colony at Abbotsbury (Dorset), with 102 nesting pairs and 300 non-breeders (504 birds). The Loch of Harray and the contiguous Loch of Stenness on Orkney held 140 pairs and 382 non-breeders (662 birds) in HY21 and a further 20 pairs in HY31, so that more than 700 Mute Swans were present on the two lochs. Many pairs on the Loch of Harray have abandoned the territorial habit and nest colonially, this being the only site where such behaviour has been recorded in Britain under natural conditions.

Large numbers were found in TG40 and TG30 (south-east Norfolk, and Suffolk) containing Halvergate, Claxton and Strumpshaw marshes. Other squares in East Anglia holding more than 20 pairs or 100 non-breeders were found in the valleys of the Waveney, Alde, Brett, Stour and Colne, at Abberton Reservoir and at the Ouse Washes. Similar densities occurred in six squares in the coastal marshes of Kent and Sussex and five

Table 1. 1990 Mute Swan totals (provisional).

		Pairs with nests/broods	Additional estimated pairs	Pairs with territory only	Non-breeders	Additional estimated non-breeders	Total birds
England	pairs	2,565	393	934			
	birds	5,130	786	1,868	10,986	931	19,701
Scotland	pairs	650	277	186			
	birds	1,300	554	372	2,164	817	5,207
Wales	pairs	95	18	45			
	birds	190	36	90	432	92	840
Overall	pairs	3,310	663	1,165			
total	birds	6,620	1,376	2,330	13,582	1,840	25,748

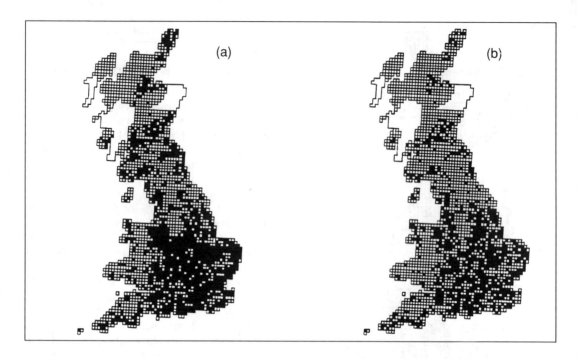

Figure 2. *10km squares with one or more pairs of Mute Swans (a) and 10km squares with one or more non-breeding Mute Swans (b). Note: one bird in Shetland has been omitted from (b).*

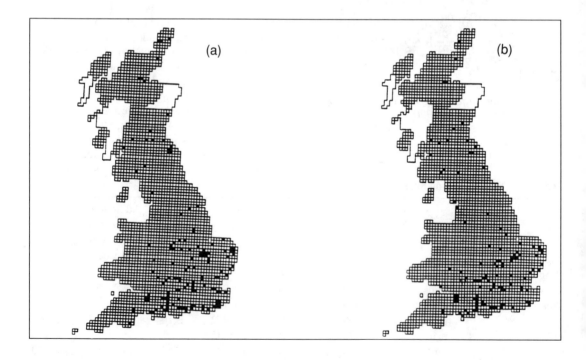

Figure 3. *10km squares with nine or more pairs of Mute Swans (a) and with 36 or more non-breeding Mute Swans (b).*

squares along the Thames. More than 100 non-breeders were also counted in squares TL37 (Barleycraft Gravel Pit, Huntingdonshire), SP86 (River Nene, Northamptonshire), SU09 (Cotswold Water Park, Wiltshire/Gloucestershire), ST44 (Tealham Moor, Somerset), and SO70 (WWT Slimbridge, Gloucestershire).

One of the most important areas in Britain for Mute Swans is the valley of the Avon and its tributary the Wylye in Wiltshire, Hampshire and Dorset. Here, six adjacent squares produced a total of 188 territorial and breeding pairs and 1,052 non-breeders, or about 3.7% of the British paired population and 6.8% of the non-breeders.

Apart from the two introduced and almost self-contained populations in Orkney and the Outer Hebrides, there were few dense concentrations of breeding Mute Swans north of the Fens or west of the Somerset Levels. Exceptions to this were NT84 in the valley of the Tweed (Borders District), and SE42 at Fairburn Ings in Yorkshire.

10km squares with moderate and low densities of Mute Swans

These high concentrations of birds are only found over a small proportion of the range of the species in Britain, with much lower densities being more usual. There were four pairs or less in 74% of occupied squares. A total of 368 squares held only one pair of birds and a further 240 squares held two pairs, so that 52% of occupied squares held just one or two pairs.

Why might the populations have increased?

Table 2 provides a comparison of population totals

of Mute Swans derived from all national breeding season surveys undertaken to date. The population has apparently increased considerably since previous surveys and now stands at 25,750 birds, the highest level yet recorded. Given the incomplete coverage in all the surveys, however, this conlusion must remain tentative until formal analyses are complete.

The increase both in numbers and in breeding success on the Thames have coincided with a decline in exposure to anglers' lead weights (Sears 1988). Sears & Hunt (1991), using post mortem examinations and measurements of lead levels in the blood of live birds, describe dramatic declines in the incidence of lead poisoning and consequent population increases. It would appear that in parts of England the reduction in exposure of swans to lead since the ban on the sale of most sizes of fishing weight in 1987 has played a major role in the recovery of their populations. Lead poisoning still occurs in many areas but, as anglers use up their stockpiles and as lead discarded in the past becomes more deeply buried in sediment, continuing reductions in the number of lead poisoning incidents can be expected.

Another important factor affecting Mute Swan populations is winter weather. It has long been known that severe weather causes increased winter mortality of Mute Swans (Boyd & Ogilvie 1964, Ogilvie 1967) and Esselink & Beekman (1991) have shown that mild winters are not only associated with low mortality but are also followed by high reproductive output. Meteorological Office data show that the winters of 1988-1990, the three years following the ban on the sale of lead weights, were exceptionally mild throughout

Table 2. Provisional Mute Swan population estimates from four British breeding season surveys.

	1955/56	1978	1983	1990
England	15,600-17,300	13,340	14,800	*20,000
		19%	+11%	+35%
Scotland	3,500-4,000	3,680	3,250	*4,900
		2%	12%	+51%
Wales	780	590	700	840
		24%	+19%	+20%
Total Britain	19,900-21,600	17,600	18,750	25,750
		15%	+7%	+37%

*300 birds on the Tweed (Borders District) subtracted from Scotland total and added to England for comparability with other surveys.

Note that these figures, especially the comparisons with earlier surveys, may need to be adjusted in the light of more detailed analyses.

Britain. Three mild winters in succession will undoubtedly have contributed considerably to the increase in Britain's Mute Swan population at the end of the 1980s.

Lead poisoning from anglers' weights was not identified as a cause of mortality of Mute Swans in Scotland, and lead for fishing was in any case not banned there, yet there appears to have been even more marked increase in the Scottish population than in England and Wales. A possibility is that increased sowing of winter cereals in Scotland has improved the winter food supply for swans, enabling a higher proportion of birds to survive the winter. Scottish birds, at least on the east coast, also appear to be more mobile than over much of their range (A. Brown and A. Bramhall, pers. comm.) and it seems possible that a proportion of the increase originates from immigration. Equally, it is possible that neither of these factors has been important and that the whole of the increase in Scotland has resulted from the mild winters.

References

Boyd, H. & Ogilvie, M.A. (1964). Losses of Mute Swans in England in the winter 1962-63. *Wildfowl Trust Ann.* Rep. 15, 37-40.

Campbell, B. (1960). The Mute Swan Census in England and Wales, 1955-56. *Bird Study* 7, 208-223.

Delany, S.N., Greenwood, J.J.D. & Kirby, J.S. (1992). *National Mute Swan Survey 1990.* Rept. to JNCC.

Eltringham, S.K. (1963). The British population of the Mute Swan in 1961. *Bird Study* 10, 10-28.

Esselink, H. & Beekman, J.H. (1991). Between-year variation and causes of mortality in the non-breeding population of the Mute Swan *Cygnus olor* in the Netherlands with special reference to hunting. Pp 110-119. In: Sears, J. & Bacon, P.J. (Eds.) *Proc Third International Swan Symposium, Oxford 1989.* Wildfowl Suppl. No.1. Pp. 110–119.

Goode, D. (1981). *Report of the Nature Conservancy Council's Working Group on Lead Poisoning in Swans.* NCC, London.

Ogilvie, M.A. (1967). Population changes and mortality of the Mute Swan in Britain. *Wildfowl Trust Ann. Rep.* 18, 64-73.

Ogilvie, M.A. (1981). The Mute Swan in Britain, 1978. *Bird Study* 28, 87-106.

Ogilvie, M.A. (1986). The Mute Swan *Cygnus olor* in Britain 1983. *Bird Study* 33, 121-137.

Rawcliffe, C.P. (1958). The Scottish Mute Swan Census 1955-56. *Bird Study* 5, 45-55.

Sears, J. (1988). *A Report on Lead Poisoning in Mute Swans in the Thames area during 1988.* Edward Grey Institute, Oxford.

Sears, J. & Hunt A. (1991). Lead poisoning in Mute Swans, *Cygnus olor*, in England. Pp 383-388. In: Sears, J. & Bacon, P.J. (Eds.) *Proc. Third International Swan Symposium, Oxford 1989.* Wildfowl Suppl. No. 1. Pp. 383–388.

Population size and breeding success of Slavonian Grebes in Scotland

Colin Crooke[1], Roy Dennis[2], Malcolm Harvey[3], & Ron Summers[1],

[1] North Scotland Office, RSPB

[2] Inchdryne, Nethybridge, Inverness-shire

[3] Clachbhan, Loaneckheim, Kiltarlity, Inverness-shire

Summary

Slavonian Grebes started to colonise Scotland in 1908. During the period 1971-1990 productivity was low (0.66 young per breeding pair) but the population showed a slow increase averaging 1.2% per year to 74 breeding pairs, or 160 adults including non-breeders. They have ceased breeding in four counties that were previously occupied and a number of lochs in the core areas in Inverness-shire are no longer used. A number of factors including human disturbance, predation, changes in water quality, poor weather, forestry and building developments may have affected productivity and, at least in part, explain site abandonment.

Colonisation

The Slavonian Grebe has a circumpolar distribution but the sub-species *arcticus* breeds only in northern Norway (c500 pairs), Iceland (500-750), sporadically in the Faeroes and in Britain where it is restricted to the Highlands of Scotland (Fjeldså 1973a, Cramp & Simmons 1977). It tends to breed on moderately nutrient-rich lochs, and generally nests in beds of emergent Bottle Sedge.

Slavonian Grebes were first recorded nesting in Inverness-shire in 1908 and spread to neighbouring counties; Sutherland and Caithness in 1929, Morayshire in the 1950s, Aberdeenshire in 1960 and Perthshire in 1973 (Thom 1986). At present they breed only in Inverness-shire and Morayshire.

Population monitoring

In order to monitor the population of this rare bird, the breeding range was split into four areas; Inverness-shire north and south of the Great Glen, Morayshire and Strathspey (Inverness-shire). Initial surveys (starting in 1971) involved visiting known and potential sites using detailed local knowledge. Thereafter, Morayshire and the area north of the Great Glen were surveyed annually but there was no coverage south of the Great Glen in 1973 and 1977 and in Strathspey in 1977 and 1983. Complete surveys, which involved visits to every loch in the study areas, were carried out north of the Great Glen in 1972, '73, '77 and every three years thereafter, south of the Great Glen in 1971, '72, '74, '83, '86 and '89, in Strathspey in 1973-76, 86 and 89, and in Moray in 1983, '86 and '89. Once a loch had been found to have Slavonian Grebes it was checked annually thereafter. The complete surveys added few new sites. For example, the complete surveys north of the Great Glen in 1977, 1983 and 1986 added two new sites and one pair at each. Therefore, the under-estimates of the total population in years between complete surveys were probably small.

As years were missed in Strathspey and south of the Great Glen, population indices were derived for each year from the equation; population in year/population in the base year (1971) x 100; using the data for those areas where it was available.

Growth rate of the population was obtained from regression analysis using the natural logarithm of the population index as the dependent variable and the year as the independent one.

Lochs were visited at least twice each year, in late May and July, to count pairs and young respectively. By late May pairs had settled down and a reasonably accurate count could be made. Initially, lochs were scanned from a suitable distance (>100 m) to avoid disturbance, followed by the observer(s) carrying out a complete circuit of each loch if appropriate, and watching from suitable vantage points overlooking sedge beds. Grebes can be difficult to detect, particularly when concealed in emergent vegetation. A pair was

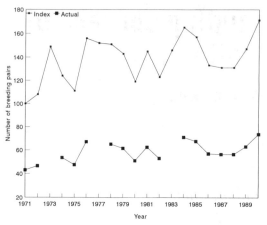

Figure 1. *Annual changes in the breeding population, and its index, for Slavonian Grebes in Scotland. The index shows an average annual increase of 1.2% (±0.5% SE) (t_{19} = 2.46, P=0.024).*

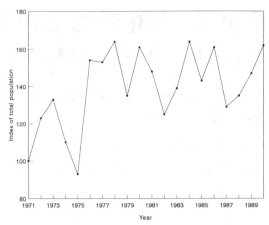

Figure 2. *Annual changes in the index of the total population of adult Slavonian Grebes in Scotland. As the base number for the total population was 99, the index was almost identical to the actual population. It shows an average annual increase of 1.5% (±0.6%) (t_{19} = 2.62, P= 0.017).*

assumed to be breeding if one or two birds were present on more than one occasion at sites where suitable nesting habitat, primarily Bottle Sedge, was available.

While it was relatively easy to gather data on the number of occupied lochs, it was sometimes difficult to interpret counts in terms of number of breeding pairs at each site, especially on the few lochs with several pairs.

Occasionally, there were only single birds present or numbers on a loch fluctuated between visits suggesting movements of unpaired birds. Also, we believe that some apparently non-breeding pairs moved between lochs and failed breeders may also move. A higher frequency of visits and longer periods of field observations would have helped to obtain more accurate counts.

Additional visits were made to count the number of young reared. Since birds lay replacement clutches after failure, subsequent visits were sometimes extended to late August. Although the fledging period is c. 8 weeks (Cramp & Simmons 1977) young were considered to have been reared when they were at least seven weeks old. Thus, some birds may not have been completely independent at seven weeks but it is likely that this will be close to the number fledged. Breeding success was measured as the number of young reared per breeding pair.

Population increase

In the first year of the survey 99 adult birds, including 43 breeding pairs were found. There was

a slow increase, averaging 1.2% per annum for pairs and 1.5% for individuals, to 1990 totals of 74 breeding pairs or 160 adults including non-breeders. The size of the breeding population in each year is shown in Figure 1 and the index of the total population (breeders and non-breeding adults) in Figure 2.

Range and sites

After colonisation in 1908 there was an expansion of range, followed by contraction and shift. Extinctions have occurred in Perthshire, Caithness, Aberdeenshire and Sutherland whilst expansion has occurred in Strathspey.

Also, a number of lochs in the core area in Inverness-shire are no longer used. During the survey period, a total of 74 lochs were used by Slavonian Grebes for breeding but only 17 - 34 were used in any one year (Figure 3). Cessation of breeding at some lochs coincided with a change in habitat. Two lochs have been afforested around their banks and another two have had houses built close to their shores.

In 1990, half of the occupied lochs had more than one pair of grebes so the population was aggregated (Figure 4). Fifty six percent of the breeding population occurred on 6 lochs, and 3 of these produced 46% of the young.

Breeding success

Breeding success averaged 0.66 chicks fledged per breeding pair, or 0.33 per breeding adult (Figure 5). In northern Norway the ratio of juveniles to adults in August ranged from 0.37 to 1.00, whilst in Iceland this ratio ranged from 0.42 to 0.63 (Fjeldså 1973b). Although these figures are not directly comparable with the 0.33 for Scotland, because counts were done in different months, it does indicate that the productivity in Scotland is low.

Factors affecting breeding success

Most information on factors affecting breeding success was based on circumstantial evidence. Desertions of nests were probably due to disturbance from fishermen, birdwatchers and unlicenced photographers who have been observed close to sedge beds for long periods of time or walking through them. Picnickers and swimmers can also cause disturbance. Egg collectors stole clutches in some years, as marked eggs were later found in confiscated collections. An adult grebe was found dead and X-rays showed that it had been shot with an airgun.

Cattle graze sedge beds and may reduce the area of suitable habitat or even trample nests. Coots take over nest platforms and kill young (Thom 1986). Predation has been recorded. In 1991, Crows were observed taking eggs at Loch Ruthven (A.MacLennan pers comm.). Pike have been suspected of taking chicks. In 1985, adult grebes were found dead and partially eaten, and feet only have been found. Pine Marten, Mink or Otter could have been responsible. Fish may compete with grebes for food (Eriksson 1979) and during the surveys it was noted that grebes abandoned one formerly regular breeding site at the same time that it was stocked with Rainbow Trout. Changes in water quality associated with forestry (Robinson & Blyth 1982) or acid rain (Battarbee 1989) may also have had an effect. The relative importance of these different factors is unknown so further study is required.

Future conservation

The population is of national importance. As it is still very small and therefore vulnerable, the RSPB will continue to monitor it. One way to help safeguard the species is to give special protection to the main breeding lochs (56% of the population bred on 6 lochs in 1990). Ideally, all qualifying sites should receive adequate statutory site safeguard through the establishment of SSSIs (39% of grebes bred on SSSIs in 1990). Some of the main groups of lochs are now listed as proposed Special Protection Areas, and a management plan for all

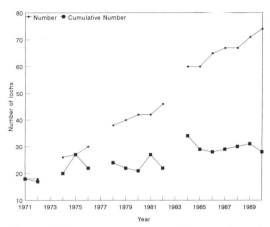

Figure 3. The number, and cumulative number, of lochs used by Slavonian Grebes in Scotland.

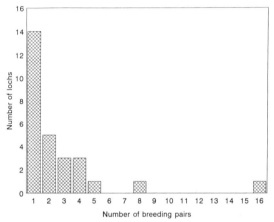

Figure 4. The number of lochs with different numbers of breeding pairs of Slavonian Grebes in 1990.

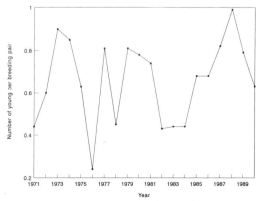

Figure 5. Annual variations in the breeding production of Slavonian Grebes in Scotland. The number of young produced per breeding pair showed no trend with time (Spearman Rank Correlation = 0.137). The average value was 0.66 ± 0.23 (SD).

sites is being initiated. The RSPB has created a reserve at Loch Ruthven which helps to take bird-watching pressure off other sites.

Who helped

The following people have helped with field work: R.A.Broad, A.Burch, M.Cook, R.Evans, A.Fox, M.Hancock, A.M.MacLennan, A.Mee, S.Moore, C.Pell, M.Pollard, J.Porter, D.Pullan and A.Thompson. Drs R.E.Green, A.M.MacLennan and T.J.Stowe commented on the draft of this paper.

References

Battarbee, R.W. (1989). Geographic research on acid rain. I. The acidification of Scottish lochs. *Geographical Journal* 155, 353-377.

Cramp, S. & Simmons, K.E.L. (1977). *The Birds of the Western Palearctic Vol 1*. O.U.P., Oxford.

Eriksson, M.O.G. (1979). Competition between fresh water fish and Goldeneye *Bucephala clangula* (L.) for common prey. *Oecologia* 41, 99-107.

Fjeldså, J. (1973a). Distribution and geographical variation of the Horned Grebe *Podiceps auritus* (Linnaeus, 1758). *Ornis Scandinavica* 4, 55-86.

Fjeldså, J. (1973b). Territory and the regulation of population density and recruitment in the Horned Grebe *Podiceps auritus arcticus* Boje, 1822. *Vidensk. Meddr dansk naturh. Foren.* 136, 117-189.

Robinson, M. & Blyth, K. (1982). The effect of forestry drainage operations on upland sediment yields; a case study. *Earth Surface Processes and Landforms* 7, 85-90.

Thom, V. M. (1986). *Birds in Scotland*. T. & A. D. Poyser, Calton.

S C Porter, RSPB/Slavonian Grebe

Trends in the numbers of breeding Bitterns in the UK

K W Smith & G A Tyler

Research Department, RSPB

Summary

Having recolonised Britain and increased during the first half of this century, by 1990 the Bittern had declined to 20 'booming' birds at a total of 12 sites. The largest declines have occurred in the Norfolk Broads but losses have also been widespread elsewhere. The most likely explanation is the degradation and succession of the Bittern's reedbed habitat and steps are being taken to secure the appropriate management of the remaining sites and the creation of new ones.

Colonisation and decline

The Bittern is one of our most threatened and vulnerable breeding species. Although wintering birds can turn up in the most unlikely places (Bibby 1981), as a breeding bird in Britain the Bittern is largely restricted to extensive reedbeds (Bibby & Lunn 1982). The last review of breeding numbers was published in 1978 (Day & Wilson 1978) so it is timely to review the trends since then.

Bitterns ceased to breed in Britain in the late 19th century probably as the result of persecution and, although 'booming' birds were heard in 1900, they were not again proved to breed until 1911 (Turner 1924). Figures 1 and 2 show the numbers of 'booming' Bitterns and the numbers of occupied sites from 1911 until 1990. Two features are clear in both figures; that the numbers of sites and birds were at their highest in the 1950s, and that subsequently there has been a serious decline in both numbers and occupied sites. In 1990 there were only 20 'booming' birds at 12 sites, probably the lowest numbers since the 1920s.

In Figures 1 and 2 the numbers of birds and sites in Broadland have been distinguished from those elsewhere. The recolonisation of Britain in the early decades of this century occurred entirely in the Broads, but by the 1950s birds were found in many sites elsewhere. By the early 1980s a catastrophic decline had taken place in the Broads with only six or seven sites occupied and by 1990 this was down to only three. The numbers of birds outside the Broads actually increased between the 1950s and

1980s but in the last few years these too have crashed.

Bitterns are extremely secretive and, even in their strongholds, are not often seen. Estimating numbers has always been difficult and has usually been limited to counts of 'booming' birds. Because 'booming' is often sporadic and birds can move locations over the course of the breeding season, it has been difficult to be certain of the numbers

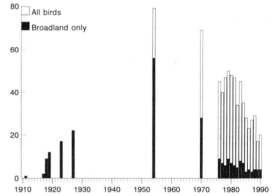

Figure 1. *The numbers of 'booming' Bitterns in Britain each year from 1910 to 1990. The data are those given by Day & Wilson (1978) and, from 1977 onwards, the annual reports of the Rare Breeding Birds Panel (Spencer et al. 1992) and, more recently, surveys co-ordinated by the RSPB.*

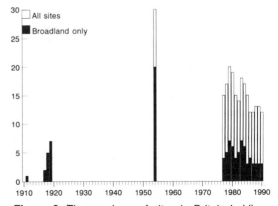

Figure 2. *The numbers of sites in Britain holding 'booming' Bitterns each year from 1910 to 1990.*

of birds present. In the last few years techniques have been developed to allow the recognition of individual Bitterns by the acoustic characteristics of their 'booms' (McGregor & Byle in press) and these have been applied to virtually the whole British population (Gilbert & McGregor 1991). Unfortunately it is not possible to look in the same way retrospectively at the historic figures, so these remain the best available estimates of past numbers.

Causes of decline

The possible causes of the decline in breeding Bittern numbers were discussed by Day & Wilson (1978) and included hard weather, disturbance and habitat deterioration.

It is probable that loss and degradation of habitat is the main factor which has caused the virtual loss of breeding Bitterns from the Broads.

In the 1970s, George (1977) drew attention to the loss of reedswamp from the margins of Broads and associated waterways, often in areas formerly used by Bitterns. This is now thought to be the result of poor water quality, increased boat traffic and, at some sites, grazing (George 1992). Radio-tracking studies of Bitterns at Leighton Moss, Lancashire (Tyler 1992a) have shown that they feed in wet reedbed close to naturally encroaching reed edges where, presumably, they can fish in shallow water. At the time when Bitterns were re-colonising the Broads, reedswamp was expanding rapidly into areas of shallow water and, as 'hover', across deeper water (Ellis 1965), providing much wet reedbed and advancing reed-open water interface. Subsequently, with the reedbeds in retreat, the edges have become less suitable whilst the remaining reedbed has itself tended to become too dry for Bitterns.

At other sites vegetation succession and the consequent drying out of the reedbed appear to have affected Bittern numbers. In 1990/91 the RSPB carried out detailed habitat surveys in reedbeds currently occupied by breeding Bitterns and those outside the Broads which had lost their birds in the last ten years (Tyler 1992b). The differences were striking. The sites which had retained their Bitterns had more open water and the reed stands were wetter than the sites which had lost their birds. Also, at the sites with Bitterns, the reedbeds contained fewer wetland plant species representing the next stages of the succession.

Although the current Bittern breeding sites are nature reserves, it is clear that the appropriate management is needed to ensure the continued well-being of the birds. The next decade will be critical if the Bittern is to remain as a British breeding species. Action is already taking place at the key sites but seems unlikely that numbers can easily be restored in the Broads in the foreseeable future, if ever. So, to return the Bittern to its status of the 1950s, the creation of some major new reedbeds offers the most practical course of action, a task which will present an exciting challenge to the bird conservation organisations in this country.

Further information

Advice and information on the creation and management of sites for Bitterns can be obtained from the Conservation Management Advisory Unit, RSPB, The Lodge, Sandy, SG19 2DL.

Acknowledgements

J. Day and M. Seago kindly made available their historical data on Bittern numbers and sites, whilst B. Bishop, M. Blackburn, F. Russell, N. Sills, J. Sorenson, R. Starling, C. Waller and J. Wilson provided more recent information. The work on the sound recording of Bittern booms has been pioneered by P. McGregor, P. Byle and G. Gilbert, the latter as part of a Science and Engineering Research Council CASE studentship at the University of Nottingham. J. Day suggested improvements to an earlier draft of this paper.

References

Bibby, C.J. (1981). Wintering Bitterns in Britain. *British Birds* 74, 1-10.

Bibby, C.J. & Lunn, J. (1982). Conservation of reedbeds and their avifauna in England and Wales. *Biol Conserv* 23, 167-186.

Day, J.C.U. & Wilson, J. (1978). Breeding Bitterns in Britain. *British Birds* 71, 285-300.

Ellis, E.A. (1965). *The Broads.* New Naturalist, Collins, London.

George, M. (1977). The decline in Broadlands aquatic fauna and flora - a review of the present position. *Trans. Norfolk and Norwich Nat. Soc.* 24, 41-53.

George, M. (1992). *The Land Use, Ecology and Conservation of Broadland.* Packard, Chichester.

Gilbert, G. & McGregor, P.K. (1991). *Individually distinct bird calls: their role in monitoring rare bird populations.* Unpubl. rept. University of Nottingham.

McGregor, P.K. & Byle, P. (in press). Individually distinct Bittern booms: potential as a censusing tool. *Bioaccoustics.*

Spencer, R. & The Rare Breeding Birds Panel (1992). The Rare Breeding Birds Panel. *British Birds* 85, 117-122.

Turner, E.L. (1924) *Broadland Birds.* Country Life, London.

Tyler, G.A. (1992a). *Home range and habitat use of radio tagged bitterns at Leighton Moss.* Unpubl. rept. RSPB, Sandy.

Tyler, G.A. (1992b) *The relationship between the numbers of breeding bitterns in UK reedbeds and measures of the habitat.* Unpubl. rept. RSPB, Sandy.

Study of population dynamics of Uist Greylags

Carl Mitchell

Research and Conservation Department, WWT

Background

The Greylag is our only native breeding goose and used to breed in the East Anglian Fens, Lancashire, the Lake District and probably other parts of Britain before the marshes and fens were reclaimed for agriculture. By the early 20th century Greylags were restricted to north-west Scotland. Although between 1930 and 1970 feral flocks were established in many parts of Britain, almost all of the indigenous birds are confined to the Outer Hebrides, Coll and Tiree and the mainland and islands of north-west Scotland. Here increases in some local populations have brought complaints of damage to agricultural crops.

On the Uists and Benbecula under the Integrated Development Plan (IDP) the area of high quality grass and cereals (mainly Rye and Small Oats) has increased since 1983 by c.1,000 ha. Since the mid-1980s geese have caused problems to crofters in the area by grazing reseeded grass in winter which provide an important "spring-bite" for stock and eating and trampling ripe cereal crops in late summer. The Uist population is thought to represent about two thirds of the total indigenous non-feral population of Greylags and was estimated at 2,000 birds in 1991 (Elliott 1991). Although the native Greylag is listed on Schedule 1 of the Wildlife and Countryside Act 1981 in view of its considerable conservation interest, it may legally be shot in this area during the open wildfowling season. Against this background the North Uist Crofters' Union approached the Dept. of Agriculture and Fisheries for Scotland (DAFS) with a view to reducing the goose population.

Population monitoring

A study of the Uist population and its impact on crofting agriculture was carried out by the North of Scotland College of Agriculture (NOSCA) with IDP funding between 1986 and 1987 (Patterson 1987). Regular counts through North Uist, Benbecula and South Uist were undertaken during this study and birds were caught and ringed. This initial study showed a need for continued monitoring and for investigations into population dynamics, initially through a joint NOSCA/NCC project and latterly by WWT and the Nature Conservancy for Scotland (NCCS, now Scottish Natural Heritage). The work includes an attempt to assess the significance of hunting and assist in developing a management strategy.

To monitor change in numbers, counts along fixed routes are now carried out twice annually by NCCS and WWT staff and local volunteers, in late August after the birds have left their breeding areas but before the start of the shooting season, and again in early February after the shooting season. The counts show the population slowly increasing from 1986 to 1991 (Figure 1) although increased experience in the counters and favourable weather conditions may have improved recent coverage.

Breeding primarily occurs around the NNR at Loch Druidibeg, South Uist and on North Uist, both on islands in freshwater lochs and offshore. Breeding success is assessed by surveys of nests to determine clutch size early in the season, followed by later survey of broods in July and at the time of the August census. Brood sizes have remained sta-

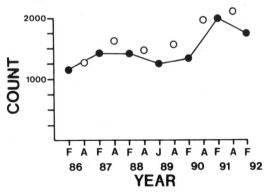

Figure 1. *Greylag Goose counts in the Uists 1986 to 1992. ● Winter count (post-shooting season) F = February, and ○ Summer count (pre-shooting season) A = August.*

Table 1. Greylag Goose brood sizes in the Uists 1986 to 1991. Mean ± standard error (sample size)

Year	North Uist	South Uist	Tiree and Coll[4]
1986[1]	3.1 ± 0.21 (32)	4.3 ± 0.30 (17)	
1987[1]	2.3 ± 0.46 (13)	4.5 ± 0.37 (14)	
1988[1]	3.7 ± 0.33 (33)	4.2 ± 0.28 (41)	
1989[2]	3.0 ± 0.42 (10)	3.5 ± 0.62 (8)	3.6 ±0.34 (23)
1990[3]	3.7 ± 0.24 (36)	4.2 ± 0.34 (38)	
1991[2]	2.7 ± 0.19 (34)	3.7 ± 0.47 (13)	3.8 ± 0.26 (56)

Sources of data:
1 - Patterson *et al.* (1990)
2 - Mitchell (unpublished data)
3 - Mitchell (1991)
4 - A.C. Knight (pers comm.)

ble through the period 1986 to 1991 (Table 1).

The various causes of mortality can be assessed in a number of different ways. The differences between the August and February counts and data from local shooting bag statistics give some indication of the over-winter mortality and whether the results of shooting are additive to other forms of mortality or substitutes for them. Ringing recoveries can also be used to estimate mortality rates and a more accurate independent assessment of survival can come from the French SURGE models which rely on resightings of individually marked birds (Clobert *et al.* 1987).

Movements of Uist Greylags

Population studies must take account of the possibility of immigration and emigration so ringing is also necessary to determine whether our fundamental assumption of negligible movement to and from the Uists is a reasonable one. Ringing between 1968-72 at Loch Druidibeg had suggested that Uist Greylags were highly sedentary. Of 15 recoveries, 14 were from South Uist with most shot in the vicinity of the reserve (I. Newton pers comm.). Since 1986, study of the movements of individual Greylags has been greatly facilitated by a colour-ringing programme. To June 1992, 490 Greylags had been ringed, 487 of which had also been marked with solid colour rings or two letter-engraved rings. During this period 47 (9.5%) were recovered dead, 37 (78.7% of the recovered sample) having been reported as shot. The resighting rate of individual colour-ringed geese is relatively high for an area where there are few birdwatchers, with an average of 3.8 sightings of each bird known to be alive.

Whilst remaining essentially within the area of the Uists, Greylags show pronounced seasonal movements. The majority of those ringed in the principal catching areas of Lochmaddy and in the Sound of Harris wintered to the west of North Uist, moving back to the breeding areas from January onwards mainly along the north coast of North Uist. Some birds ringed in North Uist were seen or recovered in South Uist and Benbecula demonstrating that exchange can occur between the islands and that the island group as a whole should be regarded as holding a single population (Figure 2).

Colour-ringed individuals often return to the same wintering areas in subsequent seasons: of 137 individuals seen in two or more winters, 83 (60%) have been seen at the same site on at least two occasions. However, there are several records of movements during the course of a single winter - some birds moving from North Uist to South Uist and back again.

Whilst the majority find winter feeding in the Uists, there are rare occasions where birds have been recorded elsewhere. A single individual ringed as a moulting adult in July 1986 was shot at Hunavatnssysla, Iceland (65°54'N 20°50'W) in September 1987 - this bird was probably of Icelandic origin that had oversummered in the Uists. A moulting adult ringed in July 1986 was found dead four years later on the Isle of Coll, having apparently been seen alive there for some time (N. Galbraith pers comm.); another has been found dead on Lewis. The latter recoveries pose interesting questions about the validity of the assumption that the Uists Greylag population is closed. Interchange with Coll and Tiree, Harris and Lewis and mainland north-west Scotland has yet to be fully investigated, although co-ordinated counts in these areas were begun in 1990. There has, however, been a remarkable increase in the Coll and

Tiree population in recent years, from no more than 250 birds in 1987 (Shepherd *et al.* 1988) to 829 birds counted in August 1990 (A. Knight and M. Green pers comm.). Whilst this increase probably reflects reduced shooting pressure on Coll and Tiree, it is possible that some of the increase is due to immigration by birds formerly resident on the Uists.

References

Clobert, J., Lebreton, J.D., & Allaine, D. (1987). A general approach to survival rate estimation by recaptures or resightings of marked birds. *Ardea* 75, 133-142.

Elliott, Mary M., (1991). Greylag Goose counts in the Uists from 1986 to 1991. *Hebridean Naturalist* 11, 54-58

Mitchell, C. (1991). *Greylag Geese on the Uists (for the period June 1990 - March 1991).* Unpubl. rept. NCC, Peterborough.

Patterson, I.W. (1987). *The Uist population of Greylag Geese Anser anser and its impact upon crofting agriculture.* Scottish Agricultural Colleges, Perth.

Patterson, I.W., Boyer, P.R. & Massen, D. (1990). Variations in clutch size and breeding success of Greylag Geese breeding in the Uists, Scotland. *Wildfowl* 41, 18-22.

Shepherd, K.B., Green, M., Knight, A.C. & Stroud, D.A. (1988). *The breeding birds of Tiree and Coll in 1987/88 with special emphasis on breeding waders.* NCC, CSD Rep No. 827.

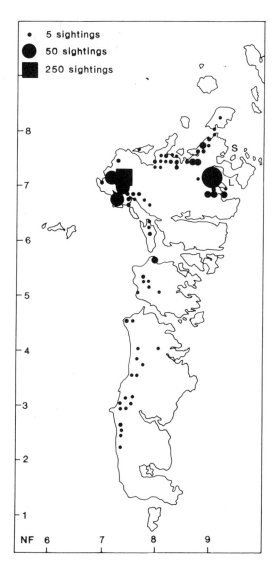

Figure 2. *Principal ringing areas (L = Lochmaddy, S = Sound of Harris) and locations of all sightings of individually colour-ringed birds within the Uists.*

Dr G Fisher/Graylag Geese

National Waterfowl Counts 1990/91

J R Ferns & J S Kirby

Research and Conservation Department, WWT

Summary

The distribution and abundance of wintering wild-fowl recorded throughout Britain and Northern Ireland in 1990/91 is summarised in this account. The information is derived from the results of the 44th consecutive season of monitoring through the National Waterfowl Counts scheme (NWC - formerly known as National Wildfowl Counts). The monthly counts are undertaken by a dedicated network of volunteer ornithologists at a variety of wetland habitats, co-ordinated via a regional organizers. Data for the following groups were collected in 1990/91 and are presented here: divers, grebes, Cormorant, swans, geese, ducks and Coot. The total numbers of wildfowl recorded, monthly fluctuations and indices are all presented in tabular form.

Total numbers of most wintering wildfowl species in 1990/91 were maintained or increased in comparison with 1989/90 counts. Only a few species e.g. Tufted Duck and Coot showed significant declines in terms of overall numbers. The reasons behind these increases in total numbers must be related at least in part, to the improvements in coverage, although, the huge January count of Mallard was probably weather related. Most species reached maximum abundance in mid-winter (December to February). The indices for Britain reflect relative stability in most populations, with only four species showing large population increases, i.e. Mute Swan, Gadwall, Shoveler and Goldeneye and two showing marked declines, i.e. Whooper Swan and Pintail. The reasons behind some of these trends are not clear and here the counts are useful in illustrating the need for further work on the ecology of many species.

Coverage in 1990/91

The coverage achieved for the NWC scheme is obviously critical to the results obtained and their interpretation. A total of 2,504 wetland sites in Britain and Northern Ireland were covered at least once during the 1990/91 season, including 2,442 in January and 1,460 in all seven of the priority months, September to March. This is considerably higher than the total of 1,910 sites achieved in

1989/90. Furthermore, the coverage in Britain improved in every month compared with the previous season. This can be attributed to two main factors, most significant being the efforts expended by counters in north-west England to cover additional sites for a special project and computerisation of the count data from estuaries at a finer level. There was good coverage in north-west England but gaps in eastern and north-east Wales, in central and east Kent, East Anglia, northern England and throughout many regions of Scotland. On the coast, incomplete counts were received from the Humber Estuary, Rough Firth and Dulas Bay.

Total numbers and population indices

A word of caution is necessary regarding the uses to which waterfowl counts can correctly be applied and the limitations of these data, especially in the summary form. The data are preliminary in the sense that they are uncorrected for differences in site coverage and count quality.

Tables 1 & 2 show the total numbers of each species of wildfowl, grebes, Cormorant and Coot recorded in September to March of 1990/91 for Britain and Northern Ireland separately.

The numbers of grebes counted in each month of 1990/91 were mostly similar to the numbers in 1989/90, e.g. the monthly maximum count for Little Grebe was only 362 birds higher than that of last year and Great Crested Grebe was up by 606 birds. The peak count of Cormorants in Britain was relatively high, with a maximum of around 15,000 in 1990/91 compared with 13,500 in 1989/90, whilst that for Northern Ireland was on the low side. Amongst the swans, Mute Swans in Britain surpassed the peak number counted last season (12,616) by some 2,600 birds, whilst both Bewick's and Whooper Swans were recorded in similar numbers in 1989/90 in both Britain and Northern Ireland. The numbers of Pink-footed, Greenland White-fronted, Icelandic Greylag, Barnacle and Dark-bellied Brent were highest during the months of specific surveys for them, and in all cases exceeded the totals of the previous year.

The numbers of both feral Greylags and Canada Geese appeared to be relatively high in Britain in 1990/91.

For the "freshwater ducks", the peak British count of Mallard in January (214,458) exceeded the previous seasons maximum by a staggering

Table 1. Total number of wildfowl, grebes, Cormorant and Coot counted in Great Britain in each month of 1990/91. The numbers of sites counted are given in brackets.

	Sep (1,595)	Oct (1,694)	Nov (1,756)	Dec (1,779)	Jan (2,295)	Feb (1,790)	Mar (1,737)
Little Grebe	2,878	2,570	2,385	2,434	2,411	1,931	1,552
Great Crested Grebe	8,803	8,126	7,770	7,823	8,365	7,156	7,179
Cormorant	12,861	12,785	13,866	12,661	12,620	12,485	9,305
Mute Swan	12,751	13,801	13,585	13,328	15,220	12,119	9,983
Bewick's Swan	11	321`	4,761	5,966	7,905	7809	973
Whooper Swan	29	1,344	3,972	4,285	4,556	3,252	2,463
Bean Goose	0	3	116	446	509	308	0
Pink-footed Goose	3,495	175,724*	194,752*	82,767	100,541	93,781	74,508
European White-fronted Goose	27	207	898	3,005	498	4,025	2,352
Greenland White-fronted Goose	19	637	14762*	13111	9056	1625	15180*
Greylag Goose (Icelandic)	1,057	76,286*	114,678*	29,548	50,105	30,915	19,528
Greylag Goose (feral)+	12,176	9,210	10,118	12,017	15,334	9,623	7,391
Canada Goose	34,741	37,994	35,540	32,807	35,457	34,388	20,432
Barnacle Goose++	246	10,340	2,603	33,523*	3,430	7,771	24,768*
Dark-bellied Brent Goose	4,466	101,513	91,140	116,276	105,474	124,067	50,445
Light-bellied Brent Goose	142	1,419	2,706	2,705	1,723	732	65
Shelduck	21,965	42,589	61,149	64,594	78,097	79,949	56,905
Mandarin	78	209	167	69	134	49	61
Wigeon	55,145	151,479	158,200	213,665	238,369	221,411	107,909
Gadwall	5,700	6,683	6,973	7,497	6,843	5,288	3,402
Teal	67,747	91,119	93,517	121,403	135,423	100,854	37,246
Mallard	153,779	156,374	159,812	176,708	214,458	140,863	57,282
Pintail	9,026	23,041	18,463	22,509	16,019	23,091	3,913
Garganey	17	2	0	0	0	0	11
Shoveler	8,975	8,862	6,445	6,748	6,806	5,074	4,482
Pochard	11,640	23,920	35,335	33,863	37,419	36,138	12,121
Tufted Duck	34,525	37,827	46,825	46,333	48,425	46,422	34,581
Scaup	454	603	1,206	2,353	6,028	6,492	2,826
Eider	25,574	24,130	18,735	19,272	16,184	44,232	17,957
Common/Velvet Scoter+++	1,412	2,800	4,650	5,899	2,993	9,072	4,612
Long-tailed Duck	6	542	1,472	1,865	1,796	1,625	644
Goldeneye	391	2,669	8,442	13,076	16,756	17,102	12,663
Smew	1	1	19	60	67	270	32
Red-breasted Merganser	2,008	2,809	2,824	3,891	3,777	3,884	3,103
Goosander	809	1,050	1,918	3,249	2,918	3,064	1,516
Ruddy Duck	1,850	1,917	2,088	3,076	3,087	2,387	1,859
Coot	85,806	80,174	85,453	83,388	79,026	69,845	34,853

+ In all months except September, the feral component of this species is approximated by totalling counts from English (exc. Northumberland) and Welsh sites only and adding 1,500 (after Shimmings *et al.* 1989) for the feral birds in Dumfries & Galloway.

++ Includes mainly birds from the Greenlandic and Svalbard breeding populations, and a few feral birds also.

+++ In some instances, these species are inseparable.

33,396 birds (perhaps due to cold weather immigration or the expansion of coverage in the scheme). In Northern Ireland, Wigeon reached over 18,600 in October compared with just 12,500 in 1989/90 and, whilst Pochard exceeded the previous years figure by over 4,400 birds, Tufted Ducks were relatively less abundant by some 7,200 birds. Goldeneye were noticeably more abundant in Britain (over 17,000 compared with 12,700 in 1989/90) and Northern Ireland (15,200

vs 12,170), and Ruddy Ducks continued to increase, reaching almost 3,100 birds in total. There was clearly an influx of Smew to Britain in February related to the cold weather earlier in that month.

The number of seaducks, particularly Eider, scoter spp. and Long-tailed Duck, was characteristically very variable due to difficulties in observing them adequately on a regular basis. Steps are being taken to improve the monitoring of these species. These include the collation of opportunistic

Table 2. Total number of wildfowl, grebes, Cormorant and Coot counted in Northern Ireland in each month of 1990/91. The number of sites counted are given in brackets.

	Sep (114)	Oct (124)	Nov (125)	Dec (116)	Jan (147)	Feb (135)	Mar (134)
Little Grebe	687	560	722	656	500	542	289
Great Crested Grebe	750	759	1,518	1,034	942	1,040	1,088
Cormorant	1,310	1,079	1,278	1,529	869	1,283	766
Mute Swan	1,956	2,060	1,996	2,184	2,032	1,666	1,493
Bewick's Swan	0	84	343	480	347	584	113
Whooper Swan	5	828	1,875	1,658	1,593	1,476	1,284
Greenland White-fronted Goose+	0	17	13	3	3	53	55
Greylag Goose++	169	377	407	523	1,107	1,094	1,113
Light-bellied Brent Goose	14,468	15,903	10,206	4,198	3,843	3,274	3,549
Canada Goose	147	245	252	89	61	150	82
Barnacle Goose	71	68	65	64	62	56	58
Shelduck	54	514	1,474	2,416	3,128	3,738	2,675
Wigeon	8,246	18,660	10,864	5,892	9,052	4,453	1,929
Gadwall	241	169	240	148	153	170	122
Teal	1,866	3,802	4,241	5,548	6,133	4,254	1,688
Mallard	10,864	9,556	7,551	7,313	7,430	5,703	2,526
Pintail	70	88	127	251	253	134	134
Shoveler	127	274	202	161	88	59	28
Pochard	1,420	5,870	26,128	41,364	9,606	10,049	881
Tufted Duck	4,684	7,981	23,138	20,442	19,174	12,682	8,981
Scaup	4	95	583	753	615	1,821	1,579
Eider	164	816	1,207	1,382	489	630	647
Common/Velvet Scoter+++	299	0	2,480	945	483	0	191
Long-tailed Duck	2	0	32	37	44	69	18
Goldeneye	982	475	12,630	12,088	10,298	15,201	5,204
Red-breasted Merganser	584	520	442	450	426	550	544
Goosander	0	0	1	1	0	0	0
Ruddy Duck	6	34	30	2	0	14	31
Coot	8,304	8,426	7,385	5,504	4,844	4,234	2,442

+ See the appropriate Species Account for census details for the whole of Ireland.
++ It is not possible to separate the feral from the wild component of this population in Northern Ireland.
+++ In some instances, these species are inseparable.

records and the initiation of boat surveys in key areas. The recorded maximum for Coot in Britain was almost 13,000 fewer than in 1989/90.

Monthly fluctuations

Since the number of sites counted is not the same in all months, monthly count totals may not necessarily reflect true changes in relative abundance during the season. However, this can be examined by using only counts from sites counted in all seven months (September to March). Once these totals are calculated, the number present in each month can be expressed as a percentage of the maximum number present, thus revealing patterns of seasonality for the considered species. Such calculations are shown in Tables 3 & 4, for Britain and Northern Ireland separately. Non-migratory,

scarce and irregularly counted species are omitted.

In both Britain and Northern Ireland, mid-winter (December to February) was the period during which most species reached maximum abundance, the rise to this peak being steady in most cases, but especially dramatic for the swan and goose species. Other species, however, were relatively more abundant earlier in the season, during the September to November period. These included the grebes, Shoveler and Coot in both countries, Cormorant in Britain only, and Wigeon, Gadwall and Mallard in Northern Ireland only. Such patterns are perhaps indicative of either emigration from the UK or movements away from the sites counted and, for these, detailed count information from other countries, particularly Eire, would be invaluable.

Table 3. Indices for wildfowl populations in Britain, 1960/61 to 1990/91.

		Mean 60/61 -64/65	Mean 65/66 -69/70	Mean 70/71 -74/75	Mean 75/76 -79/80	Mean 80/81 -84/85	Mean 85/86 89/90	88/89	89/90	90/91
Mute Swan	Sep	105	96	103	93	119	145	158	169	174
	Jan	88	106	90	85	89	99	102	113	124
Bewick's Swan	Jan	15	50	72	153	215	272	233	244	218
Whooper Swan	Nov	69	77	104	148	164	188	235	225	178
	Jan	202	146	118	114	116	160	180	174	159
E. White-front Goose	Jan	62	85	56	39	40	59	68	43	37
Canada Goose	Sep/Jan	47	72	127	175	275	407	444	451	438
Dark-b. Brent Goose	Jan	61	87	134	305	455	475	523	406	445
Shelduck	Jan	92	106	102	132	13	128	125	125	123
Wigeon	Oct	111	112	138	149	183	194	235	219	219
	Jan	83	91	84	85	97	113	113	96	107
Gadwall	Oct	42	50	146	149	259	461	553	515	599
	Dec	86	81	164	336	781	1,275	1,464	1,488	1,562
Teal	Dec/Jan	94	76	115	150	193	188	199	259	251
Mallard	Sep	73	83	92	82	92	93	94	101	97
	Dec	78	89	86	80	90	95	91	91	90
Pintail	Dec	27	54	151	177	147	129	134	123	75
Shoveler	Oct/Nov	91	97	144	193	201	204	180	208	211
	Jan	50	63	113	139	127	99	107	123	141
Pochard	Jan	64	105	124	122	101	93	102	114	93
Tufted Duck	Sep	44	64	110	122	134	122	135	122	111
	Dec	73	91	119	123	123	142	170	130	131
Scaup	Jan	61	110	114	33	11	16	24	6	11
Goldeneye	Jan	115	92	126	109	98	107	114	104	127
Red-b. Merganser	Jan	49	101	115	245	222	210	195	129	107
Goosander	Jan	92	80	121	285	213	311	311	363	174
	Feb	171	115	153	123	171	186	191	148	184

Table 4. Proportions in each month of the peak population present on British sites that were counted in all seven months of 1990/91. The number of sites included was 1,364 and bracketed figures give averages for the 1986/87 to 1990/91 period.

	Sep	Oct	Nov	Dec	Jan	Feb	Mar
Little Grebe	100 (100)	90 (96)	76 (86)	78 (76)	70 (77)	61 (64)	51 (62)
Great C. Grebe	100 (100)	93 (93)	82 (87)	85 (75)	92 (70)	77 (74)	80 (81)
Cormorant	100 (95)	99 (100)	97 (97	86 (89)	85 (90)	86 (88)	74 (82)
Bewick's Swan	0 (0)	3 (1)	58 (36)	76 (71)	100 (99)	96 (77)	9 (17)
Whooper Swan	1 (1)	28 (36)	74 (86)	100 (75)	99 (90)	87 (81)	69 (63)
E. White-front Goose	1 (0)	4 (1)	19 (9)	63 (50)	100 (91)	82 (93)	18 (33)
Dark-b. Brent Goose	4 (1)	91 (57)	71 (73)	95 (90)	83 (93)	100 (96)	43 (48)
Shelduck	26 (18)	59 (50)	78 (67)	82 (76)	95 (93)	100 (97)	76 (81)
Wigeon	27 (19)	61 (56)	82 (75)	98 (88)	100 (100)	99 (73)	51 (44)
Gadwall	84 (76)	99 (90)	92 (92)	100 (96)	91 (83)	74 (69)	50 (47)
Teal	54 (51)	73 (69)	74 (81)	92 (98)	100 (82)	74 (66)	28 (37)
Mallard	86 (87)	84 (89)	85 (91)	90 (97)	100 (94)	71 (66)	31 (36)
Pintail	42 (38)	98 (84)	79 (83)	98 (93)	65 (75)	100 (62)	18 (17)
Shoveler	100 (89)	96 (96)	71 (75)	76 (69)	72 (57)	54 (61)	50 (51)
Pochard	31 (31)	67 (63)	94 (88)	93 (98)	100 (95)	95 (92)	33 (42)
Tufted Duck	76 (79)	82 (80)	99 (96)	99 (98)	100 (97)	98 (87)	77 (75)
Goldeneye	3 (1)	13 (11)	59 (55)	80 (77)	94 (91)	100 (99)	89 (92)
Goosander	29 (24)	27 (23)	61 (45)	90 (80)	68 (87)	100 (78)	49 (63)
Coot	100 (88)	95 (96)	96 (95)	92 (92)	82 (84)	76 (66)	39 (44)

Population indices

Because not all sites are counted in every year, population changes cannot be derived from simply comparing the total numbers counted in each year. Consequently, a simple method of indexing population change has been derived and has been applied to wildfowl counts for many years.

Table 5 gives index values for individual species in Britain for each of the 1988/89 to 1990/91 seasons, and for earlier five-year periods for comparison. Indices are not, as yet, calculated for Northern Ireland. The values are obtained by comparing only counts for sites covered in the relevant month in consecutive years, and by relating the ratio of the two monthly totals to an arbitrary standard, nominally 1970/71, when the index was set at 100. The months chosen for each species are those in which the greatest numbers are usually present. For species which may peak in either of two months, the average indices for these months are given, and for those with significant populations at different times of the year (usually autumn and mid-winter), separate sets of indices are given. Species for which complete censuses are attempted

each year (e.g. Pink-footed Goose) and species counted irregularly (e.g. seaducks) are omitted.

Indices for 1990/91 suggest relatively large population increases in Britain for Mute Swans, Gadwall, Shoveler and Goldeneye. Amongst these, the increase in Gadwall in both October and December was particularly marked. For Goosander, the trends went in opposite directions according to the month chosen, with a large decrease in January and an increase in February. Indices for the remaining species suggested relative stability or population declines, though most declines were relatively small. Declines of 21% for Whooper Swan in November and of 39% for Pintail in December were the only two that exceeded 20%.

Species accounts

Detailed information for the wintering wildfowl species are provided in the *Species Accounts* elsewhere in this volume.

Principal sites

The peak counts for each site holding more than 10,000 wildfowl, grebes, Cormorant and Coot

Table 5. Proportions in each month of the peak population present on Northern Ireland sites that were counted in all seven months of 1990/91. The number of sites included was 96 and bracketed figures give equivalent figures for 1989/90.

	Sep	Oct	Nov	Dec	Jan	Feb	Mar
Little Grebe	100 (77)	70 (89)	94 (100)	89 (77)	66 (54)	76 (37)	34 (26)
Great C. Grebe	100 (70)	63 (72)	41 (35)	37 (100)	64 (18)	51 (27)	97 (68)
Cormorant	81 (100)	59 (93)	66 (83)	100 (90)	51 (55)	77 (35)	50 (54)
Bewick's Swan	0 (0)	14 (0)	59 (76)	82 (100)	60 (78)	100 (48)	19 (9)
Whooper Swan	0 (0)	45 (27)	100 (60)	86 (69)	79 (91)	75 (99)	63 (100)
Shelduck	2 (7)	14 (9)	39 (77)	63 (100)	73 (98)	100 (90)	70 (87)
Wigeon	44 (25)	100 (95)	55 (100)	25 (56)	43 (76)	20 (33)	10 (30)
Gadwall	100 (54)	70 (88)	99 (79)	61 (95)	62 (100)	71 (45)	51 (58)
Teal	34 (50)	65 (57)	69 (66)	86 (100)	100 (90)	67 (42)	26 (45)
Mallard	100 (100)	82 (90)	65 (68)	62 (50)	61 (55)	49 (29)	22 (21)
Pintail	28 (16)	35 (31)	50 (100)	98 (93)	100 (95)	53 (82)	53 (19)
Shoveler	47 (39)	100 (100)	73 (53)	59 (37)	31 (72)	21 (29)	9 (36)
Pochard	3 (4)	14 (29)	63 (77)	100 (100)	23 (44)	24 (11)	2 (3)
Tufted Duck	20 (18)	34 (63)	100 (25)	89 (100)	83 (66)	55 (37)	38 (30)
Scaup	0 (0)	6 (5)	37 (0)	47 (100)	20 (30)	91 (34)	100 (60)
Goldeneye	7 (0)	3 (9)	87 (28)	82 (100)	68 (34)	100 (43)	34 (84)
Coot	100 (82)	95 (100)	81 (77)	63 (70)	54 (54)	47 (32)	27 (28)

were calculated by listing the highest count for each species, irrespective of the month in which it was made, and then totalling these counts. Peak counts in 1990/91 at 14 sites exceeded the appropriate five year average by over 30%, thus revealing considerable increases in the importance of these sites. These were Medway Est. (+152%), Loch Eye (+143%), Loch of Skene (+85%), Tay Estuary (+65%), Wash (+57%), Ribble Estuary (+50%), Crouch/Roach (+48%), Swale (+47%), Loch of Harray (+44%), Poole Harbour (+42%), Forth Estuary (+40%), Loch Leven (+37%), North Norfolk Marshes (+33%) and The Fleet/Wey (+32%). Conversely, seven sites supported much smaller numbers than expected: Martin Mere (-59%), Hamford Water (-49%), Burry Inlet (-47%) and Cromarty Firth (-42%). The ranking of sites according to the total numbers of birds they support should not be taken as a rank order of the conservation importance of these sites. This is because certain sites, perhaps low down in terms of their total numbers, may nevertheless be of critical importance to certain species or populations at certain times, for example during the main migratory periods.

How is the work being done?

The NWC programme receives financial support from the Joint Nature Conservation Committee (JNCC), the RSPB and the Department of the Environment for Northern Ireland (DoE(NI), and is organized by staff from WWT headquarters in Slimbridge, Gloucestershire. Many thousands of rivers, canals and ponds. Most counts take place during the autumn and winter period, between September and March, although valuable information from other times of the year is currently also received. To complement the monthly counts, volunteer ornithologists throughout the UK take part, and the success of the programme to date reflects their enthusiasm for ensuring the safeguard of the UK's wildfowl and their habitats.

Instigated in 1947, the core activity in the counts programme comprises the once-monthly counts on estuaries and coastal bays, reservoirs, lochs/loughs, gravel pits, freshwater marshes. Additional surveys of certain swans and geese are organized in most years, as some species prove difficult to census completely by the monthly counts alone. 'Special Surveys' of breeding and moulting waterfowl are also carried out. The

WWT works closely with the BTO, as both organizations collect information on the waterfowl occupying coastal sites.

Where can more information be obtained?

Summary statistics of the most recent NWC census data, and its applications are published in *Wildfowl and Wader Counts* (Kirby *et al.* 1991). New participants to NWC are always very welcome. Volunteers receive newsletters, a comprehensive annual report, and there regular regional conferences.

Further information may be obtained by contacting the Waterfowl Counts Officer, WWT, Slimbridge.

References

Kirby, J.S., Ferns, J.R., Prys-Jones, R.P. & Waters, R.J. (1991). *Wildfowl and Wader Counts 1990-91*. WWT, Slimbridge.

Shimmings, P.J., Owen, M. & Burn, J.L. (1989). Feral Greylag Geese and other breeding wildfowl in south-west Scotland. *Scottish Birds* 15, 162-169.

Barnacle Geese

British censuses of Pink-footed, Icelandic Greylag and Dark-bellied Brent Geese: 1990/1991

J S Kirby & P A Cranswick

Research and Conservation Department, WWT

Summary

The 31st British census of Pink-footed and Icelandic Greylag Geese in 1990/91 produced the highest totals of both species in Britain, but may still under-estimate true population sizes. Counts of Dark-bellied Brent Geese in 1991 at 41 coastal sites in Britain also produced the highest total yet. The principal concentration was present on the Wash which is outstanding in its importance for this sub-species. Further details are provided here.

Coverage and timing

National goose censuses take place as part of the National Waterfowl Counts (NWC) programme which is organised by the WWT and financially supported by the JNCC, RSPB and the Department of the Environment for Northern Ireland (DoENI). The information gathered is widely used for both research and conservation purposes. In particular, the data are essential to the JNCC for supporting the protection of individual sites under both national and international legislation. Also, the JNCC, and other conservation bodies, draw heavily on these data when preparing management plans for sites or species. Here we provide a brief overview of the results of the censuses of Pink-footed, Icelandic Greylags and Dark-bellied Brent Geese which took place during the autumn and winter of 1990/91. More detailed information is presented in Kirby & Cranswick (1991) and Kirby (1991a,b).

The census of Pink-footed and Greylag Geese was the 31st in Britain. The methods used were similar to those of previous years, with most observations being made by volunteer counters, and the majority of geese being counted at roost sites. Also, as usual, additional counts were made over the 2-11th November by M.A. Ogilvie who, together with a small number of experienced observers, assessed breeding success by recording the proportion of young birds and brood sizes in sample flocks. The census differed from previous ones in two main ways: (a) coverage was extended to include some parts of south-west Iceland (with counts mainly between 20 October and 11 November); (b) in Britain, two discrete counts were undertaken, on 20/21st October and 10/11th November, instead of just a November count. This was done due to recent detailed studies in central and south-east Scotland that have suggested that early to mid-November was no longer the best time to census Pink-footed Geese (Newton *et al.* 1990). This species is certainly more concentrated shortly after arrival than is the case later in the season, and generally occupies sites which are well counted, the use of which may be more predictable than later in the season. The aim, therefore, was to carry out two counts in 1990 to see which provided the higher national estimate.

The census of Dark-bellied Brent Geese was carried out on 20th January and 17th February 1991, for the fourth consecutive winter. It involved counting the geese in intertidal areas, but also feeding on grasslands and in arable crops, frequently at some distance from the coast. The 41 sites included in this census are the principal sites for this sub-species in Britain (see Kirby & Salmon 1990a), and all areas within each of these were searched for geese on the specified dates and the numbers and precise localities of flocks recorded, together with habitat details and notes on their activity and behaviour.

The conditions for counting over the October census weekend were generally satisfactory, with the majority of observers indicating that good counts had been made. This was certainly not the case in November, however, since localised patches of fog, mist and heavy rain resulted in poor visibility and reduced counting accuracy in a number of areas, particularly in southern Scotland and around the Moray Basin. Visibility and weather conditions in January and February were generally good, and few problems were encountered, though the count weekend in February was particularly cold.

Pink-footed and Greylag Geese

Total numbers

In Britain, 144 areas were checked for geese in October and 192 in November, coverage for the latter count being the most complete ever. Virtually no birds were found at the additional sites counted in November, and thus direct comparison of totals for the two months was possible. The maximum count of 194,752 Pink-footed Geese was obtained in November (Table 1) and was the largest total yet recorded. It compares with 182,969 recorded in the previous November (Kirby & Salmon 1990b) but is still likely to be an under-estimate (perhaps by more than 10,000 birds) due to the poor weather conditions in some areas. The October count total of Pink-feet constituted ca. 90% of that recorded in November.

For Greylags, the November count produced 114,678 birds (Table 1), also the largest total yet recorded in Britain. As with the Pink-footed Goose, this was likely to under-estimate the population size, due to poor weather conditions in some areas and disturbance. However, this total places the population back on the steady increase observed in recent years, an increase that was apparently interrupted in 1989 when only 83,577 birds were recorded (Kirby & Salmon 1990b). For Greylags, only a little over two-thirds of the November total had apparently arrived by the October count date. Counts in Iceland produced relatively few Pink-feet or Greylags, and field-workers there considered that almost all geese had left Iceland by the last days of October.

Although it would be wrong to draw too many conclusions from this first year of two counts, it should be noted that the higher numbers of both species were recorded in November, the time when the annual census traditionally takes place. Indeed, it would appear that an equally comprehensive national count of Pink-feet can be obtained in either October or November, though it may be necessary to cover more sites (and thus use more observers) in November than in October to achieve a similar result. An October count alone would not be desirable for Greylags though, as only part of the population was present by that time. Thus, in order to estimate total population sizes of both species, continuation of the November census would appear to be desirable and will also ensure

continuity with previous national censuses, though it could be supplemented with an earlier census.

Distribution

Table 1 provides a regional breakdown of the census results. In October, about 62% of Pink-feet were found in just three regions, Perth & Kinross, the Lothians and Borders, but by November the proportion counted in these regions had dropped to around 37%. Numbers had increased markedly by this time in Banff & Buchan, Lancashire, Norfolk and, to a lesser extent, Caithness.

Greylags were more widely dispersed than Pink-feet, with many more regions contributing relatively large numbers of birds to the grand totals in both months (Table 1). However, there were notable concentrations, with Ross & Cromarty/Sutherland, Moray and Perth & Kinross together holding just over 53% of the Greylags counted in October. In November, each of these regions contributed relatively fewer to the total count (21.8% in total), and there were obvious increases in NE Scotland as a whole and in SW Scotland/NW England.

Principal sites

Of the areas checked, only 13 supported more than 5,000 Pink-feet in either October or November. The peak counts (all October unless stated otherwise) at these were as follows: Loch of Strathbeg (37,100, November), Ribble Estuary (20,700, November), West Water Reservoir (21,300), Aberlady Bay (17,500), Loch Leven (16,000), Montrose Basin (12,700, November), Hule Moss (10,030), Carsebreck/Strathallan (9,900), Snettisham (9,300, November), Dupplin Lochs (8,200), Solway (7,259), Martin Mere (6,365, November), Loch Tullybelton (5,500) and Fala Flow (5,500). For Greylags, five areas held more than 5,000 individuals: Loch Eye (16,607, November), Dinnet Lochs (15,989, November), Loch of Skene (15,764, November), Loch Spynie (6,100, October) and Haddo Country Park (5,900).

Whilst these single counts go some way towards highlighting the significance of particular sites to geese, their importance is not fully assessed by the results of the national census alone. For example, there were 42,000 Pink-feet at Dupplin Lochs on the 7th October, but only 8,200 on the October and 5,470 on the November count dates. In the Borders, West Water Reservoir held 23,500 Pink-feet at the end of September and 24,700 on the 6th/7th October, somewhat higher than the 21,300 and 12,430 recorded on the

Table 1. Total numbers and regional distribution of Pink-footed and Greylag Geese in Britain in October and November 1990.

	No. of areas checked		Pink-footed		Greylag	
	Oct	Nov	Oct	Nov	Oct	Nov
Shetland	-	-	-	-	-	-
Orkney	3	4	6	120	1,040	3,970
Western Isles	1	0	1	-	0	-
Caithness	6	6	0	3,064	0	2,860
Ross & Crom./Suther.	13	13	20	330	20,342	8,550
Inverness/Nairn	6	7	530	410	2,720	9,790
Badenoch & Strathspey	1	1	37	8	523	1,592
Moray	3	3	47	280	9,240	7,250
Banff & Buchan	2	2	15,900	37,110	130	3,650
Gordon/Aberdeen	3	3	2,230	3,600	7,120	21,890
Kincardine & Deeside	1	1	20	610	6,610	15,990
Angus/Dundee	10	11	4,930	15,370	4,940	3,980
Perth & Kinross	13	21	48,400	31,800	11,270	9,260
Central	5	6	8,250	5,690	848	2,430
Fife	6	7	1,190	5,350	60	2,920
Argyll & Bute	4	9	0	4	1,070	4,981
Glasgow area	6	28	0	24	1,030	2,890
Clydesdale	2	2	5,000	5,200	250	190
Wigtown	4	10	40	40	1,750	2,370
Stewartry	5	5	2	1	910	930
Nithsdale	2	3	0	0	0	70
Annandale/Eskdale	2	4	7,260	2,780	432	598
Lothians	10	9	28,780	20,690	1,212	2,120
Borders	9	10	31,366	19,530	1,478	3,090
Northumberland	6	6	40	246	2,100	2,010
Cumbria	3	4	0	17	800	730
Lancashire	8	8	9,650	31,960	0	0
Humberside	-	-	-	-	-	-
Lincolnshire	6	5	15	168	0	0
Norfolk	4	4	2,010	10,350	380	430
GRAND TOTALS	144	192	175,724	194,752	76,286	114,678

October and November count dates respectively (A.W. Brown, in litt.). It is clear that site assessments could be greatly improved by having numerous counts available for a particular site, made throughout the autumn to spring period, rather than relying on one or a few counts made around the time of the census. This represents a high priority for the future.

Breeding success

The proportion of young Pink-feet observed in flocks in Scotland, Lancashire and Norfolk (21.5%, n=12,716) shows a return to what appears to be a normal level of breeding success after a poor year in 1989 (13.0%). The figures obtained varied regionally, perhaps due to differences in flock size, habitat and observer differences. This may well apply to regional differences in the brood size data also, which was measured as 2.22 overall in 1990 (n=370) compared with 1.72 in 1989.

The proportion of young Greylags in 1990 also reflects a relatively good breeding season at 20.7% (n=3,997), and compares with 12.3% in 1989 and 22.5% in 1988. Although the number of Greylags aged in 1990 was smaller than for Pink-feet, the brood size data revealed a remarkable degree of consistency between most regions, and was calculated at 2.51 young/pair overall (n=148).

Dark-bellied Brent Geese

Total numbers and distribution

Table 2 gives total numbers of Dark-bellied Brent Geese counted in Britain in January and February 1991, together with figures for the previous three winters for comparison. The peak count, of almost 109,400 in February, should be viewed as incomplete due to partial counts from a number of sites, notably Southampton Water and the Medway. Indeed, the actual number present in that month was probably around 115,000, representing the highest total yet recorded in Britain. The total number in January 1991 was considerably lower, probably around 100,000, so there had undoubtedly been a sizeable influx between these dates.

The counts made at numerous sites in 1991 were relatively high compared with previous winters. This was especially true of the peak totals from the Thames (12,419), Crouch/Roach (8,388), Hamford Water (6,889), Deben (2,051), Exe (1,526), Poole Harbour (1,512), Brading Harbour (1,245) and Yar (1,200). There are currently 16 British sites that regularly hold numbers in excess of the level required for international importance (1,700) (Table 3). Of these, the Wash is outstanding in its importance. Five additional sites, including the tiny Newtown estuary on the Isle of Wight, hold numbers which makes them·of national importance for this sub-species.

Breeding success

During September to December 1990, some

Table 2. Total numbers of Dark-bellied Brent Geese counted at coastal sites in Britain in January and February 1991, with earlier years for comparison. Incomplete totals are preceded by an asterisk.

	January	February
1988	95,802	92,162
1989	102,552	94,712
1990	*83,749	*73,624
1991	94,440	109,371

44,574 Dark-bellied Brent Geese were aged at various localities on the British coast and 21.4% were juveniles, thus revealing a moderate level of breeding success for the population in summer 1990 (Kirby 1991a). The average brood size was 3.0 juveniles per pair overall (n=762). Using these data, it was predicted that 94-141,000 geese would resort to Britain in mid-winter 1990/91. The peak total actually recorded in 1991, of around 115,000, falls approximately in the middle of the predicted range.

More information

Much more information on the goose censuses and the NWC programme in general, including copies of *Wildfowl and Wader Counts* (Kirby *et al.* 1991) and other reports and papers, is available on request from the Waterfowl Counts Officer at WWT, Slimbridge. Similarly, persons may access the count data themselves, for research or conservation purposes, and we would be happy to advise on data availability and interpretation.

Table 3. Principal sites for Dark-bellied Brent Geese in Britain. The sites are ranked according to average January/February maxima, 1988-1991.

Sites with internationally important numbers:

Wash	21,773
N Norfolk	10,691
Thames	9,169
Chichester Hbr	9,132
Blackwater	6,852
Langstone Hbr	6,678
Hamford Water	4,860
Crouch	4,843
Colne	4,725
Medway	2,931
Pagham Hbr	2,660
Swale	2,464
NW Solent	2,403
Dengie	2,196
Portsmouth Hbr	2,136
Southampton	2,072

Sites with nationally important numbers:

Stour	1,302
Humber	1,284
Exe	1,182
Newtown	1,154
Poole Harbour	963

Remaining sites:

Deben	898
Beaulieu	830
The Fleet/Way	722
Burry Inlet	696
Yar	448
Brading Habour	416
Alde complex	353
Christchurch Harbout	184

Can you help?

The national goose censuses and the NWC programme in general, is always needing more volunteers to contribute these very valuable counts. If you could spare anything from one to several weekends per year then please contact the Waterfowl Counts Officer at WWT, Slimbridge. We would be delighted to hear from you and believe that every birdwatcher can make a real and valued contribution to our research and conservation efforts.

References

Kirby, J.S. (1991a). *An assessment of breeding success in the Dark-bellied Brent Goose in 1990*. WWT rept. to NCC, Slimbridge.

Kirby, J.S. (1991b). *Numbers of Dark-bellied Brent Geese in Britain, January/February 1991*. WWT rept. to JNCC, Slimbridge.

Kirby, J.S. & Cranswick, P.A. (1991). *The 1990 national census of Pink-footed and Greylag Geese in Britain*. WWT rept. to JNCC, Slimbridge.

Kirby, J.S., Ferns, J.R., Waters, R.J. & Prys-Jones, R.P. 1991. *Wildfowl and Wader Counts 1990-91*. The Wildfowl & Wetlands Trust, Slimbridge.

Kirby, J.S. & Salmon, D.G. (1990a). *Numbers of Dark-bellied Brent Geese in Britain, mid-winter 1989/90*. WWT rept. to NCC, Slimbridge.

Kirby, J.S. & Salmon, D.G. (1990b). *National census of Pink-footed and Greylag Geese in Britain, November 1989*. WWT rept. to NCC, Slimbridge.

Newton, S.F., Bell, M.V., Brown, A.W. & Murray, R. (1990). Pink-footed Goose numbers at arrival sites in eastern and central Scotland. *Scottish Birds* 16, 35-36.

Mike Weston/Dark-bellied Brent Geese

Birds of Estuaries Enquiry 1990/91

R J Waters & R P Prŷs-Jones[1]

Estuaries Unit, BTO

How is the BoEE carried out?

The key aim of the Birds of Estuaries Enquiry (BoEE) is to monitor the waterfowl populations present on all main estuaries of the United Kingdom, together with a selection of stretches of open coast shore. Towards this end, co-ordinated counts by about 1,000 volunteer participants are carried out throughout the year on selected dates near the middle of each month, timed to coincide with the best tidal conditions for censusing estuarine birds. The programme is carried out in close liaison with the WWT, the results for wildfowl being made available for incorporation with those of the National Wildfowl Count scheme. The Enquiry is organised by staff of the BTO Estuaries Unit and is co-sponsored by BTO, RSPB, English Nature (EN), Scottish Natural Heritage (SNH), Countryside Council for Wales (CCW) & DoE(NI) (through JNCC). Prater (1981) provides full details of BoEE methodology, and Prys-Jones (1988) gives a brief overview of the aims, history and results from the BoEE and associated projects since its start in 1969.

Coverage achieved in 1990/91

The main period of the year covered in this report is the winter (November-March), although additional information relating to spring (April-June) and autumn (July-October) is provided in the Species Accounts sections for those species with notable passage populations.

The level of coverage in 1990/91 was exceptionally good, with winter counting being achieved for the first time on every one of the 117 estuaries (Figure 1). Complete counts were made at least once at all sites except the Humber, Rough Firth and Dulas Bay, with most sites receiving complete coverage in at least three of the five winter months.

Wintering wader populations in 1990/91

Table 1 shows the total populations of each wader

1. Current address: British Museum (NH), Sub-department of Ornithology, Akeman St., Tring, Herts HP23

species counted in each winter month of 1990/91 in both Britain and Northern Ireland, together with the numbers of BoEE sites covered in each month. Because of their behaviour, recorded totals of Jack Snipe and Snipe are likely to be much smaller than the populations actually present, but for other species the figures should provide reliable estimates of the populations on the sites covered.

1990/91 was a third successive year of record-breaking numbers, probably as a result of a combination of the increasingly complete coverage achieved and of a succession of generally mild winters. For the first time, a monthly UK count (January 1991) exceeded 1.7 million waders, and numbers in each winter month were higher than in any previous year. Counts of over 9,000 Black-tailed Godwits in November and over 1,500 Avocets in January were substantially the highest UK winter totals of these species ever recorded by the BoEE. See Table 1.

The February counts for Oystercatcher, Grey Plover and, most notably, Bar-tailed Godwit also appear to be records for any winter month. These February peaks followed a very cold spell, which caused a major movement of Bar-tailed Godwits into the UK, presumably from the Wadden Sea area. This cold spell caused an opposite response among Lapwing, Golden Plover and Black-tailed Godwit, which all recorded much lower totals in February than January.

Last, but not least, Dunlin numbers in each month of the winter were well up on the equivalent totals recorded in winter 1989/90; not since the mid-1970s have UK mid-winter monthly totals for this species exceeded 500,000.

Population trends among wintering waders

The geographical coverage achieved by the BoEE varies somewhat from year to year; it is therefore not satisfactory to derive population changes for species between successive winters simply from the countrywide totals of birds counted. Instead, indices of relative population change are obtained by comparing counts from those UK sites covered in each successive pair of Januarys, with the

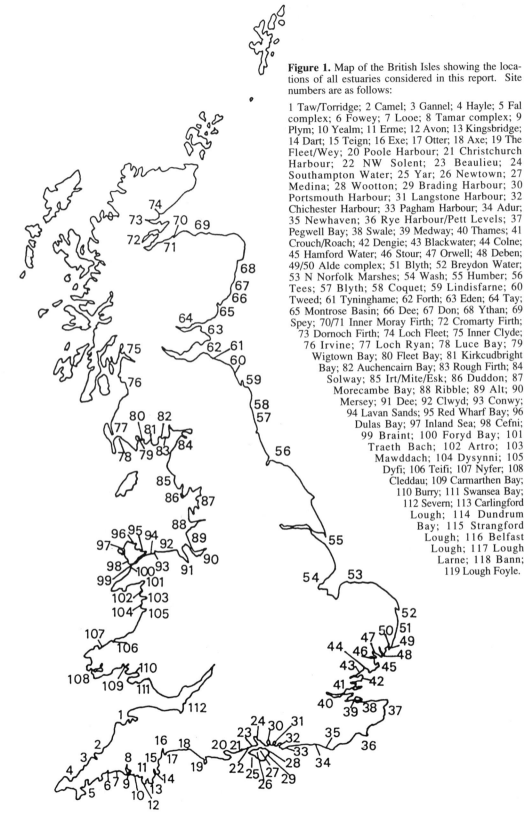

Figure 1. Map of the British Isles showing the locations of all estuaries considered in this report. Site numbers are as follows:

1 Taw/Torridge; 2 Camel; 3 Gannel; 4 Hayle; 5 Fal complex; 6 Fowey; 7 Looe; 8 Tamar complex; 9 Plym; 10 Yealm; 11 Erme; 12 Avon; 13 Kingsbridge; 14 Dart; 15 Teign; 16 Exe; 17 Otter; 18 Axe; 19 The Fleet/Wey; 20 Poole Harbour; 21 Christchurch Harbour; 22 NW Solent; 23 Beaulieu; 24 Southampton Water; 25 Yar; 26 Newtown; 27 Medina; 28 Wootton; 29 Brading Harbour; 30 Portsmouth Harbour; 31 Langstone Harbour; 32 Chichester Harbour; 33 Pagham Harbour; 34 Adur; 35 Newhaven; 36 Rye Harbour/Pett Levels; 37 Pegwell Bay; 38 Swale; 39 Medway; 40 Thames; 41 Crouch/Roach; 42 Dengie; 43 Blackwater; 44 Colne; 45 Hamford Water; 46 Stour; 47 Orwell; 48 Deben; 49/50 Alde complex; 51 Blyth; 52 Breydon Water; 53 N Norfolk Marshes; 54 Wash; 55 Humber; 56 Tees; 57 Blyth; 58 Coquet; 59 Lindisfarne; 60 Tweed; 61 Tyninghame; 62 Forth; 63 Eden; 64 Tay; 65 Montrose Basin; 66 Dee; 67 Don; 68 Ythan; 69 Spey; 70/71 Inner Moray Firth; 72 Cromarty Firth; 73 Dornoch Firth; 74 Loch Fleet; 75 Inner Clyde; 76 Irvine; 77 Loch Ryan; 78 Luce Bay; 79 Wigtown Bay; 80 Fleet Bay; 81 Kirkcudbright Bay; 82 Auchencairn Bay; 83 Rough Firth; 84 Solway; 85 Irt/Mite/Esk; 86 Duddon; 87 Morecambe Bay; 88 Ribble; 89 Alt; 90 Mersey; 91 Dee; 92 Clwyd; 93 Conwy; 94 Lavan Sands; 95 Red Wharf Bay; 96 Dulas Bay; 97 Inland Sea; 98 Cefni; 99 Braint; 100 Foryd Bay; 101 Traeth Bach; 102 Artro; 103 Mawddach; 104 Dysynni; 105 Dyfi; 106 Teifi; 107 Nyfer; 108 Cleddau; 109 Carmarthen Bay; 110 Burry; 111 Swansea Bay; 112 Severn; 113 Carlingford Lough; 114 Dundrum Bay; 115 Strangford Lough; 116 Belfast Lough; 117 Lough Larne; 118 Bann; 119 Lough Foyle.

Table 1. Total numbers of waders recorded by BoEE counts in the United Kingdom during winter 1990/91.

BRITAIN

	November	December	January	February	March
Oystercatcher	247,131	257,761	269,761	277,091	161,707
Avocet	1,141	1,418	1,564	1,044	718
L. Ringed Plover	0	0	1	0	0
Ringed Plover	11,880	10,935	10,202	8,310	4,313
Kentish Plover	0	0	1	0	1
Golden Plover	56,309	52,238	42,912	25,885	20,502
Grey Plover	36,259	37,170	40,779	43,186	36,422
Lapwing	138,080	173,511	130,534	44,858	15,032
Knot	292,117	247,973	278,735	247,342	121,508
Sanderling	6,717	5,111	6,405	4,818	7,451
Little Stint	10	5	9		10
Curlew Sandpiper	10	1	0	0	0
Purple Sandpiper	1,312	1,246	1,832	2,039	1,185
Dunlin	423,977	526,991	567,173	533,782	231,945
Ruff	111	39	106	134	100
Jack Snipe	56	48	19	37	22
Snipe	2,027	2,382	2,516	1,358	906
Woodcock	2	0	0	16	0
Black-tailed Godwit	9,440	8,056	7,028	4,724	7,922
Bar-tailed Godwit	37,645	39,401	43,458	71,912	19,034
Whimbrel	11	6	5	1	8
Curlew	56,463	58,663	67,774	62,544	65,807
Spotted Redshank	109	84	60	51	51
Redshank	74,429	72,784	69,093	62,870	47,725
Greenshank	198	188	166	157	161
Green Sandpiper	44	45	31	14	10
Terek Sandpiper	1	0	0	0	0
Common Sandpiper	25	34	28	8	5
Turnstone	15,651	15,923	17,199	15,927	15,900
Total	**1,411,155**	**1,512,013**	**1,627,011**	**1,408,109**	**758,435**
No. sites counted	136	146	150	144	135

NORTHERN IRELAND

	November	December	January	February	March
Oystercatcher	13,622	13,115	13,698	12,598	7,901
Ringed Plover	1,310	1,007	1,140	1,053	385
Golden Plover	7,242	6,231	7,485	4,370	5,929
Grey Plover	135	142	184	152	66
Lapwing	12,284	12,903	19,106	18,480	622
Knot	2,020	6,673	1,566	896	565
Sanderling	18	13	57	40	63
Purple Sandpiper	111	122	132	101	130
Dunlin	8,658	11,721	16,268	12,286	3,830
Ruff	1	3	4	4	0
Jack Snipe	3	1	0	0	0
Snipe	126	209	157	84	69
Black-tailed Godwit	99	181	152	164	135
Bar-tailed Godwit	510	937	2,709	4,063	2,623
Curlew	3,499	4,346	6,017	4,909	4,422
Spotted Redshank	0	1	1	2	0
Redshank	5,606	4,989	4,488	5,975	4,712
Greenshank	78	74	94	75	51
Turnstone	2,422	2,356	2,940	2,676	2,486
Total	**57,744**	**65,024**	**76,198**	**67,929**	**33,989**
No. sites counted	9	10	10	9	7
UK Totals	**1,468,899**	**1,577,037**	**1,703,209**	**1,476,038**	**792,424**

results for January 1973 having been arbitrarily assigned a value of 100. Species which occur only in small total numbers are excluded, as are Lapwing and Golden Plover for which a large but variable proportion of the populations occur inland. For all species, it should be borne in mind that whereas long-term trends in index values almost certainly indicate real changes in wintering population levels, short-term fluctuations may merely reflect changes in population distribution caused by factors such as the weather.

Over the 21 years covered by the January population index, striking increases in wintering numbers have occurred among Oystercatchers and Grey Plovers whereas Dunlin have tended to decline (Table 2). In the case of Oystercatchers and Grey Plovers, the trend over recent years remains upwards; for Dunlin, however, a major decline starting in 1974 appears to have "bottomed out" by the mid-1980s, with signs of a subsequent recovery. Between 1990 and 1991, the January indices of Grey Plover, Sanderling, Dunlin and Bar-tailed Godwit all increased by over 10%, whereas those for Curlew, Redshank and Turnstone declined by over 10%. More detailed information on species covered by BoEE counts may be found in the *Species Accounts* section elsewhere in this volume.

Principal wintering wader sites

The peak wader counts for winter 1990/91, along with the average peak winter wader counts for the five-year period 1986/87 - 1990/91, are listed in Table 3 for all estuarine sites covered by the BoEE. The only non-estuarine site supporting more than 10,000 waders, the Outer Ards

(Northern Ireland), is also included. For each site, the 1990/91 peak winter count was calculated by summing the highest counts for each species between November and March, irrespective of month. The resulting totals thus represent standardised minimum estimates of the overall numbers of waders using each site during the winter. The sites are listed in descending order of their five-year average peak winter counts, which provide the estimates of regular wintering population size used in assessing their national or international importance in conservation terms.

Most sites supported higher than average wader populations in winter 1990/91, but peak numbers at four of the large sites stand out as exceeding their five-year averages by over 50%. Three of these, North Norfolk Marshes, Breydon Water and Hamford Water, are in East Anglia, but the species responsible for the increases were different at each site. On the North Norfolk Marshes it was a high population of Knot, whereas on Breydon Water there were large numbers of Lapwing; at Hamford Water, an array of species showed increases, with that for Ringed Plover being particularly striking. The fourth estuary, the Mersey, supported exceptional populations of Lapwing, Grey Plover and Dunlin. Dunlin also showed marked population increases on other major west coast sites such as Morecambe Bay and the Severn.

Developments in 1990/91

An important new initiative in late 1990 was the establishment of a new database on wader productivity. It had become increasingly clear that interpretation of the observed variations and trends in UK wintering wader numbers, revealed by the

Table 2. January indices for wader populations in the United Kingdom, 1971–91.

	Mean 1971 to '75	Mean 1976 to '80	Mean 1981 to '85	1986	1987	1988	1989	1990	1991
Oystercatcher	116	158	173	203	171	215	238	244	222
Ringed Plover	107	129	141	162	105	129	169	149	149
Grey Plover	115	157	173	221	199	299	386	326	366
Knot	112	84	83	92	82	88	92	119	113
Sanderling	129	120	107	104	85	103	81	87	108
Dunlin	101	93	71	64	55	64	77	78	92
Bar-t.Godwit	101	137	184	166	190	161	142	105	123
Curlew	119	103	93	75	69	108	101	110	84
Redshank	100	97	77	78	69	100	109	108	85
Turnstone	118	143	130	192	144	173	181	179	160

Indices for all species set at 100 for 1973.

BoEE, could be much improved if we had better understanding of annual variations in the breeding success of the species and populations present. This cannot be gathered on their far-flung breeding grounds, but can potentially be deduced from knowledge of the proportions of first-year birds in wintering populations, as is being done by the WWT for geese. BTO ringers already collected this information for most of the many waders they catch, and the problem therefore lay in making results from existing studies available in a form suitable for easy extraction and analysis. This co-ordination of the efforts of ringers and BoEE counters represents an exciting development which will hopefully yield much new information.

Many studies were carried out by the Estuaries Unit under various contracts during the year in question. Notable among these were on-going major projects on the Severn and Mersey estuaries, where proposals to build large tidal-energy barrages have stimulated detailed investigation of the ecology of the intertidal bird populations present. Similar work was also carried out in Cardiff Bay, where there was a proposal to construct a non-permeable barrage which would submerge the area under a freshwater lake. The long-term data from the BoEE have formed an invaluable basis for these studies, but in addition the collection of comprehensive information on low-tide feeding distributions has been necessary. The wider value of these latter studies was strikingly revealed following major oil spills on the Mersey in August 1989 and on the Severn in February 1991. In each case, the Estuaries Unit was well placed to conduct assessments of oil impact because of the comprehensive pre-spill information it held on bird distribution, largely gathered through the efforts of our volunteer counters.

An ever-increasing number of development proposals seriously threaten a number of our estuaries. Detailed knowledge of low-tide feeding distribution of intertidal birds is essential when assessing the likely impacts of these schemes. The Estuaries Unit studies on the Severn and Mersey have revealed that, even on large and complex estuaries, it is possible for co-ordinated teams of volunteer counters to obtain this information. With strong backing from the RSPB and JNCC, we are therefore hoping to initiate a programme of low-tide counting which would result in coverage of all the main UK estuaries at intervals of five or so years, and the maintenance of a computerised database of results. Plans for a pilot survey of a number of estuaries during winter 1992/93 are cur-

rently being formulated, and in the meantime we would welcome receiving information as to sites at which locally-based projects are planned or already underway.

Where can more information be obtained?

A comprehensive summary of the results of the BoEE is published jointly with that from the Wildfowl and Wetlands Trust's NWC in an annual, 80 page booklet *Wildfowl and Wader Counts*. The latest issue, for 1990/91, is available for £5.00 (inc. p & p) from the BTO.

Help needed

Coverage for the BoEE remains good, with all estuarine sites counted in 1990/91. However, additional offers of assistance are always extremely welcome from any birdwatcher for both the BoEE and other Estuaries Unit projects. If you are willing to help provide the facts to conserve our estuaries by turning out at least once each winter month, please contact Ray Waters, Estuaries Unit, BTO.

References

Moser, M.E. (1987). A revision of population estimates for waders (*Charadrii*) wintering on the coastline of Britain. *Biol.Conserv.* 39, 153-164.

Prater, A.J. (1981). *Estuary birds of Britain and Ireland*. T. & A.D. Poyser, Calton.

Prŷs-Jones, R.P. (1988). Birds of estuaries: the BTO Estuaries Programme. Pp. 247-252 In Pemberton, J.E. (ed.) *The Birdwatcher's Yearbook and Diary 1989*. Buckingham Press, Buckingham.

Table 3. Overall wader counts at BoEE sites in winter.

Site No.+	Site	Peak winter count, 1990/91	Average peak winter count, 1986/87 to 1990/91
54	Wash	279,882	228,703
87	Morecambe Bay	204,906	174,824
88	Ribble	121,864	122,016
55	Humber	(127,082)	103,636
40	Thames	108,521	94,890
91	Dee (Eng/Wales)	100,837	92,132
84	Solway	87,447	79,061
112	Severn	74,131	63,05
89	Alt	46,944	59,525
62	Forth	48,095	41,539
115	Strangford Lough	36,830	41,316
31	Langstone Harbour	36,744	40,965
39	Medway	45,378	39,216
90	Mersey	75,576	36,024
32	Chichester Harbour	38,621	35,902
110	Burry	36,798	35,806
38	Swale	29,760	32,615
59	Lindisfarne	21,979	28,081
46	Stour	30,331	27,063
43	Blackwater	37,140	26,851
86	Duddon	27,764	25,963
44	Colne	21,131	22,886
53	N Norfolk Marshes	34,768	21,949
70/71	Inner Moray Firth	25,476	21,359
42	Dengie	26,714	20,746
56	Tees	18,992	16,351
*	Outer Ards	13,751	16,063
16	Exe	18,981	15,702
47	Orwell	16,297	15,054
119	Lough Foyle	16,378	13,550
116	Belfast Lough	12,994	13,311
65	Montrose Basin	17,503	13,128
75	Inner Clyde	11,471	12,714
49/50	Alde complex	12,242	11,893
41	Crouch/Roach	11,721	11,799
45	Hamford Water	19,153	11,472
94	Lavan Sands	12,733	11,435
64	Tay	10,417	11,274
20	Poole Harbour	14,373	11,006
24	Southampton Water	11,835	10,608
30	Portsmouth Harbour	10,834	10,387
108	Cleddau	10,212	10,205
72	Cromarty Firth	12,342	10,150
48	Deben	9,285	9,798
1	Taw/Torridge	8,420	9,646
63	Eden	11,530	9,519
8	Tamar complex	8,971	8,983
52	Breydon Water	18,940	8,505
109	Carmarthen Bay	12,149	8,308
73	Dornoch Firth	10,314	7,726
79	Wigtown Bay	8,128	7,407
33	Pagham Harbour	4,785	7,266
114	Dundrum Bay	5,366	6,789
111	Swansea Bay	6,413	6,179
36	Rye Hbr/Pett Levels	6,868	6,139
22	NW Solent	6,877	6,082
2	Camel	6,766	5,534
74	Loch Fleet	4,035	4,976
113	Carlingford Lough	4,251	4,582

Table 3. Continued ... /2

Site No.[+]	Site	Peak winter count, 1990/91	Average peak winter count, 1986/87 to 1990/91
61	Tyninghame	4,785	4,567
76	Irvine	5,497	4,538
68	Ythan	2,660	4,364
37	Pegwell Bay	4,082	4,252
97	Inland Sea	4,129	4,189
23	Beaulieu	3,618	3,892
51	Blyth (Suffolk)	5,869	3,731
5	Fal complex	3,034	3,570
93	Conway	2,378	3,387
118	Bann	3,801	3,090
105	Dyfi	2,883	3,063
26	Newtown	3,680	3,053
117	Lough Larne	3,702	2,997
82	Auchencairne Bay	2,028	2,984
4	Hayle	3,014	2,791
92	Clwyd	2,105	2,516
85	Irt/Mite/Esk	2,778	2,391
34	Adur	2,271	2,387
77	Loch Ryan	2,460	2,223
13	Kingsbridge	1,892	1,941
95	Red Wharf Bay	2,289	1,872
98	Cefni	1,982	1,831
101	Traeth Bach	2,851	1,828
100	Foryd Bay	1,844	1,651
21	Christchurch Harbour	3,139	1,628
78	Luce Bay	1,831	1,348
35	Newhaven	1,064	1,325
99	Braint	1,322	1,315
19	The Fleet/Wey	899	1,235
29	Brading Harbour	1,044	1,073
60	Tweed	1,063	890
57	Blyth (Northumberland)	1,284	888
58	Coquet	1,438	845
27	Medina	711	816
9	Plym	884	786
81	Kirkcudbright Bay	722	766
103	Mawddach	768	753
104	Dysynni	599	677
3	Gannel	590	602
18	Axe	214	594
83	Rought Firth	(591)	(591)
66	Dee (Scotland)	639	588
106	Teifi	77	393
96	Dulas Bay	(239)	360
25	Yar	353	349
12	Avon	260	324
15	Teign	210	323
107	Nyfer	145	298
28	Wootton	460	292
102	Artro	224	275
67	Don	136	213
17	Otter	122	196
7	Looe	90	176
6	Fowey	82	145
10	Yealm	145	137
11	Erme	113	118
14	Dart	47	101
80	Fleet Bay	129	60
69	Spey	26	26

+ see Figure 1
* non-estuarine site

The following non-estuarine sites were also counted at least once in 1990/91: Aln, Alnmouth-Boulmer, Amble-Chevington, Applecross Bay, Ardrossan-Seamill, Arran (Brodick, Cordon, Kildonan, Kingscross, Machrie-Waterfoot), Arun-Middleton, Ayr-Prestwick, Beadnell-Howick, Blyth-Seaton Sluice, Boulmer-Howick, Budle Pt.-Seahouses, Burghead, Carnoustie-Easthaven, Clwyd coast, Colonsay, Cresswell-Chevington, Cuckmere, Isle of Cumbrae, Deveron, Doon, Eye, Glyne Gap-Galley Hill, Goring/Ferring/Kingston, Loch Gruinart, Guernsey, Helford, Holy Loch, Hunterston, Loch Indaal, Jackson's Bay, Jersey, Killough, Loch Gilp, Lossiemouth, Newbiggin-Blyth, Newbiggin-Cresswell, Norman's Bay, Orkney (Newark, Widewall), Rosehearty-Fraserburgh, Saltwick Bay, Seahouses-Beadnell, Spey coast, St.Mary's Island, Thanet, Troon-Barassie, Turnberry-Dipple, Tyrella/Minerstown.

R. T. Mills: Wader Flock

National beached bird survey, February 1991

Lennox Campbell

Research Department, RSPB

After a break of six years, a UK-wide beached survey was carried out in February 1991. Results suggest some reduction in oiling in southern waters but winter mortality incidents, not related to oil-pollution, continue around the north of Britain.

Although the sporadic occurrence of large numbers of dead seabirds on British beaches has been recorded for more than a century, comprehensive surveys of dead and, in particular, oiled birds were not undertaken until after the 1939-45 war, when they were organised by the RSPB in conjunction with ICBP. In 1966 the newly-formed Seabird Group and the RSPB extended these surveys by encouraging volunteers to count more frequently and to carry out a February count to coincide with schemes already operating in Belgium and the Netherlands. By 1971 the national Beached Bird Survey was fully established, with a minimum of 5 systematic counts per year on specified weekends. In 1977 Beached Bird Surveys were formally incorporated into the Nature Conservancy Council's oil-spill contingency plans and the RSPB was contracted by NCC to analyse and review the results of the on-going survey. This review (Stowe 1982) demonstrated the importance of weather in determining the numbers of birds found on beaches and, after allowing for weather conditions, was unable to find any significant trends in the total numbers of dead birds found or the proportion that were oiled.

In 1985, following an internal review of conservation priorities and after discussions with other potential funding agencies, the RSPB decided to discontinue the full programme but regular surveys continued in several parts of the country, notably those carried out by SOTEAG in Shetland and organised by RSPB regional offices in Orkney, the north and west of mainland Scotland and north-east England. These counts continued to be co-ordinated with the International Beached Bird Survey (IBBS) February counts.

In 1990, in response to political initiatives in the context of the North Sea Ministerial Conferences and approaches from other countries,

the RSPB decided to run a national beached bird survey to coincide with the international count date at the end of February 1991.

Most surveys were carried out over the weekend of 23-24 February 1991, although in Northern Ireland as a whole and on some other individual sections elsewhere counts were carried out within the period spanning the preceding and following weekends.

In total just under 1400 kilometres of coastline were covered. The most notable gaps were in eastern and south-western Scotland, north-west England and Lincolnshire. The total lengths surveyed in south-east England and north-west Scotland were also rather small. Despite this, the overall total distance surveyed compares well with the average of 1905 kilometres for counts in the 1970's reported by Stowe (1982).

Results

Excluding records of detached wings, 1683 dead seabirds, wildfowl, divers and grebes of 42 different species were recorded, of which 239 (14.2%) were noted to have been oiled. A total of 111 dead waders and miscellaneous land-birds were also found, eight of which were oiled. The ten most frequent species are shown in Table 1, with details of the proportions oiled and comparable data from the 1970s. Regional breakdowns for the two most numerous groups of species, auks and gulls, are shown in Table 2.

The data show a broad north-south divide in both the density and the proportion of dead birds oiled. In the north, notably Shetland and Orkney, relatively high densities of mainly un-oiled seabirds were recorded, whereas in the south, although densities were comparatively low, many of the corpses were oiled.

Winter mortality incidents involving un-oiled seabirds, mainly auks, started to become a frequent feature in northern Britain during the early 1980s and their occurrence in Orkney and Shetland has recently been reviewed by Heubeck et al. (1992). Mudge et al. (1992) present similar data for the

Moray Firth. The count in February 1991 coincided with one such incident, hence the predominance of auks in the north and in the overall totals. The majority of birds involved in these incidents have been found to be emaciated and, although perhaps compounded by adverse weather conditions, reductions in or changes to the distribution of fish populations are believed to be implicated.

In Stowe's analysis of the data up to 1979 the proportion of birds found to be oiled also tended to be higher in the south, notably south-east and southern England. However his average values for most parts of the country were appreciably higher than the rates of oiling in 1991, most markedly so in the north. This finding is in line with the general view that oil pollution around British coasts and in particular that arising from identifiable oiling incidents is now much less frequent than in the 1970s and early 1980s. That it remains relatively high in the south and south-east of England is consistent with findings for other countries, such as the Netherlands, on the southern shores of the North Sea (Camphuysen 1989).

The future of UK beached bird surveys

Although only a limited amount can be concluded from the results of a single national survey, the data from February 1991 provide a useful update on regional patterns in the densities of beached birds and the frequencies of oiling. They have also filled in an obvious gap in the coverage of the International Beached Bird Survey, co-ordinated by Henrik Skov of Ornis Consult in Denmark. The survey has also emphatically proved that, despite the lapse in time since the national survey was abandoned, volunteer manpower continues to be a realistic means of obtaining information on beached birds throughout much of the country.

In response to the renewed interest, the Seabird Group, BTO, JNCC, RSPB and others are together considering whether there is a need to re-establish a full national programme of surveys. As a contribution to this the RSPB is undertaking a further analysis of the national database to include the years between Stowe's report and the end of the survey in 1985. In the meantime a further national survey has been carried out in 1992.

Acknowledgements

As with all previous beached bird surveys, the February 1991 count would not have been possible without the dedication and enthusiastic support of the considerable number of volunteers who, at short notice, were willing to take part. Their support is gratefully acknowledged. Thanks also to the RSPB staff who organised the survey and to Martin Heubeck of SOTEAG for making available the data from Shetland.

References

Camphuysen, C.J. (1989). *Beached Bird Surveys in the Netherlands, 1915-1988.* Techn. Rapport Vogelbescherming 1, Wergroep Nordsee, Amsterdam.

Heubeck, M., Meek, E. & Suddaby, D. (1992).The occurrence of dead auks (Alcidae) on beaches in Orkney and Shetland, 1976-91. *Sula* 6, 1-18.

Mudge, G.P., Crooke, C.H. & Aspinall, S.J. (1992). Non-oiling Guillemot mortality incidents in the Moray Firth, 1983-86. *Seabird* 14, 48-54.

Stowe, T.J. (1982). *Beached Bird Surveys and Surveillance of Cliff-breeding Seabirds.* Unpublished report to the Nature Conservancy Council. RSPB.

Table 1. The 10 most numerous species recorded on the British national beached bird survey in February 1991. Proportions oiled and comparable summary data from Stowe (1982) are also shown.

	February 1991			Data from Stowe (1982)	
	Rank	Total dead	% oiled	Rank	% oiled
Guillemot	1	513	14.6	2	58.3
Razorbill	2	227	12.3	4	60.8
Puffin	3	154	4.5	23	47.0
Black-headed Gull	4	122	23.8	3	8.7
Herring Gull	5	110	18.2	1	8.9
Fulmar	6	78	10.3	9	12.9
Shag	7	57	12.3	12	15.4
Little Auk	8	55	3.6	x	x
Kittiwake	9	52	9.6	8	18.1
Common Gull	10	41	46.3	5	11.0

x = species not in top 25 in Stowe 1982.

Table 2. Numbers, density and proportion oiled of corpses of auks and gulls found on the national beached bird survey in February 1991.

Region	Distance covered kms	Auks: Number	Density	% oiled	Gulls: Number	Density	% oiled
Shetland	47.8	211	4.4	4.3	12	0.3	0
Orkney	48.1	263	5.5	1.1	16	0.3	0
Moray Firth	64.3	64	1.0	1.6	15	0.2	0
Firth of Forth	32.5	77	2.4	9.1	14	0.4	0
NE England	136	50	0.4	26.0	20	0.1	15
East Anglia	77	81	1.1	48.1	39	0.5	48.7
SE England	26	9	0.3	55.6	2	0.1	0
SW England	199.2	53	0.3	58.5	24	0.1	33.3
Wales	458.5	68	0.2	20.6	127	0.3	20.5
NW England	29.8	1	**	0	26	0.9	11.5
Northern Ireland	105.5	9	0.1	33.3	53	0.5	0
W Scotland	128.5	20	0.2	0	31	0.2	0
NW Scotland	53.3	89	1.7	1	9	0.2	0

TOTAL DISTANCE
COVERED   1,397.5

Detached wings not included. Oiled includes lightly and heavily oiled categories combined.

Anon/The Solent

Species Accounts

The following Species Accounts, which were compiled by Richard Winspear, collate information for most of those birds which are subject to regular monitoring in Britain . They are incomplete in several respects; notably, they include neither birds occurring solely on migration and vagrants, information on which can be gleaned from county bird reports, nor most rare breeding birds, whose breeding numbers are collated by the Rare Birds Breeding Panel and published in *British Birds*. It is intended to attempt to expand the coverage of these Accounts in subsequent years.

The Accounts for waterfowl are based on information drawn from Kirby *et al*. 1991, those for seabirds from Walsh *et al*. 1991 and those for raptors from the data collected by the Scottish Raptor Study Groups and first published by the SOC in Scottish Bird News No. 22. Data derived from the CBC, WBS and CES ringing programme were taken from *BTO News*. Many other sources are cited in individual accounts and are referenced at the end of the Section.

Most of the data published here derive from the skilled fieldwork of many hundreds of amateur birdwatchers. It is they who furnish us with the up-to-date information on bird numbers and population trends, both nationally and at key sites for important bird groups, which is essential to the planning and implementation of conservation action.

Criteria for International and National Importance

Criteria for international importance have been agreed by the contracting parties to the Ramsar Convention on the Conservation of Wetlands of International Importance. Under it, a wetland is of international importance if it regularly holds 1% of a flyway population of a species or sub-species, or regularly holds at least 20,000 waterfowl. Britain and Ireland's wildfowl belong to the Northwest European population (Pirot *et al*. 1989) and the waders to the East Atlantic flyway population (Smit & Piersma 1989).

A British wetland is considered to be nationally important if it regularly holds 1% of the British population of one species or sub-species.

The Species Accounts for waterfowl give the current qualifying levels for both these categories of importance. However, the national category applies only to Great Britain as equivalent figures have not yet been produced for Ireland. Sources of qualifying levels for international importance are: wildfowl – Pirot *et al*. (1989); waders – Smit & Piersma (1989) and Scott (1982). Sources of qualifying levels for national importance are: wildfowl – Owen *et al*. (1986) updated where necessary from National Waterfowl Count data; waders – Moser (1987) and Prater (1981).

Key
+ the British population is too small for a meaningful figure to be obtained
* 1% of the British population is less than 50 birds. In this case 50 is normally used as a minimum qualifying level for national importance

Br	Broad
Est	Estuary
Fth	Firth
Gp	Gravel pit
Hb	Harbour
Lo	Loch or Lough
prs	pairs
R	River
RSGs	Raptor Study Groups
Rsr	Reservoir

Little Grebe
Tachybaptus ruficollis

Present population trend:
Uncertain; little evidence of change.

Percentage change in WBS index, 1989-1990:
+19% (-7% to +55%) based on < 20 plots.

Latest estimate of breeding population:
9,000-18,000 pairs in Britain and Ireland (Sharrock 1976); 73% of occupied squares were then in Britain.

Wintering:
The NWC scheme only covers a rather small proportion of the population of this species in the UK. The peak count in the UK was 3,565 in September, a slight increase on the peak count of 1989-90 probably due to the increase in the number of small freshwater sites visited. Numbers in both Britain and N Ireland peaked in September and declined steadily thereafter.

Sites supporting average maxima of 50 or more over the past five seasons (with peak count for 1990-91) were Lo. Neagh/Beg (324 Sep.), Strangford Lo. (122 Dec.), Swale Est. (108 Nov.), Thames Est. (88 Dec.), Chew Valley Lake (100 Sep.), R.Soar:Leicester (68 Dec.), Medway Est. (100 Jan.), Deben Est. (87 Dec.), Rutland Water (40 Oct.), Southampton Water (27 Mar.) & Upper Lo. Erne (67 Nov.). Other sites holding more than 50 individuals in 1990-91 alone include the Wash (112 Feb.), Clandeboye Lake (73 Nov.) & the Hampshire Avon between Blashford and Hucklesbrook (60 Aug.).

Great Crested Grebe
Podiceps cristatus

Present population trend:
Increasing.

Latest estimate of breeding population:
6,000-7,000 adult birds in Britain (Hughes *et al.* 1979).

Wintering
Qualifying 1% level for national importance: 100 international importance: ?(not set)
Latest estimate of winter population: likely to exceed 10,000 individuals. The total number of this species counted in Britain was higher than in 1989-90, almost certainly because of the increased site coverage and the expansion of the species on gravel pit complexes and reservoirs in lowland England. In contrast, fewer were recorded in N Ireland than was the case in 1989-90. Numbers were highest throughout the UK in September and declined thereafter.

A total of 18 sites currently support over 150 Great Crested Grebes on average. These are (with peak count for 1990-91): Lo. Neagh/Beg (612 Sep.), Belfast Lo. (1,162 Nov.), Forth Est. (524 Sep.), Rutland Water (1,038 Jan.), Chew Valley Lake (440 Aug.), Grafham Water (744 Nov.), Queen Mary Rsr. (526 Oct.), Upper Lo. Erne (137 Nov.), Swale Est. (28 Sep.), Medway Est. (206 Feb.), Morecambe Bay (229 Sep.), Pitsford Rsr. (243 Dec.), Carlingford Lo. (259 Feb.), Borth/Ynyslas (186 Dec.), Conwy Bay (no count), Colne Est. (214 Jan.), Stour Est. (200 Oct.) & Abberton Rsr. (161 Nov.). In addition, up to 400 birds were seen regularly off Greatstone-on-Sea, Dungeness during the winter and a further 4 sites held more than 150 in 1990-91: Blithfield Rsr. (233 Dec.), Lo. Leven (212 Nov.), Hanningfield Rsr. (186 Dec.) & Stewartby Lake (171 Feb.).

Fulmar
Fulmarus glacialis

Breeding numbers:
In the two regions where populations are monitored, Shetland showed a small decrease (-2.4%) and Caithness an increase (+9.0%) compared to 1989. Elsewhere most populations seem to have been increasing or roughly stable during 1986-90. In particular, there was a significant upward trend recorded on the Farne Islands, Skomer and various colonies on the Isle of Man. There is evidently a continued upward trend at least at colonies outside of Scotland.

Breeding success:
An average of 0.4 chicks/site fledged from 30 colonies monitored in 1990: a non-significant decline on the 1989 average. The biggest reduction were seen at Fair Isle, the Isle of May and Tantallon (SE Scotland). The least successful colonies (rearing only 0.16-0.27 chicks/site) were Fair Isle and colonies in Caithness, the Firth of Forth, the Channel Islands and the Isle of Man. Orkney was the most successful region with 0.5 chicks/site. Reduced availability of sandeels is clearly still having an influence on breeding success in Shetland colonies where averages of 0.52 and 0.54 chicks/site were recorded in 1986 and 1987, respectively. Despite this, success was higher in Shetland than at many colonies further south (unlike, for example, Kittiwake). Perhaps the role of food availability is more complex in this species which, even in Shetland, is not wholly dependent on sandeels.

Manx Shearwater
Puffinus puffinus

Breeding numbers and success:
There was a non-significant (3%) decrease in used burrows on Rhum (NW Scotland) indicating little change in breeding numbers (Furness 1990). Egg-laying was confirmed in only 23 of the 55 study burrows (42%) in 1990. Although this was higher than the 1989 figure of 24%, it is below the 60-70% usually recorded during 1976-88 (Swann 1990). The estimated breeding output of 0.52 chicks/egg in 1990 is close to the average for 1976-88 (0.57) and above the 1989 figure of 0.31.

Gannet
Sula bassana

Present population trend:
In general, breeding numbers at the smaller colonies continue to increase rapidly including Foula (Shetland) (+c40%) and Great Saltee (Wexford) (+10.5%). Slight decreases on 1989 numbers were recorded at Fair Isle (-4.9%) and Bempton (-3.9%) but the longer term trends at both sites have been significantly upwards.

Breeding success:
Five colonies averaged 0.62 chicks fledged per nest in 1990. This is slightly below average and three out of four colonies were less productive than in 1989. On Hermaness, the sandeel proportion in gannet diet during the nestling period declined markedly from 1981 to 1988 without any obvious change in breeding success (Martin 1989), evidently reflecting the availability of suitable alternative fish species (especially herring and mackerel).

Latest estimate of breeding population:
A complete survey in 1984–85 recorded 157,400 nest-sites at 14 colonies (Wanless 1987), updated slightly to 158,400 for 1984–88 (Lloyd *et al.* 1991).

Cormorant
Phalacrocorax carbo

Breeding numbers:
Sampled populations in four out of six regions decreased between 1989 and 1990. This contrasts with 1988-89, when numbers in most regions increased. The general trend of population indices for most regions during 1986-90 has been one of increase. Shetland is perhaps an exception, having more stable numbers during 1986-89. A 15% decrease at the Shetland colonies in 1990 was the biggest annual change seen there during 1986-90, and corresponded with a 10% decline at the other North Sea colonies monitored.

Breeding success:
No systematic monitoring is undertaken, but, as in previous years, no reports of major breeding failure were received.

Latest estimate of breeding population:
6,700 apparently occupied nests recorded on UK coasts in 1985-87 (Lloyd *et al.* 1991), a 9-10% increase since 1969-70. About 800 pairs breed inland.

Wintering
The total count of Cormorants in 1990-91 reached 13,866 in Britain and 1,529 in N Ireland, representing an increase and a decrease, respectively, on the totals of 1989-90. In Britain, the population appears to be expanding, especially in inland areas and this is naturally alarming to fisheries managers (the species is shot under licence in many

parts of the country). The species reached its highest level of abundance in September on British NWC sites, declining slowly subsequently, but did not peak until December in N Ireland.

Sites with average maxima >200 birds (with peak 1990-91 count) are: Lo. Neagh/Beg (904 Dec.), Morecambe Bay (991 Sep.), Medway Est. (1,280 Feb.), Forth Est. (962 Nov.), Inner Clyde (408 Jan.), Inner Moray Firth (112 Oct.), Solway Est. (492 Sep.), Poole Hbr. (417 Oct.), Queen Mary Rsr. (467 Feb.), Ranworth/Cockshoot Br. (329 Jan.), Lo. Leven (800 Feb.), Abberton Rsr. (320 Sep.), Rutland Water (350 Feb.), Dee Est. (286 Sep.), Tees Est. (480 Sep.), Ouse Washes (163 Mar.), Swale Est. (263 Oct.), Blackwater Est. (208 Nov.), Grafham Water (450 Feb.), Belfast Lo. (284 Nov.), Outer Ards (153 Feb.), Wash (263 Oct.) & Upper Lo. Erne (192 Feb.). A further nine sites supported over 200 cormorants in 1990-91: Lindisfarne (720, Nov.), Queen Mother Rsr. (419 Dec.), Hanningfield Rsr. (374 Dec.), Queen Elizabeth II Rsr. (320 Nov.), Carmarthen Bay (303 Sep.), Blithfield Rsr. (278 Dec.), William Girling Rsr. (232 Oct.), Rostherne Mere (222 Jan.) & Alton Water (208 Dec.).

Shag
Phalacrocorax aristotelis

Breeding numbers:
All sampled regions showed a reduction in breeding numbers between 1989 and 1990, in most cases continuing a decline noted in 1989 or earlier. The only significant trend seen during 1986-90 was for several colonies in SW Scotland (average -14% per year). Fluctuations between years were most marked for SE Scotland (mainly colonies in the Firth of Forth).

Breeding success:
All three Shetland colonies studied in detail produced less than one chick nest-with-eggs in 1990. For North Sea colonies as a whole, productivity declined by an average of 0.43 chicks/nest (not statistically significant). In contrast, the three west coast colonies sampled showed an improvement or no change in success in 1990 (average change +0.21 - not significant), all rearing at least one chick/nest. The difference in success of east and west coast colonies may reflect food availability.

Latest estimate of breeding population:
The UK population was c.37,300 apparently occupied nests in 1985-87 (Lloyd *et al.* 1991), a c22% increase since 1969-70.

Grey Heron
Ardea cinerea

Present population trend:
Increasing.

Latest estimate of breeding population:
About 10,155 pairs in the UK in 1985: England and Wales 5,770 pairs, N Ireland 585 pairs (Carter *et al.* in prep.); Scotland 3,800 pairs (Marquiss 1989). The population in England and Wales increased by 2.8% in 1989-90, continuing the upward trend.

Mute Swan
Cygnus olor

Present population trend:
Stable.

Percentage change in CBC index, 1989-1990:
All habitats = +14% (-15% to +54%) based on < 30 plots.

Percentage change in WBS index, 1989-1990:
+13% (-12% to +47%).

Latest estimate of breeding population:
3,150 breeding pairs in Britain, plus 12,600 non-breeders (Ogilvie 1986).

Wintering:
Qualifying 1% level for national importance: 180
international importance: 1,800

The total count of Mute Swans in Britain clearly reflect a continuation of the population increase in this species following the ban on the sale of lead weights for angling and the later prohibition of its use by water companies and others. Perrins & Sears (1991) estimated that up to a fifth of Mute Swans in Britain die from collisions with overhead wires. WWT is currently discussing this problem with electricity companies.

Sites with average maxima of over 180 Mute Swans (with peak count for 1990-91) were Lo. Neagh/Beg (1,205 Sep.), the Fleet/Wey (1,029 Oct.), Abberton Rsr. (635 Aug.), Ouse Washes (414 Jan.), Colne Est. (255 Jan.), Christchurch Hbr. (150 Aug.), Upper Lo. Erne (470 Jan.), Lo. of Harray (1,205 Oct.), Tweed Est. (368 Dec.), Stour Est. (207 Sep.), Somerset Levels (256 Jan.), Lo. Bee (307 Jan.), Rutland Water (246 Sep.), Lo. Eye (324 Dec.), Thames Est. (159 Jan.), Strangford Lo. (195 Sep.), R. Welland: Spalding (111 Feb.) & R. Avon: Fordingbridge (211 Oct.). Other sites holding over 180 Mute Swans in 1990-91 were Lo. of Skene (275 Nov.), Derwent Water (266 Jan.) & Fairburn Ings (197 Sep.).

Bewick's Swan
Cygnus columbianus
bewickii

Wintering:
Qualifying 1% level for national importance: 70
international importance: 170

Bewick's Swans bred well in 1990, with nearly 20% juveniles in the wintering flocks at WWT centres. Bewick's Swans reached Britain exceptionally early in autumn 1990 with over 100 individuals at Slimbridge, 740 at Welney & 975 in the Martin Mere area by the end of October (Rees *et al.* 1991). Such early movements were thought to be due to a shortage of Potamogeton, and relative drought in the Lauwersmeer area of the Netherlands. Peak numbers were not particularly high in 1990-91; the maximum in the UK as a whole was almost 8,400. Peak numbers occurred in January in Britain and February in N Ireland. Sites holding a five winter average of over 150 (with peak count in 1990-91) were: Ouse Washes (5,100 Jan.), Nene Washes (653 Feb.), Martin Mere/Ribble Est. (167 Jan.), Severn Est. (340 Feb.), Lo. Neagh/Beg (523 Feb.), Walland Marsh (no count), R. Avon: Ringwood (169 Feb.), Walmore Common (164 Feb.) & St Benets Levels (182 Feb.). Elsewhere, the following sites supported over 150 Bewick's Swans in 1990-91: Black Fen (250 Feb.), Lo. Foyle (195 Dec.) & Ludham How Hill (155 Feb.).

Whooper Swan
Cygnus cygnus

Wintering:
Qualifying 1% level for national importance: 60
international importance: 170

Breeding success in 1990: moderately successful with 16.4% young in flocks at Welney, 17.6% at Martin Mere and 16.9% at Caerlaverock (Rees *et al.* 1991). Whooper Swans were slow to arrive in the autumn of 1990 with the main influx at WWT centres not occurring until November.

Sites holding a five year average of >200 birds (with peak numbers in 1990-91) were: Lo. Foyle (988 Nov.), Lo. Neagh/Beg (1,110 Dec.), Upper Lo. Erne (896 Jan.), Lo. of Harray (927 Nov.), Ouse Washes (578 Mar.), Lo. Eye/Cromarty Fth. (1,115 Nov.), Martin Mere/Ribble Est. (538 Nov.), Solway Est. (96 Mar.), Lo. of Strathbeg (129 Jan.) & Lo. Leven (180 Dec.). A further two sites held over 170 Whoopers in 1990-91: Montrose Basin (501 Feb.) & Lo. of Skene (314 Dec.).

Bean Goose
Anser fabalis

Wintering:

Qualifying 1% level for national importance: +*
international importance: 800

Parslow-Otsu (1991) provides an account of the history, recent status and population of Bean Geese in east Norfolk. There is now evidence that this group is an isolated population of the race *fabalis* breeding in Scandinavia. A record total number of Bean Geese was present in the Yare Valley, peaking at 485 in January. The only other record of more than 10 birds came from Lo. Ken (20 birds in Jan.). Smaller numbers appeared at numerous other localities.

Pink-footed Goose
Anser brachyrhynchus

Wintering

Qualifying 1% level for national importance: 1,100
international importance: 1,100

Relatively good with averages of 21.5% young and 2.2 young/pair in autumn flocks (Kirby & Cranswick 1991). The November census count of 195,000 represents the highest total yet.

Sites that currently hold a five year average maximum of >10,000 Pink-footed Geese (with peak count in 1990-91) are Lo. of Strathbeg (37,100 nov.), Westwater Rsr. (24,700 Oct.), SW Lancashire (31,805 Nov.), Dupplin Lo. (42,000 Oct.), Montrose Basin (15,000 Dec.), Slains Lo./Ythan Est. (13,190 Apr.), Solway Est. (17,421 Mar.), Lo. Leven (16,000 Oct.), Hule Moss (16,755 Sep.), Carsebreck/Rhynd Lo. (9,900 Oct.) & the Wash (25,330 Jan.). The following sites had maximum counts >10,000 in 1990-91: Aberlady Bay (17,500 Oct.) & Castle Lo. (16,380 Feb.).

European
White-fronted Goose
Anser albifrons albifrons

Wintering

Qualifying 1% level for national importance: 60
international importance: 3,000

Despite the spectacular increase of the Siberian breeding population in recent decades, the number wintering in Britain continues to decline. The flyway population is around half a million birds, but improvements in feeding conditions and protection in the Netherlands, and recently in the Nord-Rhein Westfalia region of Germany, means that few need to migrate to traditional wintering areas further from the breeding grounds. This is a phenomenon known as 'short-stopping', well known among geese in N

America. Total numbers recorded in Britain in 1990-91 reached only 4,025, almost 1,800 fewer than in 1989-90, and the population index fell to its lowest level for a number of years.

The principal sites for this species (with peak 1990-91 count) are: Severn Est. (2,600 Feb.), Swale Est. (2,280 Mar.), Thames Est. (85 Jan.), R.Avon:Sopley (105 Jan.), North Norfolk Marshes (215 Feb.), Middle Yare Marshes (295 Jan.), Minsmere (no count), R.Tywi:Dryslwyn (30 Feb.) & Alde complex (15 Feb.).

Greenland
White-fronted Goose
Anser albifrons flavirostris

Wintering:

Qualifying 1% level for national importance: 100
international importance: 220

Breeding success in 1990: 19.0% young amongst flocks on Islay and 18.8% amongst flocks in Scotland as a whole compared with 19.3% in the previous winter. Numbers have doubled since the sub-species was protected, beginning in Scotland in 1981. The Greenland White-Fronted Goose Study and the Irish National Parks and Wildlife Service estimated a total of 29,388 birds in 1990-91 compared with 26,845 and 27,341 in the autumns of 1989 and 1988 respectively.

Sites holding a five year average of >220 birds are as follows (with peak 1990-91 count): Islay (8,857 Mar.), Machrihanish (1,240 Mar.), Rhunahaorine (797 Dec.), Tiree (941 Dec.), Stranraer Lo. (600 Feb.), Coll (792 Nov.), Lo. Ken (306 Dec.) & Endrick Mouth (350 Dec.). A further 3 sites supported 220 birds or more during the 1990-91 season: Danna/Keils (245 Dec.), Appin/Eriska/Benderloch (314 Mar.) & Colonsay/Oronsay (250 Mar.). The Greenland White-fronted Goose will be the subject of the first International Management Plan in Europe which is being drawn up by the JNCC.

Greylag Goose
Anser anser

Latest estimate of population:

The non-migratory native Greylag population in the far north and west of Scotland numbers almost 2,000 including non-breeders.

Breeding success in 1990:

Breeding success, averaging 3.72 young/pair on North Uist and 4.16 young/pair on South Uist, was similar to previous years (Mitchell 1991).

Wintering:

Qualifying 1% level for national importance:
Icelandic 1,000
international importance: Icelandic 1,000

Autumn age counts of Icelandic Greylags in 1990

revealed 20.7% young overall and 2.5 young/pair on average, suggesting that they had bred very well (Kirby & Cranswick 1991). The November census revealed almost 115,000 birds. This is considered to be an under-estimate of the true population size.

Sites holding a five year average of >5,000 birds mainly from the Icelandic stock, are as follows (with peak 1990-91 count): Dinnet Lo./R. Dee (16,000 Nov.), Inner Moray Fth. (8,525 Nov.), Lo. Eye/Cromarty Fth. (18,593 Oct.),Lo. of Skene (19,150 Jan.), Lo. Spynie (6,100 Oct.) & Lo. of Strathbeg (925 Feb.). The latter count was well below average. The 1990-91 peak count also exceeded 5,000 at the following sites: Haddo House Lo. (5,900 Oct.) & Tay/Isla Valley (6,262 Oct.).

Canada Goose
Branta canadensis

Present population trend:
Strong long-term increase.

Latest estimate of breeding population:
Approaching 50,000 birds in Britain, including non-breeders (Salmon et al. 1988).

Wintering:
The peak count in Britain of almost 38,000 in October 1990 exceeded the equivalent figure of the previous season by almost 4,000 birds. Canada Geese remain a considerable nuisance on farmland and amenity grassland. Counts at key sites seem to indicate that numbers remain constant at least in some areas.

The following sites have average maxima of >600 birds (with peak 1990-91 count): Kedleston Park Lake (1,060 Nov.), Stratfield Saye (1,701 Nov.), Bewl Water (546 Feb.), Abberton Rsr. (618 Aug.), Rutland Water (740 Feb.), Dorchester Gp. (767 Oct.), Twyford Gp. (182 Sep.), Blithfield Rsr. (896 Sep.), Drakelow Gp. (650 Dec.) & Harewood Lake (550 Dec.). In addition, the following sites held more than 600 birds in 1990-91: Fleet Pond (804 Oct.), Bar Mere (800 Nov.), Kings Bromley Gp. (714 Feb.), Dinton Pastures (682 Sep.), Tundry Pond (674 Sep.), Capesthorne Hall (653 Sep.), Eversley Cross and Yateley Gp. (636 Dec.), Eccup Rsr. (622 Sep.),Ellesmere Gp. (608 Oct.) & Kirby Bellars Gp. (602 Feb.).

Barnacle Goose
Branta leucopsis

Wintering:
Qualifying 1% level for national importance:
Greenlandic 200, Svalbard 100
international importance:
Greenlandic 320, Svalbard 100

Greenland population:
Numbers of juveniles present in the Islay flocks, averaging over 20%, indicated an excellent breeding season. The peak count at Islay (30,208 Dec.) is the highest ever

counted there. The only other sizeable flocks likely to comprise birds from this population included Craiglin Lo. (375 Mar.). Unlimited numbers continue to be shot under Scottish Office licence on Islay: 1,300 birds were killed in 1990-91. A number of schemes to scare birds onto SSSIs have met with limited success. This population remains, in world terms, very small.

Svalbard population:
The proportion of juvenile birds in flocks averaged 12.0%. The population at Caerlaverock appears to have stabilised at around 12,000 birds. Peak counts for 1990-91 were at Caerlaverock (12,100 Oct.), Lo. of Strathbeg (356 Oct.), Gladhouse Rsr. (275 Oct.) & Portmore Lo. (115 Oct.).

Dark-bellied Brent Goose
Branta bernicla bernicla

Wintering:
Qualifying 1% level for national importance: 900
international importance: 1,700

Breeding success in 1990: moderately good, with 21.4% juveniles and an average of 3 young/pair in autumn flocks in Great Britain (Kirby & Haines 1990, Kirby 1991). The maximum count of 124,000 birds in Britain in February 1991 is by far the highest total yet.

Sites with average maxima >1,700 (with peak 1990-91 count) were: the Wash (21,273 Dec.), Thames Est. (33,109 Oct.), North Norfolk Marshes (11,888 Nov.), Chichester Hbr. (9,406 Jan.), Blackwater Est. (9,918 Dec.), Langstone Hbr. (6,133 Dec.), Hamford Water (6,889 Feb.), Colne Est. (4,924 Feb.), Crouch Est. (8,388 Feb.), Medway Est. (6,809 Feb.), Swale Est. (4,823 Dec.), Portsmouth Hbr. (5,318 Jan.), Pagham Hbr. (3,181 Nov.), Exe Est. (2,665 Nov.), NW Solent (3,335 Feb.), Dengie (1,950 Oct.) & Humber Est. (2,733 Dec.). In addition, counts of >1,700 were made in 1990-91 at the Fleet/Wey (2,800 Dec.) & Deben (2,051 Jan.).

Light-bellied Brent Goose
Branta bernicla hrota

Wintering:
Qualifying 1% level for national importance:
Canada/Greenland +*
Svalbard 30*
international importance: Canada/Greenland 200
Svalbard 40

Birds present at Strangford Lo. (13,237 Sep.) & Lo. Foyle (6,007 Oct.) in N. Ireland originate from the population breeding in arctic Canada and Greenland, whilst those at Lindisfarne (2,700 Dec.) are of the Svalbard population.

Shelduck
Tadorna tadorna

Present population trend:
Probably still increasing.

Percentage change in CBC index, 1989-1990:
All habitats = +45% (+4% to +107%) based on < 30 plots.

Latest estimate of breeding population:
12,000 nesting pairs in Britain, and 26,000 non-breeders (Owen *et al.* 1986).

Wintering:
> *Qualifying 1% level for national importance: 750*
> *international importance: 2,500*

The peak counts in Britain and N Ireland occurred in February and were up on the 1989-90 figures in both cases. However, the long-term index showed relatively little change on recent seasons.

Sites holding a five year average of >2,000 birds (with peak 1990-91 count) are: the Wash (16,275 Feb.), Medway Est. (10,149 Feb.), Dee Est. (1,149 Nov.), Humber Est. (5,856 Oct.), Morecambe Bay (6,143 Oct.), Ribble Est. (3,113 Jan.), Mersey Est. (5,757 Dec.), Severn Est. (3,598 Dec.), Forth Est. (4,025 Aug.), Chichester Hbr. (2,321 Feb.), Thames Est. (2,535 Jan.), Poole Hbr. (3,451 Jan.), Blackwater Est. (3,398 Jan.) & Strangford Lo. (2,311 Feb.). In addition, over 2,000 birds were counted in 1990-91 at the Swale Est. (2,545 Jan.) and the Solway Est. (3,354 Jul.).

Mandarin Duck
Aix galericulata

Present population trend: increasing.
Latest estimate of breeding population: about 7,000 individuals in Britain (Davies 1988).

Wintering:
The peak NWC count in 1990-91 was 209 in October. The largest counts came from Virginia Water (72 Oct.), Hammer Pond (47 Nov.) & Witley Park (39 Oct.).

Wigeon
Anas penelope

Present population trend:
Little evidence of change.

Latest estimate of breeding populations:
Less than 500 pairs (Batten *et al.* 1990).

Wintering:
> *Qualifying 1% level for national importance: 2,500*
> *international importance: 7,500*

The peak NWC count in Britain was 238,369 in January; and in N Ireland was 18,660 in October.

Sites with average maxima >7,500 (with max 1990-91 count) were: Ribble Est. (59,187 Dec.), Ouse Washes (24,715 Jan.), Lindisfarne (9,040 Oct.), Lo. Foyle (15,584 Oct.), Dornoch Fth. (10,251 Oct.), Swale Est. (11,671 Feb.) & Cromarty Fth. (6;512 Dec.). Other sites with >7,500 in 1990-91 were North Norfolk Marshes (12,779 Nov.), Lo. Eye (9,815 Oct.) & Lo. of Harray (9,200 Oct.).

Gadwall
Anas strepera

Present population trend:
Increasing and spreading (Fox 1978)

Latest estimat of breeding population:
500–600 pairs (Batten *et al.* 1990)

Wintering:
> *Qualifying 1% level for national importance: 50*
> *international importance: 120*

The NWC counts in Britain and N Ireland were similar to those of 1989-90, but the population index for Britain increased in both October and December to reach the highest ever levels. This increase may be related to expansion onto artificial waters in the inland southern lowlands.

Sites with average maxima of >150 (with peak 1990-91 count) were Rutland Water (1,323 Sep.), Abberton Rsr. (402 Sep.), Gunton Park Lakes (325 Sep.), Severn Est. (345 Feb.), Ouse Washes (352 Mar.), R. Avon: Blashford (364 Nov.), Cheshunt Gp. (290 Dec.), Lo. Leven (258 Oct.), Chew Valley Lake (190 Jan.) & Stanford Meres (141 Oct.). Other sites holding more than 150 birds in 1990-91 were Eversley Cross/Yateley Gp. (338 Oct.), Hickling Broad (312 Oct.), Buckden/Stirtloe Gp. (232 Nov.), Amwell Gp. (209 Jan.), Burry Inlet (177 Oct.), The Fleet/Wey (171 Jan.), Langtoft Gp. (168 Jan.) & Hanningfield Rsr. (165 Sep.).

Teal
Anas crecca

Present population trend:
Uncertain; little evidence of change.

Latest estimate of breeding population:
3,000-4,500 pairs in Britain (Owen *et al.* 1986).

Wintering:
> *Qualifying 1% level for national importance: 1,000*
> *international importance: 4,000*

The 1990-91 numbers were similar to the high figures of 1989-90.

Average maxima of >1,000 birds (with peak 1990-91 count) were at Mersey Est. (10,375 Dec.), Ribble Est. (9,078 Nov.), Dee Est. (4,824 Oct.), Abberton Rsr (11,483 Sep.), Ouse Washes (5,225 Jan.), Woolston Eyes (4,500 Oct.), Hamford Water (7,211 Dec.), Martin Mere (1,900 Sep.), Cleddau Est. (3,148 Dec.), Thames Est. (3,407

Jan.), Severn Est. (1,820 Jan.), North Norfolk Marshes (3,223 Dec.), Lo. Leven (3,614 Oct.), Lo. Neagh/Beg (2,915 Dec.), Swale Est. (1,846 Jan.), Dornoch Fth. (1,831 Dec.) & Humber Est. (1,795 Nov.). Over 1,000 birds were also recorded in 1990-91 at Irvine shore (7,500 Feb.), Chew Valley Lake (5,500 Jan.), Blithfield Rsr. (3,410 Jan.), Alaw Rsr. (2,938 Dec.), Blagdon Rsr. (2,500 Jan.), Pulborough Levels (2,210 Jan.), Rutland Water (2,187 Sep.) & Alde complex (2,160 Jan.).

Mallard
Anas platyrhynchos

Present population trend:
Apparently now stable after period of increase.

Percentage change in CBC index, 1989-1990:
Farmland = +5% (-10% to +21%).

Percentage change in WBS index, 1989-1990: +23% (+6% to +42%).

Latest estimate of breeding population: 70,000-150,000 pairs in Britain and Ireland (Sharrock 1976); 74% of occupied squares were then in Britain.

Wintering:
> Qualifying 1% level for national importance: 5,000
> international importance: 50,000

The peak NWC count was considerably higher than the 1989-90 counts but the population indexes were similar indicating that the high total counts probably reflect more sites counted in 1990-91, especially in the north-west. Nine sites currently support over 3,000 Mallard regularly (with peak 1990-91 counts): Humber Est. (4,373 Feb.), Lo. Neagh/Beg (5,318 Sep.), Wash (5,200 Jan.), Ouse Washes (3,530 Jan.), Morecambe Bay (3,400 Oct.), Swale Est. (10,469 Jan.), Dee Est. (1,947 Dec.), Martin Mere (4,170 Dec.) & Severn Est. (3,186 Nov.).

Pintail
Anas acuta

Latest estimate of breeding population:
Probably well under 50 pairs (Batten *et al.* 1990)

Wintering:
> Qualifying 1% level for national importance: 250
> international importance: 700

Peak counts of Pintail in Britain were less than those of 1989-90 and the population index was considerably lower than recent years.

Sites with average maxima >700 (with peak 1990-91 count) were: Dee Est. (8,706 Dec.), Mersey Est. (3,200 Oct.), Wash (1,910 Feb.), Morecambe Bay (3,190 Oct.), Burry Inlet (1,784 Feb.), Martin Mere (640 Sep.), Ouse Washes (1,332 Jan.), Duddon Est. (830 Sep.), Solway Est. (2,208 Oct.), Medway Est. (1,243 Dec.) & North Norfolk Marshes (1,714 Nov.). Pagham Hbr. (839 Nov.) was the only other site to support over 700 birds in 1990-91.

Shoveler
Anas clypeata

Latest estimate of breeding population:
1,000–1,500 pairs (Batten *et al.* 1990)

Wintering:
> Qualifying 1% level for national importance: 90
> international importance: 400

Population indices in Britain showed slight increases in 1990-91.

Sites holding over 250 Shoveler, based on the five year average maxima (with peak 1990-91 count) are: Ouse Washes (625 Mar.), Abberton Rsr. (1,085 Sep.), Rutland Water (680 Sep.), Lo. Leven (540 Oct.), Chew Valley Lake (465 Sep.), Swale Est. (276 Mar.) & Woolston Eyes (260 Sep.). In Addition, a further seven sites held >250 Shoveler in 1990-91: Severn Est. (454 Aug.), Quuen Mary Rsr. (427 Oct.), King George V Rsr. (360 Oct.), Staines Rsr. (271 Feb.), Attenborough Gp. (268 Oct.) & Grafham Water (263 Feb.).

Pochard
Aythya ferina

Latest estimate of breeding population:
375–395 pairs (Batten *et al.* 1990)

Wintering:
> Qualifying 1% level for national importance: 500
> international importance: 3,500

The peak NWC count was down on the 1989-90 total in Britain but up on the 1989-90 figure in N Ireland. Pochard numbers were highest between November and January in Britain and peaked in December in N Ireland.

Sites with average maxima of >1,000 birds (with peak 1990-91 count) are: Lo. Neagh/Beg (40,928 Dec.), Abberton Rsr. (4,064 Aug.), Ouse Washes (1,135 Feb.), Lo. of Boardhouse (1,594 Nov.), Rostherne Mere (2,703 Feb.), Severn Est. (1,616 Feb.), Cotswold Water Park East (1,113 Feb.), Kingsbury/Coton Pools (1,099 Feb.), Lo. of Harray (2,245 Oct.), Cotswold Water Park West (1,046 Nov.), Poole Hbr. (1,311 Feb.), Lo. Leven (895 Sep.) & Chew Valley Lake (260 Dec.). In addition, over 1,000 birds were recorded in 1990-91 at Stanton Harcourt Gp.(1,243 Nov.), Rutland Water (1,218 Oct.) & Wintersett Rsr. (1,035 Nov.).

Tufted Duck
Aythya fuligula

Present population trend:
Fluctuates, but still increasing.

Percentage change in CBC index, 1989-1990:
All habitats = +11% (-38% to +101%) based on < 30 plots.

Percentage change in WBS index, 1989-1990:
-10% (-42% to +37%).

Latest estimate of breeding population:
Over 7,000 pairs in Britain (Owen *et al.* 1986).

Wintering:
> Qualifying 1% level for national importance: 600
> international importance: 7,500

The peak count in Britain (48,425 Jan.) was similar to the 1989-90 maximum total. In N Ireland, the peak count (23,138 Nov.) was substantially lower than the 1989-90 figure.

Sites holding a five year average of >1,000 birds (with peak 1990-91 counts) are: Lo. Neagh/Beg (22,278 Nov.), Abberton Rsr. (3,550 Aug.), Rutland Water (2,097 Sep.), Lo. Leven (3,120 Sep.), Kingsbury/Coton Pools (1,433 Nov.), Lo. of Harray (1,643 Oct.), Severn Est. (817 Feb.) & Walthamstow Rsr. (1,589 Feb.). In Addition, the following sites held >1,000 birds in 1990-91 alone: King George V Rsr. (2,500 Oct.), Besthorpe/Girton Gp. (1,801 Feb.) & Rostherne Mere (1,075 Feb.).

Scaup
Aythya marila

Wintering:
> Qualifying 1% level for national importance: 40[50]*
> international importance: 1,500

Sites holding a five year average of >130 birds (with peak 1990-91 count) are: Solway Est. (3,803 Jan.), Lo. Neagh/Beg (1,539 Mar.), Lo. Indaal (660 Dec.), Forth Est. (381 Jan.), Lo. Ryan (200 Jan.), Carlingford Lo. (352 Feb.), Dornoch Fth. (368 Mar.), Lo. of Harray (240 Sep.), Cromarty Fth. (247 Dec.), Inner Clyde (144 Dec.), Belfast Lo. (43 Feb.) & Dee Est. (3 Nov.). Low counts at the latter two sites may be due to difficulty in seeing the birds adequately on the count dates. Counts of over 130 Scaup were made at five other sites in 1990-91: Dungeness (245 Mar.), Hamford Water (219 Feb.), Lo. of Stenness (194 Mar.), Ribble Est. (178 Mar.) & the Towyn-Abergele coast (151 Feb.).

Eider
Somateria mollissima

Latest estimate of breeding population:
15,000–25,000 pairs in Britain and Ireland, with 92% of occupied squares in Britain (Sharrock 1976).

Wintering:
> Qualifying 1% level for national importance: 700
> international importance: 20,000

The peak total count for Britain was lower than that of 1989-90 but, in N Ireland, the count was almost double that of last season.

Sites holding >1,500 Eider on average (with peak 1990-91 count) are: Tay Est. (20,300 Feb.), Forth Est. (7,836 Oct.), Morecambe Bay (8,183 Nov.), Inner Clyde (2,939 Oct.), Lindisfarne (2,600 Nov.), Montrose Basin (2,100 Feb.), Ythan Est.(2,322 Mar.), Murcar (no count) & Troon (no count).

Long-tailed Duck
Clangula hyemalis

Wintering:
> Qualifying 1% level for national importance: 200
> international importance: 20,000

In Britain and Ireland, the Long-tailed Duck winters in localized concentrations in open coastal waters, mainly along the east coast of Scotland and the northern and western isles.

Sites holding a five year average of >200 birds (with peak count in 1990-91) are: Moray Fth. (8,037 Jan.), Forth Est. (451 Nov.), Lindisfarne (420 Jan.), Water Sound (365 Feb.) & Broad Bay (no count). In addition, the Eden Est. held 360 birds in December 1990.

Common Scoter
Melanitta nigra
and
Velvet Scoter
Melanitta fusca

Latest estimate of breeding population:
100–114 pairs of Common Scoter (Partridge 1987).

Wintering:
> Qualifying 1% level for national importance:
> Common Scoter 350 , Velvet Scoter 30*
> international importance:
> Common Scoter 8,000, Velvet Scoter 2,500

The peak scoter count in the Moray Firth was 2,836 in December when at least 1,818 Common and a minimum 328 Velvet Scoter were present. At other sites, peak Common Scoter counts were 2,150 (Eden Est., Feb.), 1,735 (Forth Est., Mar.), 1,100 (Lindisfarne, Dec.) & 700 (St Andrews Bay, Jan.). Velvet Scoter peaked at 400 in St Andrews Bay (Dec.) and 84 in the Forth Est. (Oct.). In Wales a single flock of 2,500 Common Scoter were counted off Pendine (Jan.), 1,226 birds in Cardigan Bay (Dec.), 2,900 between Towyn and Abergele (Dec.) and 992 in Red Wharf Bay (Dec.).

Goldeneye
Bucephala clangula

Present population trend:
Increased annually 1970–1989.

Latest estimate of breeding population:
At least 85 nests in 1989 (Batten *et al.* 1990).

Wintering:

Qualifying 1% level for national importance: 150
international importance: 3,000

Peak NWC counts in both Britain and N Ireland were substantially greater than in 1989-90. Numbers peaked in February.

Sites holding a five year average of >250 birds (with peak 1990-91 count) are: Lo. Neagh/Beg (13,591 Feb.), Forth Est. (1,831 Jan.), Inner Moray Fth. (993 Feb.), Abberton Rsr. (707 Mar.), Belfast Lo. (634 Feb.), Maidens Hbr./Turnberry (462 Jan.), Eden Est. (360 Dec.), Inner Clyde (609 Jan.), Morecambe Bay (425 Mar.), Blackwater Est. (424 Feb.), Strangford Lo. (290 Mar.), Tweed Est. (351 Jan.), Rutland Water (505 Feb.), Lo. Leven (265 Jan.) & Windermere (329 Jan.). Other sites exceeding 250 birds in 1990-91 were: Solway Est. (507 Feb.), Dipple shore (462 Jan.), Lo. of Skene (358 Nov.), Doonshore (324 Feb.), Humber Est. (310 Feb.), Irvine shore (300 Dec.) & Lo. of Stenness (259 Feb.).

Potential threats to this species include the heavy stocking of lochs with rainbow trout, depleting invertebrate numbers and the poisoning of lochs to remove unwanted fish species before restocking. The effects of acidification on invertebrates of Scottish lochs are not yet understood.

Smew
Mergus albellus

Wintering:

Qualifying 1% level for national importance: +*
international importance: 150

There was clearly a cold weather influx of Smew from the continent between the January and February count dates. Relatively large counts were recorded in February at Rye Hbr. (22), Stan Hill Rsr.s (21), Goldhanger (18) and King George VI Rsr. (18).

Red-breasted Merganser
Mergus serrator

Wintering:

Qualifying 1% level for national importance: 100
international importance: 1,000

The Inner Moray Firth holds by far the highest numbers in the UK though the peak count in 1990-91 was relatively low.

Sites holding a five year average of >250 birds (with peak 1990-91 count) are: Inner Moray Fth. (658 Oct.), Tentsmuir (220 Sep.), Forth Est. (478 Oct.), Cromarty Fth. (340 Dec.), Poole Hbr. (338 Nov.), Strangford Lo. (274 Oct.), Morecambe Bay (256 Dec.) & Duddon Est. (271 Aug.). In addition, 280 were recorded at the Fleet/Wey in February 1991.

Goosander
Mergus merganser

Wintering:

Qualifying 1% level for national importance: 50
international importance: 1,250

For NWC sites counted in all seven months of the counting season, Goosanders were most abundant in February in Britain and N Ireland.

Sites holding a five year average of >75 birds (with peak 1990-91 count) are: Inner Moray Fth. (610+ Nov.), Hirsel Lake (290 Oct.), R. Tweed: Kelso/Coldstream (147 Feb.), Thrapston Gp. (149 Feb.), Tentsmuir (no count), Chew Valley Lake (163 Feb.), Tay Est. (206 Sep.), Hay-a-Park Gp. (166 Dec.), Eccup Rsr. (101 Feb.), Castle Lo. (52 Feb.), R. Eden: Rockcliffe/Armtw. (110 Jan.), Leighton/Roundhill Rsr. (no count) & Castle Howard Lake (84 Dec.). Other localities supporting over 75 Goosander in 1990-91 were: Castle Semple/Barr Lo. (106 Feb.), R. Tweed (103 Jan.), Balgray (103 Dec.), Cults Rsr. (102 Oct.) & Montrose Basin (89 Sep.).

Ruddy Duck
Oxyura jamaicensis

Wintering:

The maximum count in Britain increased by 9.2% between 1989-90 and 1990-91, with a peak count in January 1991 of 3,087.

Sites holding a five year average of >80 birds (with peak 1990-91 count) are: Blithfield Rsr. (899 Dec.), Chew Valley Lake (435 Dec.), Rutland Water (750 Feb.), Belvide Rsr. (248 Oct.), Eyebrook Rsr. (304 Jan.), Blagdon Lake (108 Jan.), Woolston Eyes (56 Oct.), Farmwood Pool (106 Dec.), Stanford Rsr. (37 Mar.), Swithland Rsr. (184 Mar.), Llyn Penrhyn (101 Feb.) & Llyn Traffwll (84 Sep.). A further seven sites held over 80 Ruddy Duck during 1990-91: Rostherne Mere (195 Feb.), Swithland Rsr. (184 Mar.), Cheddar Rsr. (162 Feb.), Hanningfield Rsr. (123 Feb.), Hilfield Park Lake (114 Dec.), Staines Rsr. (103 Feb.) & Attenborough Gp. (81 Mar.).

Sparrowhawk
Accipiter nisus

Present population trend:
Sustained recovery from earlier major decline now completed.

Percentage change in CBC index, 1989-1990:
All habitats = +3% (-26% to +43%)

Latest estimate of breeding population:
25,000 breeding pairs in Britain, plus 30,000 non-breeders (Newton 1986).

Buzzard
Buteo buteo

Present population trend:
Modest increase, mainly through in-filling; perhaps late stage of slow recovery from earlier decline.

Percentage change in CBC index, 1989-1990:
All habitats = +5% (-25% to +48%) based on < 30 plots.

Latest estimate of breeding population:
12,000-15,000 territorial pairs in the UK in 1983 (Taylor et al. 1988); at least 100 pairs in N Ireland in 1986 (Hutchinson 1989).
The population level estimated by the CBC is the highest since 1983.

Golden Eagle
Aquila chrysaetos

Breeding success in 1990:
Results from the Scottish RSGs indicate a disasterous season for Golden Eagles over much of their range. Chicks fledged at only 42% of sites where birds were present (c.f. 55% in 1989, 47% in 1988 & 49% in 1987). Summary results from RSGs are given at in Table 1.

Latest estimate of breeding population:
424 pairs in 1982 (Dennis et al. 1984).

Osprey
Pandion haliaetus

Breeding success in 1990:
There was a total of 63 known pairs, of which 56 laid eggs: 48 clutches hatched giving 44 successful broods which resulted in 88 fledged young. Seven nests were robbed by egg collectors (one of whom was taken to court and fined £2,500) and one failed due to interference from a third osprey. A number of chicks died due to very wet weather and food shortage.

Kestrel
Falco tinnunculus

Present population trend:
Stable or declining slightly, after earlier increase.

Percentage change in CBC index, 1989-1990:
All habitats = -8% (-23% to +9%).

Latest estimate of breeding population:
70,000 pairs in Britain (Newton 1984).

Hobby
Falco subbuteo

Present population trend:
CBC data continue to add to evidence for overall increase.

Latest estimate of breeding population:
Over 500 pairs in Britain (Fuller et al. 1985).

Merlin
Falco columbarius

Breeding success in 1990:
Summary results from the Scottish RSGs indicate a relatively good year in terms of fledging success at occupied sites (57% cf 60% in 1989, 45% in 1988 and 58% in 1987), see Table 2.

Latest estimate of breeding population:
550–650 pairs in 1983–1984 (Bibby & Natrass 1986).

Peregrine
Falco peregrinus

Breeding success in 1990:
Of occupied sites checked by Scottish RSGs 51% fledged young (cf 48% in 1989, 44% in 1988 & 52% in 1987), see Table 3.

Latest estimate of breeding population:
Over 900 pairs (Batten et al. 1990).

Table 1. Golden Eagle breeding in 1990.

Home range/ site	Lewis & Harris	North-east	Central	Argyll	Highland	Uist	TOTAL
Checked	50	30	25	68	113	15	301
Birds present	41	29	25	60	84	14	253
Eggs laid	11	18+	10+	37	46	5	127+
Eggs hatched	10	16	3	21+	42	2	94+
Chicks fledged	9	15	3	18	42	2	89
Total young fledged	10	22+	3	23	52	2	112

Table 2. Merlin breeding in 1990.

Home range/ site	Lewis & Harris	Tayside	Grampian	South West	South East	Argyll	Highland	Orkney	Shetland	Uist	TOTAL
Checked	33	69+	–	24	25+	18+	53	46	29	12	367+
Birds present	11	47	58	23	25	18	43	14+	29	12	280+
Eggs laid	3	–	51	16	23	14	30	14	23	–	207+
Eggs Hatched	3	–	39	12	21	9+	22	9	8+	3	166+
Chicks fledged	3	30	36	11	19	9	21	9	18	3	159+
Total young fledged	10	95	108+	33+	59	34	69	29	52	8	497+

Table 3. Peregrine breeding in 1990.

Home range/ site	Lewis & Harris	North-east	Central	South-West	South East	Argyll	Highland	Orkney	Shetland	Uist	TOTAL
Checked	8	121	61	71	35	104	104	33	5+	8	471
Birds present	8	109	53	59+	31	24	84	17	5	8	398+
Eggs laid	0	84	51+	29	20	70	7	–	15	1	293+
Eggs Hatched	0	62+	38+	18	17+	51	4	–	7	1	222+
Chicks fledged	0	58	30+	33	15	17+	46	4	1	6	205+
Total young fledged	0	142+	67+	75	37	25+	96	4+	3	8	453+

Red-legged Partridge
Alectoris rufa

Present population trend:
Fluctuates; the trend has been upwards since the mid-1950s, latterly due to artificial stocking.

Percentage change in CBC index, 1989-1990:
Farmland = +24% (+4% to +48%)

Latest estimate of breeding population:
100,000-200,000 pairs in Britain (Sharrock 1976). No reliable estimate is possible due to the large scale of rearing and releasing, compounded by the hybrid problem.
There was a significant increase in the CBC index in 1989-90, continuing the erratic population swings.

Grey Partridge
Perdix perdix

Present population trend:
Severe long-term decrease is continuing (but see below).

Percentage change in CBC index, 1989-1990:
Farmland = +2% (-18% to +28%).

Latest estimate of breeding population:
About 500,000 pairs in Britain and Ireland in 1968-1972 (Sharrock 1976); 89% of occupied squares were then in Britain. The CBC index has halved since that period. This species enjoyed a second successive rise in the CBC index but the recent increase is negligible in the face of this species' long-term decline.

Quail
Coturnix coturnix

Present population trend:
Unknown, owing to huge year-to-year fluctuations.

Latest estimate of breeding population:
Over 600 calling birds in Britain in 1964 influx (Parslow 1973); many fewer in normal years.

Pheasant
Phasianus colchicus

Present population trend:
Stable or increasing where releases continue, but the wild population has fallen recently.

Percentage change in CBC Index, 1989–1990:
Farmland = +19% (+7% to +33%) statistically significant; woodland = +17% (+1% to +35%) statistically significant.

Latest estimate of breeding population:
3 million territorial males and 4.5 million females in Britain and Ireland; 73% of occupied squares during 1968-1972 were in Britain (Sharrock 1976).

Moorhen
Gallinula chloropus

Present population trend:
Probably stable overall.

Percentage change in CBC index, 1989-1990:
Farmland = +8% (-5% to +23%).

Percentage change in WBS index, 1989–1990:
+11% (+3% to +19%) statistically significant.

Latest estimate of breeding population:
300,000 pairs in Britain and Ireland (Sharrock 1976); 71% of occupied squares were then in Britain.

Coot
Fulica atra

Present population trend:
Increasing, in England at least.

Percentage change in CBC index, 1989-1990:
All habitats = +2% (-13% to +20%) based on < 30 plots.

Percentage change in WBS index, 1989-1990:
+11% (-1% to +24%).

Latest estimate of breeding population:
50,000-100,000 pairs in Britain and Ireland (Sharrock 1976); 75% of occupied squares were then in Britain.

Wintering:
Qualifying 1% level for national importance: 1,000
international importance: 15,000

The peak numbers in NWC counts in Britain and N Ireland were lower than the high figures reached in 1989-90. Highest counts were made in September.

Sites holding a five year average of >1,000 birds (with peak 1990-91 count) are: Abberton Rsr. (9,252 Sep.), Lo. Neagh/Beg (6,685 Sep.), Rutland Water (3,743 Nov.), Hanningfield Rsr. (3,668 Sep.), Cotswold Water Park West (3,608 Dec.), Ouse Washes (no count), The Fleet/Wey (2,647 Nov.), Cotswold Water Park East (2,396 Dec.), Lo. Leven (1,515 Oct.), Kingsbury/Coton Pools (1,310 Nov.), Cheddar Rsr. (1,416 Oct.), Stanford Rsr. (1,118 Sep.), Fen Drayton Gp. (950 Dec.), Chichester Gp. (1,099 Oct.), Fairburn Ings (1,151 Sep.), Shepperton Gp. (no count) & Brogborough Gp. (807 Dec.). Five other sites held >1,000 birds in 1990-91: Chew Valley Lake (1,070 Aug.), King George V Rsr. (1,800 Oct.), Staines Rsr. (1,131 Oct.), Dorchester Gp. (1,095 Feb.) & Aqualate Mere (1,000 Dec.).

Oystercatcher
Haematopus ostralegus

Present population trend:
Long-term increase.

Percentage change in WBS index, 1989-1990:
-6% (-21% to +11%) based on < 20 plots.

Latest estimate of breeding population:
33,000-43,000 pairs in Britain (Piersma 1986).

Wintering:
Qualifying 1% level for national importance: 2,800
international importance: 9,000

The January 1991 population index was lower than the record high figure of 1990.

Seven sites continue to rank as internationally important for Oystercatchers (with peak 1990-91 count): Morecambe Bay (56,361 Jan.), Wash (33,791 Feb.), Solway (40,095 Feb.), Dee (Eng/Wales) (35,774 Nov.), Burry (15,151 Jan.), Ribble (18,263 Feb.) & Thames (17,378).

Avocet
Recurvirostra avosetta

Latest estimate of breeding population:
Nearly 400 paris in 1988 (Batten *et al.* 1990).

Wintering:
Qualifying 1% level for national importance: 5*
international importance: 700

The rise in the wintering population continued with the peak count of over 1,500 in January being almost 50% higher than that of 1989-90. The Alde complex remains the main site with a peak count of 729 (Jan.) though the average maximum still falls short of international importance. Five other sites qualify as nationally important. These are (with peak 1990-91 count): Exe (323 Dec.), Tamar complex (240 Feb.), Hamford Water (188 Dec.), Poole Hbr. (175 Jan.) & Medway (36 Nov.). In addition, the following all supported over 50 birds during winter 1990-91: North Norfolk Marshes (110 Mar.), Swale (75 Mar.) & Blyth (Suffolk) (59 Mar.). In October, before the first BoEE count, 235 Avocets were present on the Medway.

Stone Curlew
Burhinus oedicnemus

Present population trend:
Declining rapidly.

Latest estimate of breeding population:
Not more than 160 pairs (Batten *et al.* 1990).

Ringed Plover
Charadrius hiaticula

Present population trend:
Apparently increasing.

Latest estimate of breeding population:
8,600 pairs in the UK in 1984 (Prater 1989).

Wintering:
> *Qualifying 1% level for national importance: 230*
> *(passage 300)*
> *international importance: 500*

Sites with average maxima >400 birds (with peak 1990-91 count) are: Chichester Hbr. (519 Dec.), Thames (674 Nov.), Medway (501 Nov.), Outer Ards (709 Feb.), Hamford Water (1,427 Nov.), Lindisfarne (800 Nov.), Langstone Hbr. (420 Jan.), Morecambe Bay (380 Dec.), Forth (422 Dec.) & Colne (276 Dec.). In addition to the winter population, there is a substantial spring and autumn passage through the UK. Peak passage counts exceeding 500 birds were recorded at Morecambe Bay (2,615 May), Wash (2,147 Sep.), Severn (1,573 Aug.), Hamford Water (1,462 Sep.), Langstone Hbr. (1,279 Aug.), Dee (Eng/Wales) (1,202 Aug.), Chichester Hbr. (1,149 Sep.), Thames (1,110 Oct.), Humber (998 May), Medway (984 Aug.), North Norfolk Marshes (818 Sep.), Colne (663 Oct.), Blackwater (605 Sep.), Ribble (583 Aug.), Lindisfarne (582 Oct.),Stour (530 Sep.), Orwell (505 Sep.) & Solway (502 Sep.).

Golden Plover
Pluvialis apricaria

Latest estimate of breeding population:
22,600 pairs (Stroud *et al.* 1987).

Wintering:
> *Qualifying 1% level for national importance: 2,000*
> *international importance: 10,000*

November and December counts were exceptionally high and dropped off at most important sites in the cold weather of January and February.

Sites with average maxima >2,000 (with peak 1990-91 count) are: Humber (20,168 Nov.), Strangford Lo. (4,136 Nov.), Ribble (2,451 Nov.), Forth (6,637 Nov.), Solway (2,693 Dec.), Crouch/Roach (2,223 Jan.), Wash (3,591 Dec.), Thames (2,572 Mar.), Lindisfarne (1,600 Feb.), Blackwater (3,388 Mar.) & Morecambe Bay (1,831 Nov.). Two other sites had counts exceeding 2,000 in 1990-91: Lo. Foyle (2,828 Mar.) & North Norfolk Marshes (2,671 Dec.).

Grey Plover
Pluvialis squatarola

Wintering:
> *Qualifying 1% level for national importance: 210*
> *international importance: 1,500*

February saw an all-time BoEE record count of 43,186 birds in the UK and the January index was second only to that of 1989.

Sites with average maxima of >1,500 birds (with peak 1990-91 count) are: Wash (7,432 Feb.), Thames (6,388 Feb.), Medway (3,435 Mar.), Ribble (2,720 Mar.), Humber (2,490 Nov.), Chichester Hbr. (1,718 Mar.), Stour (1,999 Jan.), Morecambe Bay (1,466 Feb.), Blackwater (4,085 Mar.), Swale (1,559 Jan.) & Dee (Eng/Wales) (2,004 Jan.). In addition, the Mersey (2,620 Feb.), Hamford Water (1,780 Dec.) & Dengie (1,700 Feb.) held > 1,500 birds in 1990-91.

Lapwing
Vanellus vanellus

Present population trend:
Marked downward trend in the south; probably caused by a major switch from spring to autumn tilage; probably downward overall.

Percentage change in CBC index, 1989-1990:
Farmland = -2% (-25% to +27%).

Percentage change in WBS index, 1989-1990:
+4% (-16% to +29%).

Latest estimate of breeding population:
Shrubb & Lack (1991) estimate a total population in England and Wales of c125,000 pairs with a major concentration in north-west England. A decline in central and southern England has probably been caused by a major switch from spring to autumn tillage.

Wintering:
> *Qualifying 1% level for national importance: 10,000*
> *international importance: 20,000*

The exceptionally high peak count of January 1990 was not repeated this year and the February count was low, probably due to the very cold weather.

Sites holding a five year average of 5,000 birds (with peak 1990-91 count) are: Humber (26,506 Nov.), Ribble (32,590 Dec.), Morecambe Bay (12,247 Nov.), Strangford Lo. (10,651 Jan.), Thames (7,668 Jan.), Swale (4,915 Jan.), Solway (3,504 Dec.), Dee (Eng/Wales) (5,083 Dec.), Tees (9,824 Dec.), Forth (7,529 Nov.), Wash (3,007 Dec.), Alde complex (3,393 Jan.) & Outer Ards (3,915 Feb.).

Knot
Calidris canutus

Wintering:
> *Qualifying 1% level for national importance: 2,200*
> *international importance: 3,500*

Winter numbers were unusually stable for a species which usually shows considerable mobility within the winter period. The peak count at the Wash this year was the highest count of any wader species at a single site in the BoEE.

Sites with average maxima of >5,000 birds (with peak 1990-91 count) are: Wash (164,176 Nov.), Ribble (30,567 Dec.), Alt (28,000 Nov.), Humber (35,292 Nov.), Thames (23,100 Jan.), Morecambe Bay (30,958 Mar.), Dee (Eng/Wales) (16,916 Jan.), Solway (15,305 Feb.), Forth (7,163 Dec.), North Norfolk Marshes (13,298 Feb.), Dengie (6,540 Jan.), Strangford Lo. (6,376 Dec.) & Duddon (5,570 Feb.).

Sanderling
Calidris alba

Wintering:

Qualifying 1% level for national importance: 140
(passage 300)
international importance: 1,000

The January 1991 index for Sanderling reached its highest level since 1983.

Sites with average peak winter counts of >250 birds (with peak 1990-91 count) are: Ribble (2,200 Mar.), Thanet (566 Mar.), Alt (488 Dec.), Dee (Eng/Wales) (1,011 Nov.), Humber (559 Mar.), Wash (302 Jan.), Duddon (383 Feb.), Tay (380 Nov.), Chichester Hbr. (253 Mar.), Tees (130 Nov.), Swansea Bay (415 Mar.), Solway (255 Nov.) & Clwyd coast (458 Dec.). Passage counts tend to be much higher. Sites recording over 1,000 birds during passage periods in 1990-91 were the Ribble (5,043 Jul.), Morecambe Bay (4,354 May), Humber (1,868 May), Wash (1,455 Aug.) & Lindisfarne (1,400 Aug.).

Little Stint
Calidris minuta

Wintering:

The only BoEE sites with peak counts exceeding 2 Little Stint in winter 1990-91 were the same as those in the previous year: Chichester Hbr. (6 in Nov.) & the Swale (4 in Jan.). During autumn passage, counts of over five were made at ten sites, all in September: Morecambe Bay (15 birds), Dee (Eng/Wales) (15), Chichester Hbr. (12), Severn (11), Rye Hbr./Pett Levels (110, Humber (110), Swale (10), Exe (8), Langstone Hbr. (8) & Forth (7). Only one spring count involved more than five birds, with Breydon Water holding eight individuals in May.

Curlew Sandpiper
Calidris ferruginea

Wintering:

The only record of more than one Curlew Sandpiper in winter 1990-91 was of a surprising eight on the Humber in November. In autumn 1990 six sites recorded peak passage counts of 25 or more: Severn (54 birds in Sep.), Forth (42 Sep.), Thames (37 Jul.), Exe (31 Sep.), Humber (28 Sep.) & Christchurch Hbr. (25 Sep.).

Purple Sandpiper
Calidris maritima

Wintering:

Qualifying 1% level for national importance: 160
international importance: 500

Over 95% of Purple Sandpipers wintering in Britain occur away from estuaries (Moser 1987) so the identification of any population trends from BoEE counts must be made with caution. Only five BoEE sites recorded over 100 birds in 1990-91: Tees (261 Feb.), Budle Point-Seahouses (243 Nov.), Rosehearty-Fraserburgh (235 Jan.), Spey coast (228 Feb.) & Isle of Thannet (102 Mar.).

Dunlin
Calidris alpina

Latest estimate of breeding population:

About 9,150 pairs mostly in the peatlands of Caithness, Sutherland and Lewis and the machair of the Western Isles (Batten *et al.* 1990)

Wintering:

Qualifying 1% level for national importance: 4,300
(passage 2,000)
international importance: 14,000

The January index and total BoEE counts indicated an increase in Dunlin numbers in 1990-91. The count of 76,602 Dunlin at Morecambe Bay in Jan. 1991 is the highest-ever winter count at any BoEE site.

Sites holding a five year average of >14,000 birds (with peak 1990-91 count) are: Morecambe Bay (76,602 Jan.), Wash (43,233 Jan.), Severn (58,705 Feb.), Langstone Hbr. (27,720 Jan.), Thames (29,925 Dec.), Humber (26,133 Dec.), Mersey (52,100 Dec.), Medway (26,442 Nov.), Chichester Hbr. (24,235 Jan.), Dee (Eng/Wales) (24,670 Dec.), Ribble (19,038 Mar.), Blackwater (19,025 Feb.) & Stour (16,429 Jan.).

Two recent surveys by Meltofte (1991) and Owen (1991) have confirmed that our wintering Dunlin are of the *alpina* race. They migrate to the Wadden Sea during March, fatten up there and leave for their N European breeding grounds in mid-May. After breeding the adults migrate directly to the Wadden Sea and the Wash in July/early August, where they moult. After moult, most birds move on during October and November to their wintering grounds in the British Isles. Juveniles migrate more slowly across the Wadden Sea and the British Isles during September to November. Using data from Dunlin ringed on the Wash in autumn, Branson (1991) calculated that adult birds from this group had a life expectancy of around 3 years. Juveniles had a significantly lower expectancy, averaging between 0.8 and 1.5 years.

Ruff
Philomachus pugnax

Wintering:

Qualifying 1% level for national importance: 15*
international importance: 10,000

Around 1,400 Ruff are thought to winter in Britain and Ireland (Sorensen, in Lack 1986). The UK totals recorded by the BoEE in recent years of around 100 therefore represent only a small fraction of the national wintering population, most of which is found at the muddy margins of lakes and pools.

Six sites recorded counts >20 birds in the 1990-91 winter: the Alde complex (41 Feb.), Hamford Water (41 Jan.), North Norfolk Marshes (34 Mar.), Swale (29 Mar.), Southampton Water (24 Feb.) & Chichester Hbr. (22 Nov.). Pagham Hbr. used to have a nationally important wintering population, the highest count being 540 in Dec. 1978, but no birds were recorded there in the winter months of 1990-91. On autumn passage, counts exceeded 50 birds at three sites: Humber (133 Sep.), North Norfolk Marshes (79 Sep.) & Breydon Water (51 Oct.).

Jack Snipe
Lymnocryptes minimus

Wintering:
Double figures were recorded at Langstone Hbr. (13 birds in Oct.), Morecambe Bay (12 Oct.) & Orwell (10 Nov.). British totals were unusually high in 1990-91 for this species which is probably the most under-estimated species counted by BoEE due to its habit of sitting tight.

Snipe
Gallinago gallinago

Present population trend:
Downward on lowland farmland; trends in other habitats are unknown.

Latest estimate of breeding population:
30,000 pairs in Britain (Piersma 1986).

Wintering:
Qualifying 1% level for national importance: (not set)
international importance: 10,000

BoEE totals were rather less than the typical values of recent years. Sites recording > 200 birds in the 1990-91 winter were Morecambe Bay (240 Nov.), Breydon Water (236 Jan.), Thames (200 Dec.) & Dee (Eng/Wales) (200 Dec.). By analysing numbers of Snipe shot, Hoodless

(1991) summarises the decline of the wintering population in Britain. The decline began around the turn of the century and has been most marked in E Britain, with extensive drainage of wetlands considered to be the major cause. The severe winter of 1962-63 had a drastic effect on numbers but, since then, the population appears to have been relatively stable.

Woodcock
Scolopax rusticola

Present population trend:
Some decline is suspected, perhaps in southern counties only.

Percentage change in CBC index, 1989-1990:
All habitats = -8% (-51% to +69%) based on < 30 plots.

Latest estimate of breeding population:
Tentatively 18,000-46,000 pairs in Britain and Ireland (Sharrock 1976); 77% of occupied squares were then in Britain. Existing estimates are unreliable, in part because "pair" is an inappropriate unit in this species. The CBC index is now only about half the level of a decade ago.

Black-tailed Godwit
Limosa limosa

Wintering:

Qualifying 1% level for national importance: 50
international importance: 700

U.K. totals for Black-tailed Godwits were higher than in 1989-90 in all winter months except February. The November count was more than 1,000 above the previous record winter count made in February 1990. The drop in numbers recorded in February 1991 coincided with the severe cold weather at that time.

Sites with average maxima >400 birds (with peak 1990-91 count) are: Hamford Water (2,241 Nov.), Stour (2,372 Nov.), Ribble (977 Mar.), Poole Hbr. (1,236 Mar.), Dee (Eng/Wales) (1,233 Nov.), Langstone Hbr. (651 Nov.), Colne (378 Dec.), Chichester Hbr. (367 Mar.), Exe (782 Jan.), Blackwater (743 Mar.) & Southampton Water (311 Jan.). In 1990-91 seven sites recorded passage counts over 700: Blackwater (1,932 Apr.), Hamford Water (1,584 Sep.), Wash (1,486 Sep.), Ribble (1,261 Sep.), Dee (Eng/Wales) (1,221 Oct.), Langstone Hbr. (1,185 Sep.) & Stour (1,124 Oct.).

The first foreign recovery of a British-bred Black-tailed Godwit (from the Ouse Washes) occurred recently, when one was shot in Guinea-Bissau (W Africa) in November.

Bar-tailed Godwit
Limosa lapponica

Wintering:
Qualifying 1% level for national importance: 610
international importance: 1,000
The cold spell in January and February 1991 triggered an influx of birds, particularly from the Wadden Sea.

Sites holding a five year average of >610 birds (with peak 1990-91 count) are: Wash (14,834 Feb.), Ribble (9,940 Feb.), Alt (7,095 Feb.), Lindisfarne (4,900 Nov.), Thames (11,517 Feb.), Solway (3,650 Feb.), Forth (2,722 Feb.), Lo. Foyle (3,427 Feb.), Morecambe Bay (2,568 Feb.),Inner Moray Firth (1,987 Feb.), Tay (1,696 Feb.), Humber (2,002 Jan.), Chichester Hbr. (1,056 Feb.), N. Norfolk Marshes (1,653 Feb.), Eden (680 Jan.), Cromarty Fth. (1,309 Dec.), Dee (Eng/Wales) (2,480 Dec.), Dengie (1,000 Jan.), Langstone Hbr. (844 Jan.) & Dornoch Firth (1,515 Feb.).

Whimbrel
Numenius phaeopus

Wintering:
Qualifying 1% level for national importance: +(passage 50)
international importance: 700
Passage counts of over 50 birds were made at nine sites in 1990-91. The largest counts were at the Wash (252 Jul.), Exe (138 Apr.), Tamar complex (135 Jul.), Burry (122 May) & Rosehearty-Frazerburgh (101 Aug.). As in most years only a very small number of sites recorded even the odd bird during the winter months.

Curlew
Numenius arquata

Present population trend:
Uncertain; expansion of breeding range suggests an overall increase.
Percentage change in CBC index, 1989-1990:
All habitats = +8% (-12% to +32%) based on < 30 plots.
Percentage change in WBS index, 1989-1990:
-12% (-29% to +8%) based on < 20 plots.
Latest estimate of breeding population:
33,000-38,000 pairs in Britain (Piersma 1986).
Wintering:
Qualifying 1% level for national importance: 910
international importance: 3,500
There was a substantial decline of 24% in the January index. The last time Curlew declined to such an extent was in January 1984, also a period of severe winter weather. The following three winters also contained major cold spells and the index for Curlew remained at a low level for four years. However, the fall in the January index in 1991 was somewhat distorted by the high peak count in January 1990.

Sites holding a five year average of >2,000 birds (with peak 1990-91 count) are: Morecambe Bay (13,174 Mar.), Solway (5,171 Mar.), Humber (2,320 Mar.), Thames (3,301 Mar.), Wash (3,578 Feb.), Severn (2,505 Feb.), Dee (Eng/Wales) (2,892 Mar.), Lo. Foyle (1,925 Jan.), Forth (2,137 Nov.) & Duddon (1,992 Mar.).

Spotted Redshank
Tringa erythropus

Wintering:
Qualifying 1% level for national importance: 2*
international importance: (not set)
UK totals for Spotted Redshank in winter 1990-91 were at similar levels to the previous winter.

Five sites recorded winter counts in double figures: Wash (31 birds in Nov.), Tamar complex (19 Dec.), Medway (19 Nov.), Dee (Eng/Wales) (14 Dec.) & the Fal complex (10 Nov.). In 1990-91 only the Wash recorded a passage count of over 50 birds: 67 in July, 192 in August and 104 in September.

Redshank
Tringa totanus

Present population trend:
Probably downward, certainly so in the south. The indices given below indicate an improvement in 1990.
Percentage change in CBC index, 1989-1990:
All habitats = +6% (-34% to +69%) based on < 30 plots.
Percentage change in WBS index, 1989-1990:
+5% (-10% to +23%) based on < 20 plots.
Latest estimate of breeding population:
30,000-33,000 pairs in Britain (Piersma 1986)
Wintering:
Qualifying 1% level for national importance: 750
(passage 1,200)
international importance: 1,500
Numbers declined after the onset of the cold spell in January 1991. Similar declines have occurred during very cold spells in previous winters. In February 1991 large numbers of dead waders were found at east coast estuaries, predominantly Redshank (1,500 on the Wash). This species seems unwilling to move away from adverse weather conditions.

Sites holding a five year average of >1,500 birds (with peak 1990-91 count) are: Dee (Eng/Wales) (7,330 Jan.),

Morecambe Bay (6,379 Nov.), Humber (4,776 Nov.), Thames (4,569 Nov.), Wash (3,872 Nov.), Medway (3,450 Jan.), Forth (4,393 Nov.), Mersey (4,335 Dec.), Lindisfarne (2,600 Jan.), Swale (1,472 Dec.), Inner Moray Firth (2,827 Jan.), Strangford Lo. (2,420 Nov.), Severn (2,166 Dec.), Inner Clyde (2,441 Feb.), Montrose Basin (2,717 Jan.), Solway (2,049 Feb.), Deben (1,191 Nov.), Cromarty Fth. (2,304 Dec.), Chichester Hbr. (1,718 Dec.), Belfast Lo. (1,043 Nov.) & Tay (711 Jan.).

Greenshank
Tringa nebularia

Present population trend:
Downward due to afforestation of peatland breeding grounds (Batten *et al.* 1990).

Latest estimate of breeding population:
960 pairs in Scotland in 1985 (Stroud *et al.* 1987).

Wintering:
> Qualifying 1% level for national importance: 4*
> international importance: ?(not set)

As usual, the sites recording counts of 20 or more birds in the winter months were all from N Ireland or the west of Britain as follows (with peak 1990-91 count): Strangford Lo. (36 Jan.), Lo. Foyle (30 Jan.), Tamar complex (26 Nov.), Lavan Sands (23 Mar.), Kingsbridge (Devon) (22 Nov.) & Dee (Eng/Wales) (66 Aug.). Much larger numbers pass through during autumn passage, with 11 sites recording more than 50 birds: the Wash (252 Jul.), Chichester Hbr. (150 Sep.), Blackwater (123 Sep.), Thames (97 Sep.), Strangford Lo. (66 Sep.), Medway (80 Jul.), Morecambe Bay (72 Aug.), Tamar complex (67 Sep.), Dee (Eng/Wales) (66 Aug.), Stour (62 Sep.) & Langstone Hbr. (62 Aug.). Much of the UK wintering population is believed to breed in Scotland (Hutchinson, in Lack 1986). A study plot of 15km^2 in NW Scotland contained between 4 and 13 breeding pairs between 1964 and 1989. A steady decline has occurred over the past 10 years with habitat change quoted as the most likely cause (Thompson & Thompson 1991).

Green Sandpiper
Tringa ochropus

The only BoEE sites recording peak counts of 5+ Green Sandpipers in the winter 1990-91 were the Tamar complex with 6, and 5 at each of the following: the Severn, Rye Hbr./Pett Levels, Thames and Orwell. This essentially inland wader species is also scarce during spring, but in autumn far larger numbers are present. In the autumn of 1990 only the Thames recorded over 20 birds, with a peak of 28 in August.

Common Sandpiper
Actitis hypoleucos

Present population trend:
Stable.

Percentage change in WBS index, 1989-1990:
+6% (-6% to +19%).

Latest estimate of breeding population:
17,100-20,100 pairs in Britain (Piersma 1986).

Wintering:
U.K. totals of Common Sandpiper dropped to only 8 birds in February 1991, possibly as a result of the severe winter weather at the time.

The five sites holding more than two birds in the winter months reflect the strong southerly distribution of this species in winter: Tamar complex (8 birds in Dec.), Thames (5 Nov.), Cleddau (5 Dec.), Taw/Torridge (3 Dec.) & Southampton Water (3 Dec., Jan.). Slightly larger numbers occur in spring but the highest counts are made in autumn. In autumn 1990 Morecambe Bay (91 Jul.) & the Wash (57 Aug.) were the only sites recording over 50 birds.

Turnstone
Arenaria interpres

Wintering:
> Qualifying 1% level for national importance: 450
> international importance: 700

The January index was 11% down in 1990-91. Typically, the UK count totals varied little across the winter months.

Sites holding a five year average of >700 birds (with peak 1990-91 count) are: Morecambe Bay (1,944 Jan.), Outer Ards (1,612 Jan.), Forth (1,188 Mar.), Thanet (1,253 Jan.), Wash (1,131 Nov.), Dee (Eng/Wales) (853 Jan.), Thames (766 Dec.) & Guernsey (936 Mar.). Autumn counts of >700 were recorded at nine sites: Morecambe Bay (1,554 Oct.), Outer Ards (1,508 Oct.), Wash (1,292 Oct.), Dee (Eng/Wales) (906 Sep.), Guernsey (873 Oct.), Humber (815 Sep.), Duddon (803 Sep.), Medway (794 Oct.) & Thanet (779 Sep.). 2,580 Turnstone on Morecambe Bay in April is one of the highest BoEE counts ever made for this species, but was the only spring count over 700 in 1991.

Arctic Skua
Stercorarius parasiticus

Present population trend:
Possibly a threefold increase since 1969-70 (but coverage and methodology had improved).

185

Breeding numbers:
Monitored colonies in Shetland have shown a general decline during 1986-90, including a 4-5% decrease in 1990. Most of the 1989-90 change occurred on Fair Isle and Foula, with little or no change detected at other, smaller colonies on and around the main islands. Foula in particular has shown an ongoing and statistically significant decline in recent years. Counts from colonies outside Shetland have been less directly comparable between years, although an increase was noticed at North Hill, Papa Westray (Orkney) up to 1989. However, there was probably little or no change between 1989 and 1990 at the few Orkney colonies censused or on Handa (Sutherland).

Breeding success:
Many of the colonies monitored in Shetland produced no fledged young in 1990, and both average and overall productivity was less than 0.1 chick/territory. The most successful colonies, Hermaness (Unst) and Black Park (Yell), produced only c0.4 chicks/territory (though both figures were higher than in 1989). Excluding Fair Isle, productivity was equally bad in 1988-89. On Fair Isle, where low productivity was not recorded until 1989, Arctic Skuas had their least successful year yet in 1990 (0.3/territory). Arctic Skuas bred more successfully in Orkney than in Shetland in both 1989 and 1990, but still averaged only 0.4-0.5 chicks fledged/territory. No instances of total failure were seen, and a few colonies almost achieved 1 chick/territory. As in 1989, the most successful colony in 1990 was on Handa.

Latest estimate of breeding population:
c3,350 apparently occupied territories in 1985–1987 (Lloyd *et al.* 1991)

Great Skua
Stercorarius skua

Present population trend:
Only limited information is available for 1990. On Foula (Shetland), the 1990 census showed a 6% decline since the last census, in 1986. On Fair Isle there was little change between 1989 (72 apparently occupied territories) and 1990 (73 apparently occupied territories). In Orkney, RSPB's North Hoy reserve held c400 apparently occupied territories in 1990, compared to c250 in 1984, an apparent 60% increase (Meek 1990). Increases on 1989 figures were noted on Handa and St Kilda.

Breeding success:
The most successful colony monitored was on Handa, where an average of 1.2 chicks fledged/territory. Productivity at four Shetland colonies was moderate or poor in 1990 (range 0.22-0.70/territory). The overall productivity in Shetland was similar to 1989, but much better than for Arctic Skua. Success was higher (0.83/territory) on Hoy (Orkney).

Latest estimate of breeding population:
About 7,900 apparently occupied territories in 1985-87 (Lloyd *et al.* 1991), possibly twice as high as in 1969-70 (though count methods have varied).

Black-headed Gull
Larus ridibundus

Present population trend:
1989-90 population changes were very variable between regions, and were usually based on small numbers of colonies. Trends during 1986-90 as a whole generally indicate stable or increasing populations (significant increase for monitored colonies in NW England).

Breeding success:
Little systematic monitoring is undertaken. Available information for 1990 includes: poor success at some inland Shetland colonies and variable success in Poole Harbour (Dorset). The marked variation in success reflects such factors as predation and flooding by high tides.

Latest estimate of breeding population:
About 82,000 prs. bred at coastal colonies in 1985-87, a c12% increase since 1969-70 (Lloyd et al. 1991). The inland population may be c130,000 prs.

Common Gull
Larus canus

Present population trend:
At six colonies in northern Argyll and Bute (SW Scotland), 611 nests containing eggs were counted in late May/ early June 1990, a 10% increase since 1989 (555 clutches). More limited information from elsewhere includes increases from 67 to 91 apparently occupied nests at several colonies in Co. Down (NE Ireland) and from 73 to 86 apparently occupied nests on Canna and Eigg (NW Scotland).

Breeding success:
On Fair Isle (Shetland), 9 pairs averaged 0.9 chicks/ fledged pair (1.1 in 1989). Several inland colonies in Shetland had a poor season.

Lesser Black-backed Gull
Larus fuscus

Present population trend:
Coastal numbers increased by c.30% since 1969-70.

Breeding numbers:
The most detailed counts available are from Wales and SE Scotland, where numbers have shown no obvious trends (and marked fluctuations) during 1986-90. Growth in the NW England/Isle of Man sample reflects a marked increase on the Ribble Estuary (Lancashire) from 340 pairs in 1987 to c810 pairs in 1990.

Breeding success:
For the second year in succession, the population on Skomer (Wales) suffered almost total breeding failure (c13,460 prs. reared an estimated 300-500 chicks to fledging, or 0.02-0.04/pair) (Orsman & Sutcliffe 1990). Success was almost as low on nearby Skokholm. Birds on the Isle of May (SE Scotland) averaged c0.54 chicks fledged/pair (compared to 0.98 in 1989).

Latest estimate of breeding population:
A total of 62,900 prs. bred on UK coasts in 1985-87, with a further 21,000 prs. estimated for inland and urban colonies (Lloyd et al. 1991).

Herring Gull
Larus argentatus

Present population trend:
Most monitored populations appear to have been stable or declining during 1986-90, with fluctuations. 1989-90 changes were very variable between regions, probably in part reflecting the small number of colonies included. The significant decline in SE Scotland (mainly Firth of Forth) sample over 1986-90 may not be typical of all colonies there. (No 1986-90 counts of pairs were available for most Forth islands, where counts of adults suggested a more stable population up to 1989.)

Breeding success:
Few detailed figures are available. Success was relatively high on the Isle of May (c1.2 chicks fledged/pair), Rye Harbour (E Sussex) (c.1.1), Canna (Lochaber) and Rockcliffe Marsh (Cumbria), but poor at St Abb's Head (Berwickshire). Success was probably poor on Skomer (Dyfed), although better than for Lesser Black-backed Gulls there.

Latest estimate of breeding population:
Herring Gull numbers on UK coasts decreased by c.44% between 1969-70 and 1985-87, when 161,500 prs. were recorded (Lloyd et al. 1991). An estimated 15,000 prs. breed in inland or urban colonies.

Great
Black-backed Gull
Larus marinus

Present population trend:
No clearcut trends are evident for the small population samples counted during 1986-90. 1989-90 changes were also variable.

Breeding success:
No systematic information is available. In Orkney, success appeared to be quite good on Hoy but poor on Papa Westray (Meek 1990).

Latest estimate of breeding population:
UK population c18,900 prs. in 1985-87, with probably no overall change from 1969-70 (19,100 prs.) (Lloyd et al. 1991).

Kittiwake
Rissa tridactyla

Present population trend:
Population changes for 1989-90 were more variable between regions than for 1988-89, with both east and west coast samples showing increases and decreases. Shetland populations continued to decrease, and colonies counted in both 1981 and 1990 had declined by 49%. Other east coast population samples have generally increased during 1986-90. Breeding numbers in several west coast regions appeared to show some recovery from the marked fall in numbers seen in 1989 but a significant decline was also noted for the small sample in SW Scotland.

Breeding success:
For Britain as a whole, productivity was significantly lower in 1990 than in 1989. North Sea colonies, in particular, showed a significant reduction in success since last year. Most of this reduction occurred at Scottish colonies south of Caithness, with these colonies averaging only 0.6 chicks fledged/nest in 1990. Success actually improved (to 0.9/nest) at Orkney/Caithness colonies. Some reduction was seen on the east coast of England, but these colonies remained very successful (1.2/nest). In Shetland, productivity was even worse than in 1989, and was similar to 1988 levels (c0.1/nest). For the first time, monitored nests on Fair Isle failed totally, and only two chicks were thought to have fledged from this large colony (c19,000 prs. in 1986-88). Productivity in west coast colonies was also lower than in 1989, but not significantly. Colonies off NW Scotland showed the greatest reduction. West Scottish colonies were still, on average, twice as successful (0.8 chicks/nest) as colonies around the Irish and Celtic Sea (0.4/nest).

Latest estimate of breeding population:
A total of 503,400 apparently occupied nests was recorded at UK colonies in 1985-87, about 24% higher than in 1969-70 (Lloyd et al. 1991).

Sandwich Tern
Sterna sandvicensis

Present population trend:
Twenty-six British and Irish colonies have been monitored annually since 1986. These include over 70% of the total population and have been used to calculate indices of population change both regionally and nationally. After a net loss of 2,400 prs. from the 26 study colonies in 1989, there was a slight increase (4%) in the total number of

pairs in 1990. Blakeney was the largest colony in 1990, with 3,000 pairs. No significant trends have been evident either regionally or overall during 1986-90. Some of the marked fluctuations seen (especially in the smaller Scottish and west coast samples) may simply reflect movements between colonies.

Breeding success:
Productivity was recorded for 16 colonies in 1990. The overall figure of 0.79 chicks fledged per pair is higher than in 1986 and 1988-89, but lower than in 1987.

Latest estimate of breeding population:
The coastal population increased from 11,100 prs. in 1969-70 to 16,600 prs. in 1985-87 (Lloyd et al. 1991).

Roseate Tern
Sterna dougalli

Present population trend:
Although numbers in Britain continue to decline, there is evidence of birds having shifted to the colony on Rockabill Island, Dublin Bay. Taking the population of Britain and Ireland as a whole, it now looks as though the decline in numbers which has persisted since the late 1960s may have ended. The population appears to have stabilised over the past five years. In 1990, no Roseate Terns nested on Inchmickery and only four pairs nested on the Farne Islands. On Coquet Island, numbers remained at similar levels to 1989. Numbers on Anglesey remained low compared with the early 1980s.

Breeding success:
At the main Anglesey colony no chicks fledged because of predation of eggs and chicks by Herring Gulls. At the other Anglesey colony, and at colonies in NE Ireland, bad weather reduced fledging success to almost zero. On Coquet Island 19 chicks fledged (0.82/pair).

Latest estimate of breeding population:
Only 109 pairs attempted to breed in 1990. Roseate Terns have been declining in numbers in Britain and Ireland for the past 30 years (Cramp et al. 1974; Thomas et al. 1989; Lloyd et al. 1991). The British and Irish population in 1990 is estimated at c490 pairs. This is similar to the 1989 estimate of 470 pairs.

Common Tern
Sterna hirundo

Present population trend:
There was little apparent change in the overall numbers in Britain between 1989 and 1990. However, monitored colonies in E England, and in England/Wales as a whole, declined significantly during 1986-90. Scottish regions

generally showed little change between 1989 and 1990, except where the population monitored was small. The trend of population decline in Wales since 1986 reversed in 1990, mainly as a result of one large colony which gained 86 pairs.

Breeding success:
There was a higher success rate on 28 monitored Scottish colonies in 1990 (up to 0.4 chicks fledged/pair) than in 1989, though this is still well below average. At least 12 of the 29+ Scottish colonies monitored in 1990 suffered total failure due to mammalian predators, poor weather and gull predation. Productivity at English colonies (0.49/pair overall in 1990) was markedly higher than at Scottish colonies, but slightly lower than in previous years. In Wales three monitored colonies failed completely. At the largest Welsh colony, Shotton Pools (286 pairs, Clwyd), there was mass desertion during incubation for unknown reasons.

Latest estimate of breeding population
About 13,000 prs. bred on UK coasts in 1985-87, with little overall change since 1969-70 (Lloyd et al. 1991). Inland population 1,000 prs.

Arctic Tern
Sterna paradisaea

Present population trend:
In Shetland breeding numbers had fallen by c35% since 1989. Orkney numbers seem to have shown little change. Population trends are unclear due to shortage of data for 1986-88. Elsewhere, there were no major changes in numbers between 1989 and 1990 at the larger colonies.

Breeding success:
1990 was the seventh successive year of disastrous breeding success for Arctic Terns in Shetland. Most colonies failed before eggs hatched and very few live or dead chicks were seen. The few chicks which did hatch mostly died within a few days during a period of bad weather. In Orkney, breeding success was low. At the largest colony, on Papa Westray (7,200 adults), only one chick fledged (Meek 1990). Bad weather around the time of hatching was believed to be a major contributing factor. Away from Orkney and Shetland, breeding success was uniformly poor in major Scottish colonies. Some of these failures resulted from predation, but bad weather also contributed (possibly, in part, by reducing foraging success). The few colonies in England and Wales were generally more successful.

Latest estimate of breeding population
UK population estimated as c.78,000 pairs in 1985-87 (Lloyd et al. 1991), a 50% increase on 1969-70 counts. However, over 80% of the recent total was from a 1980 survey of Orkney and Shetland (Bullock & Gomersall 1981), where surveys confirmed a major decline in 1989 and 1990.

Little Tern
Sterna albifrons

Present population trend:
Numbers in monitored colonies in England and Wales fell slightly, by 2.5%, in 1990. The nine colonies monitored in Scotland (mainly on the east coast) decreased by 20%. Numbers at monitored colonies in Britain and Ireland as a whole have shown a slow, but significant, decline during 1986-90.

Breeding success:
Productivity was even lower in 1990 than in 1989, averaging 0.40 young/pair, largely the result of predation at many colonies.

Latest estimate of breeding population:
UK population c2,400 prs. in 1985-87 (Lloyd *et al.* 1991), a c40% increase since 1969-70.

Guillemot
Uria aalge

Present population trend:
Of the seven regions where colonies were monitored in detail, only Caithness (N Scotland) and Wales showed an increase between 1989 and 1990. Little change was seen for regions bordering the Irish Sea, where numbers apparently fell markedly in 1989. Large decreases were noted on Handa (NW Scotland) (-22%) and in Shetland colonies (-18%). This is the third successive year in which Shetland numbers have fallen markedly, with a significant decline seen for 1986-90 as a whole. Numbers also fell at monitored colonies in SE Scotland and on the Farne Islands (NE England).

Breeding success:
Productivity was again high in 1990, averaging 0.68 chicks fledged/regularly occupied site on nine colonies. Nevertheless, productivity fell at seven of the eight colonies monitored in both 1989 and 1990. This represented a small, though statistically significant, overall decrease.

Latest estimate of breeding population:
A population of 1,077,000 adults attending colonies was recorded in 1985-87, about twice the 1969-70 total (Lloyd *et al.* 1991). Guillemots are currently the most abundant breeding seabird in the UK.

Razorbill
Alca torda

Present population trend:
No significant trends were detected in any region for 1986-90 as a whole.

Breeding success:
Few colonies are monitored in detail. On the Isle of May (SE Scotland), productivity continued to be high (0.76 chicks fledged/egg). Birds on Handa were also quite successful, although less so than in 1988 and 1989. On Rathlin, where there was apparently total breeding failure in 1989, at least some chicks were reared in 1990. Productivity on Fair Isle (Shetland) was moderately high. Elsewhere in Shetland, Foula birds showed slightly improved success compared to 1988 and 1989 (when very few chicks appeared to survive to fledging) (Furness 1990b). Productivity seemed reasonable at Sumburgh Head and Compass Head in south Mainland, with relatively high weights. However, Hermaness chicks were again severely underweight, and fewer than 50% (perhaps 10%) were considered likely to fledge. Chick growth-rates were also poor on St Kilda (Walsh 1991).

Latest estimate of breeding population:
About 158,600 adult Razorbills were counted at UK colonies in 1985-87 (Lloyd *et al.* 1991). Changes since 1969-70 were difficult to assess, but the population had probably increased.

Black Guillemot
Cepphus grylle

Present population trend:
Numbers of adults associated with breeding habitat at Yell Sound appear to have increased by about 17% since 1988. Counts for Noss and parts of Fair Isle indicate a slight decrease since 1989. Indices for Shetland as a whole indicate stable or increasing numbers during 1986-90.

Breeding success:
In Shetland, birds on Foula again appeared to fail completely. The Fair Isle population was moderately successful (0.73 chicks fledged/pair), less than in 1989 but more than in 1987-88. No detailed information was available for other colonies, but good numbers of fledged birds were seen around Shetland during August. In Orkney, success in the Holm of Papa Westray was higher than in 1989, although lower than pre-1988 levels.

Latest estimate of breeding population:
Counts during spring 1985-87 indicated a population of c38,000 adults at or near colonies (Lloyd *et al.* 1991). Count methods differed between 1969-70 and 1985-87 surveys, but the population had probably increased.

Puffin
Fratercula arctica

Present population trend:
No significant changes in numbers were recorded at Hermaness (Shetland), Fair Isle or the Isle of May (SE Scotland). A significant decline in the number of occupied

burrows (estimated at 36%) has occurred on Dun, St Kilda (Western Isles) since 1987 (Walsh 1991).

Breeding success:
On Fair Isle, where, in contrast to other Shetland colonies, Puffins have reared good numbers of chicks in recent years, a reduction in success was seen in 1990 (0.57 chicks fledged/egg). At other Shetland colonies, there was some suggestion of an improvement in success in 1990, although no detailed monitoring was undertaken from the egg stage. At Hermaness and Sumburgh Head, chick survival in study burrows was assessed by RSPB from mid-July onwards, using an endoscope. About 55% of these chicks were believed to have fledged at both colonies (with some losses at Sumburgh possibly being due to stoats). Total or near total failure had been recorded in several previous years, but the extent of the improvement in 1990 is not known, as losses of eggs and very small chicks were not assessed. Observations of low feeding rates (and of dead chicks being ejected from burrows) at Hermaness suggested that feeding conditions for puffins there were still poor (Martin 1991). Puffins elsewhere had a moderately successful season by recent standards.

Latest estimate of breeding population:
An estimated 450,000 prs. of Puffins bred in 1985-87 (Lloyd *et al.* 1991). Total numbers may have increased slightly since 1969-70.

Stock Dove
Columba oenas

Present population trend:
Now stabilising after partial recovery from earlier large decline.

Percentage change in CBC index, 1989-1990:
Farmland = +2% (-14% to +21%); woodland = +5% (-11% to +24%).

Latest estimate of breeding population:
100,000 pairs in Britain and Ireland (Sharrock 1976); following increase in the 1970s, this figure may now apply to Britain alone (Hudson & Marchant 1984).

Woodpigeon
Columba palumbus

Present population trend:
Some decline during 1970s; partial recovery since.

Percentage change in CBC index, 1989-1990:
Farmland = +8% (-2% to +19%); woodland = +3% (-9% to +17%).

Latest estimate of breeding population:
Perhaps 2.5 million pairs in Britain in 1983 (Inglis, in Lack 1986).

Collared Dove
Streptopelia decaocto

Present population trend:
Now more or less stable following earlier spectacular increase.

Percentage change in CBC index, 1989-1990:
Farmland = +6% (-10% to +24%); woodland = -23% (-41% to 0%) based on < 30 plots.

Latest estimate of breeding population:
Over 100,000 pairs in Britain.
There was a significant decline in the CBC woodland index following the high numbers in 1989.

Turtle Dove
Streptopelia turtur

Present population trend:
Recent decline, following earlier increase.

Percentage change in CBC index, 1989-1990:
Farmland = +8% (-30% to +66%) based on < 30 plots; woodland = -8% (-38% to +36%) based on < 30 plots.

Latest estimate of breeding population:
At least 125,000 pairs in Britain (Sharrock 1976), before recent decrease.

Cuckoo
Cuculus canorus

Present population trend:
Uncertain; information is conflicting.

Percentage change in CBC index, 1989-1990:
Farmland = -14% (-31% to +6%); woodland = -34% (-51% to -12%) statistically significant.

Latest estimate of breeding population:
20,000-30,000 laying females in Britain and Ireland; 73% of occupied Breeding Atlas squares were in Britain (Sharrock 1976). The typically promiscuous mating system makes it unwise to refer to "pairs".
CBC indices now the lowest since the early 1970s.

Barn Owl
Tyto alba

Present population trend:
Declining since the 1930s; not necessarily a continuous trend.

Latest estimate of breeding population:
4,400 pairs in Britain (Shawyer 1987).

Little Owl
Athene noctua

Present population trend:
Fluctuates; no clear recent trend but possibly increasing. CBC results indicate a decline in 1990 to the lowest level on record.

Percentage change in CBC index, 1989-1990:
All habitats = -29% (-51% to 0%).

Latest estimate of breeding population:
7,000-14,000 pairs in Britain (Sharrock 1976).

Tawny Owl
Strix aluco

Present population trend:
Higher levels reached during the early 1970s have not been sustained.

Percentage change in CBC index, 1989-1990:
All habitats = +2% (-19% to +29%).

Latest estimate of breeding population:
50,000-100,000 pairs in Britain (Sharrock 1976).

Kingfisher
Alcedo atthis

Present population trend:
Decline since the mid-1970s.

Percentage change in WBS index, 1989-1990:
0% (-24% to +32%)

Latest estimate of breeding population:
5,000-9,000 pairs in Britain and Ireland (Sharrock 1976); 72% of occupied squares were then in Britain.

Green Woodpecker
Picus viridis

Present population trend:
Small decline in the 1980s, after earlier stability.

Percentage change in CBC index, 1989-1990:
Farmland = -17% (-48% to +28%) based on < 30 plots; woodland = -11% (-24% to +3%).

Latest estimate of breeding population:
10,000-15,000 pairs in Britain (Hudson & Marchant 1984).

Great Spotted Woodpecker
Dendrocopos major

Present population trend:
Perhaps now beginning to fall from high levels of the late 1970s and early 1980s.

Percentage change in CBC index, 1989-1990:
Farmland = +9% (-18% to +46%); woodland = -3% (-16% to +13%).

Latest estimate of breeding population:
30,000-40,000 pairs in Britain (Sharrock 1976); perhaps too high then but applicable by 1982 (Hudson & Marchant 1984).

Lesser Spotted Woodpecker
Dendrocopus minor

Present population trend:
Declining from 1970s peak.

Percentage change in CBC index, 1989-1990:
All habitats = + 6% (–33% to +67%) based on <30 plots.

Latest estimate of breeding population:
3,000–6,000 pairs in Britain (Cramp & Simmons 1985). The small increase in the CBC index opposes the trend of recent years.

Skylark
Alauda arvensis

Present population trend:
Recent decline, following a long period of relative stability.

Percentage change in CBC index, 1989-1990:
Farmland = +5% (-2% to +13%).

Latest estimate of breeding population:
Around 2 million pairs in Britain (Hudson & Marchant 1984). The CBC index remains at about half the level of the late 1970s despite the small increase in 1990.

Sand Martin
Riparia riparia

Present population trend:
Major decline beginning in late 1960s; recent partial recovery.

Latest estimate of breeding population:
100,000-500,000 pairs in Britain during 1984-1988 (Marchant *et al.* 1990).

Swallow
Hirundo rustica

Present population trend:
Considerable decline since 1980.

Percentage change in CBC index, 1989-1990:
Farmland = +7% (-5% to +21%).

Latest estimate of breeding population:
At least 500,000 pairs in Britain in 1982 (Hudson & Marchant 1984). The CBC index indicates a continued slow recovery from the low points of 1984 and 1987.

House Martin
Delichon urbica

Present population trend:
No major change is known.

Percentage change in CBC index, 1989-1990:
All habitats = -16% (-39% to +13%) based on < 30 plots.

Latest estimate of breeding population:
300,000-600,000 pairs in Britain and Ireland (Sharrock 1976); 73% of occupied squares were then in Britain.

Tree Pipit
Anthus trivialis

Present population trend:
Fluctuates; some downward drift since 1970.

Percentage change in CBC index, 1989-1990:
All habitats = -16% (-33% to +5%) based on < 30 plots.

Latest estimate of breeding population:
100,000 pairs in Britain (Hudson & Marchant 1984). The CBC index is now at the lowest ever level.

Meadow Pipit
Anthus pratensis

Present population trend:
Decline since the early 1980s though CBC index increased in 1989 and 1990.

Percentage change in CBC index, 1989-1990:
All habitats = +4% (-6% to +14%).

Latest estimate of breeding population:
1-1.5 million pairs in Britain (Hudson & Marchant 1984).

Yellow Wagtail
Motacilla flava

Present population trend:
Some decline during the 1980s, after an earlier peak.

Percentage change in CBC index, 1989-1990:
All habitats = +4% (-17% to +30%) based on < 30 plots.

Percentage change in WBS index, 1989-1990:
+16% (-12% to +54%) based on < 20 plots.

Latest estimate of breeding population:
At least 100,000 pairs in Britain in 1982.
WBS indicated that both 1989 and 1990 were relatively good years.

Grey Wagtail
Motacilla cinerea

Present population trend
Downward since the mid-1970s.

Percentage change in CBC index, 1989-1990:
All habitats = -4% (-36% to +43%) based on < 30 plots.

Percentage change in WBS index, 1989-1990:
+13% (0% to +28%).

Latest estimate of breeding population:
25,000-50,000 pairs in Britain and Ireland (Sharrock 1976); 67% of occupied squares were then in Britain.

Pied Wagtail
Motacilla alba

Present population trend:
Fluctuates somewhat according to winter weather conditions.

Percentage change in CBC index, 1989-1990:
Farmland = +6% (-13% to +28%).

Percentage change in WBS index, 1989-1990:
-6% (-15% to +5%).

Latest estimate of breeding population:
300,000 pairs in Britain (Hudson & Marchant 1984).

Dipper
Cinclus cinclus

Present population trend:
Stable or increasing.

Percentage change in WBS index, 1989-1990:
-8% (-17% to +3%).

Latest estimate of breeding population:
30,000 pairs in Britain and Ireland (Sharrock 1976); 70% of occupied squares were then in Britain.

Wren
Troglodytes troglodytes

Present population trend:
Fluctuates according to winter weather conditions.

Percentage change in CBC index, 1989-1990:
Farmland = +1% (-4% to +6%); woodland = -4% (-9% to +1%).

Latest estimate of breeding population:
3-3.5 million pairs in Britain in 1982 (Hudson & Marchant 1984).

Dunnock
Prunella modularis

Present population trend:
Shallow but progressive decline since the mid-1970s.

Percentage change in CBC index, 1989-1990:
Farmland = -3% (-8% to +3%); woodland = -4% (-12% to +4%).

Latest estimate of breeding population:
2 million territories in Britain (Hudson & Marchant 1984). There was a significant decline in the number of Dunnocks caught on CES sites.

Robin
Erithacus rubecula

Present population trend:
Some recent cold-weather fluctuations; otherwise stable.

Percentage change in CBC index, 1989-1990:
Farmland = +11% (+4% to +19%) statistically significant; woodland = 0% (-4% to +5%).

Latest estimate of breeding population:
3.5 million pairs in Britain (Hudson & Marchant 1984).

Nightingale
Luscinia megarhynchos

Present population trend:
Long-term range contraction; numbers fluctuate.

Latest estimate of breeding population:
Fluctuates, now probably 4,000-5,000 territorial males in Britain (Marchant *et al.* 1990).

Black Redstart
Phoenicurus ochruros

Present population trend:
Increase since the 1970s.

Latest estimate of breeding population:
Fluctuates from year to year, but usually below 100 pairs in England; none elsewhere in Britain.

Redstart
Phoenicurus phoenicurus

Present population trend:
Recovering well from 1970s decline.

Percentage change in CBC index, 1989-1990:
All habitats = -11% (-28% to +9%) based on < 30 plots.

Latest estimate of breeding population:
140,000 pairs in Britain (Hudson & Marchant 1984).

Whinchat
Saxicola rubetra

Present population trend:
Decline since 1950s, in England at least.

Latest estimate of breeding population:
20,000-40,000 pairs in Britain and Ireland (Sharrock 1976); 90% of occupied squares were then in Britain.

Stonechat
Saxicola torquata

Present population trend:
Long-term decline, exacerbated by cold winters.

Latest estimate of breeding population:
30,000-60,000 pairs in Britain and Ireland (Sharrock 1976), with 61% of occupied squares then being in Britain. Has declined since.

Wheatear
Oenanthe oenanthe

Present population trend:
Long-term decline in the southern half of England; elsewhere, decline up to mid-1970s now reversed.

Latest estimate of breeding population:
80,000 pairs in Britain and Ireland (Sharrock 1976); 78% of occupied squares were then in Britain.

Ring Ouzel
Turdus torquatus

Present population trend:
Pronounced decline to 1950s; no recent evidence of change.

Latest estimate of breeding population:
8,000-16,000 pairs in Britain and Ireland (Sharrock 1976); 96% of occupied squares were then in Britain.

Blackbird
Turdus merula

Present population trend:
Some decline since the mid-1970s, following earlier major increase.

Percentage change in CBC index, 1989-1990:
Farmland = -4% (-8% to +1%); woodland = -6% (-10% to -1%) statistically significant.

Latest estimate of breeding population:
4.5-5 million pairs in Britain (Hudson & Marchant 1984).

Song Thrush
Turdus philomelos

Present population trend:
Overall long-term decline; steep decline from short-lived plateau since mid-1970s.

Percentage change in CBC index, 1989-1990:
Farmland = -12% (-22% to -1%) statistically significant; woodland = -5% (-15% to +5%).

Latest estimate of breeding population:
About 1.5 million pairs in Britain (Hudson & Marchant 1984).

Mistle Thrush
Turdus viscivorus

Present population trend:
Recent decline, after previous increase.

Percentage change in CBC index, 1989-1990:
Farmland = +14% (-5% to +38%); woodland = -11% (-25% to +5%).

Latest estimate of breeding population:
About 300,000 pairs in Britain (Hudson & Marchant 1984).

Grasshopper Warbler
Locustella naevia

Present population trend:
Steep decline since 1970, but with temporary partial recovery around 1980.

Latest estimate of breeding population:
25,000 pairs in Britain and Ireland (Sharrock 1976); 73% of occupied squares were then in Britain. Considerable decline since that time.

Sedge Warbler
Acrocephalus schoenobaenus

Present population trend:
Serious decline over the last 20 years, but substantial gains since 1985.

Percentage change in CBC index, 1989-1990:
Farmland = 0% (-41% to +68%) based on < 30 plots.

Percentage change in WBS index, 1989-1990:
−10% (−19% to 0%), statistically significant.

Latest estimate of breeding population:
300,000 pairs in Britain and Ireland (Sharrock 1976); 71% of occupied squares were then in Britain. Numbers now much reduced.

Reed Warbler
Acrocephalus scirpaceus

Present population trend:
No major change is known; perhaps increasing.

Percentage change in CBC index, 1989-1990:
All habitats = 0% (-10% to +11%) based on < 30 plots.

Latest estimate of breeding population:
40,000-80,000 pairs in England and Wales (Sharrock 1976); none elsewhere in Britain.

Lesser Whitethroat
Sylvia curruca

Present population trend:
Marked fluctuations, but no clear trend. There was a significant decline on CES sites in 1990.

Percentage change in CBC index, 1989-1990:
Farmland = -6% (-29% to +24%).

Latest estimate of breeding population:
At least 50,000 pairs in Britain.

Whitethroat
Sylvia communis

Present population trend:
Fluctuating around new lower level, following 1969 crash.

Percentage change in CBC index, 1989-1990:
Farmland = +15% (+4% to +26%) statistically significant; woodland = -1% (-15% to +15%).

Percentage change in WBS index, 1989-1990:
+11% (-9% to +37%).

Latest estimate of breeding population:
400,000-500,000 pairs in Britain (Hudson & Marchant 1984). Increase in WBS index surprising as there is a corresponding decrease in the index for Sedge Warbler which also winters in the Sahel and until recently showed remarkably similar population trends.

Garden Warbler
Sylvia borin

Present population trend:
Recent recovery from 1970s decline. There was a significant increase on CES sites.

Percentage change in CBC index, 1989-1990:
Farmland = -23% (-48% to +12%); woodland = +2% (-15% to +22%).

Latest estimate of breeding population:
200,000 pairs in Britain (Hudson & Marchant 1984).

Blackcap
Sylvia atricapilla

Present population trend:
Consistent increase over the last 30 years at least.

Percentage change in CBC index, 1989-1990:
Farmland = +9% (-5% to +24%); woodland = +1% (-7% to +9%).

Latest estimate of breeding population:
800,000 pairs in Britain (Hudson & Marchant 1984).

Wood Warbler
Phylloscopus sibilatrix

Present population trend:
No recent change is known.

Percentage change in CBC index, 1989-1990:
All habitats = +16% (-6% to +44%) based on < 30 plots.

Latest estimate of breeding population:
17,200 ± 1370 territorial males in Britain in 1984-1985 (Bibby 1989).

Chiffchaff
Phylloscopus collybita

Present population trend:
Declined in 1970s; has fluctuated since, but is currently increasing. There was a significant increase in the number of adults caught on CES sites in 1990.

Percentage change in CBC index, 1989-1990:
Farmland = +8% (-7% to +25%); woodland = 0% (-9% to +9%).

Latest estimate of breeding population:
400,000-500,000 pairs in Britain (Hudson & Marchant 1984).

Willow Warbler
Phylloscopus trochilus

Present population trend:
Fluctuates, but little long-term change. CBC indices indicate a decline in 1990.

Percentage change in CBC index, 1989-1990:
Farmland = -10% (-18% to -1%) statistically significant; woodland = -15% (-20% to -9%) statistically significant.

Latest estimate of breeding population:
2.5 million pairs in Britain (Hudson & Marchant 1984).

Goldcrest
Regulus regulus

Present population trend:
Recent cold winters have reduced the high levels of the 1970s; strong recovery from a population crash in 1986. Farmland numbers fell in 1990 after an astonishing increase in 1989.

Percentage change in CBC index, 1989-1990:
Farmland = -21% (-44% to +9%); woodland = +4% (-6% to +16%).

Latest estimate of breeding population:
500,000-600,000 pairs in Britain in 1982 (Hudson & Marchant 1984).

Spotted Flycatcher
Muscicapa striata

Present population trend:
Fluctuates, but the long-term trend is downwards. The CBC woodland index was at a record low level in 1990.

Percentage change in CBC index, 1989-1990:
Farmland = -8% (-35% to +29%); woodland = -30% (-56% to +6%) based on < 30 plots.

Latest estimate of breeding population:
Possibly 200,000 pairs in Britain (Marchant *et al.* 1990).

Pied Flycatcher
Ficedula hypoleuca

Present population trend:
Probably stable, except where nestbox schemes promote local increase.

Latest estimate of breeding population:
20,000 pairs in Britain (Sharrock 1976); probably too low a figure, and the reality may be double that (Hudson & Marchant 1984).

Long-tailed Tit
Aegithalos caudatus

Present population trend:
Marked fluctuations associated with winter weather conditions, but no long-term trend is apparent.

Percentage change in CBC index, 1989-1990:
Farmland = +13% (-4% to +33%); woodland = +18% (+2% to +37%) statistically significant.

Latest estimate of breeding population:
Around 200,000 territories in Britain (Hudson & Marchant 1984). The CBC indices are just short of the peak levels of the mid-1970s.

Marsh Tit
Parus palustris

Present population trend:
Shallow long-term decline.

Percentage change in CBC index, 1989-1990:
Woodland = +4% (-14% to +25%) based on < 30 plots.

Latest estimate of breeding population:
140,000-150,000 pairs in Britain (Hudson & Marchant 1984).

Willow Tit
Parus montanus

Present population trend:
Some regional changes; otherwise no clear trend. 1990 CBC index indicates a decline.

Percentage change in CBC index, 1989-1990:
All habitats = -22% (-41% to +3%).

Latest estimate of breeding population:
50,000-100,000 pairs in Britain (Sharrock 1976).

Coal Tit
Parus ater

Present population trend:
Now relatively stable at new, higher densities, after earlier increase. CBC index indicates an increase in farmland.

Percentage change in CBC index, 1989-1990:
farmland = +22% (-6% to +60%) based on < 30 plots; woodland = -1% (-11% to +11%).

Latest estimate of breeding population:
500,000-700,000 pairs in Britain.

Blue Tit
Parus caeruleus

Present population trend:
Fluctuating around higher levels reached in the 1970s; perhaps now increasing again although a decline is indicated by the 1990 CBC indices.

Percentage change in CBC index, 1989-1990:
Farmland = -4% (-10% to +1%); woodland = -6% (-12% to -1%) statistically significant.

Latest estimate of breeding population:
3.5 million pairs in Britain (Hudson & Marchant 1984).

Great Tit
Parus major

Present population trend:
Gradual increase, especially since late 1970s; perhaps beginning to stabilise. The 1990 CBC indices indicate a decline.

Percentage change in CBC index, 1989-1990:
Farmland = -10% (-17% to -2%) statistically significant; woodland = -8% (-14% to -1%) statistically significant.

Latest estimate of breeding population:
2 million pairs in Britain (Hudson & Marchant 1984).

Nuthatch
Sitta europaea

Present population trend:
Long-term gradual increase. The CBC index is now at a level double that of the early 1970s.

Percentage change in CBC index, 1989-1990:
Woodland = +15% (+4% to +27%) statistically significant.

Latest estimate of breeding population:
About 50,000 pairs in England and Wales (Marchant *et al.* 1990).

Treecreeper
Certhia familiaris

Present population trend:
Fluctuates around cold winters, but overall trend is towards increase. The significant decrease in the CBC farmland index in 1990 followed a significant increase in 1989.

Percentage change in CBC index, 1989-1990:
Farmland = -31% (-51% to -5%) statistically significant; woodland = +1% (-11% to +16%).

Latest estimate of breeding population:
200,000-250,000 pairs in Britain (Hudson & Marchant 1984).

Jay
Garrulus glandarius

Present population trend:
Stable or increasing slightly.

Percentage change in CBC index, 1989-1990:
Farmland = -16% (-33% to +4%); woodland = -12% (-22% to 0%).

Latest estimate of breeding population:
100,000 pairs in Britain and Ireland (Sharrock 1976); 81% of occupied squares were then in Britain. CBC index indicates a decline especially in farmland.

Magpie
Pica pica

Present population trend:
Increasing in rural, suburban and urban habitats. Now possibly stabilised.

Percentage change in CBC index, 1989-1990:
Farmland = -1% (-12% to +11%); woodland = -2% (-11% to +7%).

Latest estimate of breeding population:
Over 250,000 pairs in Britain and Ireland (Sharrock 1976); 67% of occupied squares were then in Britain. Now much increased though the CBC index indicates this increase is stabilising.

Jackdaw
Corvus monedula

Present population trend:
Increasing since the mid- 1970s; perhaps now stabilised.

Percentage change in CBC index, 1989-1990:
Farmland = +12% (-3% to +30%); woodland = -9% (-23% to +9%).

Latest estimate of breeding population:
500,000 pairs in Britain and Ireland (Sharrock 1976); 72% of occupied squares were then in Britain.

Rook
Corvus frugilegus

Present population trend:
Serious decline (from the mid-1950s to early 1970s) has now halted; partial recovery is occurring in some regions.

Latest estimate of breeding population:
850,000-860,000 pairs in Britain (Sage & Whittington 1985).

Carrion Crow
Corvus corone

Present population trend:
Continuing increase.

Percentage change in CBC index, 1989-1990:
Farmland = +7% (-2% to +17%); woodland = +4% (-11% to +23%).

Latest estimate of breeding population:
About 1 million pairs in Britain and Ireland (Sharrock 1976); 74% of occupied squares were then in Britain. Has increased since

Raven
Corvus corax

Present population trend:
Overall, a small decline; but trends are geographically uneven.

Latest estimate of breeding population:
5,000 pairs in Britain and Ireland (Sharrock 1976); 74% of occupied squares were then in Britain.

Starling
Sturnus vulgaris

Present population trend:
Marked decline during the late 1960s, continuing in the 1980s.

Percentage change in CBC index, 1989-1990:
Farmland = -15% (-27% to -1%) statistically significant; woodland = -35% (-49% to -19%) based on < 30 plots.

Latest estimate of breeding population:
3.5 million pairs in Britain (Potts 1967); 4-7 million pairs in Britain and Ireland (Sharrock 1976), with 74% of occupied squares then being in Britain.

House Sparrow
Passer domesticus

Present population trend:
Thought to be in decline.

Percentage change in CBC index, 1989-1990:
All habitats = -8% (-21% to +7%).

Latest estimate of breeding population:
5.5-6 million pairs in Britain and Ireland (Lack 1986); 74% of occupied squares were then in Britain.

Tree Sparrow
Passer montanus

Present population trend:
Upward in late 1950s and 1960s, but strongly in decline since 1976-1977 (but see below).

Percentage change in CBC index, 1989-1990:
Farmland = + 29% (-5% to +76%) based on < 30 plots.

Latest estimate of breeding population:
285,000 pairs in Britain and Ireland in 1985 (Summers-Smith 1989); 93% of occupied squares during the Breeding Atlas period were in Britain (Sharrock 1976).

Chaffinch
Fringilla coelebs

Present population trend:
Following recovery in the early 1960s and a short plateau period, a shallow increase is occurring.

Percentage change in CBC index, 1989-1990:
Farmland = -4% (-8% to 0%); woodland = -1% (-8% to +5%).

Latest estimate of breeding population:
About 5 million pairs in Britain (Hudson & Marchant 1984).

Greenfinch
Carduelis chloris

Present population trend:
Stable; perhaps a small downward trend recently.

Percentage change in CBC index, 1989-1990:
Farmland = -1% (-9% to +9%); woodland = -3% (-24% to +24%).

Latest estimate of breeding population:
About 800,000 pairs in Britain (Hudson & Marchant 1984).

Goldfinch
Carduelis carduelis

Present population trend:
Declining, steeply outside farmland, after reaching high population levels in the 1970s (but see below).

Percentage change in CBC index, 1989-1990:
Farmland = +18% (-2% to +43%).

Latest estimate of breeding population:
300,000 pairs in Britain (Hudson & Marchant 1984). CBC index indicates a substantial increase since the 1986-87 trough.

Siskin
Carduelis spinus

Present population trend:
Expanding in the wake of afforestation.

Latest estimate of breeding population:
20,000-40,000 pairs in Britain and Ireland (Sharrock 1976); 72% of occupied squares were then in Britain.

Linnet
Carduelis cannabina

Present population trend
Steep decline since 1977 or earlier followed by a steep increase since 1988.

Percentage change in CBC index, 1989-1990:
Farmland = -3% (-16% to +12%); woodland = +20% (-5% to +54%) based on < 30 plots.

Latest estimate of breeding population:
700,000-800,000 pairs in Britain in 1982 (Hudson & Marchant 1984).

Redpoll
Carduelis flammea

Present population trend:
Now declining from high population levels achieved in the 1970s.

Percentage change in CBC index, 1989-1990:
All habitats = -15% (-47% to +34%) based on < 30 plots.

Latest estimate of breeding population:
140,000-150,000 pairs in Britain (Hudson & Marchant 1984).

Common Crossbill
Loxia curvirostra

Present population trend:
Fluctuates widely, but increasing due to coniferous afforestation.

Latest estimate of breeding population:
Fluctuates between irruptions; probably under 1,000 birds in Britain in low years, but several thousands in good ones (Lack 1986).

Bullfinch
Pyrrhula pyrrhula

Present population trend:
Has declined since mid-1970s.

Percentage change in CBC index, 1989-1990:
Farmland = -17% (-36% to +6%); woodland = +4% (-11% to +21%).

Latest estimate of breeding population:
300,000-350,000 pairs in Britain (Hudson & Marchant 1984).

Hawfinch
Coccothraustes coccothraustes

Present population trend:
No reliable information.

Latest estimate of breeding population:
5,000-10,000 pairs in Britain (Sharrock 1976).

Yellowhammer
Emberiza citrinella

Present population trend:
Long-term overall stability. CBC indices currently at lowest levels but these have varied little over the years and the present low levels are perhaps of little significance.

Percentage change in CBC index, 1989-1990:
Farmland = -10% (-16% to -4%) statistically significant; woodland = -10% (-22% to +3%).

Latest estimate of breeding population:
About 1.5 million pairs in Britain (Hudson & Marchant 1984).

Reed Bunting
Emberiza schoeniclus

Present population trend:
Steep decline 1975-1983; now stable at lower level.

Percentage change in CBC index, 1989-1990:
Farmland = -7% (-22% to +11%).

Percentage change in WBS index, 1989-1990:
+1% (-10% to +13%).

Latest estimate of breeding population:
About 400,000 pairs in Britain (Hudson & Marchant 1984).

Corn Bunting
Miliaria calandra

Present population trend:
Decline since the early 1970s, much steeper since 1981.

Percentage change in CBC index, 1989-1990:
All habitats = -11% (-32% to +17%) based on < 30 plots.

Latest estimate of breeding population:
About 30,000 pairs in Britain and Ireland (Sharrock 1976); 95% of occupied squares were then in Britain.

References

Batten, L. A., Bibby, C.J., Clement, P. Elliott, G.D. & Porter, R.F. (1990). *Red Data Birds in Britain: action for rare, threatened and important species.* T. & A.D. Poyser, London.

Bibby, C.J. (1989). A survey of breeding Wood Warblers *Phylloscopus sybilatrix* in Britain, 1984–85. *Bird Study* 36, 56–72.

Bibby, C.J. & Nattrass, M. (1986). Breeding status of the Merlin in Britain. *British Brids* 79, 170–185.

Branson, N.J.B.A. (1991). Wader mortality. *Wash Wader Ringing Group Report 1989/90.* pp 49–51.

Dennis, R.H., Ellis, P.M., Broad, R.A. & Langslow, D.R. (1984). The status of the Golden Eagle in Britain. *British Birds* 77, 592–607.

Fox, A.D. (1988). Breeding status of the Gadwall in Britain and Ireland. *British Birds* 81, 51–66.

Furness, R.W. (1990). *Numbers of population trends of Manx Shearwaters on Rhum.* NCC CSD Rept. No. 1168.

Furness, R.W. (1990b). *Seabird studies on Foula, 1990.* Unpubl. rept.

Kirby, J.S. (1991). *An assessment of breeding success in the Dark-bellied Brent Goose in 1990.* WWT rept. to JNCC, Slimbridge.

Kirby, J.S. & Cranswick, P. (1991). *The 1990 national census of Pink-footed and Greylag Geese in Britain.* WWT rept. to JNCC, Slimbridge.

Kirby, J.S., Ferns, J.R., Waters, R.J. & Prys-Jones, R.P. (1991). *Wildfowl and Wader Counts 1990–91.* WWT, Slimbridge.

Kirby, J.S. & Haines, W.G. (1990). *A preliminary assessment of breeding success in the Dark-bellied Brent Goose, 1990.* WWT rept. to JNCC, Slimbridge.

Lack, P. (Ed.) (1986). *The Atlas of Wintering Birds in Britain and Ireland.* T. & A.D. Poyser, Calton.

Lloyd, C.S., Tasker M.L. & Partridge, K.E. (1991). *The status of seabirds in Britain and Ireland.* T. & A.D. Poyser, London.

Marchant, J.H., Hudson, R., Carter, S.P. & Whittinghton, P.A. (1990). *Population trends in British Breeding Birds.* BTO, Thetford.

Marquiss, M. (1989). Grey Herons *Ardea cinerea* breeding in Scotland: numbers, distribution and census techniques. *Bird Study* 36, 181–191.

Martin, A.R. (1989). The diet of Atlantic Puffin *Fratercula arctica* and Northern Gannet *Sula bassana* chicks at a Shetland colony during a period of changing prey availability. *Bird Study* 36, 170–180

Meek, E.R. (1990). *Orkney 1990 seabird breeding success.* Unpubl. rept. RSPB, Sandy.

Meltofte, H. (1991). The Northern Dunlin puzzle. *Wader Study Group Bull.* 62, 15–17.

Mitchell, C. (1991). *Greylag Geese on the Uists.* WWT rept. to NCC, Slimbridge.

Moser, M.E. (1987). A revision of population estimates for waders (*Charadrii*) wintering on the coastline of Britain. *Biol. Conserv.* 39, 153–164.

Newton, I. (1984). Raptors in Britain – a review of the last 150 years. *BTO News* 131, 6–7.

Ogilvie, M.A. (1986). The Mute Swan *Cygnus olor* in Britain 1983. *Bird Study* 33, 121–137.

Onnen, J. (1991). Migration phenology, measurements and weight of the Dunlin (*Calidris alpina*) in north-west Lower Saxony, FRG. *Vogelwarte* 36, 132–145.

Orsman, C. & Sutcliffe, S.J. (1990). *Seabird studies on Skomer Island in 1989 and 1990.* NCC CSD Rept. No. 1165.

Owen, M., Atkinson-Willes, G.L. & Salmon D.G. (1986). *Wildfowl in Great Britain (Second edition).* CUP. Cambridge.

Parslow, J.F.L. (1973). *Breeding Birds of Britain and Ireland.* T. & A.D. Poyser, Berkhamstead.

Parslow-Otsu, M. (1991). Bean Geese in the Yare valley, Norfolk. *British Birds* 84, 161–170.

Partridge, K. (1987). *The Common Scoter Melanitta nigra in Ireland and Britain – a review of the breeding population with special reference to Lough Erne.* Unpubl. rept. RSPB, Sandy.

Perrins, C.M. & Sears, J. (1991). Collisions with overhead wires as a cause of mortality in Mute Swans, *Cygnus olor. Wildfowl* 42, 5–11.

Piersma, T. (1986). *Breeding Waders in Europe. A review of population size estimates and a bibliography of information sources.* Wader Study Group Bul. 48, Suppl.

Pirot, J.-Y., Laursen, K., Madsen, J. & Monval, J.Y. (1989). Population estimates of swans, geese, ducks and Eurasian Coot *Fulica atra* in the Western Palearctic and Sahelian Africa. In: *Flyways and*

Reserve Networks. IWRB, Proc. Third Ramsar Conference, Regina, Canada, 14–23. CWS/IWRB.

Prater, A.J. (1981). *Estuary Birds of Britain and Ireland.* T. & A.D. Poyser, Calton.

Rees, E. C., Bowler, J.M. & Butler, L. (1991). Bewick's and Whooper Swans *Cygnus colombianus bewickii* and *C. cygnus*: the 1990–91 season. *Wildfowl* 42, 169–175.

Salmon, D.G., Prys-Jones, R.P. & Kirby, J.S. (1988). *Wildfowl and wader counts 1987–1988.* WT/NCC/BTO/RSPB, Slimbridge.

Scott, D.A. (1982). Biogeographical populations and numerical criteria for selected waterfowl species in the Western Palearctic. *Ric. Biol. Selvaggina 8 (suppl.),* 1135–1150.

Shawyer, C.R. (1987). *The Barn Owl in the British Isles: its past, present and future.* Hawk Trust, London.

Shrubb, M. & Lack, P.C. (1991). The numbers and distribution of Lapwing (*V. vanellus*) nesting in England and Wales in 1987. *Bird Study* 38, 20–37.

Smit, C.J. & Piersma, T. (1989). Numbers, midwinter distribution and migration of wader populations using the East Atlantic flyway. Pp 24–63. In: Boyd, H. & Pirot, Y.-J. (Eds.). *Flyways and Reserve Networks for Waterbirds.* IWRB Spec. Publ. 9.

Stroud, D.A., Reed, T.M., Pienkowski, M.W. & Lindsay R.A. (1987). *Birds, Bogs and Forestry: the peatlands of Caithness and Sutherland.* NCC, Peterborough.

Swann, R.L. (1990). *Canna seabird studies 1990.* NCC CSD Rept. No. 1166.

Taylor, K., Hudson, R. & Horne, G. (1988). Buzzard distribution and abundance in Britain and northern Ireland in 1983. *Bird Study* 12, 268–286.

Thompson, P.S. & Thompson, D.B.A. (1991). Greenshanks (*Tringa nebularia*) and long-term studies of breeding waders (*Charidii*). *Ibis* 133 (suppl. 1), 92–112.

Walsh, P.M. (1991). *St. Kilda seabird studies 1991.* NCC CSD Rept No. 1236.

Walsh, P.M., Sears, J. & Heubeck, M. (1991). *Seabird numbers and breeding success in 1990.* NCC CSD Rept. No. 1235.

Wanless, S. (1987). *A survey of the numbers and distribution of the North Atlantic Gannet Sula bassana and an assessment of the changes which have occurred since Operation Seafarer 1969/70.* NCC, Peterborough.